12/23

STRAND PRICE
$5.00

D1071559

IN MY OWN TIME

IN MY OWN TIME

An Autobiography

HUMPHREY BURTON

THE BOYDELL PRESS

© Humphrey Burton 2021

All Rights Reserved. Except as permitted under current legislation
no part of this work may be photocopied, stored in a retrieval system,
published, performed in public, adapted, broadcast,
transmitted, recorded or reproduced in any form or by any means,
without the prior permission of the copyright owner

The right of Humphrey Burton to be identified as
the author of this work has been asserted in accordance with
sections 77 and 78 of the Copyright, Designs and Patents Act 1988

Quote from Leonard Bernstein on pp. 303–4 © 1970 Amberson Holdings,
LLC. Used by permission of The Leonard Bernstein Office.
'Chrissie Burton' acrostic poem on p. 454 © 1990 Amberson Holdings,
LLC. Used by permission of The Leonard Bernstein Office.

First published 2021
The Boydell Press, Woodbridge

ISBN 978 1 78327 481 9

The Boydell Press is an imprint of Boydell & Brewer Ltd
PO Box 9, Woodbridge, Suffolk IP12 3DF, UK
and of Boydell & Brewer Inc.
668 Mt Hope Avenue, Rochester, NY 14620–2731, USA
website: www.boydellandbrewer.com

A catalogue record for this book is available
from the British Library

The publisher has no responsibility for the continued existence
or accuracy of URLs for external or third-party internet websites
referred to in this book, and does not guarantee that any content
on such websites is, or will remain, accurate or appropriate

This publication is printed on acid-free paper

CONTENTS

CONTENTS

Part Three: Going It Alone, 1967–1975

Part Four: In and Out at the BBC, 1975–1990

Part Five: Changing Course, 1990–2001

Part Six: Coda: The Twenty-First Century

PREFACE

I STARTED WRITING these memoirs when I was in my sixties and I suppose in search of a role. I had recently said goodbye to Leonard Bernstein, who had died in New York the previous year after a long illness. With his departure my occupation was gone; I had thought of myself as a Boswell to his Dr Johnson, filming his concerts and taping his memories, such as his conducting studenthood under Serge Koussevitzky and Dimitri Mitropoulos. My biography of Bernstein, written in the 1990s, is also part autobiography, since the footnotes abound with succinct asides such as 'the author was present on this occasion'. But what prompted me, while holidaying in Goa, to start again, this time on a narrative of my own memoirs? It was, I suppose, the challenge after I had finally taught myself to type! I had always smiled indulgently at my friend and successor Richard Somerset-Ward, who did most of his office administration by typing memoranda at his own typewriter. Now I was similarly liberated. But to do what? Off and on, I had been a programme maker at the British Broadcasting Corporation (BBC) and ITV (launched in 1955 as Independent Television) for almost fifty years, and I had grown depressed by the absence of giants, or at the least the absence of substantial presences on my professional landscape. Might it be useful to explore what I had personally done since I joined the Corporation in 1955, notably in the field of music, and en route do a little giant-spotting?

It seemed to me that my educational background – four years at a progressive co-ed school community, mixed with two spells at boys' grammar schools, plus an unusual blend of European and English influences on the classical music side – all helped to give me a positive and inquisitive attitude towards the arts. They were what made me – so it seems to me – a plausible candidate to lead the BBC department devoted to the arts; the Corporation had on its books at that time the most talented and probably the largest programme-making team that ever existed in the media world. If that claim sounds grandiose or self-important, I apologise – but that was how I saw the situation in 1975 when, at the age of forty-four, in effect halfway through my working life, I had been installed in the driving seat to supervise the production of literally hundreds of programmes about music and the other arts, all being broadcast by BBC Television.

Some outstanding people helped me on my road to self-knowledge, notably Huw Wheldon, editor and presenter of *Monitor*; Ruth Railton, intrepid creator, from scratch, of Britain's National Youth Orchestra; and Leonard Bernstein, who used television to share his love of music with an entire nation. Older television directors with whom I worked were also invaluable teachers. I'm thinking particularly of my *Monitor* director colleagues John Schlesinger and Peter Newington. I also owe a great debt to Anne James, my production secretary, who for thirty years from 1955 kept records of what was filmed for *Monitor* and took priceless photographs when she was working as Ken Russell's assistant on *Elgar*. Another photographer to whom I'm deeply grateful is my wife Christina, a former Swedish TV journalist; she has created a set of massive photo albums chronicling our life together since she came to London with our infant daughter Helena in 1967. Other colleagues with splendidly helpful recall include the Proms television director Rodney Greenberg, the *Omnibus* producers Barrie Gavin and Leslie Megahey and the logistics expert of *BBC Young Musician*, Roy Tipping. For broadcasting dates I have relied quite often on the BBC website entitled BBC Genome. If you enter a programme title in its search function, out will come the details of the relevant *Radio Times* billing. A wonderful service! For the study of specific programmes I'm not sure where I would be were it not for YouTube; so much of what I have directed and so many other programmes to which I refer can be viewed on one's own computer nowadays, all thanks to YouTube. My general point is that curious readers should always check what is available on YouTube. As Herr Baedeker observes so often, it is 'worth the detour'.

I provide dates and sources for most of my productions and for the photographs that have been distributed through the book. The images were assembled by Maureen Murray, to whom I owe another substantial debt: Maureen is an old friend with whom I previously produced an entire coffee-table book published by Oxford University Press and inspired by our shared admiration for the composer William Walton.

Some of this book's early chapters conclude with personal accounts given by witnesses I did not interview but from whom I asked for personal memories; among them were Graham Offen and Geraldine Bishop, both of whom were school contemporaries who alas died rather young. I thank also Caspian Dennis, my agent at Abner Stein, and his tireless assistant Amberley Lowis. Thanks, too, to my daughter Helena for positive proof-reading and an inside-track assessment, and to my Suffolk neighbour Mrs Abigail Hassett who kindly typed up my National Service letters to my father. Finally thanks to my dedicated publisher Michael Middeke and his production team at Boydell & Brewer. Not many writers have a publisher whose previous preoccupation was an account of Beethoven's conversation books. Michael Middeke's Beethoven project was derived from the scribbled notes which the stone-deaf composer dashed off in scrapbooks to his visitors – in Metternich's Vienna. It was Michael who introduced me to my principal editor Christopher Feeney, who did sterling work challenging my assumptions and testing the accuracy of my chronologies.

For factual errors and misapprehensions which may have slipped through the editorial net I must shoulder entire responsibility. Originally I had the idea of calling this book *Thank You for the Music* until it was pointed out that potential readers would probably be directed to look for it on the shelves dedicated to ABBA, the Swedish vocal group which created that memorable title. But I have come to understand that the music of Schubert, Beethoven and Mozart – to name just the holy trinity – is a gift from heaven that helps us make sense of life, to make it all seem worth while and for which thanks must duly be given.

The greatest musical satisfaction of my life has come from playing (as a piano duet) the slow movement of Beethoven's second symphony, most recently with my dear duet partner and Suffolk neighbour, the composer Jonathan Rutherford. An earlier partner, equally committed, had been David Attenborough, a neighbour when I lived in Richmond back in the 1960s. And I must also salute another neighbour, the pianist Nadia Lasserson, who owns a caravan here in Aldeburgh. Our duet sessions have helped to keep me more or less sane: Mozart sonatas, Bach transcriptions, Warlock's *Capriol Suite* and Ravel's *Mother Goose Suite* – that is our basic repertoire, as it must be for hundreds of duet enthusiasts.

I try in this book to show how important music has been in determining what I have done with my life. I never had a life plan and mostly made my life choices without stopping to weigh the pros and cons – quitting the BBC, for example, when propositioned by David Frost – and, to bring in the title I finally selected, those life choices were mostly made by intuition, or is it instinct? – but at the least they were made, as I declare, *in my own time*.

Aldeburgh, Spring 2020

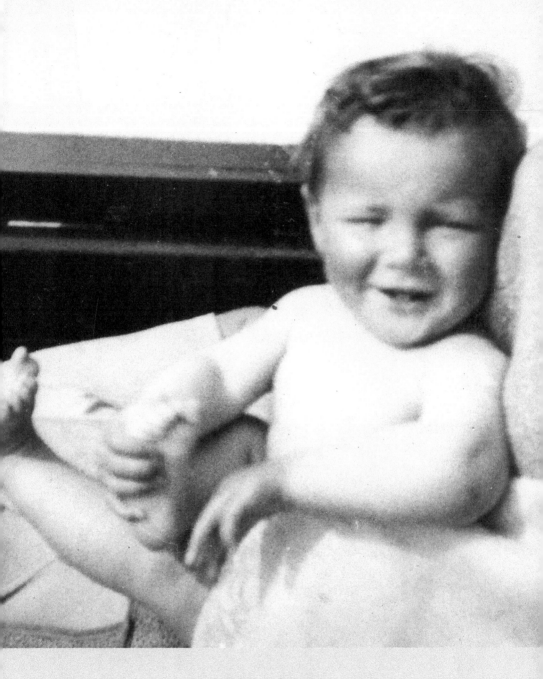

PART ONE

Early Years,
1931–1955

CHAPTER 1

CHILDHOOD

'Bill', aged two, in our Bratton house near Trowbridge, Wiltshire.
On the back my mother wrote 'shape of things to come'.

I CAN'T REMEMBER my mother ever giving me a hug, which prompts me
to conclude that one forgets all too easily the pleasant things in life. However,
I am sure I enjoyed a reasonably secure childhood, at least until I was eleven,
when on April 27th 1942 a Nazi plane dropped a huge bomb (one of many
that fell that night on what I had come to think of as my home city Norwich)
in the garden of the house next door, blasting the roof off and blowing out
the windows of our own home in Stone Road. We were inside but survived

unhurt, thanks to the protective steel cage provided by the Morrison shelter which had been recently installed under the stairs. I remember my mother's gasp when she emerged in the morning and could see the sky through the shattered rafters.

It was only recently that it dawned on me that my parents' marriage must already have been at breaking point for some years, since in August 1939, just before the Second World War started, my mother took me and my young brother Rodney to Salisbury to live with her pacifist friend Dorothy. The reason given me for our family 'evacuation' was that Norwich was too close to a possible invasion site, but in retrospect swapping one cathedral city for another does not make much sense. What I have since worked out is that the war coincided with a personal crisis in the Burton family. My mother, Kay, had a friend named Ted Harris. He was a conscientious objector whom I assume she had met in Norwich at a Peace Pledge Union meeting, since she was an active pacifist. Ted had left Norwich to work on a farm at Teffont Magna, not far from Salisbury. Later in the war I spent a summer working with Ted on that farm and a happy experience it was: riding on combine harvesters, helping with the threshing and chasing rabbits when they were trapped in the middle of the harvested field. Of course, I didn't know then that Ted had been my mother's lover (I still don't know for sure) but I do suddenly recall her taking me for tea (I must have been aged six or seven) at his Norwich flat in the unforgettably named Unthank Road and eating butter-drenched crumpets – my equivalent of Proust's *madeleine* – presumably while Kay and Ted talked passionate pacifism and maybe embraced on the sofa.

To sketch in my beginnings, I am a moonraker, a Wiltshireman, born in 1931 in Bratton, a few miles outside Trowbridge. My father, Harry, was a scholarship boy from the inner London suburb of Fulham. At that time he was the assistant director of education for Wiltshire. From the autobiography he published in his sixties I learn that his father had been a journeyman house painter and decorator with a great knowledge of London, but no ambition and very modest earning power. My father was the youngest of five children, and must have been bright because he won a place at the well-regarded, three-centuries-old Latymer Upper School in Hammersmith and stayed there until he was seventeen. But in those days there was no automatic passage to university for clever kids if they were also poor; the First World War was raging across the Channel and instead of going to university Harry signed up for the Army Service Corps. He was discharged after five months; the combination of flat feet, a 'football knee' and poor eyesight meant he was, as described in his dismissal papers, 'not likely to make an efficient soldier'. So he bummed around London, working briefly as a bricklayer and a cinema pianist, and then became a bank clerk, entering the bland, lower-middle-class world inhabited by H.G. Wells's Mr Kipps. At the prompting of his former headmaster at Latymer, my father switched to the world of supply teaching at public schools. He got a job teaching at King William's College on the Isle of Man, an institution he described as 'an ancient grammar school'. This was towards the end of the so-called 'Great' War, which resulted in an acute shortage of teachers. His spell at King William's helped to form his lifelong belief in the benefits of free *state* education for all children. He was proud that he never paid a penny towards my education. He would have been equally proud that a daughter and a grandson of mine work as teachers in a state school in Essex.

My father was already twenty-two when he finally went up to Cambridge University. He settled for the non-collegiate Fitzwilliam House, where he took a degree in English. I presume he spent the next six years as one of Fitz's assistant directors of studies, living cheaply and having lots of fun in FHADS, the Fitzwilliam House Amateur Dramatic Society.

Everybody took to calling my father 'Philip' after he made a stage hit in a role of that name. This Burton trait of having alternative first names went back at least as far as his father, who was another Harry but whose friends, it seems, all called him Dick. I didn't miss out on this peculiar double-name game. I was called Bill until I started broadcasting in 1957, when (I blush to confess) I felt that 'Bill Burton' might look a touch common in the august columns of *Radio Times*. These days it would be a badge of honour. Apparently my father said he would call me Bill whatever my name was and my mother picked Humphrey because (again I blush, given recent circumstances) she thought it would sound well when I was knighted. Since the admirable television comedy *Yes Minister* many people appear to assume that anyone named Humphrey automatically qualifies as a 'Sir'. I certainly have been addressed as 'Sir Humphrey' more than once, particularly in the USA.

My father tried his hand at writing short stories but failed to find a publisher; instead he earned extra cash as the self-appointed university correspondent for what he described as a 'wealthy and important' London daily. I have never discovered which newspaper it was but there is a certain symmetry in the fact that I started contributing reviews to the 'wealthy and important' *Times* newspaper at about the same age. Anyway, when he married, Philip evidently decided he must find a job with a steady income. Hence, I assume, the move to the administrative post in Wiltshire.

In this picture, which hangs in the Master's Lodge at Fitzwilliam College, the FHADS had just done two plays, *Hay Fever* and *A Traveller Returns*. My mother is in the back row, fourth from the left. My father is in the second row, second from the right.

My mother Kay (officially Kathleen Alice) was the daughter of a tailor and outfitter based in London's Maida Vale; his name was Stanley Henwood. Grandfather Stanley did well in Paddington business circles, which were just down the road from their Harrow home. Kay trained as a nurse and then as a midwife. She met my father on a blind date at a Cambridge May ball. He was a hopeless dancer, she told her granddaughter Helena in an interview for a school project. So instead of dancing at the May ball she remembers that they sat in a hayloft eating ripe cherries and were married soon after.

Their wedding photograph shows a dashing 1920s couple, she with a velvet cloche hat and a happy, vacant smile, he wearing morning dress complete with silk top hat and spats.

They lived in Great Shelford, a village just outside Cambridge, until Philip landed the job in Wiltshire. He had precious little administrative experience, but looking after schools suited my father and he became an expert on the subject, publishing during the Second World War a polemic entitled *The Education of the Countryman.* His job of inspecting schools involved driving all over the county in a splendid open-topped Morris Cowley with running boards. I mention these only because I apparently fell out of the car, fortunately not at speed, and miraculously landed on one of the boards. And that is about all I do recall from my first four years, although the snap of me at an upright piano in Bratton, aged two, which adorns the head of this chapter – sunshine pouring in from the garden – suggests that music attracted me early on.

In about 1935 my father moved to a similar job with the Norfolk County Council. It must have paid decently since we lived in a handsome end-of-terrace house on The Crescent in Chapel Field, a well-to-do part of Norwich not far, I remember with pleasure, from a vast factory owned by Mackintoshes,

Harry 'Philip' Burton with his bride Kathleen 'Kay' Henwood on their wedding day, 1923.

Mackintosh Caley's chocolate factory: when the wind was in the right direction the smell in the air was even better than that of a brewery.

the makers of Rolo chocolates. Apparently 700 people worked there and it turned out literally millions of Rolo tubes every week.

Our house had a small backyard which I remember for one thing only: the trauma of my second young brother Timothy's enforced departure. Two years my junior, Tim was born with Down's syndrome and was described in those unfeeling days as a 'Mongol child'. My parents followed the conventional wisdom and had him sent away to a 'home' when he was only three. My mother wept bitterly the day he was taken off and she visited him faithfully every fortnight for the rest of her life; he was housed in a ghastly Dickensian institution which I felt was little short of a madhouse. She took me with her just once and sadly she died before the revolution took place in attitudes towards the disability of Down's. Tim spent the final twenty years of his life – he died, a cheerful soul, at the age of seventy – in a standard semi-detached house with three or four fellow 'clients', all lovingly supported by carers. I visited him every year and wished my mother could have done so, too, and thus assuaged her inevitable sense of guilt at having rejected him as a toddler. Her third and last son, Rodney, who was born healthy in 1936, must have been a great consolation for her.

I lived in Norwich from the age of four until I was twelve and think of Norwich as my home town, if for no other reason than my lifelong allegiance to Norwich City football team. Since 1942 I have never set foot in the Canaries' Carrow Road football ground and yet on Sunday mornings – before the digital age – it was to the sport pages that I always turned first when I opened the Sunday newspaper and to the Norwich result before any other – and this despite the fact that nowadays I support what would logically have been my father's home team, Chelsea. (He actually supported Fulham, which was based miles away at Craven Cottage, near Putney Bridge.)

To digress for a moment longer, I have discovered that there is also a Burton family link with the city of Coventry. Back in the 1980s I learnt that Coventry has a street named 'Humphrey Burton's Road'. Once, when my daughter Helena was a student at nearby Warwick University, her mother and I made the short detour from her digs to Coventry and sure enough, there it was: Humphrey Burton's Road. Postcode CV3 6HX. I got out of the car and advanced down the middle of this well-to-do street, half hoping the occupants would come pouring out into their gardens to hail the arrival of their patron. I had been on television pretty well every week for a decade or more, so my face would not have been totally unfamiliar to the inhabitants. 'He's here!' they would cry: 'HB has come amongst us!' The reality was both prosaic and a little weird. The street remained empty, the front doors closed. My wife, at the time a professional photographer, posed me in front of the street sign bearing my name and took a couple of snaps. Normally she is a perfectionist, but when developed her photos came out blurred. The street's architecture was 1930s

Out of focus in Coventry circa 1988.

9

in style so the naming could have had nothing to do with my passing fame as presenter of *Omnibus* or *Young Musician of the Year*. I discovered later that the town's high sheriff in the early 1600s had been named Humphrey Burton and the name had been revived by an historically conscious town clerk when Coventry was expanding 300 years later.

I have an extremely soft spot for the city of Norwich: its noble cathedral and dominating Norman castle were familiar to me as a schoolboy, likewise the gentle River Wensum with its swans, and the city's medieval quarter. Before the Second World War I went to school at Thorpe House, a private establishment on the road to Great Yarmouth, where I was a happy pupil. Then came the evacuation to Salisbury, already mentioned. The winter of 1939–40 was a great disaster for me because soon after settling in Salisbury I contracted rheumatic fever and was ill for what seemed like months. I remember my father coming into my sickroom with a pile of books wrapped up in a blanket and announcing proudly that every one of them (twenty-one titles) was a 'Just William' book by my favourite author, Richmal Crompton. My father had raided Norfolk County Council's central public library, housed in the same building as his office, to provide me with Christmas reading. It was a great birthday present, even if only a temporary loan. What I did not realise until much later is that my father must have enlisted the support of one of the county librarians to take out so many books. That would have been the librarian Barbara Ellis. She and Philip were both members of the Norwich Players, a respected amateur theatre group based at the city's historic Maddermarket Theatre, which toured its production of *Hay Fever* to American, RAF and army audiences housed in aerodrome hangars and army workshops all over the county of Norfolk. I have no idea whether Philip and Barbara became lovers, but a couple of years after the war I was informed that my parents had divorced. That news came as a tear-inducing shock to me. Philip and Barbara subsequently married and my father threw caution to the winds; he resigned from his safe administrative job in Norwich and resolved to follow his star by making a living as a journalist and writer. They set up home in London, in a tiny top-floor flat above the opticians Dollond and Aitchison in Knightsbridge, just a short walk from the Royal Albert Hall. When I passed the site on a bus a few months ago the entire building was being redeveloped with scaffolding everywhere, but just after the war it must have been a most desirable address, apart from the absence of any kind of elevator past the third of seven floors.

I loved music when I was a boy, that is for sure. My happiest pre-war memory of my father is of his playing piano duets with his friend Bobby Pask, a schoolmaster from Hendon; the piano was in our Norwich front room at The Crescent. Their favourite pieces were excerpts from West End musical comedies such as *The White Horse Inn* and *The Arcadians*. I would stand at the top end of the keyboard just behind their backs, longing to join in: they were having so much fun! I guess it is no accident that duet-playing has always been my own preferred form of music-making.

I had already started taking piano lessons before the war from Miss Ida Snowden, who must have introduced me to *Scenes at a Farm* by Walter Carroll because when we moved to Salisbury I was encouraged to display my skills in that composition to a concert pianist named Frank Merrick; he was apparently a well-known pacifist, who was visiting our host, my mother's friend Dorothy. What I remember was the praise he showered on me. I already loved playing and it seems that the enjoyment I expressed (rather than any evidence of virtuosity, which was never my forte) came across to my listeners even then.

I certainly loved the sound of music. I recall the tremendous thrill I felt a year or two later when taking possession of my first 78 rpm gramophone record, given to me by my parents on my tenth birthday. On the A side was Purcell's *Trumpet Voluntary* (actually by Jeremiah Clarke) and on the reverse the *Solemn Melody* by Walford Davies, a thoughtful academic who succeeded Elgar as Master of the King's Music and was a popular schools broadcaster up to his own death in 1941. *Music and the Ordinary Listener* was the title of one of his series for general listening, a topic that has concerned me all my professional life.

It's something of a mystery to me that although my father writes of playing Schumann and Chopin when he worked as a pianist in the silent cinema, there were no volumes of printed classical music lying about on the shelves at home. But the radio was immensely important. When our weekly edition of *Radio Times* arrived I would highlight certain programmes that must never be missed, among them *ITMA* (*It's That Man Again*) with Tommy Handley, and *Monday Night at Eight*, a 'chat show' whose hosts, I remember, were Harry S. Pepper and Ronnie Waldman, then the Assistant Heads of Variety at the BBC. I have never forgotten the words of their signature tune:

> It's Monday night at eight o'clock
> Oh, can't you hear the chimes?
> They're telling you to take an easy chair:
> Settle by the fireside, take out your *Radio Times*,
> For *Monday Night at Eight* is on the air.

The air-raid shelters were built underground beneath the school playground. The photo shows my class assembling. Geraldine is extreme left and I am fourth from the left.

There was no other broadcasting network in those heroic, wartime days except for Radio Luxembourg, a commercial station which naturally had to be shunned by our family because of the advertising. My allegiance to the BBC was total, my life dominated by the jokes and patter and catchphrases which the whole nation waited to relish every week. Among them was the unforgettable line: 'Can I do you now, sir?' delivered by *ITMA*'s famous cleaning lady, Mrs Mopp.

The BBC also produced an annual yearbook and to this day I recall the secret thrill of turning the pages to discover a portrait of the actress Constance Cummings, who had taken part in a broadcast of *Beauty and the Beast*. I would stare at her expressive eyes for what seemed like hours. This was my first emotional involvement and very poetic it was. Apart from my father ticking me off for masturbating in bed after lights out, I have no further recollection of even halfway libidinous leanings until I started to attend St Augustine's junior school in Norwich, and even then my instincts were of the most innocent nature. I became good friends with a girl called Geraldine and conceived a pure desire to kiss her. I was still summoning up courage to broach the subject with her aunt, who was our form teacher Miss Manning, when the Nazis' bomb dropped in April 1942.

A few years ago I was brought back into contact with Geraldine Bishop, by then a widow in her seventies; we shared a mutual friend in a local music club. We eventually met in Norwich and at my request afterwards she kindly wrote these impressions of me as a schoolboy at St Augustine's in the early 1940s:

He would meet me at the school gate and carry my bicycle up the steps. We were good companions. Everything seemed happy. We had frequent air-raid warnings and Humphrey and I were 'trench monitors', having to carry piles of small mats, comics, pencils and paper to the underground air-raid shelters each morning, and collect them at the end of the day. I can remember enjoying our time together performing this important duty!

In those days we always seemed to be singing: hymns of praise, of course, but also folk songs, spirituals, national and patriotic songs ('Hearts of Oak Are Our Ships!') and settings of Shakespeare – 'I know a bank whereon the wild thyme grows'. Sometimes we sang in music lessons, but often just spontaneously – at the end of the day before the bell went. Then came 27 April 1942, which changed everything. The school was bombed – flattened – and my family were bombed out of our home and Humphrey's house was badly damaged. Sometime later Humphrey came to visit and to say goodbye for the last time. I can recall my joy when the headmaster asked me to take him to the other classes so he could say goodbye to the teachers.

There are no personal photographs to remember those times but I still have an 'Autograph Album' with a poem written by Humphrey, dated 6.3.41 just before his tenth birthday. Some things one never forgets.

In wartime Norwich money was in short supply. One day I lost a florin coin (10p), which led to my father upbraiding me. Oozing sarcasm, he called me Croesus, but as I had had no classical education the snub was wasted on me.

The autograph book and its owner, Geraldine Bishop.

The sense of shame the episode generated may nevertheless have contributed to a mean streak in my make-up.

Occasionally I could be a disappointment to my mother, too. One day I insisted on crossing to the other side of the road so that I would not have to walk with her. (We were on our way to the best food bargain in Norwich, the British Restaurant.) She was too fat, I declared; I did not want to be seen with her by my schoolmates. When she related the insult to my father that evening there was much unhappiness and weeping. My objection to her size mystifies me now, since photos of her show no sign of her putting on weight – with wartime rationing that sort of thing didn't happen. Unthinking children can be terribly cruel!

But soon I was to find family warmth and sympathy in a larger-than-life family, when I became part of a community experiment inspired by the ideals of Jews and Quakers. My attendance at Long Dene School, a community attended by many Jewish refugees, was less than a year away.

CHAPTER 2

A PROGRESSIVE
EDUCATION

With my younger brother Rodney, 1937.

FROM GERALDINE BISHOP'S sweet reminiscence I learnt that I actually returned to the temporary premises occupied by my bombed-out school, if only to say goodbye to the children and staff of St Augustine's. Without the bombing, might my parents have soldiered on in their unhappy marriage? Would pacifist Ted eventually have returned from his farm and carried off my mother to a second marriage? Presumably not: by the time my parents' divorce went through, my brother recalls that Ted was married and I know that my mother was deeply involved in an experiment in communal living which, so far as I am aware, never involved any conflicting romantic attachment. She stayed fond of Ted; of that I am sure, because she later entrusted me with a pile of his red notebooks stuffed with fascinating press cuttings, mostly reviews by Ernest Newman of the Wagner concerts Ted had attended in London in his youth.

There is no doubt that my parents' decision to separate meant that my education took a knock: I had been all set to move on in the autumn of 1942 to Norwich School; instead I became, virtually overnight, a boarder thirty miles away at Thetford Grammar School – arguably a less distinguished establishment than Norwich School but a respected institution where one of my father's best friends from his Fitzwilliam days, Charles Watson, was headmaster.

Thetford is an ancient market town on the borders of Norfolk and Suffolk. It was my first experience of being away from home and I have decidedly mixed memories of school life. I was keen on sport but my rheumatic fever was thought to have left me with a weak heart and I was not allowed to play games. I became an enthusiastic linesman and an expert keeper of arcane and symbol-laden cricket scorebooks, but that skill did not prevent me from being bullied for my alleged weediness night after night in the dormitory. About school lessons my mind is a total blank.

Only music gave me any sense of joy. As so often in my childhood I can see myself playing in a specific location: in Thetford it was on an upright piano squeezed into a corner next to the long tables set for school meals in the Victorian-era boarding house. I remember, too, the three works I was learning, though not my teacher: Grieg's Arietta in E minor from the *Lyric Pieces*, Bach's little D major Prelude from Book II of the pieces he wrote for his wife Anna Magdalena, and the D major Prelude and Fugue from Book I of Bach's *Well-Tempered Clavier*. Not easy stuff for a twelve-year-old, but at least it was real music and that was probably what kept me going in those dark months.

The little Bach prelude proved to be a lifetime favourite. In 1961, when I made a film for *Monitor* about the contrasting gifts of two bright but then unknown young musicians, Dudley Moore and Peter Maxwell Davies, I got Max to play the prelude on his harpsichord to his pupils at Cirencester Grammar School and then intercut it with Dudley jazzing up the Bach for the clients to dance to at the Troubadour café in Earl's Court, where he was resident pianist. I gave the *Monitor* film the blindingly obvious title of *Two Composers, Two Worlds*. But it's a good documentary!

Dudley Moore playing Bach. (*Monitor: Two Composers, Two Worlds*, 1961.)

That the year 1943 was a grey time in my life is confirmed by a summer 'holiday' I dimly recall where I was parked at some kind of posh hostel for kids who were temporarily without parents; it was miles from anywhere, in West Sussex. The only excitement for a lonely boy keen on plane-spotting was the constant movement of aircraft based at the RAF station on nearby Thorney Island; I like to think the planes were practising parachute drops for the D-Day invasion the following year. Inside the gloomy house, where I was the only 'guest' for several weeks, there was one bright spot: dozens of bound volumes of *Punch*, stretching back to the 1920s. With nothing else to do, I became a cartoon junkie and was made aware that there are many layers of English society about which I had not an inkling.

I don't recall feeling sorry for myself, however, nor surprised at the next spin of fortune's wheel which later in 1943 reunited me with my mother. She had found a job at a progressive school called Long Dene, which was housed at Stoke Poges in a handsome manor house twenty miles west of London. Kay was first hired as a live-in midwife to deliver the second baby of the headmaster's wife Karis Guinness and thus she became a full-blown member of a remarkable community; she worked as Long Dene's principal housekeeper for the next decade. She was paid a mere £2 a week but with the job came bed, board and education for her two boys. From a strictly academic point of view, this change of education was for me a distinct turn for the worse. From Thetford, a conventional, unimaginative but solid grammar school education, I was pitchforked into a test-bed experiment. And here I must freeze-frame my narrative for a moment to pay tribute to Long Dene, an *alma mater* that alas closed down in 1954 and yet remains – we former pupils still hold annual reunions – a vivid and important stage in the process of growing up.

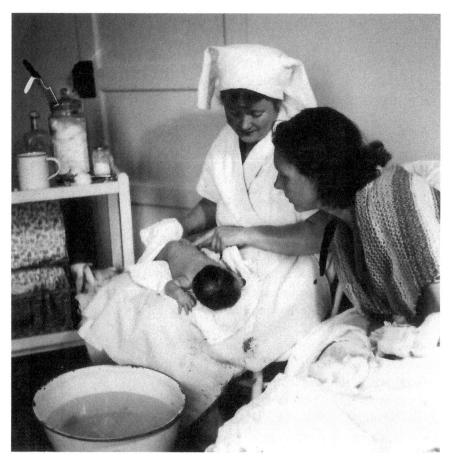

My mother the midwife. She delivered a baby daughter – Anthea – to Karis Guinness.

18

Stoke Park, the home of Long Dene School.

Long Dene had begun in a very small way before the war as 'an open air school for girls and boys 3–10 years' where (I quote from the brochure) 'the children are encouraged to conquer their own difficulties and be Independent as far as possible'. The prospectus was full of such fighting talk, which must have struck a welcome chord with free-thinking people, particularly in those incredibly unsettling days leading up to the outbreak of war in 1939.

A couple of educationalist dreamers, John Guinness and his wife Karis, took over Long Dene in the Quaker village of Jordans in Buckinghamshire – with the help of a timely legacy. The year was 1939. They had earlier been jointly in charge of the junior school at Brickwall, a progressive girls' school in East Sussex (founded by Karis's mother), which collapsed under the war's impact. Inspired by the Guinnesses' vision, new staff were recruited and Long Dene swiftly expanded into a community of like-minded spirits – many were vegetarians and most were pacifists, which is what must have attracted my mother. There were horticulturalists too, and people who knew about keeping bees and rearing goats. During the summer of 1940, with the Battle of Britain being fought out in the skies above southern England, the Guinnesses at Jordans faced a location crisis: buildings, including those housing the school, were being requisitioned every day to make room for evacuees from nearby bombed-out London. Faced with closure, John and Karis made the brave decision to relocate the school in the Manor House, Stoke Park, just a few miles away, which by an incredible piece of luck was lying empty. They moved in just a fortnight before the start of the September term. That is September 1940, when Hitler's *Luftwaffe* was softening up London and the Home Counties in preparation for the invasion. The Guinnesses arranged for outhouses and sheds to be converted into classrooms. Old railway carriages were brought in to provide more teaching space. Nobody ran away.

I knew none of this backdrop when I arrived three years later to join my mother. My chief excitement was that there were girls everywhere. First to attract my interest was a vivacious pint-sized girl from Czechoslovakia, Inka, wearing green slacks and a red pullover. Her best friend Gabi was from Germany; both were Jewish refugees with faultless English.

Schoolwork was very basic. After four years I took School Certificate in English and French, geography, history, maths and music. I had passed the Associated Board grade 5 piano examination a few weeks earlier and that provided half the necessary music marks. Today's teenagers take twice as many subjects, spreading them over a couple of years. Long Dene did not seek to rival the academic prowess of longer-established progressive schools such as Bedales, and only five of us sat the exams. We were thought of as trailblazers; in previous years there had never been more than one.

I have to concede that Long Dene's educational ambition was disappointing. I regret learning no Greek and very little Latin: later I had to teach myself Latin while in the army in order to get into Cambridge. I have a reasonably good ear for languages and could have taken advantage of the presence at Long Dene of native German-speakers to acquire a working knowledge of that noble language as well as of French. But I have never harboured any grudge against progressive education. What I gained from Long Dene was a sane way of living and an attitude of tolerance, both of which have stood me in good stead ever after. Many school periods were devoted to 'IW' – individual work – projects, initiated and later checked out by the teacher. Our class groups were not identified as a 'Grade' or a 'Form' but instead rejoiced in the names of animals and birds. The youngest pupils were Robins. Then came Ponies (six- and seven-year-olds), followed by Tigers, Kestrels, Falcons, Hawks and, right at the top, Eagles. A predatory bunch to be sure, but in name alone: in life the pupils constituted a peaceable kingdom. Children did much of the housework and most of the washing-up. The weekly school meeting, attended by both children and adults, made the rules and applied what were called sanctions to wrongdoers: I remember that when they were introduced in 1947 sanctions sparked a truly acrimonious debate.

The total community numbered about one hundred. I would guess around a quarter were adults: teachers, cooks, secretaries, handymen, medics, a goatkeeper, a cow lady, several gardeners. The Guinnesses willingly took on conscientious objectors, and Jewish refugees from Central Europe. One such young German was assigned to weed the school vegetable gardens but was brought indoors when it was discovered that he had inadvertently pulled up all the community's precious asparagus plants. Mine was the benefit: the unfortunate gardener was assigned to giving me piano lessons. His name

Self-government in action. I am seated centre in the doorway
chairing a Long Dene community meeting, circa 1944.

was Paul Hamburger, later one of the BBC's most admired and trusted staff accompanists.

Long Dene had established a rhythm of living to which, like my mother and brother before me, I quickly adapted; to echo the Old Lady in *Candide*, 'I am easily assimilated'. The manor house was quite splendid. Red-brick Jacobean with tall, stone-framed windows. On film nights, a 16 mm film projector would be installed and the entire school (so it seemed) would watch Russian classics such as *The Thin Red Line, October: Ten Days that Shook the World* and, most powerful of all, *Battleship Potemkin*. After such exposure it was little wonder that even a year studying modern European history at Cambridge could not entirely rid me of my pro-Soviet sympathies.

The grounds of Stoke Park featured spacious lawns, magnificent trees, a monumental lake and even a sunken rose garden that was said to have originally been a secret underground passage connecting the house with the church of Stoke Poges, the very spot that had inspired Thomas Gray's *Elegy Written in a Country Churchyard*:

> The curfew tolls the knell of parting day,
> The lowing herd wind slowly o'er the lea,
> The ploughman homeward plods his weary way,
> And leaves the world to darkness and to me.

I have special reason to remember that sunken garden. Because of my ailing heart I was still not allowed to play games but was always a keen spectator. One afternoon I was watching a tennis match when somebody skied a ball high out of court. Probably wanting to show off my prowess to the girls, I ran backwards like a cricketer in the outfield, ignored the warning shouts and at the very moment I triumphantly caught the ball fell backwards and eight feet down on to the flagstones of the sunken rose garden. My left arm took the brunt: I could see bits of bone sticking out of the flesh as I was carted off to hospital, where the wards were full of soldiers who had been wounded in the D-Day Normandy invasion a few days earlier. Long hot nights ensued, sleep often impossible amid the groans of the injured men. My own injuries were not in the same category, though they turned out to have long-term consequences: three bones were broken in my wrist and the first attempt to get them all realigned was not a success; the bones had to be broken and reset and I never recovered full mobility in my left arm: the bones still click when I rotate my hand and I had difficulty controlling my fingers when later I tried to learn the viola.

I recall sitting out on the lawn one hot afternoon at Stoke Park during that same summer, nursing my wrist in a huge plaster cast while I listened to the most lovely music coming from an open window in the house; a radio was playing at full strength and it was Mozart, the D minor Piano Concerto (K466), I learnt afterwards from the announcer, with Edwin Fischer the soloist. I listened spellbound. A few months later I saw that the same work was to be performed at the Community Centre in Slough by a group called the RAF Symphony Orchestra. Aircraftsman Denis Matthews was to be the soloist. I cycled over from school and that was the first symphony concert I ever attended. The players were all in blue uniforms and the Mozart was just as wonderful a second time. The Finale had such a jaunty tune, rounded off by a nonchalant trumpet. I didn't know it at the time but this RAF band contained many of Britain's best orchestral musicians, among them the great horn virtuoso Dennis Brain and the violinist Leonard Hirsch, who five years later was coaching the string players when I was a member of the National Youth Orchestra. The RAF ensemble had been carefully assembled under the knowledgeable eye of the connoisseur and impresario Walter Legge, who was then in charge of classical music for ENSA, an acronym standing for Entertainments National Service Association. The new orchestra provided the nucleus of players for Legge's dream, to create a world-class ensemble. It was founded in 1945 and he named it the Philharmonia Orchestra. And I can claim to have been in one of the first audiences to have heard it – a schoolboy who had ridden over on his bicycle from an unconventional vegetarian commune named Long Dene.

In the winter of 1944–45 the school was faced with another crisis. The end of the war was in sight and the owners of Stoke Park wanted their property back: situated close to a famous golf course, it had more earning potential as a country club than as a co-ed school. As it happens, our daily lives had become seriously uncomfortable: all through the summer and autumn of 1944 we had been hearing the menacing airborne clatter of the V1 doodlebugs. We would hear them in the distance almost every day and came to dread the moment when the rackety engine spluttered into silence and the missile's deadly descent began. But we survived unscathed: not many doodlebugs were aimed this far west of the metropolis. Later we discovered that Hitler had an even deadlier weapon up his sleeve, the sinister V2 rockets; they started raining down on southern England at the very moment the Guinnesses launched their hasty search for new premises. Once again their luck held. In the county of Kent, across a lake from a pretty National Trust village called Chiddingstone, they found a stately pile which had already served as a school before being requisitioned by the army; the estate boasted playing fields, a much bigger market garden than Stoke Park's and a 300-acre farm. It was perfect for the community experiment to continue! There was just one little drawback – the location. Chiddingstone Castle was less than thirty miles south of London, right in the firing line from northern France of that dreaded V2 rocket.

For me the move to Chiddingstone was unforgettable. Most of the children were sent home for an extra-long half-term holiday, but as a staff family member I had to help load up the pantechnicons that transported the entire school from Buckinghamshire to Kent. The castle's main building was a seventeenth-century manor house that had been given a Gothic Revival makeover in the Victorian era: the walls were refaced in sandstone and embellished with towers, the roofs decorated with battlements and turrets.

My school friend Brenda, who lived in faraway Cornwall, had also taken part in the move, and once we had arrived she and I decided to explore on foot. Beyond the school's front gate and up a country road we found a path leading into a wood. Ignoring all the 'No Trespassing' signs, we plunged in past a lurid gamekeeper's warning – dead birds strung up on a wire fence – and soon came to a lake; we followed a path past a large locked boathouse and beyond it glimpsed a splendid Tudor mansion. When we heard a shout from somebody in the garden we beat a quick retreat, fearful of being taken for poachers, and only when recounting our story to the grown-ups back at Long Dene did we discover that we had strayed into the grounds of Hever Castle, the family seat of Anne Boleyn. Four hundred and ten years later it

Chiddingstone Castle from the south. Three months after Long Dene moved here in spring 1945, a V2 rocket exploded in a cowshed a few hundred yards to the east.

24

The harbour at Mullion Cove, Cornwall.

was the country residence of a banking grandee, Colonel W.W. Astor, who was the owner of *The Times*.

For Brenda and me this modest romantic adventure was a bonding experience: I was an earnest student and she the dreamer who preferred going off on her own expeditions. She and her mother, a dancing teacher, lived precariously in a couple of wooden huts parked in a farmer's field just outside the coastal village of Mullion on the Lizard peninsula in Cornwall and for the next three years I went to stay with her nearly every holiday.

I fell in love with the craggy beauty of the cliffs between Mullion and the Lizard and the grandeur of the surf rolling in from the Atlantic. We had such fun swimming and surfing all day in Poldhu Cove or tramping along the flower-strewn cliff paths and inspecting the granite monument honouring the spot on the clifftop where in 1901 Guglielmo Marconi had sent the first wireless signals across the Atlantic. Brenda and her friend Gloria Bax (who was cousin of the dramatist Clifford and niece of the composer Arnold) would take me riding over the moors, venturing cautiously over the disused runways of the massive abandoned airfield of Predannack. Or we would walk over the golf course to the tiny cove of Gunwalloe, whose little church was remarkable for having a separate bell tower built into the side of the headland. In the churchyard was a wooden cross marking the grave of an unknown German

25

airman. I never knew why but it filled me with such foreboding that I felt the need to make a pilgrimage to that churchyard every summer. After supper we would listen to music on a battered wind-up gramophone with steel needles. My favourite music was Mendelssohn's *Hebrides* overture, closely followed by Rossini's *Semiramide* overture and Tchaikovsky's First Piano Concerto, all on 78 rpm discs. Having only one record for the Tchaikovsky, I was for years under the impression that the first movement concluded rather quietly with a cadenza; I had no idea that Brenda's family possessed only the first of the set of two or maybe it was even three discs of the complete concerto.

Once with Brenda's mother in command, the three of us embarked on a walking expedition that had us following the curve of Mount's Bay past the romantic castle-topped St Michael's Mount itself, and on through Penzance to Lamorna Cove. Next day we visited the spectacular Minack cliff theatre, which had recently featured in a romantic film drama called *Love Story* starring Stewart Granger and Patricia Roc; the centrepiece of the film's musical score was a miniature piano concerto called *Cornish Rhapsody*; the composer, Hubert Bath, has since been forgotten by everybody except Classic FM. From nearby Logan Rock our hike was a tough slog around the south-western tip of England to reach the slightly disappointing headland of Land's End, followed by friendly Sennen Cove. And then on the third day we walked north past the little airstrip where De Havilland passenger planes flew to the Scilly Isles. We were able to drink in the majestic sight to the north of Cape Cornwall – what a pity that magnificent headland didn't qualify as the legitimate land's end! We then explored the lighthouse at Pendeen and the pitheads of ruined tin mines before embarking on the final lap along Cornwall's north coast to Gurnard's Head – D.H. Lawrence country, I was later to discover – before we arrived at the truly beautiful town of St Ives, with its twin bays. For years afterwards we talked fondly about what for us had been a marathon exploration.

Sport at Long Dene School was fun. Its animator was the second master, Pat Job. He taught sciences but games (and garlic) were his passion. 'Quick's the word and Sharp's the toffee' he would cry as he whipped the hockey ball away from you in a needle match. We also played boys' soccer, occasionally fixing up games with other schools. Among our opponents was the Rudolf Steiner school across the county border near East Grinstead – we were told to avoid undue violence when playing these gentle souls – and a burly group of boys from Christ's Hospital, brought over by Philip Dore, one of that school's music masters, who for a time also taught me music once a week at Long Dene. He eventually married Suzanne, one of our school's gardeners.

26

Long Dene's First XI cricket team in 1947.
I am centre back row, with Pat Job on my right.

Long Dene vs. Christ's Hospital cricket match. Left to right sporting C.H.
borrowed robes: Colin Clyne, Trevor Morgan, me, John Pick and David Ogdon.

Music was even more important for me than games or girls, and many musicians contributed to my growing awareness of what 'being musical' implied. The aforementioned Philip Dore, for example. A fine organist, he encouraged me to sight-read with him (on the piano) Bach's wonderful Choral Preludes, myself picking out the bass line which the feet would have delivered in an organ loft.

Some of my fellow pupils at Long Dene were very musical. Peter Pick played the trumpet well enough for us to knock out the Haydn concerto together. Trevor Morgan was a decent clarinettist – we discovered Benny Goodman and played through a piano and clarinet version of his *Slipped Disc*, but I fancy we were stronger in arrangements of Schubert's Octet and the Mozart Clarinet Quintet, two fine clarinet melodies. Along with those classics, our *pièces de résistance* were the excellent Five Bagatelles for clarinet by Gerald Finzi.

My 1947 diary shows just how important music was becoming in my life: 'is there anything diviner than the Mozart G minor?', I rhymingly ask, with no fear of contradiction. The same month I subscribed to a new magazine called *Music Lover* and confess to my diary that 'Bolero got right under my skin'. In May I was having 'jolly good fun' in the school orchestra, conducting and playing viola. My diary also noted that I heard Walton's new quartet on the BBC's recently inaugurated Third Programme. And the Brahms *German Requiem* at the Royal Albert Hall.

Among the music staff nobody meant more to me than Lotte Kalischer, a Jewish refugee from Germany who after the war settled in Sweden. She played the violin with the sweetest of tones, getting me to partner her in Beethoven's 'Kreutzer' Sonata (a great thrill!), and she must also have been a good pianist because she passed on to me two German-printed cloth-bound volumes of the Beethoven symphonies arranged for piano duet. These are precious publications from which I still play every month. Lotte was also an excellent choir trainer. Blessed with eclectic taste, she would have us singing Tudor madrigals one week and Benjamin Britten's lovely *Hymn to St Cecilia* the next, mere months after its publication. 'Blessèd Cecilia, appear in visions to all musicians; appear and inspire' is how it begins, and W.H. Auden's invocatory words did that very thing, inspiring Britten to one of his loveliest melodies, and beginning for me a lifetime's devotion to his music.

Had my voice already broken? I cannot remember – I am generally pretty vague about the onset of puberty – but a few years later Lotte inspired what was by then my green baritone voice to sing its way lustily through the choruses of

Haydn's *Creation*. 'The heavens are telling the wonders of God': I was already a confirmed agnostic but not, it seemed, when it came to music.

Lotte may well have learnt about Britten from other members of the Long Dene staff. Liza, who looked after the cows, was a Benjamin Britten enthusiast. I remember her being beside herself with excitement when she invited me to listen to her latest record purchase, Britten's *Serenade for Tenor, Horn and Strings*, the original Peter Pears and Dennis Brain recorded version with the Boyd Neel Orchestra. I quickly bought my own copy from Decca, and equally quickly wore it to a frazzle with constant repetition. Two slightly older British composers were favoured by another very sympathetic member of the Long Dene staff named Norman Wormleighton. A Quaker pacifist, he joined the community as a gardener but was teaching the Hawks year group English by the time we were preparing for School Certificate in 1947. Music was his passion and his prize possession was a splendid EMG acoustic gramophone with an exceptionally large horn. The turntable's pick-up used needles but not the horrid metal ones employed by ordinary wind-ups and radiograms; Norman's were state-of-the-art triangular needles made of reddish balsa wood which needed special razor-sharp clippers to guarantee a durable but sensitive point. No oboe player ever cut his reeds with more devotion than that with which Norman prepared his needles, and the resultant sound was truly beautiful: one did not have to make any apologies for the recording process. Norman's gods were William Walton and Michael Tippett. To this day I hear in my mind's ear the sound of Walton's melancholy, dark-hued Viola Concerto as transmuted by the Wormleighton gramophone with its extraordinary papier mâché horn. Walton became my personal hero. I bought records of the Sinfonia Concertante, the Violin Concerto and *Belshazzar's Feast*. I discovered Frank Howes's lucid Musical Pilgrim analyses published by Oxford University Press. The first LP I ever bought (I'm fast-forwarding to 1953) was of Walton's searing First Symphony. My best work for *Omnibus* (fast forward another fifteen years!) was an interview with Walton about the love affair which inspired that symphony.

I owe an extra debt to the Wormleightons because apart from Norman's civilised way of living, which was quiet and gentle, exuding inner strength without any bombast, he was blessed with a wife, Susan, who in many ways was his opposite. She gave dancing lessons, in which we all joined enthusiastically if not very gracefully and without inhibition or prejudice. Susan had studied with the great German dancer Kurt Jooss, whose famous company had been given a wartime home at Dartington Hall in Devonshire. Bursting

29

with energy and jolly-hockey-sticks good humour, Susan persuaded us to use our bodies in an expressive way. I remember dancing quite a long solo to Gershwin's *American in Paris*, while a dozen of us must have participated in three movements from *The Planets*. Wearing garish make-up, we stomped around the tiny stage of Chiddingstone's Village Hall in basic Isadora Duncan-style costumes (designed by Susan), doing joyful back-stretches and yearning attitudes for 'Jupiter, the Bringer of Peace' and menacing foot-stamping stuff, fists clenched before our eyes, for 'Mars, the Bringer of War'.

I sometimes played piano for Susan's dancing improvisation classes, and several other talented women living at Long Dene encouraged me to develop my piano technique and expand my musical horizon. Tall and willowy Pamela Gaylord put Chopin on my map, if only the easier Preludes and Nocturnes, and also Scarlatti and Mozart. From Mary Davies I acquired a taste for Debussy and Schumann (the *Kinderszenen*). Mary had been a pupil of Alfred Cortot before the war, so keyboard touch was desperately important for her, though I despaired of ever achieving the relaxation and limp wrists she demanded. Even the headmaster's wife, Karis, gave me a lesson or two: she was an excellent performer herself, much given to flowery improvisation à la Rachmaninov, but I fear she rather disapproved of the way I pulled the tempo around in Debussy's *Clair de lune*. When I left Long Dene, her farewell report warned that I was too susceptible to praise and tended to skate over difficulties. It was hurtful at the time but a necessary corrective that I should have taken to heart immediately.

When VE day was declared on 8 May 1945 – Victory in Europe at last! – I found a very personal way to celebrate. I located a long stepladder and pushed it up through an unbolted trapdoor into the castle's topmost turret, dislodging on my way assorted pigeon nests and the piles of birdshit that had accrued over six years of war. The war had not meant a great deal to me personally, and yet that afternoon I felt possessed by some elemental force. The turret was falling to pieces but after scrambling up more rickety stairs I burst out into the open air, shouting for joy to anybody in earshot, 'The war is over!'. I don't know where I found it, but I even hoisted a celebratory flag. We school pupils decided that the most effective way to celebrate would be to make the next day a holiday for the staff. We even took breakfast to them in their rooms.

The end of the war enabled new and younger musicians to come down for the day from London to teach, among them a gifted horn player, Michael Maxwell, and the viola player Patrick Ireland, already a fine soloist and later a founder member of the Allegri Quartet (about whom I made one of my first documentaries, in 1961). Patrick was an exceptionally beautiful man with the nicest possible temperament. He gave me my viola lessons in the reverberant stone lobby of the castle's north door, a flattering acoustic, and listened patiently to me as I waded through a transcription of Gluck's Lament for Orfeo, 'Ché faro?', but he could not get me very far on the viola, much as I loved the soulful sound it made when he played it. I blame the sunken garden and the injury to my wrist.

Another welcome staff member was a Frenchman of gipsy origin (so we were told), Marcel Oppenheim, a classical fiddler with musical imagination and rhythmic vitality (what the Germans call *Schwung*), who introduced me to the hauntingly beautiful *Zigeunerweisen* (Gypsy Airs) of Pablo de Sarasate. But the most important post-war element for me was the arrival at Long Dene of a dynamic all-round musician named Anna Garfield Howe, who came over from Redhill once a week primarily to launch the school orchestra. I tried the trombone for a while but my lip didn't cooperate. I had a go on the timps, too, and occasionally wagged the baton, but mostly I sat at the piano filling in for the harp and any other instrument we didn't have. Mrs Garfield Howe encouraged me to compose, though she offered no serious tips on how to set about it, and I was a little upset (wrongly, I realised later) when she said my new Piano Sonata reminded her of Schubert. But in my personal hall of fame Mrs Garfield Howe, 'Gaffy', takes pride of place, if only because she enthused me with music. She was already in her eighties and was a familiar figure among musical families in Surrey. Her father, a Russian, apparently made a fortune from supervising the production of de Reszke cigarettes. She founded the Reigate Festival and her daughter Frances Kitching became a renowned Handel conductor who inspired the young musicians of Kent's rural Music College, which I attended in Maidstone as often as I could.

I had a first stab at two sublime baritone roles when I was studying at the college: Aeneas in Purcell's great *Dido and Aeneas* and Porgy in Gershwin's overwhelmingly beautiful and tender *Porgy and Bess*.

In the summer of 1947, Gaffy entered me for the Mozart concerto class at the Redhill and Reigate competitive music festival. That may sound a little dreary, but my set piece was the first movement of Mozart's F major Concerto, K459 – no pushover and a joy to perform! I practised assiduously until I could rattle off all the complex scales and rippling arpeggios and give the contrasting themes plenty of rhythmic vigour when appropriate, without ignoring the need for delicacy and the occasional stabbing accents when the harmony turned chromatic. The Schirmer edition I was given also supplied a complete

31

Life at Long Dene. The skaters on the ice must date from February 1947, the winter of the Big Freeze (I am third from the right).

The swimming pool at Long Dene, 1947; me diving.

With my contemporaries left to right: Peter Pick, me, Paul Newman, Trevor Morgan (kneeling) and John Janke.

My mother, with her sons Bill and Rodney (now aged 12), 1949.

cadenza. I knew that historically the cadenza was the passage in the movement when the soloist was given the opportunity to improvise a sort of fantasia on some of the principal themes; since I was something of a composer myself, I thought it would be legitimate to use the printed cadenza as a blueprint but nevertheless launch into variations of my own when the mood took me.

This was undoubtedly a rather substantial error of judgment. On the Reigate concert platform I enjoyed myself. Playing a concerto is an experience like surfing an ocean wave. I made a few fluffs, but nothing too blatant, and to my young mind the cadenza was little short of dazzling. You can imagine my surprise when the adjudicator rebuked me for my arrogance in daring to try to improve on Wolfgang Amadeus himself. He marked me down accordingly. Nobody had told me that the cadenza printed in the Schirmer edition was by Mozart himself – or that you mess with Mozart at your peril.

Needing an eyewitness of my early years at Long Dene, I wrote to my first girlfriend, Inka Vainstein, asking for her memories. We were in the same group for four years and writing from Prague her recollections were vivid about the school and about events that had quite slipped my mind. 'I remember', she writes, 'when you first appeared at Long Dene. It was shortly before the end of the spring term at Stoke Poges' (1943). She continues:

> You came to visit your mother Kay. Your brother Rodney was already attending Long Dene. We were all standing or sitting on the staircase in the hall rehearsing one of the Bach cantatas or Gluck's *Orpheus and Euridice*, or perhaps it was a film projection. Anyway, I remember that all the girls were very excited when you showed up and all of them, except me, showed their interest in you. For some subconsciously tactical reason I decided to more or less ignore you, although I was just as taken by you as the other girls. The result was that you noticed me, and during the summer holidays I received my first ever love letter from you. It wasn't very long and I remember one very flattering sentence: 'you are very beautiful when you smile'. And here again I acted proud and answered that we could never be more than 'friends'. But I did fall in love with you at the age of 12, and emotions at that age can be very strong. So when the term began we went for walks together in the evenings, one of the first was to the graveyard, where you stole some roses that were growing there and gave them to me. After that walk we ended near a wall of the Manor House which had ivy growing on it. You asked me if you could kiss me and I thought 'why do you ask, just do it'! Anyway, that was the first time I was kissed by a boy. It was all very romantic while it lasted, but that wasn't for very long as you soon started flirting with others. Actually I was quite unhappy until Trevor Morgan came and replaced you.

I also remember playing Brahms waltzes with you on the piano and loving it. As for memories of Long Dene as such, I loved it. I think its greatest asset was not only teaching us to love the arts, music and literature, but in forming our characters as honest and open-minded human beings. The morning discussions [school meetings] were a great lecture in democracy.

CHAPTER 3

BOYHOOD TURNS SOUR

An artful dodger ...

THIS IMAGE OF an artful dodger posed in front of one of Chiddingstone Castle's ornamental lions hints that I may have been quite a bright child. A pile of school reports, recently unearthed, shows that before the outbreak of war, at Thorpe House, Norwich, I was top of the form every term, and it was the same story at Thetford Grammar. At Long Dene I was the only one in our year who did well enough in the School Certificate to get exemption from Matriculation, allowing me to study for the sixth-form exams. But at Long

Dene there were no trained teachers at that level, so another school had to be found for me. One option was the public school at nearby Tonbridge, where even as a day boy I would surely have received the appropriate training to win a choral scholarship to Cambridge. But I had no ambition in that direction and I jibbed at the requirement that on Sundays I would have to attend services in the school chapel not once but twice: the thought of travelling ten miles each way by cycle or train was a powerful deterrent and I enrolled instead at the Judd School, a boys' grammar school which was also in Tonbridge, but at the other end of the town. Judd had an honourable history. It had been established by the Worshipful Company of Skinners in 1888, basically to provide grammar-school education for the sons of upward-thrusting West Kent farmers and shopkeepers. In my time Judd was the first English school to benefit from the 1944 Butler Education Act, being nominated as a voluntary-aided state school, government funded but with a substantial degree of independence. My acceptance there was no doubt smoothed by the fact that Judd's excellent headmaster, Frank Taylor, had attended the same Cambridge College, Fitzwilliam House, as my father. So after four years at a progressive co-ed school I was back at a grammar school, sharing daily life with 400 boys – with the crucial difference that I was not a boarder (there were none) and went home not to a conventional family but to a vibrant community of a hundred souls with whom I shared evening meals, weekends and a very social life.

It was a tough assignment to live in two worlds. And the choice of Judd, I see now, was hardly logical, since I already knew I wanted a career in the music world and Judd had no musical tradition, not even a qualified music teacher or a school orchestra. As would happen more than once in my life, I seem to have slid carelessly into a new stage, rather than forming a plan and sticking to it. True, there is an early entry in my 1947 diary indicating that my father, consulting with Judd's headmaster, had mapped out a path which led via Higher School Certificate to Oxford or Cambridge and to 'a degree in music and History or English', which is precisely what happened, interrupted by eighteen months of National Service as an army conscript. But it was more by luck than good judgment that I pulled it off.

My best subject at Judd was English, under the guidance of Mr A.J. Oakley, who encouraged me to learn chunks of Wordsworth, Milton and Shelley by heart. He taught me to write sonnets, and to contribute 'original' essays and pastiches in the style of Charles Lamb. With him we read wonderful Keats and Browning poems and studied *King Lear* and *Much Ado* but there were fewer visits to London theatres than there had been at Long Dene and I acted

School play, Judd School, Tonbridge. I am the bow-tied policeman on the extreme right. My most groan-making line: 'It was the copper that attracted the lightning'.

in only one play, George Bernard Shaw's *Passion, Poison and Petrifaction*, a farce of such marginal value that Mr Shaw omitted it from his own edition of his complete works. It was probably a blessing that on the first night of our production I skipped whole pages of the script in my nervousness.

A hint of my future film-making career in television occurred in my School Certificate exam, when I found myself spontaneously developing the thesis that John Keats had laid out *The Eve of St Agnes* in the form of a film script. I had learnt most of the poem by heart, indeed would shout whole stanzas to the roadside trees while cycling to school. My camera treatment included a selection of Keats's vivid scene descriptions, among them the sexy image of the moonlight streaming onto the kneeling heroine's breasts in her bedroom:

> Full on this casement shone the wintry moon,
> And threw warm gules on Madeline's fair breast,
> As down she knelt for heaven's grace and boon.

I was taught history at Judd by Mr 'Johnny' Allen, but all I remember now with any clarity is his emphasis on the significance of the Treaty of Brussels.

Signed in March 1948, it was supposedly a military alliance of the Western powers aimed at maintaining German disarmament but Mr Allen saw it (as I must have done, thinking of the many continental refugees I knew at Long Dene) as an important first step on the UK's road to European union. Anyway, I liked Mr Allen because when he was supposed to be discussing economic history he would sometimes talk about the stars.

The French master, 'Jimmy' Proctor, was close to retirement and something of a joke in terms of discipline, but nevertheless under his aegis we managed to enjoy two great opera-inspiring French authors, Molière (Mozart's *Don Giovanni*) and Voltaire (Bernstein's *Candide*), while another set book, *Le Grand Meaulnes* by Henri Alain-Fournier, made a deep impression on my romantic sensibilities, which were already stimulated by the high-flown poetic novels by Charles Morgan I had been reading. Morgan's novels, such as *The Fountain* and *The Voyage*, were books which entranced me but are nowadays completely forgotten. *Meaulnes*, on the other hand, is treasured by the French only slightly less dearly than the novels of Proust and Camus: the world of pure adolescent love is perfectly explored in the opening chapters, which are thought to be the best third of the book, before the plot becomes overly operatic. Fortunately this was the only section we were required to study, enough to savour an enchanted world that chimed in perfectly with my own love of moonlit nights and beautiful strange womenfolk such as Meaulnes's Yvonne de Galais. The novelist John Fowles offers a perceptive interpretation as to why adolescents are so attracted to this novel. 'Most of us,' he writes, 'remember adolescence as a kind of double negative: no longer allowed to be children, we are not yet capable of being adults.' He goes on to analyse Fournier's particular magic in *Le Grand Meaulnes*: 'to create a dreamland where these double negatives become a positive. When Meaulnes – the wanderer, the adventurer, the pathfinder – first stumbles upon the lost chateau, there is some kind of fête champêtre going on, with the partygoers dressed in costume from the 1830s. He overhears children explaining how just for the time of the festivities they are "allowed to do as we like". So the impossible dream is of a life in which we may stay children and yet run things – to play at being grown-up: this is, indeed, the novel's definition of freedom.'

Playing games had returned to being a central part of my life ever since the memorable day when a London heart specialist decreed that there was no longer anything wrong with me. That was a great moment in my life! Judd School played rugby, a game that was totally new to me, but since I could run fast it was decreed by the sports master that I would be useful playing in the wing three-quarter position. I was hopeless at tackling but with my pace I was able to score a few tries and within weeks had made it to the First XV. In the summer I played cricket and took quite a few wickets with my medium-fast bowling, mostly for the Second XI, though I was once promoted to our first team for a local derby against Tonbridge School's Second XI and survived a tense half hour at the crease. Both sports involved an inordinate amount of travelling time (plus booze and fags at the back of the coach on the way home) and occupied far too many Saturday afternoons that could have been spent playing the piano or going out with girls. But despite the grumbles I enjoyed sporting activities and never tried to 'skive off': game-playing was central to my life ever since I got my heart back and is nowadays what I miss most.

I drew the line at playing soldiers in what to my mind was the ridiculous militaristic organisation known as the Combined Cadet Force, but I enjoyed other afternoon post-school activities such as the Literary and Debating Society and the soirées organised by our art master, Mr A.P. Friend, at which we were introduced to such enjoyable modern poetry as T.S. Eliot's *Practical Cats*.

But for me the most civilising influence at Judd was Rupert Sutton, the schoolmaster violinist who agreed to supervise my musical studies. In his teens Rupert won an important violin prize at the Royal Academy of Music

Running the half mile at Judd School, Tonbridge, 1949.

but he must have suffered a crisis of confidence as a performer because records show that he gave up music and took an external degree in history at Birkbeck College, joining the Judd teaching staff a decade before the Second World War; in my time he rarely touched his fiddle. He had worked in RAF Intelligence during the war, rising to the rank of squadron leader, and had hung on to two leather-and-wool flying jackets, which made marvellous extra blankets when I stayed overnight at Springwater Cottage, the Suttons's rambling old house on the Leigh Road in Hildenborough. I would then take a two-hour piano lesson with his wife Grace on Saturday morning. In favourable weather I would cycle back to Long Dene for lunch. Pedalling away furiously, the journey would take about half an hour travelling at some 16 mph: I used to time myself, striving to break various personal speed records.

Grace and Rupert Sutton had met when they were students. She was an excellent pianist, trained by Tobias Matthay, and in my second Judd year she prepared me for the Grade 8 Associated Board exam, which as well as ear tests, sight-reading, scales and arpeggios involved learning four repertoire works: these were a tricky Bach gigue, from the Fourth English Suite, requiring lots of swagger and dexterity (and this was before the days of Rosalyn Tureck, let alone Glenn Gould or Murray Perahia, so there was no model performance to which one might aspire); the first two movements of Mozart's E flat Sonata K282, in which the challenge is to establish the correct degree of pathos in the first movement and of charm in the second; an early-period Beethoven sonata, op. 26 in A flat, a famous theme and variations, which has some hair-raising left-hand octave passages in the fourth variation; and finally the divine Menuet from Ravel's Sonatine. I can still play all four pieces but I did not do well in the exam, just scraping a Credit (120/150) which fortunately was all I needed for the performance part of the Higher School Certificate music exam. My ear tests were shamefully unimpressive.

With Grace as my perfectionist partner we worked up an impressive recital repertoire of piano music for four hands at one and occasionally two pianos. We played movements from Walton's *Façade* and the same composer's Bach transcription 'Sheep May Safely Graze'; the sparkling 'Entrance of the Queen of Sheba' (Handel); 'La Calinda' by Delius; Arthur Benjamin's catchy 'Jamaican Rumba'; Milhaud's *Scaramouche* and (more seriously) the duet sonatas by Poulenc and Hindemith. Our core repertoire also took in the gorgeous piano duet suites composed by a quartet of great Frenchmen: Bizet, Fauré, Debussy and Ravel. To these masterpieces we added Brahms's *Haydn* Variations, Schubert's A flat Variations and his top-drawer F minor Fantasia, Mozart's incomparable duet sonatas and his heavenly Sonata in D for Two Pianos K448. This four-hand repertoire became my musical bread and butter and those works have remained on my shelves and in my fingers – not to mention my heart – all my life.

It occurs to me now that I was probably the son the Suttons had never had; certainly they treated me as family (they had two daughters) and lavished care upon me way beyond the call of teaching duty. Rupert had written his history thesis on Sir Francis Drake and sported a beard to match; he dressed in a vaguely bohemian fashion, was a committed atheist, was later a CND marcher and would certainly not have been out of place at Long Dene. I guess he took me on as a favour to the headmaster but enjoyed bringing me on as a pupil. He was enthusiastic and musically well read; we studied scores together of Debussy's *Trois Nocturnes* and Dvořák's G major Symphony. But I fear Rupert didn't really know how to teach harmony or counterpoint, nor was he familiar with the university establishment – with the result that I was entered green and gauche into a scholarship examination at King's, Cambridge and inevitably lost out to well-drilled public-school entrants. It was a minor consolation that one of the examiners made encouraging noises about the suite for string orchestra which I submitted as evidence of my capacity as a composer. In four movements, the suite remained unheard until my sixtieth birthday when, as a favour to me, the St Paul's Girls' School string orchestra kindly played it through for me at a birthday party. Even on that festive occasion the audience response was muted and the work remains in manuscript. I never had any illusions about my limited talent as a composer.

However, it was Rupert who, in 1949, read about the National Youth Orchestra, then in its infancy, and persuaded its formidable director Ruth Railton to take me on. It was not a totally unjustified application as I had played timps in the Long Dene orchestra and, more seriously, at the Kent Rural Music School in Maidstone. My first day with the NYO percussionists was a defining moment: we were taken through our paces by John Dalby, the energetic Aberdeen school-master who was Ruth Railton's chief assistant and, as we tried our hands on such exotic instruments as the side drum and the castanets, it dawned on me that some of these young musicians were on a different planet from myself in terms of dexterity and musicality. It takes years to become a reasonably competent timpanist and months to acquire the skills to play a snare drum properly; a delicate trill on a triangle is no easy matter either, and to achieve an authentic soft swish of cymbals when the bronze plates are lightly drawn across each other demands considerable artistry, as does the specific rattle of a tambourine

Playing the timps at Kent Rural Music School. Frances Kitching conducts.

– you can't just shake it and hope for the best; you need to moisten the right thumb and drag it in a circular motion over the tautly stretched parchment. The glockenspiel and xylophone also call for virtuoso keyboard performers, indeed the only no-brainer is an instrument called the whip, which is not a whip at all, just two slats of wood joined by a hinge that you bang together as loudly as possible to produce a sound reminiscent of a whip crack.

My first NYO concert was to include Benjamin Britten's recent composition *The Young Person's Guide to the Orchestra* – a work to set beside Bartók's *Mikrokosmos* and Saint-Saëns's *Carnival of the Animals* as an educational masterpiece. I was allocated the whip and the triangle and also the castanets, which have a starring role for all of ten seconds and – oh joy! – the tam-tam, the big gong famous in those days as the introductory image of the feature films distributed by J. Arthur Rank; fortunately to play it, I didn't need to strip to the waist or wield a mighty hammer.

Playing in the NYO was on a par with performing a Mozart piano concerto at the Reigate Festival: fantastically exciting. The NYO's conductor in the summer of 1949 was Walter Susskind, then in his mid-thirties and bursting with vitality. He had trained in Prague and quit the city only two days before the Nazi occupation in 1939 to remake his life in Britain. He was a musician to his fingertips and conducted us in the marvellously colourful *Carnival* overture by his compatriot Dvořák (the score has a great tambourine part) and in a very stylish interpretation of Haydn's 'Military' Symphony; in this the percussion group crashed and banged on cymbals, triangle and bass drum with as much enthusiasm as a trio of Turkish janissaries guarding a harem. At the end of the evening Susskind set Leeds Town Hall alight with the blazing finale of the *Young Person's Guide*, then still a novelty in concert halls. Is there anything since Wagner that matches the moment when Britten brings back Purcell's theme in the brass, majestically riding the fugue's whirlwind orchestral waves? I doubt it. (But perhaps the arrival of the wild swan theme in the Sibelius Fifth Symphony would qualify.)

The conductor at the NYO's next course, Reginald Jacques, was twenty years older than Susskind, and could hardly match the Czech for lithe athleticism or European sophistication, but he loved his Mozart (the Symphony No. 39 in E flat). He inspired the big orchestra to deliver sensitive playing in Borodin's *Prince Igor* overture and got us smiling as we performed Walton's *Façade* Suites.

The doughty Miss Railton was impressive, too. She found time to give me some conducting lessons, passing on what I assume she had learnt at the Royal Academy before the war from Dr Malcolm Sargent: basically she taught me to beat time very clearly, using a long baton and insisting that I made a rhythmic bounce at the end of each beat, the equivalent, I suppose, of having a spring in one's step. During the course I had a little time on my hands, since I didn't play in every work, so Miss Railton co-opted me into her administrative team, making timetables and lists, checking music stands, laying out rehearsal chairs and so on. It was dogsbody work but useful experience and despite forgetting precious NYO documents on the top of a Bristol omnibus I must have done reasonably well since, a decade later, she recruited me again to be her assistant when, with Robert Mayer's financial support, she took what was known as The British Students Orchestra (top college musicians, older than the NYO) to the Brussels World Fair in 1958 and to Vienna the following year.

I think of the visionary Ruth Railton as a great force for good in my life. Although I remained unsure of myself, the general level of the NYO was extraordinarily high and being a member made one willy-nilly part of the country's musical élite: in my case it sowed the seed which thirty years later resulted in the creation of the BBC competition we called *BBC Young Musician of the Year*.

The other formative experience of my youth was a month-long stay in Paris with my penfriend Pierre Lhermette. His family lived in a handsome apartment in the 16th arrondissement, a very classy area. Another branch of the family owned a farm in Normandy, from whence arrived excellent supplies of butter and calvados. Compared with Long Dene, where the 'food reform' diet and the quite severe rationing still in force kept our calorie intake to sensible proportions, chez Lhermette the food was wonderfully rich – in my mind's eye I can still see massive sides of beef and a splendid roast fish adorning the Sunday luncheon table. René Lhermette, the *père de famille*, instructed me in the art of making a *cognac sucré* – a large lump of sugar gently dunked in a half-full brandy glass. The portly René played vigorous tennis at an indoor club (another novelty for me) and worked, I believe, in property; he owned a natty little Renault Quatre Chevaux car in which we drove around Paris in style, visiting grand cinemas in the Place Pigalle literally every other day – I was assured it was the perfect way to learn the French language. I was shown all the obvious Paris landmarks such as Notre-Dame, Sacré Coeur, Versailles and Malmaison. I particularly loved the art deco architecture of the Palais de Chaillot, from whose terrace – where Hitler had stood in triumph only eight years previously – the eye could take in the Tour Eiffel, the Champ de Mars and in the distance the Hôtel des Invalides, where thirty years later I would direct a television performance of the Berlioz *Requiem*.

Finally, I need to cast a shadow on this generally cheerful account of my adolescence. Before going to stay in Paris I had spent a couple of weeks in Cornwall with my friend Brenda. We had been friends for four years by now. Since leaving school in 1946 she had been away in Spain learning to dance the flamenco. We had seen each other every holiday and written many letters; she was the love of my teenage life. She had loads of boyfriends and I couldn't complain since I had had at least three infatuations with Long Dene girls, not to mention the local Tonbridge schoolgirls with whom I flirted on the train and kissed at Edenbridge on fireworks night. But my friendship with Brenda was different and steadfast: during those Cornish weeks spent tramping the cliffs and surfing at Poldhu Cove we became very close again; my diary shows just how intense the friendship had become.

'Our talk', I wrote, 'was quite a lot on marriage: foolish of me, for what can we think of marriage at 18 or 17? And yet I want to marry her. I love her more than anyone else I've ever loved … A year apart and we shall know for better or for worse'. The diary enlarges on my memory. It records that Brenda came down to see me at Long Dene within days of our Cornish holiday, 'a neat beret

Brenda.

perched on her lovely face and smiling eyes in her tired embrace. Full lips that needed no warming. I love this girl' (25 August 1948).

I convinced my teenage self that marriage to a dancer who loved music was not very different from marrying a musician. Brenda had decided to study ballet and dance in London and that autumn we exchanged more long letters; one Sunday in October I spent the day with her: my diary records: 'I had one of the loveliest days of my life. We went to her home [a bedsit in Bayswater] and then by bus down to Trafalgar Square after having coffee in some Charing Cross dive. We went in the Abbey [Westminster] – a wholly irreligious farce, with people walking about in the middle of the Service. And we walked about the cloisters [enjoying] the quiet old goodness of London. Then we went up Whitehall and heard a violinist chappie playing Bach in the street ... After dinner [i.e. lunch] at a Salad Bowl and a walk in the Park, we went to the Royal Albert Hall where we heard [Wilhelm] Backhaus. He played Beethoven beautifully. Walked across Hyde Park to Speakers Corner, crazy place. And then we made love for two hours at home, four floors up, looking across roof tops, oblivious to everything but each other. Now [I was writing the following day, back in Kent] I can still remember her wrapped up in her big coat, smiling goodbye and looking beautiful as hell – or heaven. Her atmosphere is still about me; I can sense her near me and her thoughts on me. I know she is thinking about me lots of the time. ... At school nothing much happened: I was tired. Choir practice: I only listened, though I'm going to conduct.'

We must have become lovers the previous year. Only a few days into my new life at Judd School, in September 1947. I noted that she had written in a letter: 'love me enough not to take me'.

The next holiday I noted a change in our relationship. 'I love her all the more. Yes, I do! Yet how far away she can take herself from me, by a mere look, or an uncalculated phrase. She doesn't know she's done it half the time. But when she looks at me, or clutches me tight, or drives me on, on, on irresistibly, I'm her slave' (17 April 1948).

I stopped writing my diary at the end of 1948, when I was still not yet eighteen. There's no clue on the final page as to what prompted me to give it up. Maybe it was fear. A month or so later I spent another Sunday with Brenda in London, probably very similar to the one described in the diary entry above. But a passage in the diary from the previous year suggests that I had a premonition that something would go wrong: 'What,' I wrote, just seventeen years old, 'do I know of making love? More than I ought – so much more. More than is good for me, so much that when I go out only one thing is inevitable. I used to believe that my goodness was sufficient counterbalance to my evil, that God would never punish me irrevocably. I daren't believe that any more. I'm not good enough. Unless I come off this mad course I'm leading I may end in disaster and drag others, whom I love, with me.'

Unfortunately God did not persuade me to abandon the 'mad course' and He was no help when disaster duly struck with the news in March that Brenda had fallen pregnant. I was miserable and guilt-ridden. The only precaution we had ever taken was for me to withdraw without experiencing orgasm. I was careful about it but Mother Nature obviously decided that my evil outweighed my goodness.

I cannot account for the Victorian nature of my moral code. At the beginning of the pregnancy I was in denial. When I took part in the school cross-country race at the end of March I persuaded myself that if I could win the race, the pregnancy news would not be true. I came second – my best-ever result. My schoolboy life proceeded as if nothing had happened. I prepared for Higher School Certificate. I joined the National Youth Orchestra. I took my Grade 8 Associated Board exam. I won an athletics trophy.

All this while I was shadowed by the guilt that I had not taken proper precautions, that I had brought Brenda's dance training to a halt, that I had ruined her life; also that I didn't have the courage to tell my closest school friends or even my mother – in fact, my mother died over three decades later, blissfully ignorant of her son's teenage misdemeanour and her new status as a grandmother. It was Brenda's mother who took control. I was to say nothing; my only confidante at Long Dene was to be Lois Pinchbeck, the needlework and geography teacher, who was an old friend of Brenda's mother. Other friends were told that Brenda had decided to return to Spain for more studies: flamenco was already her speciality, so that made sense. In fact she lived for months in seclusion near Minehead, on a Somerset farm owned by friends of family friends. I saw her fleetingly in the summer. But during my autumn

Me, sitting cross-legged, with Foster, Offen and Dolding –
after unexpectedly winning the relay cup, Spring 1949.

Brenda the
Spanish dancer.

half term, when she was big with child, Brenda and I spent a night together in a Somerset guest house near Porlock. In our room we were tender and loving. Her skin was smooth, her belly round and she gleamed with good health and serenity: I was very moved. We went for a gentle walk in a valley near the cottage where the poet Coleridge claimed (while writing his poem *Kubla Khan*) to have been disturbed by 'a person on business from Porlock'. I liked this detail because at Long Dene I had sketched a 'symphonic poem', no less, inspired by Coleridge's opium-fuelled vision of the stately dome in Xanadu. I told the landlady that I was on leave from the army. I doubt whether she believed me but she was sweet and understanding. I had spun my mother an elaborate story about hitch-hiking to Birmingham to see a violinist friend from the NYO. Nobody challenged me. Late in November Lois told me Brenda had had a baby boy. I still chide myself for not insisting that I should see him for myself and for not offering her support. I had been sidelined. After two weeks she bravely handed the baby over to an adoption society, a decision which must have been shattering for her. She then went back to complete her dancing studies. I am ashamed that I did not have the imagination to reach out to her at such a desperate time. A couple of summers later, when I was on leave from the army, my diary notes that I saw her dancing professionally in a summer show at Portsmouth but I have no memory of that encounter. In her twenties Brenda married an ex-RAF officer, met locally, with whom she had two children. However, this is not the end of our story, as will be revealed later on.

For the time being I had escaped scot-free from censure or responsibility. But I felt guilty as hell: nursing my shameful secret cast a blight on my final two terms at Judd, indeed on my entire young manhood. On Judd School speech day that year I was instructed to deliver, in French, some resonant lines from Jean-Jacques Rousseau, beginning: '*L'homme est né libre et partout il se trouve dans les fers.*' The rhetoric was impressive but I cannot discern any connection between conditions at Judd School in 1949 and the Social Contract of 1762. The reading was selected by the deputy headmaster. I have no idea what prompted his choice. He knew nothing about my private life. However, I certainly felt trapped by the social conventions of my own time and bitterly regret that I did nothing to make contact with Brenda, a failure which must have greatly upset her.

Despite the trauma I did well enough in the Higher School Certificate examinations to be awarded a state scholarship; the problem was that it was for a place at far-off, undervalued Durham University. But between them my father and my headmaster managed to get it transferred to their own Cambridge *alma mater*, Fitzwilliam House. After a single term at Judd as head boy I left school at Christmas 1949 and waited in an intellectual and emotional no man's land for my National Service call-up papers, due any day and guaranteed to release me in time to go up to Cambridge in the autumn of 1951. Despite my mother's pacifism I made no attempt to avoid joining the army: I simply went with the flow.

I recall only one positive event from that winter: the screening in Tonbridge of the MGM musical *On the Town*. I wrote an ecstatic review for the *Tonbridge Free Press*; I think it was the first time ever that my words appeared in print. In those days I was quite serious about wanting to become a music critic. I was an avid reader of the leading music writers of the day, especially those erudite double-barrelled critics from the posh Sunday papers Edward Sackville-West and Desmond Shawe-Taylor. It was after attending a lecture given by the music critic of the *News Chronicle*, Scott Goddard, that I asked how one set about becoming a critic. Mr Goddard generously responded by inviting me to be his guest when he reviewed opera and concert performances in London. He was the kindest of men and a very good writer. With him I saw several exciting productions, including my first Verdi opera, *Simon Boccanegra*, vividly sung in English at Sadler's Wells; on another occasion, at the Nag's Head pub, across Floral Street from the Royal Opera's stage door in Covent Garden, he introduced me to Constant Lambert, who was gloomily drinking alone at the bar before going on to conduct; he and Goddard had been students together at the Royal College. I was in seventh heaven to meet a friend of William Walton's and the author of that much-loved polemic *Music Ho!*, but Lambert's poor health was sad to behold. He died soon afterwards, two days short of his forty-sixth birthday. One of the first documentaries I commissioned for BBC2 was directed by Francis Coleman in 1965: *In Search of Constant Lambert*.

To round off this chapter I quote briefly from the letter I received from a fellow pupil at The Judd School named Graham Offen. Graham's father owned a butcher's shop in Edenbridge and also kept the King Henry VIII pub in the village of Hever. 'Blondie', as we called Graham, was two days older than me and died in 2008. I boarded with him when the school was in quarantine. In a letter written over a decade ago, Offen recalls the social impact of Long Dene on the innocent young men of Kent:

'On several occasions we were invited by Bill to take unofficial Judd soccer and cricket teams to play against Long Dene School. Long Dene was a very progressive school and it came as a bit of a shock to us country boys to notice that all the teachers were addressed by their Christian names … Musically', Offen continues, in jocular vein, 'Bill was extremely active … His composing talents were less well known but long before Winifred Atwell or Russ Conway had become household names, Bill had collaborated with one of his classmates (yours truly) to produce a catchy Western Ballad, for two pianos, with lyrics impressively entitled "Cowboy Joe". Sadly it never made the Top Ten Thousand and is in fact still awaiting general release.'

'Cowboy Joe' has completely slipped my mind but Graham and I obviously had fun – simple, gauche, innocent fun. We were schoolboys. But now – and this troubled me deeply – I was also the father of an illegitimate son. The future seemed depressingly bleak.

CHAPTER 4

NATIONAL SERVICE

No.3 Troop 7 Selection Regt. R Signals March 1950. Inst. Cpl Hinds. Cpl Harrison. L/Cpl Burness

Fourth from the left standing in the middle row, a grim Signalman Burton H.

IT WAS IN March 1950, shortly before my nineteenth birthday, that I at last received joining instructions and a travel warrant. So the die was cast. I took a train from King's Cross to Darlington where regular soldiers, older men, met us. They shouted orders at all and sundry as if we were already in uniform and eventually corralled us innocents into 3-ton lorries for the short drive to the North Yorkshire moors and Catterick Camp: the reality of National Service was upon me.

The first days were the worst. Basic training was a total melting pot, all walks of life and social backgrounds lumped together in a vast stone barracks. Terrible coarse language. Impenetrable accents. A shock to the system.

I kept my father in the picture throughout my National Service and will use excerpts from my letters to provide impressions of my army life, which was, to say the least, a formative experience.

Catterick Camp, Yorks 29.3 [1950]

Dear Philip,

I doubt whether the Army is as bloody as it was in your day, though these first few days have certainly been pretty dreadful. We suffer no real hardship: there is drill, and P.T., getting up at 5.45AM and eating pretty awful food; but I feel quite fit – the point is that there is absolutely no chance to sit down and really think, or even write letters. Every moment finds something to do, especially when you spend hours bullshitting boots you will only wear once or twice.

At the moment I'm in with the mob, but on Saturday the élite transfer to a Potential Officer's Training Regiment, which is much tougher work, we're told. In these fairly modern barracks we're well off in that we eat in the same building, wash-house next door, with lots of basins and generally boiling hot water; only 14 in the room, radiators, quite good beds, a Naafi next door. The Corporals to our Troops are quite fair, if you work hard, but they swear so much! (As do the other blokes in this room.) The routine at the moment is mainly drill alternating with weapon training; up at 6 or earlier; 5.30 onwards is spent cleaning, which takes ages. I am being very conscientious because it may help later. The immediate future is fairly clear – on Saturday to the new Regiment; approx. six weeks square bashing etc. And then a W.O.S.B [War Office Selection Board]. If I pass that (which I doubt) then I move on to O.C.T.U. [Officer Cadet Training Unit]; otherwise I shall apply for a transfer to Intelligence Corps or Education. If I don't get them I shall stay a Signaller for a while, but I'm not crossing that bridge yet!

On Saturday – my birthday – we had a hell of a day, mainly because of a very powerful inoculation in the right arm, which made it useless for two days and caused six blokes to faint in my troop!

Latin is, for the time being, impossible but I shall apply for an Educational Course when I get settled down. ['Latin' refers to my need to learn enough while in the army to pass the Cambridge entrance exam; no Latin, no Cambridge, simple as that!]

No piano, no wireless, no Remington shaver, no peace! But so far I'm still alive and hoping to make the best of it. Any used magazines etc will be extremely welcome.

My best wishes to the family; I trust everyone is well.

　　Much love,
　　　　Bill

Drill – 'square-bashing', as it was called – meant hours of patterned marching every day in heavy boots whose toecaps had to be polished like mirrors for the daily parade. And it was bitterly cold on those Yorkshire moors, as this letter suggests:

I was had up on Parade last week – we have one every day, it's the most frightening part of the day, and today I nearly died of frost-bite from the bitter wind and snow cutting across the square. Shaving in cold water is a pretty frequent occurrence and it means a new blade every other day.

Inevitably there were ignominies: mine came early, on the firing range. I had never held a rifle in my life. It was astonishingly heavy, more so when dummy bullets were added. I soon discovered that I couldn't close my left eye, which you have to do in order to take aim through the sight with your right eye. The NCO thought I was malingering and called an officer. He began by suggesting that since I *could* wink with the other eye I should try to hold the gun left-handed. This is not recommended practice. I've seen left-handed violinists [for example James Barton of the original Allegri Quartet], but left-handed marksmen are rare and I was never one of them. The officer held a piece of cardboard between me and my weapon but my six shots at the target all went well off the board and thereafter I was rarely invited to fire a shot, certainly not in anger. Though I still had to keep the blasted gun in immaculate, well-greased condition. And carry it on assault courses.

A few of my contemporaries were assigned to the Intelligence Corps, but I don't recall being offered that attractive option, which carried with it the chance to learn Russian. This was the destiny of several slightly younger contemporaries such as Michael Frayn and John Drummond, who doubtless attended schools with a good military network and greater clout. The Education Corps was rumoured to be another cushy destination, but staying in the Signals meant I would be learning some physics, and that would be useful in my music degree course at Cambridge:

I'm quite happy just to lie down and relax when the weekends come along. Next Sunday most of my squadron are going on a Victory Parade at York Minster. I escaped the hypocritical affair, which entails large amounts of bulling, creasing and extra drill, because my battle-dress tunic is the wrong type. We get 3 days leave at Whitsun, Friday evening till Tuesday Reveille, and I should like to spend some of the time at Hitchin [my father's new home town] – hitching down on Friday night, though I doubt whether I'll be there before 11pm or midnight.

We spend most of our time talking about our last leave or working out when the next one will be.

This week has been very easy for us, I'm happy to say; we've not been on the Assault Course, and we've done only one period of P.T. This morning we went on a tactics exercise, running about through brambles, crawling through mud on our stomachs, people firing blanks and throwing thunderflashes left right and centre. I carefully didn't fire a round because I didn't want to boil out my rifle tonight.

Tomorrow I start training for Athletics; I hope to do quite well because it is a useful method of getting out of objectionable jobs. Getting out of things is quite an obsession!

The most interesting part of training is Method of Instruction, where we learn the right way to give lectures and give 10 minute ones ourselves. Mine will be on Hitch-hiking, I think: its theory and practice. I should be able to work out some nice cracks.

This week I am 'Course Corporal' – I wear two temporary stripes and am in command of my course, making them get to periods on time, calling the roll and so on, quite a responsible job.

The blokes in 86 Course – 2 weeks ahead of us – are starting to get their WOSB postings, so in about three or four weeks' time I shall know the rough shape of things to come for the next 16 months.

It's amusing how quickly I became an old lag in those early spring days at Catterick:

I am now working in the Post and Pay office. I do about an hour's work every day … I read 5 newspapers nearly every day which is very instructive; go on parade once a week; wear shoes all day and generally feel I'm wasting time. My chief reading just recently has been the Kinsey Report, which four of us bought for ten bob and sold for a quid a week later (I know a good investment when I see one!) and a Penguin on Tudor England. I plan to follow that with some Oscar Wilde – Everyman edition – and, of course, Teach Yourself Latin, though that's not easy. A friend brought back some piano duets last weekend and we had a very pleasant evening playing Mozart and Schubert – since then we've not been able to get near a piano unfortunately. I hear occasional concerts, but the wireless situation is not too good and I feel very starved musically and somewhat depressed about my musical capabilities; I hope a little leave will either dispel doubts or convince me that I am not really good enough to read music and that I must do something else with my life, but I think this is just a passing phase of depression – I have got a Credit in Music, H.S.C. [Higher School Certificate] and a Credit in 'Finals' piano, so I can't be altogether useless.

One of my 'very ordinary' medals for athletics.

Though I must admit that the thought of writing an 8 part double fugue rather terrifies me! [As well it should: I never mastered the art of writing fugues.] With all my scientific knowledge acquired in the Signals I ought to get quite a good job with HMV or Decca if I ever felt like it, which I doubt. [I never explored this career path.]

… The Korean situation was very much in the forefront of our thoughts last week, with a lot of people talking madly about war, talk which worried me terribly. But somehow the crisis seems to have passed, even though the Americans are getting pushed back all the time – Korea seems so far away from this playing at soldiers business we do here.

I was pathetically anxious to do well and I set off to the War Office Selection Board in Hampshire with high hopes for my selection at the Barton Stacey camp. One was required to prove one's intelligence, leadership, physical strength, stamina and social skills. And also, more demanding, one's practical side. As leader of a small group I had to work out how to cross a river using a piece of rope that was not quite long enough for the task. I forget the details but recall that I didn't have a clue, so asked for advice from my colleagues in the group, one of whom came up with a sensible solution which meant we all crossed over without getting our feet wet. He probably prospered as a plumber; I duly became a second lieutenant. Some well-earned leave followed the WOSB and I was scarcely able to conceal my self-satisfaction when I next wrote to my father:

I'm relieved to say that I passed the Selection Board as 'recommended for O.C.S.' (Officer Cadet School), though not without a considerable number of butterflies in the stomach! The thought of spending 18 months 'learning a trade' with hundreds of other 'failed WOSB types' appalled me. It's not snobbishness; I just wanted to be treated as a human being, and have my intellectual tendencies recognised and partially catered for rather than laughed at or ignored. One boy from Eton was failed – 'not thrustful enough' – so a good school isn't an automatic pass. Which is of course a good thing.

Back at Catterick, the summer of 1950 passed quite agreeably and after only four months in the army I had a stripe on my sleeve.

We get the rise when we pass WOSB and are waiting to be posted to the Officer Cadet School at Aldershot, which for me won't be till July 28th I think. Normally such time is spent attached to courses still in training, helping instructors etc, but there are so many of us at the moment that seven blokes are constituting a Working Party (not quite the same as fatigues, thank heavens) painting lockers in Barrack Huts, creosoting the Assault Course, putting up swings for a regimental fête in a fortnight's time (in which I shall be running if I'm still here) and erecting and designing a superb slippery pole affair for the same event. We also have several pleasant privileges; get up later, don't queue for meals, don't fold up blankets every morning, don't go on parade at all. So I hope to get some Latin learnt and investigate a little more carefully the artistic (?) life of Catterick and also the beauties of Richmond (architectural not human, of course). I had a very pleasant leave, though it slipped past awfully quickly, partly because I broke it up somewhat by going down to Portsmouth for the week-end to see Brenda in her show – the resident summer show on the South Parade Pier. [My father knew nothing of Brenda's pregnancy and the birth, the previous November, of the son she had named Nicholas.]

The Officer Cadet Unit at Mons Barracks in Aldershot turned out to be another six-week melting-pot experience. Whether one's final destination was the lowly Service Corps or the Coldstream Guards one had to go through the gruelling test that was Mons. I was never fitter in all my life, and with my white blancoed belt, my immaculate shiny boots and my chic beret, sporting a white plastic disc which allowed the Royal Signals's regimental emblem of Mercury the winged messenger to stand out in gilded glory, I had never been so smartly turned out as I was at Mons barracks. Or in such good company. A few beds along in the barrack room slept the Hon. Desmond Guinness and across the aisle his cousin the Hon. Martin Oranmore and Browne. I was never again to sleep in such high society. But on the parade ground we all quailed under the bullying voice of the regimental sergeant major, RSM Brittain. His bellowed orders and withering comments were alleged to have reduced blue-blooded aristocrats and the sons of foreign royalty to nervous wrecks, but I confess I quite enjoyed being treated as a gentleman after the coarseness of Catterick and I never heard him call anybody 'a 'orrible little man', which was said to be his catchphrase, like something out of *ITMA*. A letter to my father soon after arriving sets the scene:

> … a basic six weeks course in infantry tactics (regardless of our eventual corps), which entails a great deal of outdoor work, all night schemes [exercises], dawn attacks, map-reading and what have you. There are about 90 periods of tactics in the six weeks, and about 70 of drill, and the rest of the time we do Administration, Military Law, Method of Instruction, Messing, officer qualities and so on. There's no doubt that things are well and highly organised but it's an awful strain to begin with, up at 5:30 and never in bed before 11:15.

In another letter I expressed my resentment about the way Russia was always cited as the potential enemy (it was less than five years since the end of the war we had won with the help of the Russians).

While I was at Mons the Labour government extended National Service from eighteen months to twenty-four. If I had to stay in the army until March 1952 that would put the kybosh (as we said in those days) on my planned entry to Cambridge but luckily those with guaranteed college places were eventually given exemption. The downside was that my posting, once I finished officer training, would be in the UK, not to an exotic location such as Cyprus or Jamaica. But it wouldn't be to war-torn Malaya or Korea either; that was the relief. My last letter to Philip from Aldershot chronicles a minor triumph:

> I've not got much news except that I was in the boxing after all [I had dislocated my knee a few days earlier] and fought this afternoon, losing quite a close but very rough fight!! My nose bled considerably and my face feels far too big for the bones but I wasn't dishonoured, in fact I knocked my opponent silly in the 2nd round.
>
> Otherwise there have only been the exams and final gradings. I, the inexperienced cadet, was second best in my platoon of 24 which pleased me somewhat, and in the exams I was fairly high up, with 95%, 70% and 81%. So I've not disgraced the family name.

I made no secret of my dislike of army life:

> One of the silliest things is haircuts. We have to have them at least once a week at 1/6 a time; in the last four weeks I've had mine cut five times. Farcical because it just grows again quicker.

In September it was back to Catterick Camp but now as a future officer and a gentleman earning 22 shillings [£1.10] a week.

> In many ways life here is very good in comparison with all my previous regiments etc. I have been playing the piano quite a lot in the Naafi with friends – Mozart trios, sonatas and things with a clarinet and violin. Most pleasant. [Mozart's *Kegelstatt Trio*, allegedly composed while he was playing a game of billiards, was included; it was an appropriate choice for the Naafi canteen.]

I realise now that attendance at the Officers Training Wing was tantamount to going to a technical college for half a year; I told my father that I was in favour:

… It's marvellous to start using one's brain again after six months and the course will be interesting even if hard work. We've just started on Line Equipment – field telephones of all shapes, sizes, fullerphones (morse code transmitters), exchange systems and dreadfully complicated circuit diagrams full of squiggles and squirms: and horrible equations and so on. It has absolutely no relation to music or history but I'm determined to master it all – after all it might mean a good job at the Post Office in later life! [Groan! What a ludicrous observation: I can't have been serious.]

The young officers produced 'Someone at the Door' [by Campbell Christie] last week; it was really very good and the girl in it was astonishingly good to look at. When I'm commissioned (a favourite phrase!) I shall take a great deal more interest in out of school activities, quite apart from music; one thing: I do hear a nice lot of music on the radio in the evenings whilst I'm busily polishing my boots or learning Fleming's Right Hand rule [the latter was a way of memorising the rules – I quote – for working out the direction of motion in an electric motor or the direction of electric current in an electric generator].

They wouldn't give us driving licenses – not sufficient practice and experiences, which was quite true really.

Our trip to the Lakes was absolutely terrific even though it rained most of Sunday. I never realised how much Arthur Ransome had affected my childhood memories!

My love to the family and I hope you're all well.
     Bill

I seem very keen to emphasise to my father that life in the army is not a picnic:

The driving course [I told him] lasted a fortnight, at the end of which I knew quite a lot about the workings of the car and could drive motor-bikes and trucks by night or day. The final run was about 150 miles, all over the Yorkshire moors: Ripon, Pateley Bridge, Skipton, Ingleton, Hawes, Leyburn and back, across all the dales. The last 50 was in the darkness, starting about 11.30 p.m.

I thought that having passed Basics my exam worries were over but I immediately ran into a lot more trouble with the next fortnight's course which was Line Equipment, all sorts of telephones and telephone exchanges, complicated circuit diagrams and so on. We had two exams on Friday and haven't yet had the results; I think I've done well enough to get by. Now we are on Line construction, laying cable, learning how to lay it across roads and rivers and what to do under fire and so on. It is reputedly interesting work and more fun than the last two subjects. You will notice that I've not seen any wireless sets yet – I shan't see one until I'm commissioned.

… I saw the Garrison theatre's production of 'The Chiltern Hundreds' on Saturday night. Poor production it was, though I didn't think it [the play] very funny anyway. The weekend before I spent a '48' at Great Ayton with the Newmans, very enjoyable too – I saw a grim film by Rossellini 'Germany Year Zero' very moving indeed. The rest of the time I spent eating, drinking and playing Canasta – and of all things beagling for the first and last time in my life.

Getting commissioned was akin to a first communion or a confirmation (not that I have experienced either of those rites): I remember the parade ground at Catterick, and the swagger of the assembled troops. Two months earlier, when course 251 passed out, my future BBC colleague Ned Sherrin had taken the parade, his voice trembling with emotion or maybe nervous tension as he barked out his orders. Naturally Ned had been assigned the leading role that morning: he was already a star. And then it was the turn of my 259 course. I would like to say that I followed in Ned's boot-steps at our passing out parade but dammit I can't remember.

Nov 17th 1950: I seem to have got through all my exams safely and not fainted on the Assault Course or broken down on the 10 mile bash. But nobody would deny that it's been hard work, especially the last fortnight. I have an average mark of 79% for all the exams so far which is quite good and I was actually top of the 'Organisation and Administration' course which we had last week. The Assault Course has been very tough – practices every day in order to get within the set time. It's full of nasty obstacles and most of us suffered cuts and bruises in a small way – I took a lot of skin off my hands (which was unfortunate as we have a Boxing Tournament all next week) but it's all over now. The forced marches were nearly as bad: 10 miles in 2 hours 5 minutes in full equipment! I was lucky and got a second wind.

I bought a second hand Sam Browne [an elaborate officer's leather belt] yesterday for 50/– [£2.50] – it needs a hell of a lot of work unfortunately. Our pay will eventually be 13/– a day, so even with mess bills (which are pretty substantial) I should be able to save a fair amount once I've paid off all my accounts for buying clothes. But they have grapefruit for breakfast in the Mess so it's definitely worth being an officer!!

I hope your play is going well. I am taking part in 'Murder on the Second Floor' [a 1929 play by Frank Vosper] which we are producing for Xmas. I don't think a lot of it but we have a very good producer. Rehearsal all this afternoon. This evening I'm going to see 'To Have and Have Not', a Humphrey Bogart film which a friend says is worth seeing. [He was right. The co-star of this 1944 classic was Lauren Bacall, with whom, forty years later, I was to work at Tanglewood on a salute to Leonard Bernstein. When introduced she observed to my wife that she, too, had had a husband called 'Humphrey'.]

Otherwise things aren't too bad though we had one hell of a rush last week. There was a Boxing Competition on two evenings, moving house on another, sewing on pips, filling in forms, starting accounts, and so on. The Boxing was dreadful; I won two fights before being beaten in the semi-finals, thank heavens, and our course won the competition in the end. It's a dreadful 'sport'; I had a badly cut lip, a swollen nose and a bruised eye at the end of my last fight.

I rushed south for a '48' last weekend, mainly to buy service dress and accessories. I was at Long Dene for Sunday, Brenda was there too, which was very pleasant as I've not seen her for about 6 months.

… Life as an officer and a gentleman is quite pleasant. The food is excellent and armchairs and newspapers abound. Also I'm living in comparative luxury: sharing a room with one chap; table and armchair each; plenty of drawer and wardrobe space; a batman who makes my bed (I still have a conscience about it, but he does it very well!) and does all my kit, very badly unfortunately.

The shadow of the pending Latin exam hovers over all my Catterick letters. Without that pass in the 'Littlego' I would be barred from taking up my state scholarship. How was it, I ask myself now, that this problem had not been identified and dealt with while I was still at school? Still, I took my pleasures when I could and they included dashing down to London in my posh uniform:

… I also saw Peter Pick – had dinner with him in a rather dingy Soho restaurant – he is going to Canada before Xmas to join his family and this was a farewell meeting. [Peter had been my closest friend at Long Dene and I only ever saw him once again, on a flying visit to Toronto in the 1970s.]

We had a Christmas Party on Thursday. The sight of about 150 officers all trying frantically to enjoy themselves was frightening. The only games seemed to consist of leaping around a room using all the furniture as an obstacle course plus squirting soda siphons all over best uniforms. 'Natural horseplay' of course – but when there's nothing else but eating and drinking and that from 8pm to 1.30am it's a bit sickening. At least I found it so and I wasn't alone and I'm no snob. I expect it was the fact that my dinner was cold by the time it reached me that depressed me.

At the only army cocktail party that sticks in my mind I was allocated the task of serving drinks, presumably because I was the newest officer on the block. I wasn't allowed to drink myself until the guests had gone; I then spotted a trayful of undrunk cocktails which I learnt were called 'White Ladies', a lethal mixture of gin, Cointreau and lemon juice with crushed ice and sugar round the rim of the glass. Being thirsty, I downed perhaps half a dozen in quick succession and of course was horribly sick. It was close on sixty years before I touched another drop of gin in any form.

The Christmas holiday gave me time to recover and I made a significant detour on my way back to camp:

Last night I went to Hull for the National Youth Orchestra's concert – an expensive trip but well worth it. I realised just how rusty my music has become: but it was marvellous to hear an orchestra in the flesh again, especially my own orchestra!

Hull itself looks pretty battered, but I enjoyed the visit very much; the music was a welcome tonic, as was seeing old friends whose interests are the same as mine. Do you know I hadn't been to a concert since March 5th!

We spent two days on radio schemes driving around N. Yorkshire last week and it was quite dangerous at times. Next week we are out nearly all the time, sleeping away from Catterick for four nights. We set up wireless stations at Ripon, Pocklington near York, Scarborough and Harrogate and try to keep in contact all the time with each other … I've borrowed a handsome fur-lined flying jacket from Rupert Sutton [my music teacher] that is helping me to keep warm.

… It's been quite good fun but working shifts has meant rather odd hours for sleep and the incessant noise on one's eardrums of wireless atmospherics and interference is rather maddening.

It was while shivering in a signals van that I heard Vaughan Williams's Fifth Symphony for the first time. What a haven of peace that broadcast was, after all the horrid white noise I'd endured in my headphones! VW's music encouraged me to keep going, as did a letter from Fitzwilliam in which:

Mr Peter Tranchell [my future director of studies and supervisor] has reported that he is of the opinion that I am 'well suited to take the Music Tripos' and he has definitely accepted me for October provided the Latin is passed. So that is one weight off my mind. And all exams are over now in this particular academy, which is another relief.

When training was completed the big question in all our minds was: Where next?

The news came on Tuesday and it really was very gloomy. We are all being posted to the Signal Training Centre i.e. Catterick! the reason being that we are getting the early release and have only seven months to go. But quite frankly all the desire I had to do well in the Army has just gone, now that I

At Beverley with my sergeant and troop of boy soldiers.

know that 11 months' training has resulted simply in being posted here for another 7 months.

The despondent mood lifted when at the last moment I was posted away from Catterick after all, but only as far as the minster town of Beverley in Yorkshire's East Riding, where the Royal Signals maintained a training regiment for boy soldiers. I was about to become something pretty close to a schoolmaster.

I haven't yet decided whether I like my new home or not but there's no doubt that it will always be interesting and fairly amusing. Talk in the mess seemed to be chiefly on the subject of new boys bed-wetting (apparently quite widespread) but it ranges from boys stealing kit and 'losing it' (flogging it on the quiet in Beverley probably) to their breaking out and running away – and getting four strokes and 28 days at Colchester detention barracks when they are brought back. The whole place is rather unsavoury in fact; there must be something wrong with a boy who chooses to come into the Army at the age of 16 and some of them come from unhappy homes or have no home at all; but there are a few brainy ones who are really keen on Signals work, – who have come here to make an early start.

... I shall probably be a troop officer. This means looking after about 80 boys, their discipline, turn-out, cleanliness and hygiene, personal problems and administration. It's not easy and it's long hours, because it's out of school that we can help most; the CO is very keen on hobbies and in the evenings there are all sorts of things we attend – P.T., basket ball, stamp-collecting, choir, games practice, fencing, boxing, cycling, library, table tennis, radio club and so on. It also means a lot of brow-beating and heavy father stuff on occasion but at least it's not the harsh discipline of the men's army.

Anyway I'm just learning the ropes for a fortnight watching how things are done. The officers are a good lot – some I know from O.T.W. [Officer Training Wing] days – they try hard, though I don't think there are many psychologist-trained amongst them ... I shall try hard too, because the boys deserve a better fate but I still think it's a bad cause because this regimentation and militarisation at an early age is all wrong. But I keep my personal opinion to myself for the time being!

Anyway I'm jolly glad to be here because

i) It's away from Catterick and the snow

ii) It's more interesting

iii) It's near Hull (for Latin lessons)

iv) (Quite the most important thing) We get two weeks' holiday at Easter and four weeks – repeat 4 WEEKS – in the summer (July–August) which means that I can go to the Kent Summer School and Weekend of Music if I can afford it.

My opinion of the Boys' Regiment further improved after a fortnight's exposure:

I think I was pretty despondent about the job then: it looked as if it was going to be all social service and adjustment of mentally retarded or unbalanced boys, with a little juvenile delinquency thrown in. But after ten days I've decided that it's not as bad as I thought: the bed-wetting is not so prevalent as I'd been led to believe and although there is a fair amount of petty stealing and a little viciousness it's confined to a small section of the boys ... I don't think there's any doubt that this is a better job than I would have had at Catterick, more interesting and also there's the feeling here that one can really do something to help these boys. Half of them haven't got a home apart from the Army so one has to do something for them.

... I've done quite a bit of Latin since I arrived here; I'm relying entirely on the EUP Teach Yourself book which gives the answers to the questions it sets and English translations of the prose texts it includes.

... Littlego may have been a joke in your time, but it's not funny to me!

My faith in the Latin language was restored, I told my father a week later:

> ... by reading 'The Georgics of Virgil' translated by Cecil Day Lewis, because they made me realise that Latin really was living once. I've been comparing the Latin text with Day Lewis's version and it is very good.

Money, the lack of it, was a constant preoccupation for my father as well as myself:

> I was glad to hear that the cheques and work were beginning to flow at last; I shall encourage my boys to hear your Forces broadcasts though I believe we shall be on a Summer camp at that time, being hale and hearty and living in tents.
> ... We are having a minor Festival Week in Beverley Minster, with four concerts, one choral, one organ, one piano and one string orchestra. Beecham and the R.P.O. are playing soon at Bridlington and I hope to be going to that. [I did: Beecham conducted the RPO in Sibelius's Sixth Symphony and it was marvellous.]

My parents wrangled about maintenance payments. I wrote several letters addressed to them both. This one from Humphrey the Peacemaker reads like Polonius in reverse:

> None of us are [sic] in dire hardship thank heavens, and I am sure that all this trouble can be sorted out. It is ridiculous that half of it need never have occurred; if letters had been more carefully read and more speedily answered, if there had been a telephone call or two to sort things out, if Kay hadn't kept silent for so long and if Philip had pointed out more clearly why he was unable to pay the allowance as before [Philip had been summoned for failure to pay his rates in Hitchin] then the bitterness, even the unpleasantness could have been avoided. And until last Autumn things were going very well, at least as far as Rodney and I had been concerned, and I am very grateful to you both for making the family split as gentle as possible.
> And now I beg you both to admit that you have made mistakes and to go half way to heal the breach. For it makes me sad to see this additional disruption to the family.

In the summer of 1951 the Labour government created the Festival of Britain, a national thanksgiving which marked the nation's final emergence into peace after the grim decade of the Second World War and its austerity aftermath. The mood was celebratory, not dissimilar to the euphoria that gripped the British in 2012, the year of the London Olympics. Back in 1951 the Royal Festival Hall was opened on the south bank of the Thames and an ambitious exhibition ran all through the summer, with the pleasure gardens in Battersea Park serving as an additional attraction. I was an early visitor:

20th May 1951

London was looking absolutely beautiful; the sun was shining; the people were dressed in gay colours and the flags and festival symbols and fresh paint made everything and everybody seem a lot more happy than usual. The Festival Site looks very impressive from the outside though I must agree with Sir T. Beecham that the Festival Hall is not very beautiful to look at; I walked along the Embankment at 11pm on Whit-Monday and saw all the coloured lights and the boats lit up on the Thames. And then I travelled back to Beverley, sitting on a W.C. most of the way as it was the only seat left in the train!

With the Littlego exam scheduled for early June, I used four days' leave to stay with my father and swot up Latin all day. The actual exams were quite civilised because for the first paper one was permitted to take a Latin dictionary into the proceedings: imagine my delight when I discovered that one of the sentences I was translating from the classics for the exam was quoted in full with its translation as an example of good practice.

My next letter was sent from Whitburn, a fishing village near Whitley Bay in Northumberland, where the entire regiment, several hundred boys, had been sent for a 'summer' camp. It was midsummer's day and raining.

June 24th 1951

The weather in Cambridge was perfect and I spent the lunch hour wandering around the backs, looking especially at the lovely views of King's Lawn and Clare College. I had a headache before I went into the second exam and a much worse one when I came out!

Life since then has certainly been hectic; very little had been laid on beforehand [at the camp] and as Administration Officer I had to lay on coke for the boilers, people to collect swill and rubbish, people to empty the latrines, all done by various contractors. I had to write detailed instructions for Orderly Sgts, Orderly Cpl, Piquet Commander, Piquet Naafi NCO, Duty Boy Warrant Officer and so on.

The weather couldn't be worse. We are about 400 yds from the sea and for the last two days it's been raining and misty and freezing cold. (I have a snorter myself.) The boys are all under canvas, but fortunately I am in a hut with a proper bed, which I must admit I prefer.

Coming up from Beverley I became more and more depressed as we approached Sunderland (quite apart from the responsibility of all those boys to look after) – the countryside seemed to be comprised entirely of slag heaps and pit heads. We emerged into the Sunderland main street and became a great centre of attraction before being driven away in trucks to the camp. At Beverley we had marched down to the station (1½ miles) with the band playing, everyone in field service marching order – large packs, small packs, pouches, rifle etc., the OC at the head of the column and me just behind him.

The camp itself is situated between Sunderland and South Shields, at Whitburn. The sea, I am told, is very cold. The local women are of very easy virtue (so the boys tell me). We are taking precautions against civilian mobs of hooligans who cause rough houses down at the fair. On the whole I'm enjoying myself and it's all good experience. But I wish that result would come through!

Eventually the news arrived via my father that I had passed the wretched Littlego. I should not complain since mugging up Latin did at least give me an idea of how the language worked and today I remember more Latin than I do of the physics I struggled with at Catterick.

Thanks very much for sending the telegram and for your letter; I was overjoyed to hear the news … relieved, slightly surprised, very glad and anxious now only that my early release will go through.

… The camp at Whitburn finished on Tuesday. In a way I'm glad to be back [in Beverley] but it was certainly very enjoyable up there in so far as I was doing interesting work, lots of it, right in the thick of things, always having to change plans and timetables because the transport had broken down or the rations hadn't arrived, or the section on the range was an hour late for lunch.

I didn't go swimming at all. I went for a walk along the cliffs one sunny Sunday afternoon and lay on the very brink watching the gulls. The boys went out on a 48 hour exercise centred on a lovely village called Blanchland (about 10 miles south of Hexham) and I drove out from Whitburn, first for miles through the mining areas with slag heaps and warning notices about Subsidence in the Road due to mining, and finally out to the rolling foothills of the Pennines. The boys marched up to 30 miles across country that day and through bad planning (not mine) some didn't get in until 11.30pm, but it was all a great experience for them, sleeping out with only a few blankets. … Sorry this has all been about me. I should like to see [my brother] Rodney's 'Nocturne' – he is good, though derivative, and he needs to listen to a lot more music. But certainly he's a long way more forward than I was then, though his piano playing is worse. I hope you buy a piano to play it on!

My brother Rodney had composed his Nocturne, about which I am ungenerously sniffy, as a birthday present for our father. To judge from a recent reunion at which I joined my three brothers to play music for eight hands at two pianos, Rodney today is a better pianist than me and as a composer more poetic, though my pieces from that era are probably livelier in spirit. My half-brothers Tony and Jonathan are good all-round musicians. Our father certainly had vigorous musical genes.

The boy soldiers' summer camp at Whitley Bay was the last significant episode of my army life. It pleases me now that I was on top of all that army administration. I didn't quite realise it at the time but I clearly had what it took to be a producer, to run things efficiently. Just two months remained before my return to what we called Civvy Street, and much of that time was to be spent on vacation because the boys' regiment closed for a holiday month! Preparing for undergraduate life became the major concern of the summer. I was naïve and ignorant. Luckily my father's work as an examiner in English often took him to Cambridge and he could brief me concerning such arcane undergraduate concerns as when to wear one's gown and what the difference was between a supervisor and a tutor. I wrote my next letter in August while holidaying at Long Dene.

> I saw a superb musical on Saturday called 'On the Town' – about three sailors' 24 hour shore leave in New York. It really was first class; good music (by the U.S. equivalent of Constant Lambert), good to look at, very exciting dances, funny, intelligent. A very good 1/10 worth [less than 10p].

Surprisingly, I don't mention the name of the American composer of *On the Town* – which I had already reviewed for the *Tonbridge Free Press* eighteen months previously. It was of course Leonard Bernstein.

What a change from life a year earlier, when I had been pushed to the limits, physical and mental, by the sweat and strain of officer training at Mons and Catterick! Now I was writing to my father from Cornwall, where I was holidaying with Brenda.

> August 1951,
>
> I am having a very pleasant holiday here; only one wet day in 8 … I thought the [Battersea] fun-fair very charming and entertaining, although it certainly touches the pocket more than the heart. I went to see 'The Little Hut', with Robert Morley; very slight and cynical, but very funny in a sophisticated way. Also 'Four in a Jeep' and 'Hue and Cry', the former film about Third Man type Vienna but much more moving, the latter very good.
>
> Forgive me for the catalogue and remember that it was my first 'splash' this year and after the exertions of Latin I needed it. And yet I was not really happy;

Lt. Burton, Royal Signals, Territorial Army, 1952. The military image was a bit of a sham.

I found it hard to concentrate on music, visiting exhibitions more from the idea of necessity, the right thing to do, than an inward urge to enjoy myself. I've no doubt I was happier during my first week of leave – playing the piano, swimming, tennis, seeing friends, living on the cheap.

I seem to have accepted some unsatisfactory out-of-town Cambridge accommodation without putting up a fight, a great mistake since in the year that followed I was to waste many hours cycling in and out of the city centre.

… I've done a lot more reading; 'I Claudius', 'Eastern Approaches' by Fitzroy Maclean – very exciting and amusing – and now Boswell's London journal. After this I intend to get down to some music as I'm incredibly rusty these days.

* * *

Was my National Service a waste of time? In terms of what the nation got out of me, I guess it was, since months of training were put to no use. Luckily I never had to fight. Most of the boys I looked after probably benefited from my pastoral care, though for a time I developed what amounted to an obsession for one of them, a 16-year-old named Shakespeare. I don't remember his first name or what he looked like, but I recall that when I was doing my evening rounds I would sometimes linger at the end of his bed for a chat before lights out. My fascination came to an abrupt end when Boy Soldier Shakespeare was put on a charge with other lads for bullying a younger boy and blacking his private parts with boot polish. Despite this aberration I conclude that

National Service was good for me: my letters provide the evidence. Indeed, my first year at Cambridge felt like a backward step: I lost confidence. Being at Fitzwilliam, which was then not a fully fledged college, I was saddled with a legitimate inferiority complex. And I was on very shaky ground where my musical ability was concerned. And I was pathetically nervous concerning my competence to look after myself as an undergraduate. I wrote to my father:

> I can see me meeting you in Cambridge fairly frequently even if only to hand over a pair of socks that are too difficult for me to darn! But maybe my landlady will oblige … The next 18 days are going to be quite hectic; farewell parties, packing, good-byes (I shall be genuinely sorry to say goodbye to my Troop): but I'll be doing it all with a light heart.

And that is the last letter I wrote before taking up residence in Cambridge. My father kept no more letters. So as an autobiographer I am now on my own. Memory, hold the door!

CHAPTER 5

CAMBRIDGE

Outside the Fitzwilliam Street digs of the General Secretary
of the Amalgamated Clubs, 1953.

I WAS THRILLED to be at Cambridge at last – it had been my goal for three years – but I soon perceived that I had entered a very rough-and-ready version of the dream: it was impossible to ignore the disappointing conclusion that, so far as Cambridge University life was concerned, Fitzwilliam House was not the real thing. The official position was that Fitzwilliam was a 'non-collegiate' institution, created in 1869 to look after the interests of students who either because of their religion or through lack of funds could not get a place at any of the colleges; it was not until 1969 that Fitzwilliam was granted what is called *collegiate* status. In my day, twenty years before that major change, the House had few signs of the traditional collegiate set-up: there were no elegant courtyards with 'Keep off the Grass' signs; no Perpendicular chapel; no Wren Library or Gibbs Building. 'Fitzbilly' was housed in a three-storey late-Georgian building situated on the corner where narrow Fitzwilliam Street joins broad Trumpington Street, almost opposite the great Fitzwilliam Museum. A chemist shop founded in Victorian times functions to this day on the ground floor adjacent to what in my time was the crowded dining room where we took our lunches and dinners in two rowdy shifts. The lack of style reminded me of early National Service days at Catterick and was a million miles from the candlelit elegance enjoyed at King's or Magdalene, where I sometimes dined with undergraduate friends.

Upstairs at Fitzwilliam there was a student common room with scruffy armchairs and a cluttered clubs' noticeboard. A pleasant back room was named, in Victorian style, the Parlour: here the Fitzwilliam House Musical Society gave its concerts; there was a decent grand piano on which I composed a few songs and played duets with my contemporary John Parry (father of today's distinguished choir conductor Ben Parry). I made no attempt to form my own orchestra or to continue with the conducting I had enjoyed at school; the inferiority complex I was nursing held me back. I applied to sing in none of the élite Cambridge choirs or to play percussion in the university orchestra despite my participation in the NYO. In my first term my only significant move was to join the university music society choir (CUMS) under Boris Ord but I gave it up after only a few rehearsals: we were studying the controversial *Carmina Burana* by Carl Orff. I don't suppose anybody knew that the work had been a great favourite of the Nazis but that was not my problem: my objection was to the low standard of singing – there were no auditions and the choir's accuracy of pitch was too approximate for my taste. It has long been a depressing Cambridge axiom that if a thing's worth doing, it's worth doing badly. But in my priggish way I felt then that Orff's music was not worth the time we spent on it. How could we all get it so wrong? Over a decade later Jean-Pierre Ponnelle's film of *Carmina Burana* (made for Unitel in 1970), with Lucia Popp and Hermann Prey as the principal soloists, won me over completely.

I took a few piano lessons early on from a fellow music student but he didn't know how to teach any more than I knew how to play. I never got past the second page of the Chopin Ballade (in F major) I had foolishly

Hermann Prey and Lucia Popp in Jean-Pierre Ponnelle's earthy concept of *Carmina Burana*.

chosen to study. And yet the piano provided me with arguably my greatest Cambridge excitement: among the other new musical arrivals at Fitzwilliam that September was a thrilling bass-baritone named John Noble who everybody noticed when he sang the lovely solo part in a college performance of Vaughan Williams's *Fantasia on Christmas Carols*. But what I remember best was Noble's electrifying read-through with me of the closing scene of *Don Giovanni*. We were in my lodgings in Fitzwilliam Street, where I had managed to install a grand piano. I was sight-reading Mozart's piano score and John, who was at least two metres tall and possessed of a malevolent physical presence, was belting out, *tutta forza*, the Commendatore's scary invitation to the Don to join him for dinner in the underworld. My hair was standing on end as I played Mozart's tension-screwing chromatic scales and then, wonder of wonders, I heard myself joining in the singing, taking Leporello's part and then that of the Don, spitting out defiance to the relentless stone guest. It's a marvellous moment when Mozart's anti-hero finally goes down to hell with all guns blazing. I collapsed in a heap when it was all over. Friends came in from the street, marvelling at what they had heard. John studied geography but made his university mark singing in a student production of *The Pilgrim's Progress* to which the composer himself gave great praise.

I can see now that I wasted my first year. Agreeing to be housed in suburban digs proved to be a very poor move. Bicycling in to town two or three times a day, come wind come rain, was not how I had imagined university life. I had done that cycling stuff for several years at Judd School and now I also had to contend with the freezing Fenland fog. The landlady meant well but she was no music lover. I remember her banging on my sitting room door one evening when I was listening to a Third Programme relay of *Wozzeck* from Covent Garden. 'Stop that 'orrid noise', she screamed; 'it's enough to wake the dead.' The BBC had been a faithful friend in my army days so it was with considerable reluctance that I switched off the radio.

For my second year I wangled a set of residential rooms on the ground floor in a house at the far end of Fitzwilliam Street, number 17. And for my third year, after I'd contrived to get myself elected General Secretary of the Amalgamated Clubs, which was Fitzwilliam's non-collegiate equivalent of President of the Junior Common Room, I was in clover, living in a two-room suite at number 24, just around the corner from Fitz's front door.

But the price of privileged digs was high because with the top job of General Secretary went the chores of representing the undergraduates on various committees and, most onerous because so time-consuming, of organising Fitzwilliam's fundraising campaign on Rag Day. Fierce rivalry existed between the colleges as to who could collect the most cash on Rag Day, a frighteningly aggressive version of the nation's annual Poppy Day appeal. Many traffic-stopping japes were devised and much cross-dressing was involved; we fielded a whole army of Mrs Mopps to block a zebra crossing. I guess Fitzwilliam students were encouraged to do well: it was another way of raising our visibility, part of the long-running campaign which my father had supported before me for Fitzbilly to be awarded that coveted collegiate status. On Rag Day 1953 we did better than anybody had ever done before, collecting hundreds of pounds, nearly half the total raised by the entire university. Sacks of coins had to be stored in my rooms overnight and every penny counted: such a bore! The experience gave me an aversion to fundraising which I was not to overcome until 2001 when at the Royal Albert Hall I conducted a charity performance of the Verdi *Requiem* which raised £75,000 for prostate cancer research. (I did not have to count out the cash and I promise that is the end of my flag-waving!)

For music students like me, Cambridge had only recently introduced a new BA degree as an accessible alternative to the ancient, organist-dominated degree of bachelor of music (B.Mus.). Subjects for study included harmony, counterpoint, orchestration, score reading, ear tests, acoustics and finally historical awareness, the latter a poorly served category: I never heard a note of Bruckner, Mahler or Webern. The degree is called a tripos but has only two parts and I knew before I started that I would be switching disciplines for my third year; I never regretted dropping music and taking on instead the second part of the history tripos – as my father had foretold I would do five years previously.

Cambridge's music teaching faculty was very small. We rarely saw the professor, Patrick Hadley. He lost a leg in the First World War and was said to have spent a substantial proportion of the intervening years drinking to alleviate the pain. He was an amiable *raconteur* whose compositions, much-loved by performers, were couched in the language of his teacher Ralph Vaughan Williams and sprinkled with a musical perfume derived from Frederick Delius. I felt it was wrong for Professor Hadley to have so little contact with his undergraduates; I met him perhaps twice in two years. Much more influential was Robin Orr, a dour Scot with a plummy accent who introduced us to the music of Béla Bartók (the wonderful *Concerto for Orchestra*) and Lennox Berkeley (his graceful *Divertimento*), both rich in the orchestral felicities which in his lectures on orchestration Orr taught us to love. From his faculty colleagues Cuthbert Middleton and Henry Moule (coaches in harmony and fugue respectively) I learnt little, nor did I have much luck with my first weekly supervisor, Peter Tranchell. He was younger than the others (born 1922) and more eccentric in his tastes: he told one lecture class that music was best listened to in the nude. At one of my first supervisions we played piano four hands through the entire score of Erik Satie's *Socrate*, minimal music before its time. It left me cold then and still does: I prefer Satie's cheerful piano duets and the haunting *Gymnopédies*. Tranchell made little impression on my musical development. When he died his executors sent me the autograph of the piano duets I had commissioned from him when I was running the university music club. Entitled *Three Friendly Grotesques*, they are devilishly difficult but witty and debonair – the essence of Tranchell – and it is a shame they were never published.

For my second year I was supervised by Philip Radcliffe of King's, an archetypal Cambridge don, tweed-suited, shy, sensitive, intensely loyal, deeply musical and steeped in scholarship: his study of Mendelssohn has not been surpassed. Philip had been one of the assessors who in 1949 turned me down (rightly) for a scholarship at King's but he eventually took pity on me since he accepted me as a student and supplied the calm thinking I needed to get through the big Tripos exams. An absurd system was in place: if one already had the appropriate grades in one's Higher School Certificate, as I did, one was not required to sit the Preliminary Tripos exam at the end of year one, so I had no test until the end of my *sixth* term. To acquire some exam experience we were encouraged to enter the John Stewart of Rannoch scholarship in sacred music. The subject was hardly my forte but I started attending evensong at King's College chapel every day (it was no hardship) and soaked myself in everything from Tallis and Byrd to Stanford in B flat. But I was realistic about my chances and happy to take a bet with my friend Neil Sutherland, a lanky music scholar at Corpus who also didn't fancy his chances; the deal was that we would share the prize money if either of us won. Unbelievably, Neil was successful and, dammit, the dark horse declined to share the cash. We stayed friends nonetheless; he eventually got a producer's job at the BBC – working on popular classical music shows for the Light Programme – before emigrating to Canada to become a big fish in the small pond of CBC's Vancouver studios. Sadly Neil was a heavy smoker and he died ridiculously young.

Among the other personalities in my Cambridge years was John Exton, an outstanding violinist in the NYO; he won a composition scholarship to King's which led to a career as a teacher, serving as director of music at Bedales before moving to Australia. David Gwilt, a viola-playing Scot, was like me a student of Philip Radcliffe but with greater distinction since eventually he became a major figure in the flourishing academic musical life of Hong Kong. Angus Watson, another fine NYO violinist, ended up in a top job as head of music at Winchester College. A contemporary with whom I stayed in touch was Ian Kemp, later a passionate student of Berlioz and Tippett; his daughter Francesca Kemp is one of the few producers of classical music programmes still to be found in BBC Television. In my final year I also saw a lot of Guy Woolfenden, a former horn player with the NYO. He had conducted the première of Tranchell's opera *The Mayor of Casterbridge* when only twenty. Prodigiously fluent, Guy was for thirty-five years in charge of music at the Royal Shakespeare Company, for whom he composed incidental music for every one of Shakespeare's thirty-seven plays. I also saw a good deal

78

of Christopher Bishop; we played two-piano duets at the university music club and he sang most mellifluously in the club's choir which I conducted when Louis Halsey, the top man in the field, moved to London. Christopher joined the EMI record company, where he produced orchestral LPs with such luminaries as Boult, Menuhin and Previn; that career was followed by a long spell running the Philharmonia Orchestra.

What I deduce from this brief roll call is that in my subsequent career I didn't do as badly as I feared I would when I was struggling through my counterpoint exercises. Three friends helped me on my way. Ken Naylor was like a personal coach. A student at Magdalene College, he played beautiful jazz piano and wrote luscious eight-part arrangements of popular songs for our choir to sing as encores. Ken supervised me throughout the music tripos, patiently doing ear tests every day of the week before the exam. Later he joined the Leys School, half a mile from Fitzwilliam, where he was greatly prized as a teacher. Twenty-seven years later he moved to Christ's Hospital. He edited a book of hymns and wrote dozens himself, one of which, I'm told, is still greatly loved: 'How shall I sing that Majesty?' (Coe Fen).

Sadly Ken died when he was only sixty. I had no idea he was gay until he very shyly propositioned me when we were sharing a bed in a cheap Paris hotel at the end of a car-touring summer holiday in France. (There were four of us on the tour and our Ford Popular car was so basic that when we were driving in the Pyrenees three of us had to get out and push our fellow traveller over the summit.)

Musically the high point of that French holiday was hearing Pablo Casals perform at Prades. My other travelling companion, Louis Halsey, was a countertenor in the King's College chapel choir. He founded the Moeran Singers, making it instantly the top chamber choir in the university, and I had a wonderful season singing bass with them – we were the official choir of the University Music Club, sixteen youthful, confident voices. Naturally we sang music by Moeran, but also the newly published *Five Flower Songs* by Britten which were the acme of contemporaneity, rather more taxing than Britten's *Hymn to St Cecilia*, which I already adored. Louis has had a fruitful career as a choral conductor and adjudicator; his son Simon Halsey has done even better, working with Simon Rattle on mixed-voice choirs in Berlin. Louis taught me a lot about running a small vocal ensemble. After I succeeded him, the music club choir gave a concert in Oxford that included Arnold Bax's demanding eight-part motet *This Worldes Joie* as well as a group of fine Tudor madrigals. I remember being chuffed when a member of the Oxford audience asked

Robin Lock's Ford Popular proudly
attaining the highest point of a
mountain pass in the Pyrenees.

afterwards how we undergraduates could achieve such accuracy and tonal
bloom. We were good, I'm sure, but it has to be admitted that the standard of
Oxford's choral singing was then depressingly low.

The Ford car in which we toured France was owned by the third of my
significant friends, a research scientist from Caius named Robin Lock who
was a reliable clarinettist and the Cambridge link with the Chelsea Opera
Group, which visited the university (and Oxford) three times a year to
perform Mozart operas under the inspirational baton of Colin Davis. My
first COG experience was seeing *The Marriage of Figaro*, performed in a
girls' school hall in Hills Road. Colin's wife April Cantelo sang Susanna and
the entire sunlit afternoon was a joyful revelation of Mozart's comic genius
from which I never recovered. Robin also introduced me to the joys of the
Music Camp at Bothampstead in Berkshire, a nine-day gathering of amateur
music-makers of all ages inspired and administered by Bernard Robinson, a
scientist colleague of Robin's whose gentle missionary zeal was a legend for my
generation. We all slept rough in tents and ate simply but well. Under Colin
Davis's baton we tackled such choral masterworks as Beethoven's sparkling C
major Mass. At another Camp session I sang the role of Sarastro in *The Magic
Flute* under the baton of the even younger Roger Norrington, later renowned
as the early-music maestro who wanted string players to dispense with vibrato.
Singing was then Roger's forte: he was a member of Louis Halsey's choir,
which I inherited and turned into the University Music Club choir. More
impressively, Roger later sang in Mozart's *Seraglio* under Yehudi Menuhin at

the Bath Festival. I respected Norrington's work as a conductor but confess I had no inkling then of the musical personality which deservedly took him to such high places in the world of early music.

I used to claim that my real education only began when I joined the BBC, but I can see now that Music Camp, Kent's Rural Music School, the NYO and the Chelsea Opera Group all helped form my musical tastes more effectively than my formal education had done. And to that list of influences must be added the summer school of music at Bryanston (and subsequently Dartington), where for a fortnight in the summer of 1952 I took lessons from the eminent composer Alan Rawsthorne. I have a photograph to prove it: the only problem is that the snapshot shows us drinking at the bar, the regular location for our meetings.

Bryanston Summer School was a total delight. The legendary George Enescu was giving master classes that year. Enescu sat slumped in a chair, a wreck of a man, it seemed, until he spoke or touched his fiddle, and then he sprang to life. (I knew of him only from my much-treasured pre-war 78 rpm recording of the Bach Double Violin Concerto, performed with his famous pupil, Yehudi Menuhin.) His current pupil, Manoug Parikian, was one of the

With the composer Alan Rawsthorne at the bar of the Bryanston Music School, 1952.

best violinists in Britain, and Enesco's exchanges with him were genuinely illuminating, something I remembered when I inaugurated the first series of Master Classes on BBC Television a dozen years later. If the sessions are to live up to their name it's not only the teacher who must be a master.

Bryanston's founder, William Glock, was an admirer of Colin Davis, and Davis was prominent at the summer school, conducting Frank Martin's delightful *Petite Symphonie Concertante* for harp (played, I think, by Osian Ellis), harpsichord (George Malcolm) and piano (Glock himself). The youthful Amadeus Quartet was in residence that year and we were kept up late at night by a stream of risqué stories told by the second violinist Sigmund Nissel, aided and abetted by the summer school's ebullient secretary, John Amis. What a great institution he and William Glock created!

About my sex life in my early twenties I remember very little. I had been shocked into inaction by Brenda's pregnancy and the birth of our son. In my day Cambridge had ten men for every girl and in my first year I remember rashly accepting an invitation to a May Ball at Girton College, several miles out of the town. I also remember my deep embarrassment because on the night I could not bring myself to invite my hostess, a well-built soprano who rowed for her college, to join me on the ballroom floor. I slipped away in shame, I who had spent countless evenings at Long Dene enthusiastically dancing innumerable foxtrots and quicksteps.

The girlfriend situation improved mightily in the summer of 1953, when I attended the summer school Musica Viva at Tours in the Loire valley and there fell in love with Aline Binet, the daughter of the Swiss composer Jean Binet. Musica Viva was very special. A hundred and fifty young musicians from many parts of Europe were assembled for a six-week course held in the decaying Château de Grammont just outside the cathedral city of Tours. The gathering was the brainchild of three gifted young Swiss musicians, a flautist named François Binet (Aline's brother), Lionel Rogg, already a well-known Geneva organist, and the conductor Christian Vöchting, a daemonic personality who was to die before he was forty. Christian conducted the French première of Stravinsky's new opera *The Rake's Progress*, sung in a French translation. Neil Sutherland and I, good Europeans, and intrigued, went over from Cambridge to be members of the opera chorus. I was greatly surprised when, for *Rake's Progress*, I was assigned a cameo solo part, that of the keeper of the madhouse where poor deranged Tom Rakewell ends up in the opera's final scene. To this day I can remember every note of my part, both in the French translation and in Auden's original English libretto. It was not such a difficult assignment: the jailer is on stage for hardly a minute and has only thirty-five words to sing.

The opera house in the city of Tours was taken over for three performances of the Stravinsky. The production was simple but effective. It made me see what a fool I had been not to have attempted to do any stage work while living in Cambridge.

The cast were gratified after the première to be visited backstage by the great Francis Poulenc – his country home at Noizay is close to Tours. Musica Viva also gave a week of concerts, performing in Tours's magnificent cathedral. We studied the new Britten cantata *St Nicholas* and a selection of gorgeous Russian Orthodox church music, in which the second bass parts go down to bottom C, slightly beyond my comfort zone. We sang sonorous eight-part compositions by Gretchaninoff and Archangelsky – rarities to this day – containing many scrumptious harmonies; we enjoyed ourselves hugely chanting our fervent

The Musica Viva Chorus, 1953: my friend Neil Sutherland is at the extreme right of the top row. Peter Pears's niece Sue Pears (later my good friend Sue Phipps) is in the middle of the second row from the front.

'Gospodi pomiloys' in Russian! Not even a prolonged national rail strike and an extended heatwave could mar my enjoyment of that lovely French summer of international music-making.

In my final Cambridge year I studied for part two of the history tripos. This brought me into the university mainstream – and taught me that university education could be experienced as a branch of show business. The star lecturer was J.H. Plumb, a history don who was a born entertainer and attracted huge audiences at the Senate House with his witty survey of English life in the 1700s. In the same term the history faculty's professor, Herbert Butterfield, also gave a series of powerful lectures – what a change it all was from proceedings at the disappointingly dull music faculty! The brilliant historian Dennis Mack Smith from Peterhouse had already embarked on his exploration of modern

Aline Binet and the author at the Château de Grammont outside Tours, France, August 1953.

Italian history: learning from him about Garibaldi gave me a much deeper understanding of Verdi and the Risorgimento.

I had (wisely) opted to study European history from the death of Richard III in 1485 to modern times, and I undertook to do extra papers on English economic history; this was rather a baffling decision, since I had absolutely no background in the subject. For my 'special period', I chose the outbreak of the First World War, 1912–14. This would mesh in well, I thought, with my musical studies. Fitzwilliam had an excellent director of studies for history in Dr Leslie Wayper, who was then at the outset of his long and benevolent association with Fitzwilliam. As an officer of the college, Leslie lived just opposite my flat in Fitzwilliam Street and I took great pleasure in our very civilised weekly supervisions. They were reasonably fruitful, too, since from a standing start I managed a 2.1 in my degree exam. And this despite the hazard of having a girlfriend in Cambridge.

Alas, I did not treat Aline well. I fear she was bewildered and hurt by my lack of care at the university, although fifty years later we exchanged letters and she forgave me in a tender message sent from her home in Switzerland. At Cambridge she and I talked of an engagement but sadly our affair fizzled out. I concede I was pushing my luck: I was, as I've already noted, general secretary of the college clubs and also captain of the college football team, so I had a busy life.

Captain of football? Yes, though I suspect I acquired this honour not on account of my skill as a ball-player but for the very snobbish reason that opposing team captains would at least be able to understand my English when we tossed the coin for choice of ends; some of our players came from northern English counties where the accent was so thick it could be cut with a knife. (I jest.) Overleaf is the team in 1953. Not very frightening, I concede.

In my last Cambridge year I was determined to make as much music as possible: in any week I would sing in as many as six choral groups. The Madrigal Society was far and away the best, under Boris Ord, the director of music at King's. Ord's gravelly voice concealed a warm heart and a fine musician – he could achieve better results with a small group like us than when conducting the large forces of the university (CUMS) choir and orchestra. In 1953 the Madrigal Society gave the world première of *A Garland for the Queen* as part of the coronation celebrations. Ten composers and ten poets were commissioned by the Arts Council to create a successor to *The Triumphs of Oriana* (1601), the madrigal glory of the first Elizabethan age, masterminded by the composer Thomas Morley. Michael Tippett, Arnold Bax and Herbert Howells

Fitzwilliam House 1st XI Soccer Team, 1953. As Captain, I am seated in the middle.

were among the heroes of mine who came to our rehearsals before we all went up to the Royal Festival Hall to perform the Garland cycle on the eve of the coronation.

Another of my favourite choirs, the Cambridge Singers, was formed and conducted by John Stevens, a gentle musicologist and scholar who was a fellow of Magdalene College; he had the most marvellous set of firelit rooms where we gathered to work on the medieval English carols John had unearthed and then edited; when they were published in one of the first volumes of *Musica Britannica* we went up to London to give them their première. Another great event to enjoy!

These choral activities undoubtedly had their excitements and their satisfactions yet I was surely misguided to have spent so much time singing and as a consequence to have missed out on so many other fun social activities in Cambridge. It pains me now to admit that I made no attempt to join the

Footlights (the satirical review club, dominated at the time by Leslie Bricusse) or the theatre club at the ADC Theatre, where Peter Hall and Tony Church held sway. Perhaps because of my idiotic inferiority complex I entered no trials for athletics or tennis, even at college level, and never put my name down to speak at the Union, where my father had paid for me to become a life member in my first term. Out of mild curiosity I attended the freshers' meetings of the three main political parties. Probably because I had been so firmly imprinted with socialist attitudes at Long Dene, I joined the Labour Party and have voted Labour ever since. I also appeared as a Union guest speaker on several quite noisy occasions during the 1980s and '90s when I had a bit of a reputation as a TV pundit.

In my student years at Cambridge I was both a 'hearty' and an 'aesthete'; college soccer matches on Saturday afternoons would be followed by madrigals and crumpets at Newnham College in the rooms of Helen Platt or Mary Elspeth Milford, two of my contemporaries who read music and loved singing. By my third year, as the outside world began to beckon, I became more serious about life in general and a career in particular. I started to write music criticism for both the staid *Cambridge Review* and the hip new *Broadsheet*, in which I published a reasonably penetrating preview of the forthcoming Chelsea Opera Group's *Così fan tutte*. Discussing the way the lovers switched affections in the course of the action, I mused on how closely Mozart identified with the dilemma since in real life he personally switched his attention from Aloysia Weber, who spurned him, to her younger sister Constanze. Colin Davis's impassioned conducting of *Così* was a revelation. When Ferrando, tenor, breaks down the resistance of Fiordiligi, soprano, he conjured performances from David Galliver and Ilse Wolf that were truly heartbreaking: with the Chelsea Opera Group I was experiencing world-class music-making for the price of a coffee at Espresso Bongo.

So I was starting to have opinions and to make decisions both inside the college and in the wider world. As secretary of the university music club there were concerts to organise and publicise, posters to design, personalities to be wooed, *amour-propres* to be stroked. Socially I saw myself, I fear, as being part of Cambridge's musical élite, and I was absurdly pleased with myself, to take one example, for being a founder member of the Staggins Society, a Cambridge dining club dedicated to the singing of the smutty catches and rounds composed at the end of the seventeenth century by Henry Purcell and his contemporary Dr Nicholas Staggins who, in 1674, was made Master of the King's Musick by Charles II. The great musicologist Thurston Dart was the ringleader of this bawdy all-male fellowship, aided and abetted by his friend William Oxenbury, who was another King's choral scholar with a fine countertenor voice and a certain aptitude on the river – he coxed the King's 'choral' boat. Bill had an infectious laugh and bags of energy. He became Dart's lover and lifelong companion; Dart was eventually named Cambridge's professor of music (a post Dr Staggins had held), but he soon left to found his own revisionist music faculty at King's, London, where he was reputed to have had a sign placed over the entrance to his offices reading 'abandon counterpoint, all ye who enter here'. For Staggins gatherings we put on black ties and drank a good deal of sherry and wine before launching into song. One of the favourites was this Purcell round:

> My man John had a thing that was long:
> My maid Mary had a thing that was hairy.
> My man John put his thing that was long
> Into my maid Mary's thing that was hairy.

As the verses unfold it transpires that the poet is referring to a broomstick and broom brush. We found the song in a collection entitled 'Rakish Rogues and Sultry Sirens of Sin'. Another musical round we sang told of the demise of the Earl of Lincoln, who met his death in a country churchyard. On paper it's an innocent lyric but the composer breaks up the word 'country' into two syllables and has the phrase 'in a count-' repeated by all the voices. How we all laughed!

Robert Thurston Dart, harpsichordist and scholar, was a key figure in the next chapter of my life. He was a dazzling performer and a published scholar, a big burly man with a childlike face – his revelatory book *The Interpretation of Music* had just appeared. Above all, Bob was a good companion, genuinely interested in what I was doing at the university music club, where he helped by coaching the choir in madrigals by Gesualdo and Marenzio and by playing in our Saturday evening club concerts.

It was Bob Dart who encouraged me to apply for a French government research scholarship rather than going straight into the BBC, which I had fixed up on my own initiative. He helped me devise a research topic that would attract the attention of the cultural attaché at the French embassy, Tony Mayer. I should apply, Bob suggested, for a grant to explore the development of public concerts in provincial France in the decades prior to the 1789 revolution. The only previous work on the subject had been published as long ago as 1900 so I would be on my own in the field. I went up to London for the interview, which was largely conducted, quite stringently, by the young *Financial Times* critic Andrew Porter, himself a former recipient of an award. I was somewhat chagrined to learn much later that the scholarship was eventually awarded to me not because of any hint of my intellectual prowess but on the basis of my handwriting: the attaché's wife, Thérèse Mayer, was a graphologist. I was offered five months in France (later extended to ten) and the BBC agreed to put my training appointment on hold for a year. Bingo! All thanks to Bob Dart.

I should perhaps add that I had muffed an earlier opportunity to inaugurate a really intriguing career. In the spring of 1954, when I checked into the careers office – pompously known as the University Appointments Board – three years had elapsed since the scandal of the 'Cambridge spies', Burgess and Maclean, who decamped to the Soviet Union. My appointment was to discuss my future job at the BBC. But after enumerating the various merits of the Foreign Office, the civil service and the BBC, my interviewer looked up from his papers and took off his glasses. The subsequent conversation went something like this:

'Ever thought of working for us?'

'What, the Appointments Board?'

'No, stupid' (he may not have actually said stupid but it was in his tone of voice): '*Us*, MI5.'

Myself, shaken and scared, in a trembling voice: 'Well, no sir, I can't say I have: what would it entail?'

'Well, you know, you'd take a regular day job at the Foreign Office or at the BBC but you'd really be working for us.'

I suppose I should have been flattered. Had I had any presence of mind, let alone journalistic curiosity, I would at least have expressed strong interest and taken the first step towards joining the Secret Service. Reader, I failed, I fell at the first hurdle: I have never been a spy. I was happy enough with my existing job offer from the BBC. It was not one of the much-prized fast-track General Traineeships, for which I wasn't even shortlisted – I assumed it was my Fitzwilliam background and my co-ed, progressive school education that ruled me out of contention – but the alternative BBC position on offer of studio manager specialising in classical music was in fact just what I wanted. And what was especially enticing was that there was a permanent job promised at the end of the half-year training period. Who could ask for anything more?

Madrigals Night. The scene at King's College Bridge.

Were I able to retain only one memory of Cambridge it would be of singing. To be precise, singing in the Madrigal Society's May Week concert at the end of my last year. Wrapped up in rugs against the evening dew, two dozen of us are sitting in a double row of punts moored side by side under King's College bridge, illuminated by Chinese lanterns strung out above us. As dusk descends, the summer night is filled with the sound of madrigals: 'The Silver Swan', 'Now is the Month of Maying', 'April is in my Mistress' Face' and many more, all immaculately sung under the watchful eye of Boris Ord. He is fifty-six and somewhat frail; he had initiated this marvellous tradition of madrigals on the Backs thirty-three years earlier. The sloping riverbanks are crowded with students and their girlfriends, who have 'come up' for the May balls (in June, as my mother had done to meet my father a quarter of a century previously); the clinking glasses fall silent as the enchanted listeners recline on the grass or crowd together in their punts. Comes the last song and our own punts are quietly untied and gently, very gently, propelled downstream towards Clare College bridge. Over to our right as we glide down the River Cam we can glimpse the tall towers and noble window of the chapel's east front. Nothing is heard on the evening air but the occasional splash of punt poles and the beauty of John Wilbye's madrigal, set to complex words by an unknown poet, perhaps the composer himself:

> Draw on, sweet Night, best friend unto those cares
> That do arise from painful melancholy;
> My life so ill through want of comfort fares,
> That unto thee I consecrate it wholly.
> Sweet Night, draw on; my griefs, when they be told
> To shades and darkness, find some ease from paining;
> And while thou all in silence dost enfold,
> I then shall have best time for my complaining.

Cambridge: Farewell Party. Joke calendar after a 'sweet night' has drawn on.

91

CHAPTER 6

L'ANNÉE FRANÇAISE

Le Café Mondial, the students' rallying point on the Cours Mirabeau in Aix-en-Provence.

I NEVER REGRETTED postponing the start of my working life by doing a year of research in France. The title of my government scholarship was pompous – 'boursier du Gouvernement Français' – scholar of the French Government – but it offered five months of study in France, later extended to a full year, with all expenses paid. It was a godsend for somebody as lacking in self-confidence as I was, despite my local successes at the Fitzwilliam clubs and the university music club. I was quite serious about my research: taking my cue from the historian Lewis Namier, who used statistics to chart the rise of the English middle class in the eighteenth century, I proposed to examine the records of the *académies de musique* in cities of various sizes; inspired by Namier, I would list their memberships, which were partly aristocratic and partly the well-to-do bourgeoisie, and add to the statistics the titles of the operas they performed – mostly last year's Paris hits, more often than not composed by Rameau – and the professional singers recruited from the metropolis who were hired for short seasons. Maybe it was the *attaché culturel*, Tony Mayer, who prompted me to select three towns in Provence – he owned a house east of Avignon in the attractive hill village of Ménerbes. I would perhaps have done a more thorough job had I moved around the regions and researched major cultural centres such as Bordeaux or Lyon, but it was more fun to stay in a single area, especially since Provence boasted the nation's warmest autumns.

My first port of call, Avignon, had actually not been a French town in the eighteenth century but an independent city state owned by the Vatican; it was the seat of the schismatic popes in medieval times and boasted a magnificent papal palace which I had explored two summers earlier on our French motoring expedition. When we visited the palace, Louis Halsey had sung an arpeggio in the high-vaulted hall and his fine countertenor voice had reverberated around the rafters for at least ten seconds. A group of American visitors paused to express their admiration and I heard myself boasting that 'Mr Halsey is a graduate of King's College.' 'No! Not King's College, Tennessee?' gasped one of the Southern matrons in awe.

In the autumn of 1954 I was lodged for six weeks with Vincent Laugier, an amiable and cultivated building contractor who was an expert on the local wines (among them Gigondas and Tavel) and on the local versions of the powerful liqueurs known as *eaux-de-vie* such as Marc de Gigondas and Marc de Châteauneuf-du-Pape. He took me on many explorations to check out the new vintages. I also tasted for the first time sun-dried tomatoes and aubergines cooked in olive oil and enjoyed the basic tenet of Provençal cuisine that every dish is improved by the addition of a few cloves of garlic. An unexpected bonus was Monsieur Laugier's friendship with Francis Poulenc, whose piano duet sonata I had played at Cambridge and who had graced us the previous year with a visit to the Musica Viva performance of *The Rake's Progress* in Tours. After a dinner in his honour chez M. Laugier, Poulenc needed very little persuasion to sit down at the grand piano and play us excerpts from his *magnum opus*, then still a work in progress, *Dialogues des Carmélites*.

I knew nothing of the story of the French nuns who are guillotined for their beliefs but Poulenc must have sketched in the background since we all found the Sarabande he played very touching. 'C'est beau, n'est-ce pas?', he called out to us over his shoulder as he continued playing the nuns' eloquent and courageous march towards the guillotine while singing the Salve Regina. I felt something not previously experienced: I was in the presence of an indisputable genius.

On another occasion Poulenc heard me practising the piano accompaniment of Duparc's song *L'Invitation au voyage*. 'Plus lent', he insisted, but in the gentlest of tones: it was the nearest I ever got to a master class in song accompaniment but I never forgot it. Most music is better, I feel, for being played a little slower than you expect.

My lodgings were several kilometres to the west past Villeneuve-lès-Avignon and every morning I would come in to the city by bus and head off to the Hôtel de Ville archive, passing through a little square, the Place de l'Opéra, where behind the discordant modern façade of a garage one could still discern a classical pediment and the legend 'Maison de l'Opéra'. Over a coffee in the town I met an American student who introduced me to the music of Dave Brubeck and his Quartet, starting of course with *Take Five*. Not since Benny Goodman's *Slipped Disc* – enjoyed when I was a Long Dene teenager – had I been so taken with a jazz record. Brubeck had already been

Maison de l'Opéra, Avignon.

featured on the cover of *Time* magazine but I was just a fan, absurdly ignorant of such worldly matters.

Avignon boasted a flourishing branch of a national club for young music lovers called the Jeunesses Musicales de France; for next to nothing members could attend excellent concerts with top artists. I heard, for example, a delectable performance of Poulenc's Sextet for Piano and Winds. It was stimulating to be sitting with several hundred young people, all keen on classical music, the performances introduced by intelligent speakers, with no hint of condescension – I was impressed and resolved to create something similar when I got back to England. Eventually I introduced myself to the philanthropist Robert Mayer and for five years worked as his unpaid lieutenant, serving in the British version of the Jeunesses Musicales organisation, which he called Youth and Music.

In mid-November I moved on to Aix-en-Provence, larger than Avignon and with an equally distinguished history dating back to glory days in the fifteenth century when the good king René ran his own Provençal kingdom

At a Jeunesses Musicales function, 1958. Middle foreground:
Sir Robert Mayer; to his left is Ruth Railton and to her left (smiling with glasses)
is me. They were the two most formative figures in my musical career.

and troubadours ruled the roost at his legendary court. Aix had had a particularly active musical life in the eighteenth century and I set to work with gusto; I am mystified as to how I succeeded in deciphering the flowing calligraphy of eighteenth-century academy secretaries. I lived in student digs not far from the Cité Universitaire and soon discovered that social life in Aix was lived outdoors and mostly on the lovely Cours Mirabeau, a wide avenue in the city centre. It was remarkable not only for its double row of plane trees but also, on the south side, for its handsome seventeenth-century town houses, all with large doorways decorated with impressively endowed caryatids holding up massive lintels. South of the Cours Mirabeau was Aix's 'new' town, laid out on a grid pattern rather like Edinburgh but with splashy fountains at every intersection – I walked through the Place des Quatre Dauphins every day and would pause to sip the water, which the Romans had first put to good use a couple of millennia earlier.

I was still working on a five-month research plan and since I knew I wanted at least two months in Paris I didn't linger in Aix despite the attraction of bars like the Deux Garçons, a natural refuelling stop on the way home from the *mairie* to the university, where I took some of my (frugal) meals. In December I moved my researches to the great seaport of Marseille, France's third city, just thirty kilometres from Aix by tram (it was the longest tram route in Europe according to my future friend John Drummond, who inevitably knew about such obscure matters). Here I stayed with the Vidal-Naquet family, Sephardic Jewish intellectuals, one of whose sons, Pierre, a contemporary of mine, was soon to lead the protests against the French army's use of torture in Algeria. It was a stimulating household; I enjoyed talking to Madame Vidal-Naquet, completely ignorant of the fact that her husband had been murdered by the Nazis at Auschwitz. The Marseille music academy's archive was housed in the charming seventeenth-century town hall in the celebrated Vieux Port section. A rundown, ramshackle affair in 1954, the hôtel de ville building has since had a makeover and now serves as a bijou hotel. The weather stayed wonderfully warm – I spent Christmas Eve in my shirtsleeves – but I was happy to swap climates and take up residence in Paris for the remainder of my scholarship. I persuaded Tony Mayer that I would benefit from a full year to develop my research and flesh it out with transcriptions of music by the French composers I had been unearthing. I was, after all, the world authority on my specialist subject; for what it was worth, I knew which music was top of the provincial pops back in the 1760s.

In Paris the centre of my activities was the Bibliothèque Nationale in the Rue de Richelieu, just north of the Comédie-Française. I went to performances at the famous old theatre more than once – by the end of this French year I was able to comprehend the stately alexandrines of Racine and the racier dialogue of Molière. At the national library my unofficial director of studies was François Lesure, a model of sympathetic scholarship, always ready with a relevant new manuscript for my delectation. François was to become a leading figure in French musical life, much more than a straightforward academic; his English admirers were especially grateful for his work in rescuing for posterity a number of orchestral scores by Hector Berlioz. The enthusiasm we shared for the Philidor family, in which there were as many composers as there were Bachs in Saxony, led him to bring out new manuscripts every week for my inspection. François-André Danican Philidor (1726–95) was my favourite; he wrote *opéras-comiques* and pretty instrumental suites (one of which I later transcribed for oboe and keyboard) but he is best known to the modern world for his mastery not of music but of chess: 'the Philidor defence' remains a classic ploy. About his personal life I know only that he married a woman fifty-one years younger than himself who unfortunately died soon after.

I cannot pretend that my researches into French musical life in the eighteenth century made much of an impression on the cultural history of that great nation but eventually I did publish a learned article, in French, in the *Revue de Musicologie*. I also placed an essay in England's equivalent learned quarterly, *Music and Letters*, whose editor, Eric Blom, I greatly admired as the pungent music critic of the *Observer* and annotator of the Penguin selection of Mozart's letters I had revered since childhood. Mr Blom was quite complimentary about my academic effort and I suspect it was he who helped to get me freelance work with the *Observer* later in the 1950s.

My student life in Paris was based at a small hotel in the Rue Campagne-Première in Montparnasse, just off the Boulevard Raspail. I lived in a tiny room on the top floor (no lift) which nevertheless boasted floor-to-ceiling French windows and a tiny balcony from which I could look out over the rooftops of Paris. I lived on the equivalent of a pound a day (300 francs a month being the extent of my government grant). But I must have benefited from student travel subsidies: I certainly took the Metro and rode the city buses – leaping on and off their open platforms with an aromatic Gitane between my fingers like a true Parisian. I often ate at the subsidised student restaurants and when money was really short would make do with whatever was provided free: a stale baguette could be spread with eye-watering French mustard.

My personal life centred on the atelier of Florence Jonquières, whom I'd met at the Musica Viva course eighteen months earlier. She was a weaver. Her tiny

Rue Campagne-Première, my room at the Hôtel Istria arrowed. Marcel Duchamp lived here at the beginning of the twentieth century.

Vie de bohème – supper with friends chez Florence Jonquières. Harry Guest, a Cambridge poet, is at extreme left. I am foreground, right, with my friend Claudine Effront next to me.

studio was in a courtyard in the ancient and very narrow Rue Visconti, close to the École des Beaux-Arts. She would push her looms to one side and make space for half a dozen of her musical friends to sit around munching baguettes spread with *rillettes de Tours* and knocking back cheap but decent red wine from the local branch of Nicolas while we listened to our favourite records: the top choice was a group of Monteverdi madrigals sung under the direction of Nadia Boulanger by a tiny group in which Hugues Cuénod figured large – his plangent tones in 'Chiome d'oro' were unforgettable. Another much-played LP was a wonderful work of neoclassicism by Ernest Bloch dating from 1924 entitled Concerto Grosso No. 1 in D minor for String Orchestra with Piano Obbligato – we had a brand-new LP recording by the Chicago Symphony Orchestra under Rafael Kubelík and we played it over and over again, revelling in its imposing opening, its heart-stirring Swiss folk tunes dressed out in grandly tonal classical gestures and the thrilling fugue with which it ends. (I rate the Concerto Grosso every bit as highly as Elgar's *Introduction and Allegro*.)

Florence's father was a celebrated printer, a friend of Jean Cocteau and a true artist: the books he printed were themselves works of art. He had a grand piano in his apartment, where we would foregather to make music; Ruth Hansen, the Danish soprano who had sung the role of Anne Trulove very touchingly in Musica Viva's *Rake's Progress*, was now studying in Paris and she and I spent happy afternoons working through the soprano arias in Mozart's C minor Mass and Donna Anna's 'Or sai chi l'onore' from my adored *Don Giovanni*. Also in the circle was Harry Guest, a Cambridge poet turned *boursier* with whom I shared a love of verse as well as of music and theatre. Harry became a much-admired schoolmaster: one year his English class at Lancing College included Christopher Hampton, David Hare and Tim Rice. He and I went together to see Chekhov's *The Seagull* done by the legendary Pitoëff family in their own Montmartre theatre: this was an evening of intense, spellbinding theatricality. A much more raw entertainment was provided by a Paris visit from Joan Littlewood's brand-new Theatre Workshop Company – we were knocked out by their *Arden of Faversham* and by Ben Jonson's *Volpone*, done in modern dress with a captivating turn by Maxwell Shaw as the spiv-like Mosca. In fact 1955 was for me a year of theatrical revelation; I became a regular at the TNP, the Théâtre National Populaire, which was housed in my favourite modern building, the Palais de Chaillot, overlooking the Champ de Mars and the Tour Eiffel. Maria Casarès and Gérard Philipe (both greatly admired film stars) were the TNP's leading players, alongside their grizzled leader Jean Vilar. In their hands, theatre was much more than a superior form of entertainment; it was like a way of life, boasting similar educational ambitions to those of the Jeunesses Musicales. I still possess the programme books which the TNP published in conjunction with their productions; they contained – wonder of wonders! – complete play texts.

An equal joy was the theatre company run by Jean-Louis Barrault (whom I had adored as the mime Dubureau in *Les Enfants du Paradis*) and his wife Madeleine Renaud. They had a lease on the famous wooden theatre at the bottom of the Champs-Élysées and it was here that the company's director of music, a certain Pierre Boulez, held court on Sunday mornings at his famous 'cushion' concerts. (My admiration for his pedagogic powers found practical outlet a decade later when, under my watch, Boulez began a series of revelatory musical essays for BBC2.)

More music came my way thanks to my membership of the Jeunesses Musicales. Especially fine was a chamber concert given in the round by the Amadeus Quartet. These lovely people, with whom I had joked at Bryanston the previous summer, performed Britten's recently composed Second String Quartet, which I remember enjoying as much as Walton's A minor Quartet from a few years earlier; how blessed we were in those days with masterpieces appearing nearly every month created by the world's leading composers. But my chief joy was *making* music. I sang in the Chorale Élisabeth Brasseur – it was quite an experience learning the Duruflé *Requiem* – and I teamed up to play duos with another *boursier*, the oboist Maurice Checker, who was later to play with distinction in the London Philharmonic and the Scottish Chamber Orchestra. Maurice was a charming guy, modest and a little shy but with the loveliest of smiles and the warmest of good natures: he helped me get my Philidor transcriptions into performable condition: it was just too bad that I lost interest in my musicological study as soon as I started work at the BBC. Another musical partner was Claudine Effront, who had been the organist Lionel Rogg's girlfriend when we had all met at Musica Viva in the summer of 1953. Claudine was in Paris without Lionel; she became a dear friend and the most polished duet partner of my entire life – we had plenty of time for study in that long Parisian spring. We gave a spiffing duet concert in her landlady's salon at an elegant address near the Parc Monceau – a very pleasant *quartier*. Needless to say, Bizet, Debussy, Fauré and Ravel were all represented but we expanded our repertoire to include Hindemith's difficult but very rewarding duet sonata, to this day one of my favourites.

Claudine was warm-hearted and affectionate: for the second time in my young life I found myself contemplating a lifelong relationship with a Swiss girl. We made plans to visit Italy together later in the summer but then fate intervened in the person of an Anglo-French lutenist whom I met at a summer school in Royaumont, just outside Paris. Mildred Clary was an outsize personality, a brilliant performing musician with a formidable intellect, somebody much more challenging than my companions of the Rue Visconti. With her at Royaumont I met the English musicologist Denis Stevens – a truly original musician – and sang madrigals under his direction; I even introduced his group to some of the bawdy Staggins repertoire I had acquired in Cambridge – with the filthy words discreetly bowdlerised for mixed company. Good fun! But by now I was besotted with Mildred, who was tall, alluring and utterly frank: she gave me *Toi et Moi* by Paul Géraldy, a set of love poems written in 1912 but newly re-edited: I blushed at their directness. To this she added *Letters to a Young Poet* by Rainer Maria Rilke, a book that turned my heart over. To cut a long and not very edifying story short, Mildred and I arranged to meet in Florence a few days before my expedition with Claudine was due to begin. When I reached Florence, alone, I was at my wits' end with guilty indecision. I attended an open-air concert in the Boboli Gardens; Lorin Maazel was conducting Sibelius's Second Symphony, a work I knew backwards and adored – but never before had its passions been matched by such a turmoil in my own heart. I suddenly perceived what a shit I was being vis-à-vis my unsuspecting friend Claudine. I telegrammed her at her Geneva home: 'Don't come to Italy. Will explain in person tomorrow' – or words to that effect. I took the night train to Geneva and had a very frosty interview with Claudine and her mother. I never saw dear Claudine again but she eventually married her childhood sweetheart, the organist Lionel Rogg. From a website I discovered that she was two years my senior and died in 2015.

I took the next train back to Florence with a load of guilt lifted from my mind and the prospect of a torrid summer to come. Mildred and I met as planned and went through the absurd process of trying to find a hotel that would provide a double room for a couple with different surnames in their passports. In the end we made love at dusk on a fairly secluded Florentine hillside, only for Millie to confess that she was still in love with her former fiancé, the surrealist writer René de Obaldia – to whom she returned a few months later and eventually married. For our Roman holiday she had already made plans for us to rent a flat in Rome from a film director friend, and despite the emotional setback our friendship had just undergone we persevered with this proposal; the apartment was round the corner from the Campo dei Fiori and for three weeks we shopped in the market and explored the Eternal City unencumbered by passion but hungry to see the sights, from the Coliseum to the Villa Borghese, from the Panthéon to the Baths of Caracalla, where we duly attended one of Rome's spectacular open-air opera performances. Our absentee landlord was indeed a film buff and our siesta hours were taken up with reading countless back numbers of *Les Cahiers du Cinéma*.

It turned out to be one of the best holidays of my life. But suddenly it was September and the days of wine and roses were at an end: my training as an assistant studio manager, Central Programme Operations, BBC Broadcasting House, was about to begin.

What had I learnt from my French year? That you didn't need money to have a good time. My musical research taught me about the social value of public music-making, so there was a certain relevance to the work I was to do in broadcasting and television over the next fifty years, bringing people together in the name of music. My stay in Avignon was followed up two summers later when I reported for *The Times* on the TNP's Avignon festival and actually rubbed shoulders with the great actor Jean Vilar and his colleagues at a lunch for the international press, best remembered at sixty years' remove for the wonderful *melon au sherry* which was served as an *hors d'oeuvre*. I also returned to Aix-en-Provence as the *Observer*'s critic to write about the delightful Mozart and Rossini operas performed in the Archbishops' Palace – under the baton of no less a maestro than Carlo Maria Giulini. And I found myself sitting next to Marc Pincherle, doyen of French music critics, at the second performance anywhere of Boulez's *Le Marteau sans Maître*; it was fun being *The Times*'s anonymous 'special correspondent' – I only wish I could have formed a more sympathetic understanding of Boulez's music: I confess it eludes me still, despite the enormous attraction of Boulez the man.

Looking back on my *année française* it is pleasant, finally, to recall a delightful excursion made from Paris one Sunday afternoon with my oboist friend Maurice Checker to the enchanting little village of Ville d'Avray. The visit had a logic bestowed upon it fifty years later when I discovered in the course of my biographical researches that Yehudi Menuhin and his family had lived in Ville d'Avray in the 1930s.

Menuhin was also at the back of a sentimental journey I made at the other end of my life, in 2011, to the clifftop house in Oregon of Ernest Bloch, whose music we had so enormously enjoyed in Florence Jonquières's workshop. In his memoirs Menuhin wrote of making a pilgrimage to the dying composer's last home overlooking the Pacific; the link between Bloch and Menuhin was that Bloch had dedicated his *Abodah* to the child virtuoso when they both lived in 1920s San Francisco. Christina and I visited our friend John Evans in Eugene, Oregon and with him followed in Yehudi's footsteps to salute Bloch's memory in a remote cliff-side spot on the Pacific coast, his vibrant Concerto Grosso ringing through my head. Here concludes my digression!

I may not have had much to show for my year in France and yet I had planted the seeds of a lifetime's affection. A quarter of a century later I was to be made a Chevalier in France's *Ordre des Arts et des Lettres*. I have a little ribbon and a mini-medal which I have worn perhaps ten times in the last forty years. I was told the award was for services to French music. Not, I suspect, for my serious researches into provincial musical life in the eighteenth century. Maybe for my *Monitor* films about Darius Milhaud and Paul Tortelier, or for my advocacy of a new musical instrument, *Les Structures Sonores* – an attractive array of glass rods backed by reflective stainless-steel leaves; the rods were stroked with wet fingers by the brothers François and Bernard Baschet. But my chevalier award was more likely, I suspect, for the television work I did in the cause of Hector Berlioz – my production of *L'Enfance du Christ* was televised in Ely Cathedral in the 1960s on BBC2 and the *Te Deum* in St Paul's for London Weekend Television (both conducted by Colin Davis), and finally Leonard Bernstein's Berlioz films in the early 1970s for French television and Unitel – *Harold in Italy* and the *Symphonie Fantastique* were performed at the Théâtre des Champs-Élysées and – grandest of all – the *Requiem* performed at the Invalides in the presence of the French president, Giscard d'Estaing. I describe that bizarre occasion in the next chapter.

PART TWO

Finding My Feet at the BBC,
1955–1967

CHAPTER 7

THE BBC'S NEW RECRUIT

Exterior of Broadcasting House: 'Nation Shall Speak Peace Unto Nation'.
I walked past this inscription every time I went to the BBC Concert Hall or to the
basement Studio where you could hear the Bakerloo Line trains trundling by.

IN 1955 RADIO was still very much the BBC's senior service. I had lived
with it all my life: it was my Everyman, always at my side; I listened to *Much
Binding in the Marsh* and *Breakfast with Braden* as faithfully as to a Prom or
a Third Programme Henry Reed feature. I felt, too, that the announcers were
my friends: Bruce Belfrage, Alvar Lidell, Stuart Hibberd – quite a litany. And
now, in September 1955, I was to enter that broadcasting world – in a lowly
capacity, to be sure: as a trainee studio manager. But I was not envious of
the general trainees, as the high-flyers were discreetly identified; I found it
genuinely exciting to pass through those heavy Broadcasting House doors into

the foyer's lofty hallway and read the equally lofty inscription: Nation shall speak peace unto nation. My starting salary for speaking peace was £408 per annum – at the bottom of the D scale, just over £8 a week and no help with travel to work. My early ambition was to get myself promoted to B1Minus, the lowest level for production staff; I modestly hoped to be earning a thousand pounds a year by the time I was thirty. But promotion proved swifter than I had dared anticipate and I never stayed in the same grade for longer than two years.

The BBC landscape was certainly Orwellian. Senior staff at BH were known by their initials. In the Central Programmes group my boss, H.C.P. Ops, was somebody called Brian George. He was remote: I don't think I met him more than twice. His deputies (A.H.C.P.Ops) were 'Pip' Porter, in charge of studios, a genial white-haired gentleman who was very helpful to me later on, and an equally nice man called Tim Eckersley, who was in charge of recordings: his uncle had been a founding father of the Corporation who got into trouble before the war by marrying a Nazi sympathiser. I liked Tim because his good looks and cultivated voice reminded me of the excellent actor Robert Donat.

The studio manager did what it said on the label: he or she (there were quite a few women: a higher proportion than in my year at university) literally 'managed' the studio. We studied the production script and worked out what would be required in the way of microphones, lecterns, and tables and chairs. During rehearsals and the actual broadcast we (the studio managers) opened up the mics to create radio by twiddling finely calibrated faders (knobs to you), known as 'pots' (potentiometers); we had to ensure that not too much electric energy went coursing through the microphones and out to the transmitters. The old wives' tale was that transmitters would collapse and go off the air if you let the needle on the dial stray over 6 for longer than a few seconds. (I was reasonably well informed about all this because of the work I had done in the Royal Signals.)

Training began at the Staff Training studio on Marylebone Road, a mile away from Portland Place where the real-life broadcasting happened. Our basic Studio Manager course was the only formal education I ever received at the BBC. It lasted six weeks, just like the army's square-bashing. Our final exercise involved an imaginary White Network which imitated a day's broadcasting on one of the BBC's domestic radio networks complete with its own continuity studio, 'live' contributions and pre-recorded inserts. The jargon soon came naturally and six months of probation followed as we trainees were shunted round the principal bastions of British broadcasting situated in London. First stop for me was the studio at 200 Oxford Street, then home of the General Overseas Service. Here I met the guitarist Alexis Korner, a founding father of British Blues. It was reassuring how many unconventional people could slip through the net of BBC appointments boards. Then I moved to Bush House, situated in another famous London landmark, the Aldwych. Bush is where I went on air for the first time. Nobody in the UK could hear my début broadcasts, nor would they have wanted to. In the small hours I would open the pot in a Bush studio and announce bravely that 'listeners on the 22-metre band must now re-tune'. Depending on when and where you were listening, the 22-metre band could only give better reception, I seem to remember, generally at around dawn or dusk, so listeners had to be encouraged to go in search of a stronger signal. There wasn't much in the script with which a fledgling broadcaster could establish his broadcasting style. Even more dull was the SM's other routine duty of playing in recordings engraved on giant 19-inch discs; these provided seemingly endless interviews in Swahili or Arabic. The nights were long at Bush House. But the food in the canteen was by far the best in the BBC thanks to the cross-section of exotic nations who broadcast from the basement.

Next for me came a short spell in the Aeolian Hall in New Bond Street, an historic concert hall which the BBC had taken over during the war. Here I was introduced to the showbiz world of the BBC's Variety Department. For a naïve initiate like me this was much more fun. Harry Morris, the canny chief studio manager, taught me tricks with microphones, notably how to use a rubber band to fix an empty matchbox over the standard condenser mic in order to create a more penetrative 'flat' sound. I was also coached in the art of preparing expense forms: it was a matter of fine-tuning rather than fiddling.

From cueing-up pre-recorded sound effects – my earliest duty – I soon graduated to the real thing: letting off pistols with blank caps for the shows of the comedian Alfred Marks and, in *Take It from Here*, rattling a doorknob to signal Jimmy Edwards's arrival in the household of The Glums. The conversation of dim Ron and placid Eth would be interrupted by father Jimmy's return from the pub. His first line was always: ''Ullo, 'ullo, what's goin' on 'ere?' I need hardly add that the timing of the door-rattle that preceded the catchphrase was of vital importance to the success of the sketch.

At another of the BBC's variety strongholds, the formerly elegant but now tragically decaying Camden Hippodrome, I got to do sound effects for The Goons: coconut shells for horses' hooves; creaking doors; seagulls; the

Take It from Here.
Left to right: Jimmy
Edwards, June Whitfield
and Dick Bentley.

lot. *The Goon Show* was the nation's most popular programme and this was my first taste of BBC Big Time.

One afternoon I went in early to prepare my repertoire of noises off and was surprised to hear a tenor voice ringing round the empty balconies of the shabby old auditorium: it was my favourite *Pagliacci* aria, 'On with the Motley', complete with plangent sobs in the closing bars. I was reminded of the performance of Beniamino Gigli, my childhood 78 rpm record favourite (dismissed at Long Dene as 'belly music' by my teacher Philip Dore), but then I heard the unmistakable Welsh-accented speaking voice of Harry Secombe. A singer since his army days in Naples, Harry could have had a career as a lyric operatic tenor, but being a Goon – the anarchic Neddie Seagoon to be precise – it was as satisfying as it was exciting for him to keep this genuine talent as a secret among friends. A few years later (as I relate elsewhere) I had the chance to make Harry the co-star with Kiri Te Kanawa in *Call Me Kiri*, a 'special' for BBC1. It was an unforgettable cameo; Harry was kitted out in clown's costume and sang with many a tasteful sob. In fact my studio encounter with the Goons – anarchist Michael Bentine, surrealist Peter Sellers and drop-dead-funny Spike Milligan – as well as the mellifluous Secombe

– was a highlight of my early BBC life. I was so happy to have played a small part in the show for a few weeks.

But in the summer of 1956 my probation was at an end and I duly became an Assistant Music Studio Manager, based in Rothwell House, a very dull office building near Broadcasting House where I was to live out my brief career as a broadcaster – disappointingly I showed no interest in breaking out, in getting work for example as an LP record producer, despite the exciting recordings being made by Decca and Oiseau-Lyre in the 1950s. And I felt no resentment at my lowly status. My suspicion is that I was actually quite happy.

The Music Studio Managers group was run by two true gentlemen of the BBC's old school, Raymond Suffield and Eric Docherty, both blessed with ultra-fastidious ears. My personal mentors were a pianist named Paul Reding, like me a Berlioz enthusiast, and Jimmy Burnett, who was already much in demand – moonlighting – as a freelance recording producer; Julian Bream trusted him implicitly. As the new boy in Music Studio Managers, I was assigned to nursery slopes such as the sedate morning service in the Concert Hall at Broadcasting

The Goons. Left to right: Harry Secombe, Michael Bentine, Spike Milligan and Peter Sellers.

House or to balance debutant song recitals mostly recorded at the BBC's Maida Vale studios, an historic building that had started life as a roller-skating rink and has now been awarded listed building status. I would also assist Paul Reding at symphony concerts in the big Maida Vale studio, MV1, wheeling microphone booms into place, checking the balance between woodwinds and brass, marking up the orchestral scores before the rehearsal to prepare for loud passages where the peak meter would have to be gently wound down – the routine sounds a little boring, but was actually involving and good fun.

Producers from Yalding House, the headquarters on Great Portland Street of the BBC's music division, became canteen friends, among them gifted musicians such as Peter Gould, Deryck Cooke and Roger Fiske, for whom I balanced some of the *Talking about Music* broadcasts given by that brilliant musician and teacher Anthony Hopkins. At a London Mozart Players broadcast produced by another stand-out Yalding personality, the delightfully unpredictable Viennese refugee Hans Keller, I met the orchestra's founder-conductor Harry Blech. The moment the red light went off at the end of his Haydn concert he shocked me by stripping to the sweaty waist. Also in the studio that day was the jovial, larger-than-life American scholar H.C. Robbins Landon. I took to him immediately. In the next decade 'Robbie' and I were to work on several television features about Haydn and Monteverdi. He spent so much time researching in monastery libraries behind the Iron Curtain that I began to suspect he might also be a CIA agent.

Life, it seemed to me, was proceeding very pleasantly on all fronts. It was for me a major event when I conducted a small choir at an all-Schubert concert in Leighton House organised by my pianist friend Joyce Rathbone. Helen Watts was the soloist, backed by a men's chorus when we sang Schubert's gently humorous 'Serenade'. I was also dabbling in music criticism: *The Times* took me on as a freelance fourth-string reviewer and I had the nerve to submit a laudatory piece about the BBC's recent broadcast of Stravinsky's *Le Rossignol*, naturally without revealing that it was I who had 'balanced' the transmission. I was so hungry for writing experience that when John Lawrence, the arts editor at Printing House Square, phoned me to ask if I could review Alicia Markova dancing *The Dying Swan* I foolishly accepted. I duly attended the Royal Festival Hall event and walked back over the Thames to Mr Lawrence's office – I never had the confidence to dictate my copy over the phone. I sat at the hallowed desk where before the war the great playwright and critic Charles Morgan had written his theatre reviews … but since I knew nothing about classical dancing I had no idea what to say about Markova. Pen in hand,

I stared at the blank page. Every half hour or so a printer's runner would knock at the door demanding my copy to catch the next edition. I finally scribbled something fatuous which only Londoners reading the final edition would have seen. (I recounted this incident to Dame Alicia when we were both on the panel for the *Evening Standard* opera and ballet awards but she couldn't even remember the performance, let alone my 'review'. She probably danced *The Dying Swan* more often than Pavlova herself.)

In the summer of 1956 I wangled an invitation to be *The Times*'s guest critic at the Aix-en-Provence Festival. I heard Rameau's *Platée* with the extraordinary *haute-contre* tenor Michel Sénéchal as the ugly marsh-nymph, and Rossini's *Barbiere di Siviglia* under the dynamic Carlo Maria Giulini. Both were revelations for me, setting festival standards and helping to form my adult taste. At the lovely Aix hotel in which we VIP guests (critics!) were installed, I had the good fortune to meet John Morris, the controller of the BBC's Third Programme. John was a remarkable man who had worked alongside George Orwell in the General Overseas Service – they disliked each other intensely – and had climbed almost to the summit of Mount Everest as long ago as 1923. John was a Renaissance man if ever there was one: he knew a great deal about art and literature and subsequently signed me up to do several Third Programme talks, including one on *Platée*, which we had attended together, and another on Milhaud's *Christophe Colombe*, which I didn't dare confess I had never actually seen. I went back to Aix the following year when Teresa Berganza made her stunning international début as Dorabella in *Così fan tutte* – I knew what to expect because I had already heard her at a Jeunesses Musicales conference in Madrid. That second summer I also filed copy for *The Times* about the drama festival at Avignon; the plays were by Claudel, Molière and Beaumarchais, an unsurpassable trio of writers.

Back in England, the career of my hero Colin Davis was in the doldrums: only the Chelsea Opera Group seemed to know his worth, so we were excited when the London Philharmonic offered him the second half of a symphony concert at Lewisham Town Hall. The engagement went well, as I reported in a review for the *Times Educational Supplement*, for which I was paid the princely sum of two guineas (£2.10). Ridiculously, Colin's fee for conducting was less: a measly £2 for a Tchaikovsky symphony! But at last he was on his way.

The Suez invasion threw a spanner into my gentle progress. The government clashed with the BBC. Sir Anthony Eden, the prime minister, thought it was 1939 all over again but the Labour opposition led by Hugh Gaitskell insisted on their right to oppose the crooked operation that was Suez and the BBC insisted

My hero Colin Davis rehearsing Mozart's Symphony No. 33 in B flat, K319. 'If somebody asks "How did it go?" – you don't know, because you've been too busy doing it.' From *Monitor*, October 1959.

on providing Labour with equal airtime. The Foreign Office under the odious Selwyn Lloyd objected to the BBC's even-handed reporting both at home and in its foreign-language broadcasts. The upshot was a tremendous increase in the number of BBC news bulletins. Studio managers were called in from every department to cope with the surge. Reports from our war correspondents in Egypt were broadcast within minutes of being received. The dispatches arrived in the studio not on tape but on wax disks, playing at 78 rpm. One of my jobs involved editing the reports while on the air, a hair-raising experience. I would be given a transcript marked with a cut eliminating maybe twenty seconds of the dispatch. My method was simple but fraught. With headphones clamped to my ears to keep out the noisy bustle of the control room, I would find the 'out' sentence on the disk and mark its last word in the record's groove with a yellow chinagraph pencil. On transmission the newsreader would introduce the report and I would play in the disk, scanning the grooves like a hawk for the telltale yellow mark. When the cue arrived I stopped the turntable in its tracks, deftly lifted the needle head and plonked it down again just before my second chinagraph mark; I then released the brake and gave the turntable a gentle shove to get it back to speed as the dispatch continued. The whole operation wouldn't have lasted more than a second. (I think we ran an atmosphere track on another turntable to disguise the momentary break in sound.)

Such high-tension activity was fun in the short term but I was depressed by the British government's shabby behaviour over Suez and for a few weeks I seriously thought of emigrating to Canada; I got as far as Canada's consulate in Mayfair and actually picked up the application form. But a good fairy must have wanted to keep me at the BBC (I suspect 'Pip' Porter had a hand in it) because out of the blue I was offered an attachment as a producer in the department's production unit. Unsurprisingly, the offices were in Rothwell House, the utterly undistinguished office block which also housed the music and features studio managers. So it wasn't much of a geographical move for me: the agreeable change was that now I had my own office and my own secretary. Theoretically my new outfit existed to make programmes out of the BBC's vast archive of recordings and sound effects, but my first assignment was brand new: to assemble and introduce a weekly anthology entitled (I think by me) *Transatlantic Turntable*. The hour-long shows were broadcast on Saturday afternoons on the Light Programme and derived almost totally from Voice of America tapes and the gigantic 19-inch LPs which were sent weekly to the BBC from Washington. This treasure trove included countless relays from the Metropolitan Opera in New York, among them a spellbinding account of *La Bohème* with Renata Tebaldi and Richard Tucker – both on terrific vocal form. I also found a moment of opera history, the matinée when the famous mezzo Marian Anderson sang Ulrica in Verdi's *Ballo in Maschera*, the first-ever appearance, in January 1955, of an African-American on the hallowed Met stage: there was a tremendous round of applause over the music when the curtain went up on her scene. I also waded through many wonderful hours taped at the Newport Jazz Festival and was soon spicing up my programmes by interviewing visiting American jazz musicians such as Count Basie, John Lewis of the Modern Jazz Quartet and the trumpet wizard Dizzy Gillespie, who I watched in disbelief as he drank raw eggs in a glass for his breakfast. The magazine *Melody Maker* ran a feature about me headlined 'Humphrey loves the Three B's – that's Beethoven, Bach and Basie'. When it came to having my name in *Radio Times* I decided to call myself by my given name, instead of the 'Bill' which had been my unchanging soubriquet at school and in the army. 'Humphrey' had more of a ring to it. It would be different were I starting today …

In my early months at the BBC I lived in Sidcup with my mother. The Long Dene community – my home – had gone through painful division and strife, mostly prompted by the Guinnesses's cranky belief in various brands of mysticism, before the school closed in 1954. Kay then found herself a job in her former profession, working as a midwife at the Foots Cray hospital near Sidcup, where she rented a modest house. Trundling up to London by commuter train, as I did when I started work at the BBC, was not enjoyable and after a few months I settled in digs in Ladbroke Road, Notting Hill, at the home of the publisher Livia Gollancz. Her illustrious father Victor was a great music-lover and supporter of the Chelsea Opera Group; he lived round the corner in Ladbroke Grove. Livia was an excellent horn player, formerly a professional with both the London Symphony Orchestra and the Hallé. I got to know her at Music Camp and when she played horn with the Chelsea Opera Group. A keen gardener, she used to ride around West London on her bicycle looking for manure to spread on her garden. 'Horse droppings!' she would cry when she sighted her prey, dismounting briskly and shovelling the stuff, often still warm, into a specially adapted basket attached to the bike's back wheel. The following year, when I was courting, my girlfriend Gretel would slip into my ground-floor bedsit through the front window. It was just opposite the police station but at dead of night she was never spotted. I suspect Livia also turned a blind eye.

My radio work could be quite prosaic. In the summer of 1957 I devised a radio crossword for Light Programme listeners. The puzzle's grid was published in *Radio Times*, which in those days had a huge circulation of nearly 2 million copies; the clues, mostly sound effects, were broadcast on Saturday afternoons in another show devised by Harry Rogers and myself called *Sound Mirror*. Listeners had to post in their answers. I'm hopeless at crosswords myself – solving them is a skill that jumped from my father to my sons, leaving me bereft of talent. The same summer I was given a more congenial assignment, to make a sound documentary for a series called *Holiday Hour*: I was to cover an archaeological vacation trip in central Italy. The climax of my feature was a torchlit procession and fireworks display at a village on Lake Trasimeno; the excitement could only be expressed by the actuality sound and my breathless description. For a few moments I wondered whether I might be cut out to follow in the footsteps of such eloquent radio reporters as Frank

Gretel Davis: my
midnight caller.

Gillard and Richard Dimbleby – they used the same basic equipment, after all, the good old L2 tape recorder. But there the comparison stopped. But not, for me, the fascination with cultural touring, which was to become a mainstay of my life in my sixties.

In September 1957 Gretel and I got married. Colin Davis's youngest sister, she was an actress, a former pupil at Christ's Hospital Girls' School and one of the first graduates of the Rose Bruford Training College of Speech and Drama. She acted and stage managed for several summers in provincial 'Rep' theatres and while resting lived in London with her brother and his young family; we met when she was helping Colin to organise the rehearsal schedule for the Chelsea Opera Group's production of *The Magic Flute*, for which I had been picked to sing a couple of short solo bass-baritone roles, the Second Priest and

Engagement day with Gretel, Broadcasting House very much in the picture.

the Second Armed Man. Gretel was a vivacious personality, with fire in her belly. We quite often found ourselves travelling together on the same double-decker bus from Holland Park to Oxford Circus and our friendship developed swiftly, chattering on the top deck of the No. 88. We had a church wedding near her mother's home in Wimbledon and our honeymoon was spent touring the Scottish Highlands in a Morris Minor convertible. We settled down to live in her brother's Princedale Road house while he was away conducting in Glasgow.

The music at the wedding was sung by the Elizabethan Singers, Louis Halsey's London choir – with whom I had sung occasionally, although my studio manager shift patterns at the BBC made regular attendance difficult. After singing in the Chelsea Opera Group's *Magic Flute* – a tremendous thrill! – I flirted with taking up a singing career. I remember with some embarrassment my wildly ambitious stab at the title role in Mendelssohn's *Elijah*. As I have related, I did better at Music Camp, singing a sonorous Sarastro when Roger Norrington conducted his first *Magic Flute*. But that was the high-water mark of my singing career. Flash forward two decades: I sang the role of the Second Prisoner in the Chelsea Opera Group's twenty-fifth anniversary performance of *Fidelio* in St John's Smith Square. Colin Davis was conducting and Lord Harewood was in the audience. But unsurprisingly the call to sing at his English National Opera never came – the nearest I got to that prestigious St Martin's Lane venue was to perform Mozart's 'Bei Männern' duet with my Radio 3 opera-producing colleague Elaine Padmore. This was at a fundraising event … in the foyer at the London Coliseum, so yes, I *have* sung at ENO – not on stage, however, but in the Dutch Bar.

A month after my marriage the *Today* programme was launched on the Home Service and I was soon pitching for assignments as a *de facto* arts reporter. I did an interview with the superstar Paul Anka and another with Peter Brook concerning his use of *musique concrète* to create Ariel's otherworldly sounds in his new production of *The Tempest* at Drury Lane. For the Light Programme's *Sound Mirror* I made six short features about people working at Covent Garden. One was a young dancer who had just joined the company from the Royal Ballet School; her name was Antoinette Sibley and she was to become a major star.

I always loved working backstage at Covent Garden in Floral Street. At the opera house I also made profiles of the chief electrician Sid Cheney and of the French-Canadian operatic bass Joseph Rouleau, with whom I subsequently recorded (without permission) a recital in one of the BBC's Maida Vale studios for broadcast in Joe's home city, Montreal. I accompanied him in Verdi's famous loneliness aria, 'Ella giammai m'amò', sung by Philip, the Spanish emperor, in my favourite Verdi opera, *Don Carlo*. What *chutzpah* I needed to have 'borrowed' the BBC facilities to make that recording! For the *Today* programme I went with Francis Poulenc to the Covent Garden dress rehearsal of *Dialogues des Carmélites*. After the devastating final scene when the nuns are all guillotined I followed Poulenc over the rehearsal bridge linking the auditorium with the stage and found myself taping his impromptu conversation with the soprano who had sung the tricky part of Madame Lidoine, the new mother superior of the convent. The conversation went something like this:

'Ah! Madame Sooterland!' (for it was the future Dame Joan). 'Vous avez chanté ma musique si merveilleusement bien! C'était superbe.'

'Oh, did yer think so, maestro?' came the sturdy young prima donna's reply, in a broad Australian accent. 'Ecksherly I've got a terrible cold.'

Mrs Grace Wyndham Goldie – the BBC's Queen of Hearts.

I enjoyed a momentary 'high' that morning but I was again experiencing disenchantment with Broadcasting House because after a year on attachment my position as a producer was still not confirmed – to use BBC jargon, there was no official 'post' to hold me against – and I was not being paid for my broadcast appearances. On the spur of the moment I decided to apply for a job in television that I had noticed on the board. Neither Gretel nor I possessed a television set and I had never set foot in a television studio but the new job's description seemed to fit me quite well; BBC Television's new arts magazine *Monitor* was looking for production assistants – junior directors paid on the B1Minus grade. Just what I was dreaming about! Applicants would have to supply evidence of an interest in all the arts, with specialist knowledge of either music or drama. I applied more from a sense of grievance than because I wanted to leave the senior service in favour of the buccaneering world of television. To prepare for the interview I did nothing except visit a friend's house one evening to watch the latest edition of *Monitor* and I liked what I saw, in particular an affectionate and occasionally satirical short film about an Italian opera company visiting the Theatre Royal in Drury Lane. (The film's director was John Schlesinger.) I did absolutely no other homework: I was as naive and as green as they come. At the board I was surprised to discover that *Monitor*'s editor and host Huw Wheldon was not among my interrogators. Most of the questions were posed by a sharp-featured lady who was introduced to me as BBC Television's Assistant Head of Talks, the redoubtable Mrs Grace Wyndham Goldie. I had never heard of her. She reminded me of the Queen of Hearts in *Alice in Wonderland*. She failed to scare at the board but soon she was to put the fear of God into me because, dear reader, I got the job.

CHAPTER 8

LIME GROVE:
THE PROMISED LAND

Lime Grove, looking south … not a lime tree in sight.

LIME GROVE WAS a far-flung corner of the BBC's empire, way out beyond Shepherd's Bush Green. It was rumoured to be dangerous territory, inhabited mostly by West Indian immigrants and Irish navvies. The pubs, crowded with rough trade, were no-go areas; the BBC Club, however, was always full. 'Lime Grove' sounds pleasant enough but there were no lime trees in evidence by the time I arrived in April 1958, only dull late-Victorian terraced cottages on both sides of an equally dull street, not a patch on London's bustling West End where I had been working for the previous two and a half years. What made Lime Grove unusual was the presence of a film studio complex, custom-built by Gaumont in 1932 and taken over by the Rank Organisation during the war. *The Wicked Lady*, starring Margaret Lockwood, was made here in 1945, the same year that Yehudi Menuhin (whose biography I was to write forty years later) tested for the role of Paganini in *The Magic Bow* – a part eventually assumed by Stewart Granger, who was indisputably less gifted as a violinist but had a more impressive track record as a thespian. The BBC, bursting at the seams when housed at the even more remote Alexandra Palace in north London, moved to Lime Grove in 1956, creating four television studios and a sound suite as well as a rabbit warren of offices and cutting rooms. It was to be BBC Television's HQ for a decade, supported by a pokey little studio off Kensington High Street, where the *Tonight* programme originated in 1957, and by the Riverside Studios, next to Hammersmith Bridge, on the site of another former film studio complex owned pre-war by the film star Jack Buchanan. *Hancock's Half Hour* was made at Riverside and so was Rudolph Cartier's 1959 production of Verdi's *Otello*, which famously broke down on transmission so that for several minutes the only sound that could be heard was not of opera but of the production secretary meticulously calling the shot numbers over mute images of the performers singing their hearts out. It was a true disaster.

Our Outside Broadcast units were housed in an Acton warehouse a few miles away. In the mid-1950s the BBC also took over Ealing Film Studios, which had previously been home under Michael Balcon of such great film comedies as *Kind Hearts and Coronets* and *Whisky Galore!* Because our new programme, *Monitor*, wasn't topical, the films in the series were edited not at Lime Grove but at Ealing, a further five miles west.

My first morning in television was not concerned with these geographical refinements. It did not start well. After reporting to Reception (a very modest affair by comparison with the entrance to Broadcasting House), I was directed down corridors and through a backyard to the unattractive rear entrance of a labourer's cottage. I walked up some rickety stairs to the nondescript office of Edward Caffery who, according to my joining instructions, rejoiced in the title of 'Organiser, Talks Department, BBC Television'. Yes, I was going into television to make talks – but talks with moving pictures. Edward, affability personified, introduced me to a young man who was pushing past me to leave. It was Alasdair Milne, deputy editor of *Tonight*. 'Hello, boy', he said crushingly (he was my senior by just six months) and turned on his heel. He was a Wykehamist but Winchester's motto about manners making men seemed to have passed him by. The very first of the BBC's general trainees, recruited four years earlier, Alasdair was said to have been born with a director-general's baton in his pocket. Not that it did him much good in the long run: he was humiliatingly pushed into resignation in 1987. And on that 1958 morning I was more amused than aggrieved by his *brusquerie*. Alasdair and the *Tonight* team, then led by a pugnacious Welshman named Donald Baverstock, were good journalists but came across as an arrogant bunch. But I really didn't care because at Lime Grove I was on cloud nine for months and rapidly losing my inferiority complex: the fact of the matter was that at last I was working on a level playing field. At Judd School I suffered somewhat from my inadequate Long Dene education. In the army I ended up looking after boy soldiers rather than doing something truly engrossing such as learning Russian. At Cambridge I went to lowly Fitzwilliam House rather than lordly King's College. In BBC Radio I had managed to become a broadcaster, but only while on attachment to an insignificant production unit rather than in a tenured producer post in Music or Features. But now, here at Lime Grove, I was exactly where I wanted to be: part of the *Monitor* team, working on classical music projects and going boldly forth to conquer uncharted programme territory in the fascinating, revelatory and expressive new medium of television.

Personally it was a happy time, too. In 1959 my brother-in-law took up his first London appointment as conductor at Sadler's Wells Opera. For Gretel and me this meant relocation. We found a ten-roomed house in Hammersmith Grove, a few hundred yards from the Lime Grove studios and therefore hugely convenient. We inherited a sitting tenant in the basement, an old lady who was no trouble at all; when she left, my wife's mother Lilian came to live with us, a decision which caused more tension for Gretel than it did for me. The house cost £3,200, about three times my annual salary and a substantial sum in those days, but my friend and supporter the philanthropist Robert Mayer, then eighty, kindly lent me the entire sum. I suppose for him it was a way of thanking me for the voluntary work I had been doing for his Youth and Music organisation over the previous four years. My daughter Clare was born in October 1959 and my son Matthew followed in January 1962.

The set-up at Lime Grove was agreeably informal by comparison with the establishment certainties of Broadcasting House. BH was a custom-built office block incorporating what in 1932 was state-of-the-art thinking about architecture and studio engineering. Lime Grove was a mess. It was as if the BBC staff were survivors from some terrible catastrophe which had forced the Corporation to set up temporary offices in commandeered private houses that

My daughter Clare with her brother Matthew.

were hopelessly inadequate and inappropriate for the work we were doing. When I arrived in the *Monitor* office I was assigned a plain table with a single drawer in a pokey upstairs room, presumably a bedroom before the war, which was already fully occupied by Huw Wheldon, his assistant Anne James and her filing cabinets. The production team spread via short flights of stairs through three more interconnecting rooms. To reach the canteen one had to use the iron fire escape. We didn't stay long in these cramped quarters but I vividly recall one smoke-filled production meeting in our cottage because it was attended by the poet Louis MacNeice: he was said to be exploring the possibility of secondment from radio features, where he had already worked intermittently for fifteen years. For a moment there seemed to be the marvellous possibility of working alongside a childhood hero, some of whose verse I knew by heart ('It's no go the merry-go-round, it's no go the rickshaw / All we ask is a limousine and a ticket for the peepshow'), but alas the idea came to nothing, perhaps because of the drink problem that bedevilled MacNeice's later years. We had better luck with another radio features veteran, D.G. (Geoffrey) Bridson, a familiar broadcasting name from my avid teenage listening years; he collaborated with our producer Peter Newington to make an atmospheric film portrait of the eccentric, fascist-leaning American poet Ezra Pound, then living in a crumbling castle in the Italian Tyrol. Peter's richly evocative *Monitor* films are unforgivably neglected by comparison with those of John Schlesinger and Ken Russell; among them are poetic portraits of Robert Graves, Sidney Nolan and Elisabeth Frink.

Monitor had been brought into existence by the domineering but visionary Grace Wyndham Goldie, who had already created *Panorama* and *Tonight*. Once she and her bosses Kenneth Adam and Cecil McGivern had decided that *Monitor* should become a fixture in the Talks Department output and not just a probationary series lasting a single season, the team was moved to more salubrious quarters on the seventh floor of the old film studios in offices that must once have been star dressing rooms since they were all equipped with washbasins. The make-up mirrors had been tactfully removed but the basins still ran with hot and cold water.

I worked on that corridor for four years as part of the close-knit *Monitor* team. I shall describe the set-up in a little detail in order to correct the widely held impression that *Monitor* was a film series similar to *Omnibus* or *Imagine*. As Grace never tired of proclaiming, *Monitor* did not make films, it made *programmes* – for television. Electronic cameras and film cameras were both used for every edition. The show usually consisted of three to four contrasting items (programmes) and was shown, fortnightly, on Sundays, at 10 p.m. or soon before or after. The boss, Huw Wheldon, had the newspaper-style title of 'editor'; he had the final say on what topics were to be tackled. He also presented the programme in a compelling, personal style. (I'll return to his contribution later.) Nancy Thomas, *Monitor*'s studio director, had cut her television teeth directing *The Stars at Night* and a popular quiz called *Animal, Vegetable, Mineral?* There were two junior production assistants, David Jones and myself; like me, David was one of 'Grace's boys', a university graduate whom Mrs Wyndham Goldie (not Huw) had selected. David was strong on literature and the theatre. Ann Turner, an art historian, was our permanent researcher. The production secretaries were Anne James, who basically looked after Huw and myself, Doris Jordan, who looked after Peter and David, and

127

Sally Penn, who looked after Nancy. We were the nucleus. Allan Tyrer the film editor and his assistants (Pam Andrews and later Elspeth McDougall) were all based at Ealing Studios. We were all 'BBC staff'. John Schlesinger and later Ken Russell were freelance directors hired on short-term contracts; they earned more than us but had no security of tenure. Eventually we all squeezed into four offices on Lime Grove's top floor with windows looking south over working-class Shepherd's Bush and in effect we were spokesmen for the arts on television. *Panorama* was described as the BBC's 'window on the world'. *Monitor* was intended to educate and inform about what was going on in the world of the arts, including – after a tussle – architecture. It's difficult to grasp that in the 1950s television was in such a primeval state that there was no specific commitment by the BBC to the coverage of arts subjects. Music, yes: sound radio had a music 'division' and there was the BBC's own symphony orchestra to administer. Sir John Reith had laid no such ground plan for the discussion of literature, poetry, sculpture, painting or drawing. Theatre could be re-created as plays for television, and theatrical life, which was such a vivid part of London society, was at least reflected on 1950s BBC by live relays of excerpts from West End productions, although the lively show business and movie gossip of such programmes as the shows presented by Michael Parkinson, Russell Harty and Graham Norton was entirely absent. To go further into the creative arts world was the challenge we faced. The agenda was set by Huw Wheldon.

Huw was then in his mid-forties. He grew up in North Wales and much enjoyed speaking his mother tongue, very loudly, in the company of other ebullient BBC Welshmen such as Wynford Vaughan Thomas, Cliff Morgan and innumerable Geraints and Owain Arwels, whenever they shared a round of beers at the BBC Club. Huw had had what was known as a good war, earning the Military Cross in 1944. He had subsequently worked for the Arts Council, the Festival of Britain and the BBC – as its publicity officer. The viewing public, little over half the nation in the mid-1950s, already knew Huw from a series called *All Your Own*, a young people's talent show which he hosted in an avuncular style. Peter Newington, our producer, was Huw's opposite: quietly spoken, with a nervous laugh and a saturnine expression. He was six years younger than Huw and had also served in the war, then studied at art college and at the Old Vic's famous theatre school under Tyrone Guthrie and Michel Saint-Denis. Peter had a pedigree and he had an artist's sensibility. He too had made programmes for children's television, including the first televised *Alice in Wonderland*.

In Studio G at Lime Grove, with Huw Wheldon in the chair,
floor manager Ken Riddington in attendance.

Nancy Thomas had no pretensions to being an *auteur* kind of film-maker but she was level-headed, cool and well organised – her first job had been secretary to Kenneth Clark at the National Gallery. She styled herself Mrs Thomas but we never heard anything about a husband – I learnt much later that she had married unsuccessfully during the war, but on the rebound after the love of her life had been killed on active service. Petite and self-possessed, she lived alone in a stylish apartment in Chesham Place, totally devoted to the BBC and her work on *Monitor*. She had been in the Corporation for more years than the rest of us put together, first in radio, working as secretary to George Barnes, the first head of the Third Programme, and then in television at Alexandra Palace. Later she was a passionate supporter of the Open University. For *Monitor* Nancy championed stories about architecture and art, notably masterminding a historic conversation between Roland Penrose and Max Ernst, of whose existence, let alone significance, Huw had, I suspect, been blissfully unaware.

Nancy's ongoing importance was in getting each edition on the air, a job she performed tirelessly until 1965, when *Monitor*'s last editor, Jonathan Miller, finally drove the programme into the ground. Nancy directed most of the studio transmissions, for which our always cheerful designer Natasha Kroll had devised a contemporary look: a pair of chic Italian chairs set among delicate, softly lit grey scaffolding on which would be affixed large photo blow-ups of the stars to be featured in the show. *Monitor*'s opening look was accompanied by a signature tune that became famous, the jaunty march from Dag Wirén's *Serenade*. Natasha, even older than Huw, was Russian by birth and German by education; she had had a previous career as a London shop-window designer, notably for Simpson's modernist store in Piccadilly, nowadays a bookshop but still with imposing display windows. Her riverside house at Putney was the place to be for parties on Boat Race day.

Nancy Thomas, a true BBC person.

Designer Natasha Kroll, a positive influence on the look of *Monitor*.

David Jones, like me recruited by Grace to broaden the specialist knowledge within the team, was three years younger than me and basically a theatre man. He'd gone up to Cambridge to read English straight from school and I must have seen him act at the ADC Theatre (our mutual friend Joan Bakewell speaks with awe of his Edmund in Dadie Ryland's production of *King Lear*) but at university we moved in different circles and never met; he was part of the Peter Hall/John Barton mafia. David had the most marvellously mellifluous voice and radiated not only charm but authority: he never stopped hankering for the theatre and in 1964 joined the RSC, moving thereafter between theatre, television drama and feature film-making, including Pinter's *Betrayal*. But his earlier *Monitor* documentaries also stick in my memory. They include: a portrait of the fierce Welsh poet and priest R.S. Thomas; a combative interview between Huw and Lawrence Durrell, filmed in the arena at Nîmes; and a vivid report on the Berliner Ensemble narrated by Brecht's apostle Ken Tynan.

Monitor's programmes were an eclectic mix: the films were mostly directed by a member of the team but some were bought in, among them the National Film Board of Canada's brilliant double portrait of Glenn Gould, *On* and *Off the Record*. Of the first hundred editions of *Monitor* only four consisted of a single film. Two of these were by John Schlesinger: *Private View*, about four emerging artists, and *The Class*, about the Central School of Drama. The other two were by Ken Russell: his celebration of Pop art, *Pop Goes the Easel*, and our biography of the composer Edward Elgar. Other artists profiled in shorter films included Henry Moore and Elisabeth Frink, and two vibrant commentators on art, the painter Michael Ayrton and the critic John Berger, were invited to talk about art in the studio. (Kenneth Clark, arguably the best of the pundits, was unavailable, ATV's Lew Grade having cannily put him under contract.) Many of the subjects *Monitor* tackled were new to most of our viewers but we assumed at best a genuine curiosity and at worst an intelligent ignorance; we emphatically did not dumb down. Three million viewers followed us on Sunday nights even for such esoteric topics as Pre-Raphaelite art, a Bartók quartet in rehearsal or comparisons between three productions of *Waiting for Godot*. Denys Lasdun and the Smithsons were among the architects we filmed and discussed, and studio guests with theatre as their background included writers as varied as Harold Pinter, David Storey, Brendan Behan and Orson Welles. Auden's poetry was powerfully delivered by fine actors in the studio; Christopher Logue performed stanzas from his thrilling new translation of *The Iliad*. On film Betjeman and Larkin both gave delight. A latecomer to the *Monitor* team, Patrick Garland, made an entertaining film in which Betjeman lauded Larkin and persuaded him to talk on camera. The other late recruit to the ranks of director was Melvyn Bragg (an Oxford graduate to balance the Cambridgeness of David and myself); Bragg explored his own Northern heritage with film studies of the Cumberland landscape painter Sheila Fell and the Hallé's legendary conductor John Barbirolli.

When I joined BBC radio I had a six-week induction course followed by six months on attachment to different production departments. In television I was thrown in at the deep end; I never did a course and am still vague about the properties of various camera lenses: you just had to pick things up as you went along. Within days of joining the team I was down at Ealing film studios looking at the rushes which John Schlesinger had sent back from a week-long location shoot profiling Benjamin Britten at his Aldeburgh festival, including rehearsals of his latest composition, *Noye's Fludde*. Weirdly, though I was soon to become accustomed to the procedure, we watched the rushes in total silence: music was being performed in many scenes but there was no sound – the film sound would be 'synched up' later, in the cutting room. First the film had to be checked for visual problems such as poor focus or 'hairs in the gate'; this was thought of as defective footage which ideally would be reshot. But I didn't need the sound to recognise some familiar faces in addition to those of Britten and Pears, and nor did my future colleague and friend Walter Todds, who was sitting in at the same viewing session, having just arrived on an attachment from radio's education department. 'There's Imo!' he chortled as an image of Imogen Holst came up on the screen; Walter was often up in Suffolk, he explained, and had actually sung with Holst in her group, the Purcell Singers. I knew her too, from the lectures she gave at Bryanston. By the end of the viewing Schlesinger had decided I could be useful: he co-opted me to help write the commentary, sitting on a stool at a Steenbeck editing machine in Allan Tyrer's cutting room, writing exactly the right number of words to fit the sequence of images he assembled. The film went out in June and was roundly criticised by Grace Wyndham Goldie after the run-through. 'Self-indulgent,' she declared, though the film was only thirteen minutes long. Her word was law: on another occasion when she thought the words were trite nearly a minute was lopped off the opening sequence between the dress-run and the transmission, including the first fruits of my commentary writing. Grace was unimpressed by atmospheric filming or highfalutin commentary platitudes such as this gem of mine: 'Music is an international language: its seeds are scattered indiscriminately and flourish everywhere.' She was right to insist on its excision: she was boss of a department entitled 'Talks' and the

132

language we deployed had to pull its weight. That mutilated edition of *Monitor* (its eleventh) was for me a baptism of fire.

Huw Wheldon's military style of command at our regular planning meeting was also refreshing: 'Burton,' he would bark, 'Burton, you know about music. You shall look after Madame Callas.' And there I was the following Sunday, in the diva's dressing room perched nervously on the end of a make-up chair for an entire hour, trying to pass the time of day with our star while her husband, Signor G.B. Meneghini, sat at the back of the room, attired in a black overcoat and a Homburg hat, even though it was a pleasant summer's day outside; he had probably come to collect his wife's fee, since all Italian impresarios insist on payment on the night. Madame Callas was applying her make-up for a live interview, not with Huw Wheldon but instead with David Webster, the boss at Covent Garden, where she was appearing during the summer of 1958 to mixed notices in *La Traviata*.

Huw had reluctantly accepted her terms for the interview but wasn't happy since Webster, ever the diplomat since his days managing Lewis's department store in Liverpool, would obviously take care not to fall out with the temperamental singer, whose recent last-minute cancellations had created havoc and scandal in grand opera circles as distant as New York and Rome. Having stationed myself on the studio floor for the interview, I was surprised to see Wheldon hovering in the background behind Callas, just out of shot. The show was going out live; virtually everything was live in those days except the feature films. From his grim expression I could see that Huw was disappointed by the soft line of questioning and the diva's bland responses; on this showing the great Maria Callas was more pussycat than tigress. When he could contain his impatience no longer Huw advanced, unannounced, into the cameras' line of sight. His words I remember to this day: 'Madame Callas, if I may interpose for a moment: when you agreed to do this interview you insisted that your interlocutor should be Mr Webster. May I ask why?' Callas looked him up and down and replied, glacially: 'Because Mr *Webster* is a gentleman.'

Huw must have taken a wry pleasure in a Callas story we heard three years later when *Monitor* profiled Rudolf Bing, boss of the Metropolitan Opera. Callas had had a major falling-out with Mr Bing and Bing told us how he got his own back. In response to Signor Meneghini's insistence that her substantial fee should be paid in cash, Bing arranged for the money to be delivered to her dressing room in coins of very small denomination. The backstage staff, said Bing, had enjoyed watching her husband, 'who took care of that sort of thing, struggling through the stage door with sacks of nickels and dimes on his shoulder'.

It was many months before I got to direct a multi-camera studio trans-mission, but film experience came thick and fast when I went on location with our directors. John Schlesinger was only five years older than me but he was immensely sophisticated in the ways of the world. He had read English at Balliol and then acted in several completely forgotten B movies before following his star and deciding he wanted to make films; there was no National Film School in those days so he headed for the BBC. He was making short fillers when Huw poached him from the *Tonight* stable. For *Monitor*'s opening edition John directed a charming vignette about the circus; later in the spring came a wickedly satirical report on the 1958 Brussels Expo. But music was his great love and from it stemmed his revealing documentary, already mentioned, about Benjamin Britten. This was followed a few weeks later by a film of the British Student Orchestra conducted by Alexander Gibson playing Walton's scintillating new *Johannesburg Festival* overture, which the composer described as 'a non-stop gallop … slightly crazy, hilarious and vulgar'. Despite its clumsy title, I loved it and since I was the only person who could read the score it fell to me to plan the shooting – my first step down a very long road.

Later in the 1950s I was assigned to work as a fixer for Peter Zadek, a German-born graduate of the Old Vic School on whom Huw took a flutter, so to speak, when looking for outside directorial talent to bolster the creativity of his production team. Zadek proposed a film about the Jewish East End writer and poet Bernard Kops, whose first play, *The Hamlet of Stepney Green*, had caused a big stir when mounted at the Oxford Playhouse in 1958. It was a portrait of the vanishing Jewish community in which Kops had grown up: he was not exactly an Angry Young Man but the play had a certain resonance and to capture a flavour of a close-knit Jewish family Zadek arranged for us to film an Orthodox Friday evening gathering at the Kops household. I myself had lived among more recent Jewish immigrants at Long Dene but they were all assimilated, *cultural* Jews, so my trip to the East End was the first time I experienced the strength of the Hebrew religion: I was impressed by the Kops family's shared devotion to all the ritual procedures involving the kiddush cup. (Forty years later, Leonard Bernstein's children gave me their late father's silver kiddush cup as a keepsake.) But I was also a little scared since I had nothing similar by way of a belief system upon which to fall back. After a second *Monitor* film, *Why Cornwall?*, about the poets and painters who chose to work in the royal duchy, Zadek opted to return to Germany, where he subsequently made an impressive career as an avant-garde theatre and film director: I was grateful to him for an introduction to an unknown world.

My professional education continued under the tutelage of Peter Newington. Musical subjects were set aside as I learnt the ropes about film-making. Peter did a lovely essay about Carel Weight and Ruskin Spear, two Thames-side painters with very different styles, prompting some vivid cross-cutting by the editor Allan Tyrer as the film unfolded. The music I chose for the soundtrack included *Hammersmith* by Holst and John Ireland's *London* overture. Weight's thematic speciality was spooky goings-on in the sedate surroundings of Putney, but I enjoyed even more Spear's humorous *genre* portraits of the locals in what had become my own neighbourhood of Hammersmith Broadway. Many years later I bought a Spear painting at a Royal Academy summer show; when I picked it up at his British Grove studio in Chiswick I was surprised to discover that as the result of childhood polio he was a semi-invalid: his paintings reveal not a trace of bitterness. Peter Newington moved on to make a film called *A Line on Satire*, linking three short studies of contrasting artists: Osbert Lancaster, then at the height of his influence with his Maudie Littlehampton cartoons in the *Daily Express*; Ronald Searle of St Trinian's fame, whose images of wartime POW experiences under the Japanese retain their power to this day; and André François, a Hungarian Jew who had taken French citizenship in 1939. A cross between Saul Steinberg and Jean-Jacques Sempé, his cartoons often appeared in *Punch*. If making films about artists of this calibre was an eye-opener, then exploring their work with Newington was an education because Peter's contacts were in the heart of the art world. For another programme he took me to Alderney to film a portrait of the writer T.H. White, author of *The Sword in the Stone*, the reworking of Malory's Arthurian legend which inspired the Broadway musical *Camelot*. White was interviewed by a sceptical Robert Robinson and their encounter was an entertaining clash of personalities. What I remember best from Alderney was the unwelcome involvement of White's drinking friend, the cricket pundit and poet John Arlott. I had never met such larger-than-life people. And I had never been made so aware of the perils and pitfalls of the demon booze.

Working as production assistant to John Schlesinger was equally stimulating. His first film for *Monitor*'s second season was his most elaborate so far, a portrait of a theatrical institution that was swiftly vanishing under the impact of television: the provincial repertory company. My wife Gretel had worked at Hastings Rep the previous year so I was familiar with the exotic acting world peopled by old fruits and darlings. John's research led him to the Oldham Rep in Lancashire, a company which bucked the trend and is in business to this day. He and the actor-journalist Alex Atkinson invented a story of a young stage manager clocking in for her first professional job. John had fun with obvious targets such as the hammy old pro who was the company's leading actor, but his love of the theatre shone through the sequences of *Hobson's Choice* filmed at the Oldham Lyceum. It came as no surprise that within the year John was working on film dramas (he worked on twenty-three episodes as second director of *The Four Just Men*, shown on ITV, 1959–60) or that his excellent early feature film, *Billy Liar*, had location shooting in Oldham. Closest to my own interest, however, was *Hi-Fi-Fo-Fum*, John's satirical take on the record industry. The idea was to explore the explosion in sales caused by the advent of stereo at the end of the 1950s. Business was booming, classical as well as pop – and to express that boom we filmed at Imhof's famous record shop in New Oxford Street. Imhof's had been a favourite haunt of mine since childhood: it was where I used to buy my fibre needles. We arranged to film shoppers in the famous glass-fronted, soundproofed listening booths, and as the camera tracked from one ecstatic face to the next the accompanying soundtrack switched from Maria Callas to Shirley Bassey, from The Platters to the Amadeus Quartet. I can no longer remember which recordings we used but I do know that my job was to construct that soundtrack and in those pre-digital days the task was difficult because the timing of each burst of music had to coincide exactly with the camera's arrival at the next listening booth. This was not why I had taken a music degree at Cambridge but it was fun all the same.

In another sequence I made a cameo appearance masquerading as a Third Programme reviewer of classical recordings, an area notoriously prone in those days to hyperbole and jargon. For my script I strung together various review quotes from *Gramophone* magazine such as a conductor being said to make 'a little too much play with his wind'. I reviewed three different recordings and played in the same snatch of Beethoven's Fifth every time. 'What an ear!' mocked Robert Robinson in his irreverent commentary, one of his best. Over shots of duffel-coated nerds peering into the windows of electronics shops in Tottenham Court Road, Robert penned lines which have stayed with me ever since: 'Are they in love with a woofer? Is it a feedback circuit that holds them in thrall?'

John had a cousin who worked for Decca and that got us into the company's recording studios in West Hampstead. We set up a session with a genuine pop singer and heard his manager urging the producer to 'give it all the echo you've got'. The part of the agent was played by our cameraman, Austrian-born Charles de Jaeger, famous in the business as the man who filmed *Panorama*'s April Fool spoof about the spaghetti harvest. At a genuine recording session in

Decca's big studio we captured my dear friend Thurston Dart conducting one of the Bach orchestral suites from the harpsichord. As the music continued playing, the camera followed the entire process of disc manufacturing, the most spectacular image being a vast cauldron of molten gunge which was then passed through massive rollers which squeezed out the sheets of black plastic from which the LP discs were punched.

The film's most entertaining scene showed a group of aesthetes assembling for a demonstration of a stereo enthusiast's new equipment. We filmed in the sitting room of the Davis house in Princedale Road. (I myself had some snazzy new loudspeakers, having just won a Sunday newspaper competition for the best amateur concert review; I used the prize money to buy some hi-fi equipment.) Acting their heads off under Schlesinger's direction, the music-lovers in our film included Lime Grove colleagues David Jones and Xanthe Wakefield – a production assistant on the *Tonight* team. The comedy in *Hi-Fi-Fo-Fum* is in

Monitor: Hi-Fi-Fo-Fum. Director John Schlesinger inserted himself Hitchcock-style into a scene of devout music worshippers in the listening booths at Imhof's in New Oxford Street, London.

the antics of the distraught stereo buff as he shifts his guests around the sofa searching for the ideal position for stereophonic listening. The soundtrack, taken from Decca's genuine 'demo' disc extolling the new hi-fi, offers an orchestra blaring out *The Rite of Spring* and then an express train rushing through the living room: the visitors' eyes are seen dutifully following the train's sound from left to right. Finally comes the sound of a game of ping-pong: eyes flit from left to right and back as the camera cuts to a kitten whose head turns in the same rhythm, a typical Schlesinger gag which still makes me smile. So does the film's final shot: two scruffy buskers are seen outside Imhof's hi-fi emporium wheeling an old wind-up gramophone in a broken-down pram: they walk off into the sunset like a pair of comics in a Charlie Chaplin movie. It added to the fun that the buskers were played by the cameraman Charles de Jaeger and his assistant Johnny Ray, who later worked on Ken Russell's *A House in Bayswater* and on several of my own documentaries.

By this time I had taken my first faltering steps as a director in my own right. I don't deceive myself: most of my 'shoots' were with people who were filmed only because a television studio wasn't available when they were, such as the American pianist Van Cliburn just after he won the first Tchaikovsky Competition in Moscow. Sir Thomas Armstrong, principal of the Royal Academy of Music, was drafted in by Huw as interviewer; he was a highly respected administrator but an absolute beginner in the interviewing business, so their conversation was somewhat creaky. However, Van's tremendous musicality came over unimpaired; I later filmed him playing Liszt's transcription of *Widmung* by Schumann, and it looked a lot better than the rather vulgar version featuring the lanky Texan which is currently to be seen on YouTube. When I flew to Paris with the film cans under my arm for the young virtuoso to approve my rough cut I was a little surprised by his suggestion over the house phone that since he was not yet dressed I should come up to his suite for the screening – over breakfast *en déshabillé*. Another gay proposition in Paris! Was there something in the French air? I hasten to add that my honour survived and so did his.

Another short film I directed during my first year in television featured Yehudi Menuhin talking about his friendship with Béla Bartók; we did the filming in a Maida Vale radio studio and his wife Diana gossiped incessantly between takes, placidly peeling lychees as she chattered. Yehudi played part of the searing solo sonata which he commissioned from the ailing Bartók when they were both living in New York during the Second World War. I liked Yehudi and Diana enormously and was to work many times with

Yehudi before his sudden death in Berlin fifty years later. Another *Monitor* project was about film itself. I was still a great admirer of William Alwyn, the revered composer of the score for Carol Reed's *Odd Man Out*, and I persuaded Huw to mount an item with Alwyn about the role of music in films. This involved me in the embarrassing procedure of directing Mr Alwyn to stride vigorously over Ealing Common – the idea being that the film of his progress would seem ominous or jaunty or tragic according to the music he chose to accompany it. I had to ask him to do the same walking business three or four times and he became increasingly unimpressed by my directorial gifts: it was not my proudest moment. I had better luck working with the widow of the great documentary film-maker Robert Flaherty. I had loved his films since childhood – *Nanook of the North*, a silent film about the Eskimos, was shown at Long Dene – and to cope with his widow Frances Flaherty's presentation I had to do a crash course in the pre-war documentarists; a significant opening of magic casements ensued. Flaherty had been dead less than a decade: he had made *Man of Aran* in 1934 and *Louisiana Story* in 1948. A powerful mystique had grown up around him. 'Robert Flaherty', Frances intoned significantly – we were filming on the lot at Ealing – 'did not tell the camera what to do; rather he asked it: "What can you see?"' I didn't know then that Flaherty's much-lauded *Louisiana Story*, about life among the Cajuns on the Mississippi, was entirely fictional and that it was Mrs Flaherty who had written the script. I was a bit of an innocent – and remain one to this day.

Just a year after I moved to Lime Grove I directed what I think of as my first proper film, a profile of Carl Ebert, the grand old man of Glyndebourne Festival Opera. Brought over from Germany in 1934 with Fritz Busch the conductor and Rudolf Bing the administrator, Ebert had put flesh and blood on John Christie's dream of creating an English Bayreuth in the Sussex Downs. BBC Radio had been broadcasting its productions since the 1930s and after the war installed a studio at the back of the stalls; when I became a music studio manager I booked the studio when there were no broadcasts in order to attend the summer performances. The studio was linked to the microphones which were permanently installed around the stage and the pit, and the studio boasted a one-way glass window providing a perfect view of the stage action. We didn't need to dress up; we just walked in, switched on the amplifiers and hey presto we were having fun watching the opera in our shirtsleeves, our feet up on the mixer desk, our bottle of Liebfraumilch (the standard plonk of the day) in an ice bucket at our sides. On a nice evening we could put on our togs and eat a picnic out on the lawn with the toffs. That was fun, but to make a film about Glyndebourne in May 1959, for *Monitor* – this was work: here I was, directing my first film for television. And on a rarified subject. Anthony Asquith's half-hour expedition to Glyndebourne, *On Such a Night*, had had only a limited cinema release three years earlier. His was a gentle comedy about an American tourist who discovers Glyndebourne by accident. Mine was concerned with the famous actor who had turned to opera direction late in life and was now sharing his professional secrets with us on camera. And my film would be watched by an audience of 3 million.

Seated on a bench in the opera house garden, Ebert talks to camera about how he goes about the task of mounting an opera. We watch him direct a lively rehearsal of *Così fan tutte*, the scene in the first act when the disguised lovers pretend to take poison. With only one 35 mm camera on a fixed tripod it was difficult to capture the rehearsal atmosphere but the tenor Juan Oncina is a spirited Ferrando and Geraint Evans, our Guglielmo, helps me by asking Ebert for guidance. Meanwhile, Glyndebourne's head of music staff, the great Jani Strasser, backs up at the piano – I believe this was the only time he was ever caught on camera. Elsewhere in the film Professor Ebert goes backstage to inspect the sets and costumes for *Der Rosenkavalier*, his new production which is being mounted in Sussex for the first time. He is followed at a respectful distance by John Cox, his young assistant, who twelve years later is to become director of productions in this famous theatre. Then I used the sparkling overture to *The Marriage of Figaro* to show the festival audience assembling for the show: boisterous picnicking and much quaffing of champagne were in evidence for the camera. And then Ebert confesses to us, on camera, that no production is ever as good as he would like it to be: directors are always disappointed, deceived and depressed by the difference between their dreams and the reality of what gets done on stage. On the soundtrack the gorgeous music of the Trio from *Der Rosenkavalier* wells up as the professor strolls round the now-deserted garden in the evening sunshine admiring the roses. When I watched the film recently I was appalled by my lack of ambition. There were no images of Ebert as a young actor. No production stills from the historic pre-war Glyndebourne shows. No assessment of that eccentric visionary John Christie. And worst omission of all, no opera action from the stage: we didn't have the budget to pay for an orchestra and in any case Strauss's publishers would have asked outrageous sums for permission to film even short sequences of opera. So my film was modest. But it was honest, too: a loving portrait of a man I much admired. My colleagues said nice things about it next day after transmission and *deo*

140

gratias the viewers liked it too – the edition scored a reaction index of seventy, well above our average.

Directing my own script (and we always had a script in those days, often in the form of a storyboard with hand-drawn images) made me feel I had finally found a useful role in the world of music. But the team ethos at *Monitor* meant that I didn't thereafter work solely on my own films; I contributed three or four twenty-minute film programmes in the following twelve months but also produced studio features and worked alongside John Schlesinger and Ken Russell, the acknowledged film-makers. John Schlesinger was phasing himself out. His last two *Monitor* films both took up complete programme slots – an early demonstration of my theory that all arts magazine programmes aspire to the condition of full-length documentaries. In 1960 John directed a substantial study of four young artists at the outset of their careers, entitled *Private View*; he returned a couple of years later to make *The Class*, a riveting account of Harold Lang's much-admired teaching methods at the Central School of Speech and Drama. He also contributed an elegant portrait of Georges Simenon (1959) which faithfully catalogued the crime-writer's obsessive routines preparatory to novel-writing, such as the sharpening of many pencils and the selection of characters' names from the Lausanne phone book. However, the film gave no hint (presumably because John and Huw were offered none by the wily Belgian) concerning the prolific master's secret sexual obsessions – Simenon claimed later to have regularly written eighty pages in a morning and to have slept with 10,000 women on his free afternoons.

In 1961 Schlesinger directed *Terminus*, an acclaimed documentary made at Waterloo Station for the cinema screen with backing from British Transport. I could detect in it no artistic advance on his *Monitor* films – truth to tell it was a bit of a weepy – but we all knew John's ambition was to direct features and so it soon came to pass with *A Kind of Loving* and *Billy Liar*. His success came rather too soon for BBC colleagues like me who were learning so much at his side when he was working for *Monitor*; we were soaking up ideas about the craft of film-making, of course, but also about life itself and the need to laugh at the absurdity of it all.

Also in the *Monitor* team was Ken Russell, to whom Huw gave a short-term contract on the basis of two earlier Russell films of immense charm, *Amelia and the Angel* and *Lourdes*. Ken was hired in January 1959 and by the end of the year had made seven films with us. I worked on most of them, variously collaborating as producer, pianist, fixer, commentary writer and interviewer. The titles alone give you an idea of the breadth of Ken's interests: *John Betjeman:*

141

A Poet in London; *Gordon Jacob*; *Guitar Craze*; *Variations on a Mechanical Theme*; *Scottish Painters* (Robert MacBryde and Robert Colquhoun); *Spike Milligan: Portrait of a Goon*; and *Marie Rambert Remembers*. With the exception of literature, the entire spectrum of the arts is there: all the films are vividly described in the first volume of Paul Sutton's masterly study of Ken's work.

Ken and I became friends straight away: we both loved music and enjoyed similar domestic circumstances (by which I mean we had busy and creative wives and lively children). I was better on words, at least for commentaries; Ken wrote vivid treatments and his visual imagination was beyond compare. Cameramen adored working for him – he had been a professional photographer for *Illustrated* and knew as much about lenses as they did. Our designer Natasha Kroll recognised a kindred spirit and in the cutting room Allan Tyrer was a willing and inventive partner, despite Ken's unconventional approach. At rough-cut stage Huw would occasionally refine the pictorial storytelling but he refrained from interposing his commentary voice.

In the only Russell film in which Wheldon *did* appear that year, the ballet portrait starring the flamboyant Marie Rambert, Huw turned in a gentle and very deft interviewing performance. In short, we were all on Ken's side and in every film he flourished.

In the winter of 1960 I made my first working visit to the USA. This was a big assignment. Huw and I flew to New York, itself an adventure in those days. I directed a couple of short films on my own, one of which was with the composer Milton Babbitt, now best remembered as the teacher of Stephen Sondheim but in those days a charming spokesman for the US avant-garde; we filmed him at Columbia University demonstrating his latest composition, which involved both a computer (the so-called RCA Synthesiser) and a phenomenal pitch-perfect soprano named Bethany Beardslee. The subject matter was so abstruse that Huw quietly shelved my film until after his retirement. My other programme certainly had legs: it was an interview with W.H. Auden filmed at his home in St Mark's Place, Greenwich Village. Huw had to get back to introduce the next edition of *Monitor* so the interviewing was done by a compatriot of his named Philip Burton, whom Huw knew from his Welsh Arts Council days. Burton was an inspiring teacher and stage director, recently arrived in New York: his claim to fame rests largely on the fact that back in Port Talbot he had spotted the talents of a fourteen-year-old boy named Richard Jenkins. He took the lad under his wing to the extent of adopting him as his son.

At the filming session I made little impression on Auden until I mentioned that I had sung in the French première of *The Rake's Progress*. He got very excited and called in his partner Chester Kallman from the next room to hear me sing my Warder's role, in French, all thirty seconds of it. An absurd moment.

The main purpose of our New York visit was to make a profile of Rudolf Bing. Mr Bing was the most famous British citizen in the world of opera. Then in his late fifties, he had studied music and theatre in Vienna and

Rudolf Bing on his way to work at the Metropolitan Opera where, a true Englishman with furled umbrella and bowler hat, he established the ritual of afternoon tea at 4 o'clock.

worked in opera management in pre-Nazi Germany, from whence he moved to Glyndebourne at the suggestion of Busch and Ebert. He became a British citizen in 1946, founded the Edinburgh Festival and then moved to New York, where he had been running the Metropolitan Opera for a decade. He had become a world-famous figure because of his well-publicised rows with prima donnas and recalcitrant unions, but he remained endearingly British: come rain or shine he always wore a bowler hat and carried a furled umbrella; he claimed that his most important innovation at the Met was the introduction of afternoon tea at 4 o'clock. My task, writing as well as directing, was to paint a picture of the 'Met' company in action, against which we would set Huw's interviews with Mr Bing, taking as our inspiration a quotation I came across from Ralph Waldo Emerson: any institution, he wrote, is 'the lengthened shadow of one man'. We saw Mr Bing in the wings during a performance. We filmed him watching an early rehearsal of *Simon Boccanegra*, the three star singers briskly directed by the impressive Margaret Webster. We eavesdropped at a genuine planning conference with his two able assistants Bob Herman (son of 'Babe' Herman, the great baseball star) and Herman Krawitz, a lively impresario who became a good personal friend; it was at his home (on 30 January) that I had my first sight of Leonard Bernstein on American television, presenting – it must have been in prime time because we were eating our burger supper – an essay for adults called *The Creative Performer*. Igor Stravinsky and Glenn Gould both took part. Wow! This was the sort of programme I wanted to make. (And did.)

We filmed Henry Wrong (later the Barbican's first boss but then a lowly Metropolitan aide) whispering in Mr Bing's ear while he was in the auditorium watching a stage piano run-through; the message was that a distinguished tenor was declining to attend a rehearsal. 'No', says Bing, without shifting his gaze from the stage. 'Tell him that if he doesn't make the rehearsal then he won't sing in the performance.' Henry Wrong hurries off as Wheldon's commentary intones: 'Beneath that cold exterior, there beats a heart of stone.' The entire scene was acted out specially for the BBC. You couldn't capture impromptu ruthlessness on 35 mm – everything had to be set up in advance. In fact, Bing emerged from our film profile as charm personified, though his verdict on overpaid singers was nothing if not abrasive: many of them become famous overnight, he claimed, 'by virtue of a throat disease'.

It was fun to film backstage. There were interminable negotiations with unions – we had to hire a duplicate local film crew who sat around for a couple of weeks doing absolutely nothing. Chorus, orchestra and stage staff

Elisabeth Söderström circa 1960.
A mischievous personality.

all had to be placated. There was little of the goodwill towards the BBC that exists nowadays in liberal America but Herman Krawitz was a great help in my negotiations, as was the awkwardly named Rudy Kuntner, the Met's Austrian-born lighting and stage management chief who back home had been a star pre-war soccer player.

I was particularly pleased with a shot taken during a performance of *Macbeth*. From high up in the flies the camera looked down at the action on the stage then zoomed up and panned round to find a group of stagehands playing poker in an alcove, completely oblivious to the grand opera unfolding down below.

We had our moments of panic. Unions held us to ransom more than once and at another rehearsal the *Heldentenor* Jon Vickers refused to sing while our BBC camera was turning: it transpired that he'd had a blazing row with the music department at BBC Television the previous year after they issued a press release stating that he had withdrawn from a planned production of *Salome* because he had 'knots on his vocal cords'. As a consequence Bayreuth had insisted he re-audition. (When I met him years later, Vickers told me in all seriousness that he had a private line to God.) I got on much better with the Swedish soprano Elisabeth Söderström, whom I'd watched spellbound at Glyndebourne the previous summer singing Octavian in *Der Rosenkavalier*; in the same opera in New York she took the higher role of Sophie (later in her career she excelled as the Marschallin). She also sang a heart-wrenching Marguerite in *Faust* and a spirited Susanna in *Figaro*. I couldn't film her on stage but I managed to sneak in a short scene in her dressing room in which Mr Bing purports to give her a note: I think he was as happy as I was to spend time in her delightful, mischievous company.

The day I was leaving for London I was called back to Mr Bing's office, where an astounding invitation was offered: would I consider joining the Met company as a staff director? I was flattered that they liked having me around but I didn't hesitate: much as I enjoyed what I had seen of the hurly-burly of opera house life I was too much wrapped up in my *Monitor* work to step off that particular ladder. And the television work was piling up: within weeks of my return to Lime Grove, *Monitor* transmitted the film I had directed the previous autumn about the Allegri String Quartet. When I first proposed the quartet idea Huw had been dismissive: 'Chamber music? Caviar to the general, old boy', was his verdict. But I talked him round, I guess because of my enthusiasm. Personal connections were important in this documentary. The quartet's viola player was my one-time teacher Patrick Ireland, who was married to Peggy Gray, sister of Stephen, who had been running the Chelsea Opera Group since its inception in 1950 and had recently become administrator of the Philharmonia Orchestra. The quartet's first violin was Eli Goren, whom I knew from his work with Colin Davis – soon after arriving in England from Israel Eli became concertmaster of the Kalmar Orchestra, in which Colin played the clarinet when not conducting. Huw was struck by the closeness of the four players of the Allegri; by the fact that they had rehearsed sixty-six times before giving their first concert; that all four had musician wives and all four were passing on their music to their young children. He compared them to members of a medieval guild and brought out this point in the occasional line he added – after viewing the rough cut – to my lean commentary draft. With the idea of demystifying professional musical life, I included authentic location shots of a Surrey music club, hinting at the awkward greetings which visiting recitalists receive from relieved organisers as they proffer slightly wilting pre-concert sandwiches and pour from flasks of occasionally lukewarm coffee. The music was what mattered. The Allegri played Schubert and Mozart and I also included in the film a tense rehearsal of a Bartók movement in which the clash of personalities within the quartet was striking – by this time they had forgotten all about the camera filming them. A somewhat sugary sequence had the cellist Bill Pleeth's son staying up late in his dressing gown to listen to his father and friends playing the Ravel Quartet

146

(my favourite) in a pre-recorded *Music at Night* sequence. I had filmed the session in one of my old haunts, the Concert Hall in Broadcasting House, but with the lights dimmed to create a nocturnal mood – what the Germans call *Stimmung*. I have always had a soft spot for this film portrait and was pleased when Mary Crozier, the *Manchester Guardian*'s broadcasting critic, gave it an appreciative review. The film demonstrated, she wrote, 'a positive and satisfactory use of television to show music. This particular function for the arts in general is performed by *Monitor* in its modest fortnightly time allowance; beyond the necessary introduction or explanation it leaves the chosen sculpture, painting, the stage or whatever it may be to speak for itself, and leaves the eye time to take in what it is seeing.' I think she approves ...

My jazz programmes for radio's *Transatlantic Turntable* also came in useful on *Monitor*. It was back in my earliest television days, in the autumn of 1958, that we invited the great Duke Ellington to appear in the studio, to be interviewed by two British masters of the genre, Humphrey Lyttelton and John Dankworth. Dankworth's band assembled to rehearse an Ellington classic but there was no sign of the Duke. His hotel suite was phoned: no answer. Nervous of a no-show, Peter Newington and I set off for the West End but the knock we eventually delivered on the Duke's hotel door was greeted by silence – except for the faint sound of rustling garments and scurrying footsteps. After a few more knocks the door finally opened and there stood this splendidly nude man. 'Hello, boys', he said, without a hint of embarrassment, as a bathroom door discreetly closed behind him. 'Come in and have some coffee.'

The Duke arrived at Lime Grove just in time for the show. I remember the evening for two other reasons. It was our first use of Ampex, the one-inch quad videotape which was to revolutionise the way we put programmes together, releasing us from the tyranny of live transmission. Because the picture quality on Ampex was on a par with 'live' (which the old system of tele-recording certainly was not), interviews and essays could be put on tape earlier in the day or indeed earlier in the week if you could find a studio. There was just one snag: each tape was said to cost $50,000! That is why so many good programmes were wiped by the BBC in the 1960s rather than being stored in the archive: once wiped, the tapes could be used again, whereas the programmes, once they had had their contractual repeat, were dead, or so ran the conventional accountant's wisdom. Certainly I never saw our Ellington show again. The other reason for not forgetting this feature was also to do with economics. Dankworth and Lyttelton were clearly in awe of Ellington. 'There's one thing we're dying to ask you,' said Johnny (I'm paraphrasing).

'We can't keep our bands together for more than a few weeks at a time. Yet the personnel in your great orchestra never seem to change. What's your secret?' 'It's very simple, boys,' the Duke shot back. 'I pay 'em MONEY.' (Loud laughter from the band.)

Next year, 1959, *Monitor*'s third season, I invited Dankworth to bring his jazz quartet into the studio for an improvisation session; it was an early example of the televised musical workshops which I developed when BBC2 provided more airtime. Another musical experiment was to mount a competition for young conductors. The Philharmonia Orchestra played all day in Studio G for thirty candidates, who each got a measly ten to fifteen minutes on the rostrum. The judges would have frightened the most hardened professional: the panel consisted of Walter Legge, the orchestra's forthright owner-manager, and three of the world's top maestri: Sir Adrian Boult, Carlo Maria Giulini and Otto Klemperer. Legge did not mince his words: 'this man [naturally there were no women candidates] is just managing to keep in touch with the orchestra' was one of his milder observations. Klemperer brooded like a hawk; Boult was the most constructive in his comments. Giulini said very little but his Christ-in-torment expression, soon to be familiar from telecasts of the Verdi *Requiem*, spoke volumes. Legge had devised a Beecher's Brook of a test for any conductor's control over his players; each candidate was required to bring in the orchestra precisely on the beat at the end of the soloist's cadenza in the finale of Beethoven's Fourth Piano Concerto. Half the horses fell at that fence. One contestant, already quite prominent at the Royal Opera, decided next day to give up his conducting career. Legge was unrepentant. We had discovered a real talent in James Loughran, the winner, and the programme was very popular – its appreciation index of eighty was the highest in the three years *Monitor* had been on the air, and by quite a margin.

Another studio project which was fun to work on was a set of music-theatre songs by Bertolt Brecht and Kurt Weill, written in the 1920s and '30s for shows featuring Weill's wife, the great German actress Lotte Lenya. Thirty years later, her husband long since dead, she was to sing them in the *Monitor* studio. She was accompanied by an authentic band, brilliantly conducted by Lawrence Leonard, who had recently been in charge of *West Side Story* in London. David Drew, already a Weill expert, had supervised the performing edition. That afternoon in the *Monitor* studio saw the birth of a classic video but disappointingly I have been airbrushed out of the documentation surrounding it. For a start it is not a film, as is often suggested: it was shot with four television cameras and taped on Ampex. The director was not Ken Russell but me. Ken was the producer. Allan Tyrer had the film editor credit because he and Ken assembled the back-projection newsreel montage of the Nazi persecution of the Jews against which Lenya, in shiny black leather and a sweet little beret, sang her first song, 'Mack the Knife'. When assembling the montage, Allan cut it to the pace of Lenya's 1956 recording; in the studio we had to make sure we started the telecine at exactly the right moment for it to be in synch. Thankfully Lawrence Leonard held the tempo steady. It was a chilling number, very exciting; Brecht's satire, drawing the parallel between Hitler and the highwayman Captain Macheath, had never bitten deeper. Lenya's other three songs were done in simple cabaret-style sets designed by Natasha Kroll; among them were the haunting 'Surabaya Johnny' from *Happy End* and 'O Moon of Alabama' from *Mahagonny*, which Lenya sang in a fetching straw boater. She was already sixty-three but she had fantastic allure and in a good light, which we provided, she looked a generation younger. The final number in the set, the best because it was so remorselessly bitter, was 'Pirate Jenny'. Thanks to YouTube you can see this remarkable Lenya video whenever you wish, but unfortunately without Huw Wheldon's astringent introductions, which were very much part of the show. I willingly admit that this short but tremendously powerful and historic Lenya document was Ken Russell's concept and Ken's production. With Ken at my side in the studio gallery I was very happy to be part of the team – directing the cameras.

In describing my first three years in television I mustn't give the impression that Huw Wheldon was some sort of first-stage rocket who fell away once I was launched. On the contrary, he was always there when one needed him. 'Kill your darlings' was a favourite injunction, warning one against self-indulgence in the cutting room. 'You avoid the obvious at your peril' was another and 'Never forget you have the right to fail' a third. Sometimes I worked on projects he had himself set up – falling into this category were Rudolf Bing (whose power fascinated him) and later in 1960 the prolific French composer Darius Milhaud. Somebody had tipped Huw off that the Frenchman, who had lived in California during the war, would be an interesting character to interview. Milhaud was by then confined to a wheelchair so I filmed his wife pushing him around Montmartre while the soundtrack played one of his catchy dance tunes. (Ken later ticked me off for not using Milhaud's *La Création du Monde*.) My film was hardly a masterpiece and didn't begin to get to grips with Milhaud's membership of Les Six or his teaching at Mills College, where Dave Brubeck had been a pupil, let alone his prodigious output, upwards of 440 opus numbers. Milhaud suffered from

On set with Darius Milhaud (with dark glasses), an impassive Buddha.

a wretched illness – he couldn't sweat – which made it appear as if his skin was made of parchment. He looked like an impassive Buddha and had the temperament of a sleepy pussycat. But Huw was not to be beaten: he was ready to make himself look a little silly if it would elicit a telling observation from Monsieur Milhaud. So Huw drew attention in the interview to the striking calligraphy of Milhaud's latest symphony, lying on the table between them. The conversation went like this:

'Is this a fair copy?'

'No, it is ze first draft.'

'I can't even write a letter without crossing things out.'

'Well, zat is ze difference, Monsieur Wheldon, between when you write a lett-air and I write a symphony.'

There couldn't have been a sharper contrast between Milhaud, almost seventy, and the two young musicians who featured in my next documentary, *Two Composers, Two Worlds*. I compared the lifestyles and ambitions of avant-garde Peter Maxwell Davies, then living austerely as a teacher in Cirencester, and showbiz musician Dudley Moore, who had a chaotic flat on the Harrow Road and as I have already described was making a living in London as a jazz pianist. He had been organ scholar at Magdalen College, Oxford, where he had done comedy sketches with Alan Bennett. I wasn't yet thirty but my subjects were at least three years younger; the film was shot before *Beyond the Fringe* opened in London so my choice proved quite prescient, although sadly the two musicians are now both dead. The closing sequence intercut two scenes: we saw Dudley working in candlelight with Cleo Laine at the Troubadour Club in Earl's Court, and we saw Max conducting a group of angelic Cotswold schoolgirls in a carol from his *O Magnum Mysterium*. But the film's most striking shot came earlier, in Max's monastic cell of a study: I took a huge close-up of his eyes while he spoke of his determination to go his own way as a composer, whatever it cost. The image was quite terrifying.

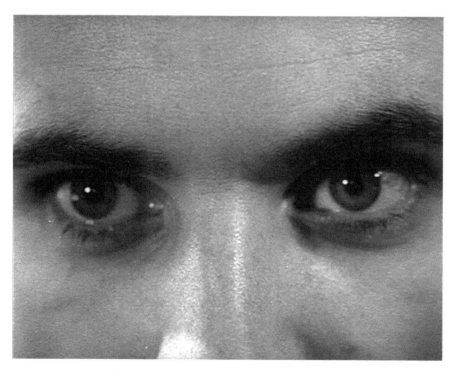

Peter Maxwell Davies – the eyes of a genius. Still frame from
Monitor: Two Composers, Two Worlds, 1961.

* * *

It has been important to me in this chapter to describe some of the productions with which I was involved in the first three years of my life in television.

Those early television programmes, studio work as well as films, have stuck in my mind like nothing else I have done. They really were formative years, those years when I started to explore the different ways that the experience of music could be shared through television with an audience of millions. At the time I had no inkling that a decade later, mostly in Vienna with Leonard Bernstein, I would devote myself to filming literally hundreds of straight performances of symphonic music. The visualisation of concert music was a discipline which I did not need to address while at *Monitor*, though I tackled it head-on a few years later in a *Workshop* programme with Michael Tippett, he suggesting what the cameras should look at as the music unfolded. Nor would I have dreamt that twenty years later I would spend much of my time in opera houses, translating stage productions to the screen. Only now can I discern a pattern to my life, and that pattern is that there should be no pattern. Even at *Monitor* I was looking for other outlets, other ways of expressing myself: my Cambridge friend Neil Sutherland, then working for the Canadian Broadcasting Corporation, thought of me as a diarist: he hired me to broadcast an hour-long London music diary once a month, using LPs for musical illustrations. For those CBC shows I did extended interviews with such luminaries as Hans Werner Henze and Colin Davis. (Colin analysed his first commercial LP recording, Mozart's Symphony No. 39, explaining why orchestral pauses had to be shorter on recordings than in concert halls, where the pauses could be seen as well as heard.)

In the summer of 1960 CBC invited me to spend a month serving as guest critic at the Vancouver Festival. It would mean being away from wife and daughter (not for the first time) but the fees would come in very handy and the work was challenging: broadcasts every day, live reactions to the concerts, interviews and mini-lectures about the works to be heard.

Vancouver proved to be very enjoyable. The resident celebrity soloist was Glenn Gould. *Monitor* had screened the remarkable documentaries about his Bach recording sessions in New York so I knew all about his quirks, how he wore overcoat, cap and muffler on the warmest of days, sat at the keyboard hunched up on a low stool and never shook hands, indeed had sued a Steinway employee for causing physical distress by putting a friendly hand on his shoulder. I found Glenn charming and intellectually irresistible; we got on like a house on fire. He was a superb interpreter of Schoenberg, of whose *Hanging Gardens* song cycle he gave a mesmerising performance with the Swedish mezzo Kerstin Meyer – she and I had met on the Lockheed Constellation flight en route for Vancouver. We also became good friends; I loved her humorous way of doing Ravel's *Histoires Naturelles*. Together we visited Glenn in his hotel room and he showed us his capacious medicine box; he had not yet given up playing in public – in fact he relished the public's warm reaction – but he was already a hypochondriac. Unsuspecting of the horrors to come – some say he died of too much medication – we laughed together as he identified the dozens of pill bottles he took with him everywhere. They included (I quote from his manager's memoire) Valium, Librax, Placidyl, Dalmane, Nembutal, Luminal, Aldomet, Indoral and other prescription drugs. I can't say I counted them: what I knew was that Glenn was an extraordinary personality and I vowed to work with him again – a resolve which materialised in Toronto some six years later.

I returned to Lime Grove in September 1961 for a fourth season of *Monitor*. It was my first, aged thirty, as a full-blown producer, following Peter Newington's decision to go freelance. To echo Wordsworth, it was bliss to be alive at the dawn of television, 'but to be young was very heaven'.

CHAPTER 9

MOVING UP THE LADDER

Left to right: presenter/editor (Huw Wheldon), film editor (Allan Tyrer) and
director/producer (Humphrey Burton) in the *Monitor* cutting room, 1962.

AFTER LESS THAN three years at Lime Grove I was promoted (without
a competition) to the rank of full producer. This meant an upgrade to the
coveted B category in the BBC's byzantine grading system. The change was
caused by the withdrawal of *Monitor*'s producer, Peter Newington. He went,
I think, because he could no longer tolerate being part of the establishment.
He resigned, directed freelance for a time and ended up teaching film and
television at the Royal College of Art. He taught me more about art than

anybody else did and I'll never forget that nervous laugh. The rest of the team remained close-knit and I spent the next two *Monitor* seasons doing much the same mixture of films and studio work as before, but now for a better salary. My first contribution to the season was a profile of Gian Carlo Menotti filmed in Spoleto, 100 miles north of Rome. Menotti's operas were impressive, particularly his *Grand Guignol* essay *The Medium* and the political music drama *The Consul*, which ran at the Palace Theatre in London for many months; his television operas *The Saint of Bleecker Street* and *Amahl and the Night Visitors* were big hits on BBC Television. Huw and I wrote to him out of the blue, proposing a conversation embedded in a portrait of his annual Festival of Two Worlds in Spoleto. To our surprise he accepted. Only when we arrived did I learn that the previous year the festival had been disrupted by a low-flying aviator hired by thugs who scattered odious leaflets over the city bearing the message: 'We salute the pederasts of Spoleto'. So Menotti was happy to have some positive publicity from the BBC about what was assuredly a splendid Italian-American festival, on a par with Edinburgh and with the added benefits of sunshine, impressive outdoor locations, a grand opera house and a resident genius. In the course of a fortnight I was able to dip with my cameras into a marvellous cultural mix: the great Luchino Visconti was directing *Elektra* while Menotti himself was mounting the first European production of the opera *Vanessa* composed by his dear friend Samuel Barber. Jerome Robbins was in town with an experimental dance company led by the brilliant Arthur Mitchell, who later founded Dance Theatre of Harlem. Robbins was even more ambitious: his Spoleto dance group was entitled Ballets USA. I got his permission to film a dance class and a scene from his latest work *Moves*, exceptional in that there was no music whatsoever, just pounding feet and rhythmical finger-and-thumb clicks reminiscent of the Jets and the Sharks: I had been a devoted fan of Robbins since seeing *West Side Story*. I cabled an enthusiastic review of *Moves* to *The Times* and was gratified to learn that my article had been reproduced in enormous print on a 20-foot street billboard. This was when Mr Robbins's company visited London a few weeks later: I never again had such a physical success in print.

The abstract backdrop for *Moves* was by the painter Ben Shahn, a deeply attractive New York Russian Jew from the generation after Chagall, with whom Huw and I struck up a friendship. This resulted the following year in my making a film about Shahn's work in the town of Roosevelt, New Jersey, a garden city which was the site of a school housing a fresco by Shahn – a major Shahn work. Back in the 1930s he had been Diego Rivera's assistant on the famous Rockefeller Center frescoes, and he had adopted the same broad-sweep style when he was commissioned to paint a chronicle of the Garment Workers' Union, whose leader David Dubinsky was one of America's labour heroes.

When Huw Wheldon joined me in Spoleto for our portrait of Menotti, he swiftly realised that in Ben Shahn he had met his match as a storyteller; it was enormous fun to be embedded in their company. In Spoleto we had other days of wine and banter with Charles Wadsworth, the tireless young organiser of the festival's daily open-air midday concert; one of *his* stars was John Ogdon, fresh from winning the Tchaikovsky competition in Moscow. Also in Spoleto that year was the equally gifted young violinist Pinchas Zukerman. We seemed never to stop filming except to sleep and to flirt, I with a dancer who told me I was the first straight man she had met in a month, and Huw – pulling rank shamelessly as I saw it – by monopolising the incredibly beautiful wife of Beni Montresor, the stage designer of *Elektra*.

Menotti himself proved to be a charming man and very articulate: it was encouraging, indeed thrilling, to meet a composer who recognised the effectiveness of television as a medium for music.

On the final day of the Spoleto shoot we pulled off a tiny cinematic coup. The 'we' in my sentence includes my camera crew led by John Ray, with whom I had worked the previous year on *Hi-Fi-Fo-Fum*. For the film's climax my script called for us to shoot a sizeable excerpt from Brahms's *German Requiem*, which was being performed as the closing event of the festival in the open-air piazza in front of the cathedral.

The conductor was the American Thomas Schippers, an Adonis figure much admired by Menotti, whom I had interviewed for *Transatlantic Turntable* in my radio days; we got on well and I had his blessing to move my film crew around during the performance. We were working with a standard blimped Arriflex camera which had a beautifully quiet motor – essential for music filming – but could run for a mere four minutes before needing a reload. So we were less than ideally equipped to deal with Johannes Brahms's long melodic lines. But we coped. After half an hour, most of what I planned was in the can. But I felt uneasy: our shots came nowhere near to matching the grandeur of the setting or of the music. I glanced up at the cathedral behind the choir and orchestra. High in the tower I noticed an opening, maybe a belfry. Could this be the location from which to shoot a final image? Leaving the crew outside, I ran to the back, found the doorway to the tower and raced up interminable flights of stairs. The view from the top was indeed breathtaking: in my mind's eye I could see a great closing shot. I scampered back to ground level, instructed the sound recordist to carry on taping until the last bar of the *Requiem* and then led my little team back up the stone staircases, between us carrying camera, spare film cassette and battery; I think I had the tripod on my shoulder. It was a double race against time: would we be ready to shoot before the *Requiem* ended (they had already begun the final movement), and with twilight falling fast, would there be sufficient light in the sky for the image to register on film? John Ray consulted his light meter and thought yes, but he soon determined that the only way to get the shot I wanted was to abandon the tripod and hang the camera halfway out of the opening in the tower: if I clung like grim death to his hips, Johnny could rest his camera on the stone window shelf and tilt it down sufficiently to frame a shot on the conductor almost vertically beneath us. Then the camera could slowly be panned up and Johnny could zoom out towards the skyline. But a quick rehearsal showed that the camera's exposure would have to be modified as Johnny zoomed out, to take account of the falling light level. We could only execute this delicate operation if the assistant cameraman stretched out into space and on Johnny's command adjusted the exposure control. This was a perilous manoeuvre. There was no chance of a second take; the light was going ever faster and the music was rising to its final climax …

There was no monitor screen for me to check on Johnny's progress: only he could see the flailing arms of Maestro Schippers in his viewfinder and attempt to get the focus sharp on the baton. With the delicacy of a surgeon wielding a scalpel, Johnny slowly widened the conductor shot to discover the strings of the orchestra desk by desk around Maestro Schippers and then the woodwinds and brass and finally the chorus filling his entire frame – and then in a continuous movement the camera zoomed out and panned further up to reveal the vast audience seated on the slope of the Piazza del Duomo, hundreds of them, raptly attentive to the closing pages of the Brahms. As the camera continued its upward tilt, the houses on Spoleto's skyline came into view and then the Umbrian hills were filling the screen, sombre but majestic even at twilight. It was beautiful: what the Americans call 'the money shot', although it had cost us nothing. Sweat, yes, but no blood or tears. I was never happier directing a film.

Three months later I was in my beloved Paris to direct a film portrait of the cellist Paul Tortelier, whose noble profile was matched by the most expressive playing. I also wanted to show *Monitor* viewers something of his work as a composer: he was an idealist if ever there was one. Although not Jewish, he

Paul Tortelier's grandmother made him practise.

and his family had recently spent a year on an Israeli *kibbutz* – and while in residence he had composed a United Nations Hymn, setting his own sincerely felt verses.

I decided to create a command performance for my film. Maud Martin, his devoted wife, led the cello section; behind the orchestra, a student choir gave a lusty rendition of the simple UN Hymn, which Paul conducted with unrelenting passion. Fifty years later I can still sing all thirty-two bars of the melody by heart, in fact I recently did just that with John Amis, my choice to conduct the interview with Tortelier. Amis asked him what had made him take up music. 'Fog', came the inscrutable reply. He was held up at an airport, he explained bafflingly. And who had had the greatest influence on his musical training? His grandmother, who made him practise: 'When I was six, I wanted to play marbles.' Tortelier was both dynamic and entertaining, and he played with exceptional eloquence – we finished the film in close-up with a ravishing performance of the Sarabande from Bach's great C minor Cello Suite. More significant for the future of music on television, we also

159

filmed Tortelier coaching his violinist son Yan Pascal in the Brahms Double Concerto and giving a cello lesson to a young English pupil, breaking off occasionally to explain to the eavesdropping John Amis what the problems were, both technical and interpretive. His language was direct, colourful and not too technical: the teaching was riveting and much admired back at Lime Grove. Twelve months later I was encouraged to invite Paul back to the BBC to give a master class in the *Monitor* studio. The live session was spellbinding and led directly to the creation of the first *Master Class* series on BBC2.

Do My Ears Deceive Me? was the title of my next big project in this fertile year, a studio feature about modern music and its incomprehensibility (as many believed) for the average music-lover. We hired the LSO under Colin Davis to play symphonic examples for the debate, and invited two of the best minds in British music, Deryck Cooke and Hans Keller, to provide opposing opinions on the merits of relatively contemporary music by Schoenberg and Stravinsky. The composer Michael Tippett also participated with his

Illuminating the *Structures Sonores* with lighting director Johnny Summers (a Baschet brother in the background), 1962.

160

customary eloquence; Colin chipped in pungent comments from the rostrum; light relief was provided by Ken Russell, who re-created a recent piece of avant-garde nonsense in which a Japanese composer, dressed all in black leather (played by Ken), entered the studio on a motorbike and threw raw eggs at a large copper sheet suspended in front of the orchestra. Hans Keller spoke up valiantly for Schoenberg's twelve-tone system; challenged by Huw Wheldon concerning atonal music's alleged absence of melody, Hans manfully whistled the opening bars of the Schoenberg Variations for Orchestra, op. 31. The evening proved inconclusive; some people's ears may have been deceived, others were enchanted. I was happy to have put Cooke and Keller on television and did so again more than once – to hear them arguing the toss as to whether George Gershwin or Cole Porter was the better composer was reminiscent of the best Yalding House canteen talk, the BBC's equivalent of a college high table.

Whistling Schoenberg was all very well, but I was keen in those *Monitor* years to explore other forms of new music. Forgotten today is the American composer Lukas Foss's exploratory Chamber Ensemble, in which four classically trained musicians improvised. Put bluntly, they were making it up as they went along. I loved Lukas but this compositional movement did not catch on. I had a soft spot, too, for the Baschet brothers from Paris. They created *Structures Sonores* – strikingly beautiful musical instruments fashioned from leaves of aluminium and rows of tuned glass rods. New York's Museum of Modern Art (MOMA) had just bought a *structure* for its contemporary art collection and Jean Cocteau commissioned the brothers to perform on them for his film *Testament of Orpheus*. If both experiments have proved to be blind alleys, they were entertaining while they lasted: I was glad to give them airtime.

I was on more familiar ground filming a competition in search of gifted young tenors at the Wigmore Hall. Knowledgeable commentary was provided by Bernard Keeffe, an engaging broadcaster who had been a professional singer himself and something of a conductor too, but was at that time working on the staff at Covent Garden. What makes a tenor? That was the question he posed and we must have answered correctly since the winner was a certain Philip Langridge, then at the beginning of almost half a century of distinguished singing. Each contestant had to sing 'Ev'ry Valley' from *Messiah* and Allan Tyrer, my ever-inventive film editor, showed what fun could be had in the cutting room by stringing the contestants together so that while the aria ran on uninterrupted, the face and voice of the tenor changed every eight bars or so. The resulting roller coaster came over as comic rather than cruel because one heard so many different singing styles in double-quick time. But Langridge's outstanding talent was unmissable.

Working on *Monitor* provided wonderfully varied experience. I spent several bitterly cold days that winter on Camber Sands, helping Ken Russell on *The Lonely Shore*, a science fiction film essay written by Jacquetta Hawkes (a leading archaeologist and wife of J.B. Priestley); it was based on the fantasy that centuries later a variety of domestic objects from the 1960s were being dug up from the sands that had covered them after some planetary disaster. What would future generations make of Hoovers, refrigerators and washing machines? (I cannot recall the answer but the images were great.) A couple of editions later I was producing the BFI's resident film historian John Huntley in a lecture concerning the coming of sound to the movies. And early in the summer of 1962 I flew to New York to direct the documentary about Ben Shahn's Roosevelt New Jersey fresco already described; en route in New York I dashed off a report on the new open-air theatre in Central Park, which was offering vibrant Shakespeare, free, under the inspirational leadership of a local firebrand named Joseph Papp. I seemed to thrive on larger-than-life personalities that year: back in London, Tyrone Guthrie spoke vivaciously about *HMS Pinafore* and my last film of the season was a profile of Julian Bream. A star since his teens, Julian was an intriguing mixture of Renaissance aesthete and cockney comedian. I took him to the bomb site in Bermondsey where his grandmother had run a pub until Nazi bombers destroyed it during the Blitz. A cunning operator, Bream spent his entire military service making music in an army band. He was so busy with gigs he bought a second-hand car to keep up with his diary. I filmed him at an unusual gig at The Singing Chef restaurant in Bayswater, where he swapped jokes with the celebrity cook of the day, Fanny Cradock. In another sequence I filmed a private drinks party at his home where I encouraged Julian to indulge his passion for Django Reinhardt, the legendary gypsy star of Le Hot Club de Paris. I remember Jacqueline Wheldon, Huw's novelist wife, was among the enthusiastic twisters on the dance floor. At the end of the shoot, Julian was scathing about my modest attempt to play a little jazz piano. 'Crikey, Bill,' he exclaimed, 'you're so fuckin' square!' It was a stinging rebuke but true; I love jazz but I can't improvise for toffee. (It is of little consolation that Yehudi Menuhin had the same problem: his famous performances with Stéphane Grappelli [of the Hot Club] were all written down for him.) For lovers of early music, my Bream documentary has a special interest: it was the first time the Julian Bream Lute Consort was

On location for *Monitor* with Julian Bream at his Kensington home, 1962.

filmed, playing some exquisite music by Dowland. In every sequence of my film portrait, Julian's charm was infectious. He balanced artistic refinement and a mission to explore with a total lack of pomposity. I was to work with him many times over the next two decades. Musically he was an angel but when faced with an unwanted camera rehearsal he could be a royal pain in the neck.

In the summer of 1962 Huw Wheldon was named boss of a new department and I was promoted (again without competition) to the editorship of *Monitor*. Huw was at the beginning of his rapid rise to the very top of the television tree and whether I liked it or not – it was never discussed between us – I was moving up in his slipstream. Apart from his obvious leadership qualities, the reason for Huw's new appointment was the publication in June 1962 of the

Group photocall at the BBC Management Conference, Evesham, 1965. I am in the middle of the very back row, leaning on the ladder. On the sofa: Sidney Newman (seated left); Huw Wheldon (centre); Joanna Spicer (right). Michael Peacock is seated front row, third from left. Frank Muir is seated front row, extreme right.

Pilkington Report. Aided and abetted by the social historian Richard Hoggart, who was a regular contributor to *Monitor*, Pilkington decreed that the next television channel, based on superior engineering – 625 lines instead of 405 – would be entrusted not to a new body (such as Channel 4 in the 1980s) but to the BBC. Furthermore, BBC2 would be the first UK network to switch to colour, undoubtedly the most important innovation since the invention of television itself.

At thirty-one I was dangerously young to be running a flagship programme like *Monitor*. I had only been working in television for four years and I was painfully aware inside myself that I lacked a strong creative personality. As an editor I did not find it easy to help my colleagues to get the best out of their material – which was one of Huw's greatest strengths. He continued to present *Monitor*, and for the big films of the year such as Ken Russell's *Elgar* and *Pop Goes the Easel*, he sat in at rough-cut screenings. But day to day it was I who ran the *Monitor* show, selecting the studio features, commissioning the individual films, deciding on running orders, drafting *Radio Times* billings, meeting the press, assessing potential subjects and potential new members of the team.

Running *Monitor* became a much less carefree existence and in the search for new ideas and personalities I made some risky programme choices: my selection of Alexander Trocchi, for example. He was a Scottish version of a 'Beat' poet, complete with a personal history of drug-taking and of writing pornography under an assumed name. Understandably, Huw wasn't too keen on him – how would his legendary mother-in-law Mrs Stroud react to this rebellious spirit who had told the Edinburgh Literary Festival that the impetus for his creative writing was sodomy? But fair play, Huw went ahead with the interview although the transmission turned out to be something of a damp squib.

The best example of Huw actually wielding a veto was when my fellow director David Jones suggested going to Australia to make a film about the novelist Patrick White, who a decade later was to be awarded the Nobel Prize in Literature. 'Australia!' Huw snorted. 'Australia?' – this time enunciated with derision – 'I wouldn't go to bloody Ealing to interview Patrick sodding White.'

Other unpredictable *Monitor* guests included William Russo, a third-stream jazz composer who had worked with Stan Kenton's much-discussed 'Wall of Sound' orchestra, and Werner Ruhnau, a visionary German architect, whose theatre-cum-opera house in Gelsenkirchen, glass-fronted, was the last word in modernity: its interior walls, moveable at the touch of a button to create different performance spaces, were in colour – a deep blue, painted by his friend Yves Klein. I had encountered Ruhnau during a tour of post-war opera houses arranged by the German cultural attaché, an effective and enthusiastic diplomat named Brigitte Lohmeyer, whose *salon* was always chock-full of interesting people. The fruits of Germany's economic miracle were evident in every city I visited: I liked the people I met, too; Ruhnau was mad as a hatter but immensely charming. Naturally I savoured the irony in the fact that the celebratory film I directed about his theatre was made exactly twenty years after German planes had bombed Norwich to bits and put an end to my childhood.

With Ken Russell and John Schlesinger both launched on feature film careers (Schlesinger never returned to *Monitor*) and David Jones veering towards what became his natural habitat, the theatre, we needed new directors: I appointed two of the most durable personalities in arts television. Both had studied at Oxford. Patrick Garland had a richly varied directorial career, taking in poetry, literature and the theatre. Melvyn Bragg swiftly became one of Lime Grove's leading young directors. He also wrote the script of Ken Russell's most controversial opus so far, *The Debussy Film* (1965). Melvyn could have followed Ken into the feature business – to be a director was, after all, his first ambition. But he found the urge to present and edit programmes irresistible and he carved out a lifetime career mixing writing and television.

My editorial selections were more instinctive than dialectical and nothing if not eclectic. In the field of classical music I persuaded the legendary teacher Nadia Boulanger to give a master class on Fauré's *Requiem*. In another choral feature I booked the brand-new Philharmonia Chorus to illustrate a subject close to my heart: the complementary roles of choirmaster and conductor. Wilhelm Pitz from the Wagners' Bayreuth Festival was the trainer and Carlo Maria Giulini the maestro – an 'A' team if ever there was one. Music of a more insidious kind was tackled by another new director, Norman James, whom I brought in on attachment from the Design Department; his film satire delivered a sharp attack on the growing curse of 'muzak', the background music in shops and cafés which was becoming such an irritant. That battle was comprehensively lost and the film is now remembered only because the actress Julie Christie made a fleeting appearance as a model. Another complaint of

'Tribute to Nadia Boulanger' opened the fourth season of *Monitor*, September 1962. Mme Boulanger stands at the piano between me and the veteran sound supervisor George Ageros (right).

mine was the ugliness of many of London's new buildings. A *Monitor* panel chose Centre Point to be the most offensive. I had nothing against critics, but I preferred to feature creative artists: three featured in an exploration I arranged of new styles in art: Bernard Cohen, Richard Smith and Joe Tilson made a decent list of cutting-edge artists, it seemed to me, but in terms of impact the feature was outclassed by Ken Russell's delightful film about a more cohesive group of young British artists led by Peter Blake. Pop art was their stock in trade and *Pop Goes the Easel* was Ken's clever title. Huw's introduction to the film was a masterpiece of disassociation: 'love them or loathe them, they are here to stay' was the gist of his introduction and the forty-five minutes that followed were a cinematic riot in which Elvis Presley, circus clowns and Brigitte Bardot all played lively parts alongside Ken's four swinging London artists, Peter Blake, Derek Boshier, Peter Phillips and Pauline Boty. Ken created a terrifying dream scene featuring Pauline, in which she is pursued around Television Centre's circular corridors by a sinister woman in a wheelchair and a posse of medics. (The venue would have been a familiar nightmare to many BBC staff members.) Pauline was to die of cancer, tragically young, only four years later. In particular I treasure the memory of Peter Blake in his pyjamas shimmying from his bed to his own Bardot Screen to the accompaniment of an insidious French pop song: 'Brigitte Bar-dot, Bar-dot (repeated twice) … the longest legs in Paris and the sweetest girl I know'. I'm not sure that Huw had ever heard of Mlle Bardot but he knew an entertaining film when he saw one.

In those far-off days there were no such people as commissioning editors. The editors of *Monitor* and *Panorama* rarely consulted a superior in the hierarchy before giving the go-ahead to a project. Within *Monitor* ideas arrived in different ways and never via publicists and PR people – those industries were still in their infancy. Television was not entirely trusted. We may have been successful with Menotti when we sent off our standard letter to the great and the good but we did not hear back from Igor Stravinsky. William Walton would have nothing to do with 'those terrible television people', as he described us. Sometimes an individual passion gave birth to a programme: David Jones pushed his admiration for the Welsh poet R.S. Thomas; Ann Turner longed to make a film about Van Gogh's drawings; Nancy Thomas's friendship with the surrealist Roland Penrose led to memorable studio encounters with Max Ernst and Marcel Duchamp. And so it was with Ken Russell's film about Edward Elgar. Before my promotion to the editorship, in 1961, Ken and I lobbied Huw for the chance to make a film about this then deeply unfashionable composer. I had always loved his *Introduction and Allegro*, while Ken, a recent convert, was drawn to his Catholicism, which, along with his lower-middle-class background and his penury-to-riches social progress, provided fruitful material for a strong storyline. Nevertheless, Ken's original outline was dismissed as 'mere gossip column stuff' by Lionel Salter, then in charge of music at BBC Television. Ken was undeterred. For *Monitor* he had already made an exciting profile of Sergei Prokofiev, mixing photographs and archive Soviet films with live action that included a concert pianist's hands playing the opening pages of the First Piano Concerto. (My own hands can be seen conducting Prokofiev's March from *The Love for Three Oranges*.) I knew Ken had evolved a workable style for film biography and we refused to accept Huw's thumbs-down ('too museumy') for our Elgar proposal: we went back to the drawing board and worked together on a new treatment to which Huw finally gave his blessing. By now I was editor of *Monitor* anyway, but this big project benefited greatly from Wheldon's involvement.

The credits at the end of *Elgar* are confusing. The first to appear is fine: 'Written and directed by Ken Russell'. That's followed by 'Commentary written and spoken by Huw Wheldon'. Then come the cast and technician credits. The last name on the screen, commonly the most important, is mine: 'Produced by Humphrey Burton'. But that's ridiculous! My contribution was nowhere near as grand. I had many fingers in the Elgar pie but it was Ken himself who produced nearly every aspect of the film with help from his designer wife Shirley and our devoted production assistant, Anne James. On the other hand, I drafted most of the words Huw delivered so magnificently. I also worked with Ken on the script: among my contributions was the use of the *Introduction and Allegro* at three vital points in Elgar's life – the boy on the pony, the young man on his bicycle and the old widower in his open car, all memorably filmed by our splendid BBC cameraman Ken Higgins on the Malvern Hills. Another suggestion of mine was more sentimental: on his sickbed the old Elgar listens to his new recording of 'Nimrod' as he reflects on crucial events in his life – a touching three-minute flashback in the finished film. His death, I suggested, should be symbolised by an endlessly rotating 78 rpm gramophone record whose needle has come to the end of the musical grooves.

In later life, when he had become a celebrity, Ken gave some colourful interviews about how the Elgar film got made. Huw rightly laid claim to making a significant creative input when he delivered a Dimbleby Lecture about creativity in 1976. The film historian Paul Sutton is preparing a detailed study. What follows here is my personal account of the making of the Elgar film.

Our starting point was Elgar's music. We listened to it for hours on end. Eventually we decided to use music as the film's backbone. We settled on ten Elgar compositions: *Introduction and Allegro*, *Salut d'Amour*, the *Serenade for String Orchestra*, the *Imperial March*, *The Dream of Gerontius*, *Enigma Variations* (for storytelling emphasis these two compositions were featured in the wrong chronological order), the Second Symphony (accompanied by extraordinary newsreel of Edward VII's funeral), *Pomp and Circumstance March No. 1*, the Cello Concerto and finally Bach's C minor Organ Fantasia, which Elgar orchestrated in 1922 when his own creative juices had dried up. In 1962 we knew nothing about Elgar's late-flowering love affair with Vera Hocking, the young Croydon violinist who warmed up the composer's declining years, inspiring the unfinished Third Symphony. Given Ken's later propensity for slightly cheesy eroticism, our ignorance was probably a blessing in disguise.

When we had settled on the excerpts we built the filming around them, starting musically with Elgar's youth. For this Ken found an early unpublished wind quintet for which we recruited a group of young players to perform seated round a table in my back garden in Hammersmith Grove; we filmed the ensemble from the kitchen window. We also unearthed some of the music Elgar composed for the staff band he conducted in his twenties (for a salary of £30 a year) at the mental hospital in Powick. Day-to-day production on location in the Malvern Hills was organised by Anne James. We used the Ealing film studio to film a few interiors, among them the touching scene when Mrs Elgar is seen ruling music staves on plain paper with a five-nibbed pen while her husband works on his *Serenade* by the light of a single oil lamp. Most of the film was shot in and around Malvern. The most expensive item on Anne's minuscule budget was the construction of three wooden crosses, which Ken had erected at the summit of the Worcester Beacon. They symbolised Elgar's ecstatic response to Gerontius's sublime outburst on the words 'Sanctus fortis, sanctus Deus'. The filming for that climactic sequence took place at dawn. Permission was not sought – it surely would not have been granted.

Because *Monitor* was officially a factual strand, there was no provision in our standard budgets for the allocation of expensive resources such as props, wardrobe, set construction or make-up. We were on our own, improvising, borrowing where we could. Anne did the make-up with ordinary powder puffs. Shirley found Victorian costumes in Notting Hill junk shops. Our studio designer Natasha Kroll came up trumps with Edwardian furniture. Casting was mostly done from among Ken's circle of friends, most notable among them being Peter Brett, who played Elgar as a young man. Earlier in the year Brett had written the script for Ken's first feature film, *French Dressing*. In Worcester Ken found a sweet-natured boy who knew how to fish and to ride a pony bareback for the childhood scenes. To play Sir Edward, the silver-haired knight of the realm, Ken chose a silver-haired old-school actor named George McGrath. These were not speaking roles because we were in a filmic no man's land, halfway between full drama and straight documentary. Theoretically this was uneasy territory but in practice Ken's method worked well. Much of the information came across the screen directly after being extracted from the composer's scrapbooks and Lady Elgar's postcards, and from newsreel footage. Equally powerful were Ken's images: lovers' hands brushing through the heads of corn, donkeys straining up a hill, bonfire smoke drifting through trees. And then there was the eloquent commentary. In Ken's early *Monitor* films commentary was the element which he preferred to delegate – this despite the gift for words he later demonstrated in his film scripts. While Allan Tyrer and Ken were editing the Elgar film's fifty-minute fine-cut, I drafted the commentary text – keeping it simple but with Huw's style in my mind's ear (something I had learnt on the job over the previous four years).

The received wisdom about commentary writing is that you should avoid duplicating the story the picture is already telling. But one of Huw's trusted maxims was that you avoid the obvious at your peril and he was at his most impressive when he brought his editorial firepower to bear on our Elgar film. He went carefully through my draft. Did Elgar really jump out of trees and scare his fiancée as a jape? Then we must be told so as a fact and not a director's fancy. Was it true that Elgar and his fiancée toiled up the Worcester Beacon dragging a pair of reluctant donkeys behind them? Did he actually telephone the Meteorological Office for weather reports before going out with his daughter to fly kites on the hills? Or before sliding down the slopes with her on tin trays? Did he really light bonfires in the Sussex woods after his wife's death? In every scene, so lovingly created by Ken, Huw's voice provided authentication, expressed in prose that imparted a Victorian and later an Edwardian atmosphere to the film and convinced viewers of its truth and even more of its romance. Huw's mellifluous voice was perfect for the assignment.

There was, however, a huge row just two days before the commentary was to be recorded at our day-long session in the BBC's Ealing dubbing theatre. The crunch came over the war sequence. Elgar loved Germany, where, thanks to the support of Richard Strauss, his music was recognised much earlier than in England. War between the two nations was anathema to Elgar.

Editor and director at odds. The disagreement between Huw Wheldon (left) and Ken Russell (right) about the use of Elgar's noble music, 'Land of Hope and Glory', raged on in the corridors of Ealing Film Studios.

Ken had found horrendous newsreel at the Imperial War Museum of the trench war in Flanders, frightening images hitherto never seen on television. Without thought of adding commentary, he cut this footage to the *Pomp and Circumstance March* which features the melody (but not the words) of 'Land of Hope and Glory'. Huw hated what he saw in the cutting room: a gallant soldier himself, and one who had witnessed the horrors of war at close quarters, he felt the sequence cheapened the sacrifice of the First World War's soldiers by setting the violent images to such hackneyed, over-familiar music. For his part, Ken wanted no words: for him the combination of war pictures and Elgar's music was the entire story. But Huw was adamant: the sequence had to be changed. The argument swung backwards and forwards all day long, through the night and into the next day. The corridor of the second floor at Ealing Studios became very familiar; likewise the view of the park from the metal fire escape at the back, where I would retreat to smoke a welcome Gauloise.

Eventually a compromise was hammered out – a decision *had* to be taken because, as I say, we were dubbing the next day. We would keep the sick-making shots of men going over the top to instant death, the desperate stretcher-bearers in the trenches, with their load of wounded Tommies, the pathetic line of blinded soldiers, victims of poison gas – we could keep all this, set to Elgar's stirring music, provided we added commentary that spoke of the ghastly irony inherent in the fact that a tune, 'a good tune, the sort of tune that comes once in a lifetime' (to quote Elgar himself) composed a decade earlier in 'the dashing, glinting days' of British imperialism (to quote Wheldon), was now being pressed into patriotic service as a second national anthem, a battle-hymn against the Germany that Elgar loved. Two more minutes of the war footage followed those words and then a final paragraph, spoken over further trench-war carnage: 'As the gates of Armageddon opened in France, Elgar, too old to serve, left London for Sussex and turned to chamber music and sonatas. Nothing, however, could sever the public's association of Elgar

The boy Elgar on his pony surveying the Malvern Hills at sunset has assumed an iconic significance.

Ken Russell directing the scene. That there is no documentary
evidence that Elgar ever rode a pony is beside the point.

to his Boer War marching song [Land of Hope and Glory] and the irony to a man who had sensed the disaster to come and felt its impact, became abominable.' Cut to the gassed soldiers as the final orchestral statement of 'Land of Hope' blares out. The sequence concluded with dizzying shots of a Flanders war cemetery, the camera's quickening zooms and dazzling pans across thousands of white crosses matching the hectic closing bars of Elgar's march. I believe it was at Huw's suggestion that Ken went to Flanders specially to film that climactic sequence.

As the editing progressed it became clear that the Elgar film represented a quantum leap forward in *Monitor*'s output and was thus a very suitable programme with which to celebrate our hundredth edition in November 1962. Reviews were mixed but the public loved it: the audience research appreciation index was eighty-six, very high, and our film was undoubtedly one of the factors that triggered the renaissance in Elgar's music, an interest that has never wavered from that day to this. The image of the boy Elgar on his pony surveying the Malvern Hills at sunset has assumed an iconic significance.

CHAPTER 10

NEW PROGRAMMES AND FOREIGN FIELDS

Briefing the cameramen outside Walthamstow Town Hall
prior to filming *Mr Copland Comes to Town*.

IN THE SUMMER of 1963 I was on the move once again, this time out
of *Monitor* altogether. The BBC's new channel, BBC2, was to be launched
the following April and to fulfil its expanded remit we needed many more
programmes and more staff to make them. A new department entitled
Documentaries and Music was hived off from Talks and housed in the
recently completed Television Centre, with Huw Wheldon as its boss. Since
Huw had a limited knowledge of classical music, I was promoted to be his

number two and given the brand-new title of Executive Producer, Music Programmes (again without ever being asked if I wanted to do the job). The BBC's previous head of music productions, Lionel Salter, was an excellent all-round musician and administrator whose television experience went back to Alexandra Palace before the war. Although not a director himself, he had written a useful grammar concerning the televising of music performance, a style guide which is consistently ignored by today's rapid-fire practitioners. However, Lionel was unadventurous in his choice of repertoire for television and being of a somewhat combative nature he had crossed swords with rather too many high-ups in BBC Television. Indeed, I heard our abrasive new controller, Donald Baverstock, complaining caustically that after examining Salter's workload he had come to the conclusion that he had scarcely enough work to fill one afternoon a fortnight. The reshuffle of which I was part saw Salter sent to Yalding House to run opera for the Third Programme (a hefty assignment) and eventually become Assistant Controller under William Glock – not a comfortable berth, I imagine, but Lionel had great resilience and was a musician to his fingertips. Meanwhile, Huw gave up introducing *Monitor*, declaring later and to my mind unconvincingly that he had interviewed everybody he wanted to interview.

My main brief for BBC Television was to devise fresh ways of putting music on to the small screen. It was a good start that Michael Peacock, the newly appointed chief of programmes for BBC2, liked classical music and jazz. Mike was a high-flyer, educated at the London School of Economics: he had edited *Panorama* while still in his twenties and then run BBC News. He and his wife Daphne and our families of young children became good friends. The first Peacock blueprint suggested that the new channel should be devoted to a different topic each day of the week, in hindsight a bizarre notion but at least it gave music many more slots than had been possible on BBC1, so I embraced it enthusiastically, coming up with a clutch of *Monitor*-type programmes that explored the process of music-making but now in sets of six programmes rather than individual features. *Master Class* was a BBC2 brand that ran for over a decade: one of my new producer recruits, the effervescent John Drummond from the BBC Paris office, was in charge of the first series, which featured Paul Tortelier. John rightly insisted that the pupils should be potential masters themselves and that the programmes should have real musical meat in addition to Tortelier's Gallic eloquence. Yehudi Menuhin, Julian Bream and Carl Ebert the opera director were among the great teachers we recruited over the seasons that followed. Another BBC2 strand, *In Rehearsal*, was based on the simplest of propositions – that it was interesting and enlightening to see musicians working something up for performance. I had done this on *Monitor* with John Dankworth and his jazz quartet; now I invited the rising star Jacqueline du Pré, still a teenager, to allow us to eavesdrop as she worked with her pianist friend Stephen Bishop on Beethoven's variations on 'Bei Männern' from Mozart's *The Magic Flute*, appropriately a love duet. It was an enchanting half hour but – like so much of the output from this period – the recording was wiped, for the unacceptable reason that since tape was so expensive it must be reused once the show had been transmitted. (The alternative was to make a copy especially for the Archive.)

My most important innovation was *Workshop*, a dull title for an eclectic hour-long slot about musicians at work, which kicked off with an essay on Paganini's Twenty-Fourth Violin Caprice. Peter Black, the *Daily Mail*'s esteemed critic, hailed *Workshop* as 'the brightest creative idea on BBC2'. Martin Cooper (the pianist Imogen Cooper's father), an urbane and witty musical historian, wrote the Paganini script with me and I also hired Arthur Hutchings, Durham University's provocative music professor, to add pungent comments. The *Radio Times* billing put it this way: 'Martin Cooper re-creates the personality of Paganini, the diabolical virtuoso, and Arthur Hutchings explores the impact of his music on two centuries of composers.' Manoug Parikian was the solo violinist and John Dankworth did a live improvisation on the famous theme. The South African pianist Yonty Solomon, who made his Wigmore Hall début the same year, was the brilliant soloist in Rachmaninov's Paganini Variations. It was a lively show, a little rough at the edges because I was squeezing in so much material, but illuminating and fun. Maybe Andrew Lloyd Webber saw it: he was only a schoolboy at the time but a decade later he created his own variant of the Paganini theme for the signature tune of the new *South Bank Show*.

I am proud of *Workshop*'s range. In *Mr Copland Comes to Town* Barrie Gavin and I filmed the great composer rehearsing the LSO in a brand-new composition and coping diplomatically with television journalists from the *Tonight* programme who had no clue what to ask him. Another of the *Workshop* team's new directors, a Canadian Buddhist of great charm named Francis Coleman, took his camera very much with my blessing *In Search of Constant Lambert*. In another programme he explored *Shakespeare in Music* – at one point Sir John Falstaff walked dreamily through the orchestra violins. From Vienna I recruited the ebullient H.C. Robbins Landon to extol the glory of Haydn the symphonist; in the development section of the 'London'

177

Aaron Copland
rehearsing the LSO in his
Music for a Great City.

Symphony's first movement, Robbie stood in front of the orchestra pointing out individual players and shouting over the music to demonstrate the way Haydn sent his theme darting from instrument to instrument in the development section. The musicians, conducted by Charles Mackerras (himself the subject of a later *Workshop* film), played on regardless of this force of nature in front of them. Robbie appeared in many more *Workshops* but came a bit of a cropper (after my time) when it was alleged that a script about Beethoven which he submitted to BBC2 in connection with the Beethoven bicentenary may have been inspired a little too closely by A.W. Thayer's classic Beethoven biography of 1866.

Workshop also tackled new music. We were still transmitting in black and white in the mid-1960s, and in an abstract studio set Pierre Boulez analysed his own abstruse Mallarmé-inspired *Pli selon pli*. This was the first of Barrie Gavin's eleven television shows with Boulez, taped over the next thirty years.

For another *Workshop* we recruited Georg Solti – a powerful presence in London since taking over at Covent Garden at the beginning of the decade – to put aspiring young conductors through their paces while rehearsing with the London Philharmonic.

A visionary teaching method for music in primary schools, pioneered by Zoltán Kodály, was revealed in another trailblazing *Workshop* produced and directed by John Hosier and Herbert Chappell. I recruited both directors from radio, and while John moved on to an important career as a music educator, Bert stayed with the BBC, combining television music production for me with brilliant work as a composer. It was his cantata *The Daniel Jazz* that had first attracted my interest. His later shows, among them *Who Needs a Conductor?* and *African Sanctus*, proved him to be equally adept as a television producer, whether in the studio, calling the shots for four or five cameramen, or out on location in the wilds of Africa, where he and Peter Bartlett, the veteran film cameraman, filmed a larger-than-life musical explorer named David Fanshawe.

Finally there was Christopher Nupen, who whizzed through BBC Television like a rocket. A product of BBC Radio's renowned features department at Rothwell House, where like me he began as a studio manager, Nupen's most famous *Workshop* was *Double Concerto*, featuring Daniel Barenboim and Vladimir Ashkenazy in the concerto for two pianos by Mozart, a delightful portrait of two young giants. At the BBC Television Centre, Nupen directed his friends Daniel Barenboim and Jacqueline du Pré (shortly before their marriage) in a tremendous performance of Elgar's Cello Concerto. How Christopher wangled a studio recording despite having no multi-camera directing experience is a mystery into which I did not delve. A wonderfully warm film about Schubert's 'Trout' Quintet followed, and then Christopher went off to create his own production company, entitled Allegro Films. I envied him his determination to do things perfectly, no matter how long the job takes, and to be answerable to nobody.

Nupen's work is still available via YouTube and on DVD but the paltry coverage of classical music provided by the BBC half a century later contains not a hint of the *Workshop* ethic.

Making a host of lively programmes in quick succession, as I did in 1963–65, seemed to me the natural order of things. After all, *Monitor* had been providing me with a fortnightly 'high' since 1958. But far from being normal, this hectic *modus operandi* was in truth very special: everybody who was there agrees that the mid-1960s was an extraordinarily exciting period to be working in television, not least because we were breaking new ground wherever we turned. And my new 'special projects' post soon involved me in expeditions to foreign fields, to the Soviet Union and before that to Scotland, which was equally foreign and exotic. Leading an English invasion of Edinburgh for its festival was, looking back, an act of breath-taking condescension but we were not going to argue when (perhaps with malice aforethought) the Welshman Donald Baverstock handed Huw and me a late-evening Scottish festival slot on what was still the Corporation's only channel, BBC1. From BBC Scotland's tiny studio on George Street in Edinburgh we were to transmit a nightly show reflecting the Edinburgh Festival. In the first half of each programme would come a miscellany of short features from around the festival and the fringe, some live in the studio, some on film. And then there would be a major concert, taped earlier in the week. The *Monitor* pedigree of this daily show was pretty obvious. My deputy was to be another Englishman, Ken Corden, a gentle and long-suffering studio director on the *Tonight* programme upon whom I had taken pity and provided with a safe haven in Documentaries and Music. His young family and mine shared a large Edinburgh house. The option of hiring Scottish presenters, the tactful thing to have done, doesn't seem to have occurred to us – quite the contrary: Robert Kee, taking time off from *Panorama*, was my choice as anchorman with Mary Holland, later the *Observer*'s acerbic Irish affairs correspondent, as the reporter. I did recruit a few Scots as researchers and directors, among them a delightfully witty Light Entertainment director named David Bell who was later to work with me at London Weekend Television (LWT).

Fortunately the locals tolerated us during this Sassenach invasion. Even 'Controller Scotland', a remote figure who was said to wear the kilt as regular daily attire, made us welcome and plied us with excellent Scotch. But at fifty years' remove I remember only one programme project from our festival magazine, and one big personality: the Queen's cousin, George Harewood, who had been the festival's boss since 1961. He accepted my invitation to make a film about a day in his life during the festival. Accordingly Robert Kee and our camera team sat with him in his office as he dealt with a crisis concerning one of his hottest bookings, the Topless Dancers of Togo. Their bare-breasted appearance had caused a sensation south of the border and was now threat-ening to unleash moral depravity at the Usher Hall. The puritanical outcry was making waves for the generally unflappable Harewood. He confided to Kee on camera that he was fed up with having to deal with these censorious fuddy-duddies – or words to that effect – adding that this fellow – Hyatt, Hignett, Hislop, he couldn't exactly remember the name – reminded him of the story of the psychiatrist who was asked if he had always wanted to follow that profession. 'Oh, no', he replied. 'I wanted to be a sex maniac but I failed the practicals.' Quite a funny story. I saw the rough cut and the film editor asked whether I was happy with that joke. I was all for it, delighted to show the world that a member of the royal family had a sense of humour. Since Huw Wheldon was in town I thought it judicious to ask his opinion. He had a good laugh too, and then said that I was the editor and it was for me to decide. I also ran the story across Lord Harewood and he was comfortable with it. So we went ahead and transmitted the film that evening. Next day the *Scottish Daily Mail* was on the phone bright and early. They had spoken to Professor Hignett, who was not a prude but a lecturer (if I remember correctly) in psychiatry at Glasgow University, and asked his opinion of the festival director's unfriendly anecdote. He was furious and – to cut a long story short – the BBC had to settle with him out of court some months later to the tune of £3,500, which was, as they say, a lot of money in those days. It turned out that Lord Harewood had got the wrong end of the stick. The professor had not been protesting on account of the threat to morality that the topless dancers represented; on the contrary, his fear was that the dancers might *not* be topless at the Usher Hall as a result of the pressure from the Mrs Grundies of Morningside: he wanted Scotland to have equal viewing rights with the English. I guess he had a point and I suppose I learnt a lesson, though I certainly would not want to have lawyers crawling over my rough cuts as happens these days.

A month later came another foreign adventure: a visit to the Soviet Union. Michael Peacock was looking for something spectacular with a Russian flavour to include in the opening evening of BBC2 to set off what he had already commissioned, a new BBC production of the American musical *Kiss Me, Kate*. (Peacock's plan had been sparked off by space exploration and the Cuban missile crisis, which had created a tremendous rivalry between the superpowers.) Mike had been tipped off about the talents of Arkady Raikin, a brilliant Russian entertainer who was said to be a mixture of Peter Ustinov the raconteur and Marcel Marceau the mime. I was to accompany our head of artists bookings, Tim Holland Bennett, on a fact-finding mission: would Raikin go down well with a British audience? Why Mike singled me out for this less than onerous task is a mystery since I knew very little about producing light entertainment, but of course I jumped at the invitation and

Arkady Raikin – lost in translation.

on a late-September afternoon I joined Tim in Helsinki, where we went on board the MS *Batory*, a battered old Polish cruise ship, for the short voyage to Leningrad.

Raikin was a Latvian Jew by birth but had been a showbiz fixture in Leningrad since his youth; he was said to be rehearsing in his home city with his troupe, preparing for an autumn tour. We were looked after by the state concert agency, Goskonsert, which was equally famous for intransigence and incompetence: it soon became obvious that Raikin was not in Leningrad – we were fobbed off on our first evening with a visit to a circus in the park (an excellent show), which was followed the next morning by the offer of a meeting with Leningrad's most famous musical son, Dimitri Shostakovich, who had been a firewatcher during the city's dreadful siege twenty years earlier. The great man never materialised despite repeated assurances that he was still a member of Leningrad's city council: I was pretty certain he lived in Moscow. On the third day our Intourist minder, who sported more than a shadow of a moustache and exuded a pervasive aroma of inexpensive perfume, reported that Raikin's group had moved to Moscow in order to do a crash course in English – exclusively for our benefit. But next day, when we arrived in that great city, which was teeming with colourful visitors from all over the Soviet Union, the Goskonsert office could find no trace of Raikin's whereabouts. Nor was Mr Shostakovich produced for us. But I had the true pleasure of attending a performance of Verdi's *Falstaff* at the Bolshoi, with no less an artist than Galina Vishnevskaya in the role of Alice Ford, singing and acting with great vivacity and charm – in Russian rather than Italian. Happily I knew the opera pretty well from having played percussion in it under Colin Davis for the Chelsea Opera Group. I was taken backstage to congratulate the alluring prima donna and I must have mentioned my slender connection with Benjamin Britten because next morning I was invited to her apartment for coffee. Her husband, Mstislav Rostropovich, wasn't there but I didn't miss the chance to boast to his wife that the BBC had recently televised Slava's performance of Shostakovich's First Cello Concerto from the Royal Festival Hall. I was impressed by the size and opulence of their Moscow flat. I learnt much later that two apartments had been knocked into one to provide appropriate quarters for the Soviet Union's most prominent musical power couple. Marshal Bulganin, the head of state, was known to be crazy about her.

Next day our quest for Arkady Raikin continued most unexpectedly with a flight to Russia's deep south, to the city of Krasnodar, capital of the Kuban region; it had finally been established that Raikin's autumn tour was to open

Power couple: Mstislav Rostropovich and Galina Vishnevskaya.

there the very next day. We stepped out of our rickety Ilyushin 18 into the inviting warmth of the subtropics: the pleasant smell of freedom was in the air. The local translator met us on the tarmac. Irina was tall, pretty and vivacious, she was the very antithesis of gloomy Galia from Goskonsert. We were immediately ushered into the theatre to attend the Raikin company's closed dress rehearsal, just Tim and myself, each flanked by a translator who whispered in our ears. However, it soon emerged that translations were rarely needed because the company had indeed been taught English versions of their lyrics, specifically for this BBC audition. 'Hello, hello', they warbled, 'we hope you enjoy our little show.' Their left-leaning Scottish coach, inevitably named Jock, joined us in the stalls: he was a tiny bundle of a fellow who had emigrated to the Soviet Union as long ago as the 1930s; he had learnt Russian and taught comedy to Russia's student comedians. Raikin's show was adorable, even in pidgin English; we laughed as loudly as we could at the sight gags, the comedy routines and Raikin's audacious quick-change acts, worthy of the English cross-dresser Danny La Rue. At the final curtain the four of us clapped and clapped with genuine enthusiasm – we must have made an incongruous sight in an otherwise empty auditorium. 'Come back tomorrow for the first night', Jock called out as we made our way out of the theatre. 'It will be something else!'

Next day we were given Kuban's standard Intourist VIP tour. A large black limousine was placed at our disposal. Galia sat up front with the inscrutable driver and Irina squeezed in between Tim and myself in the back seat; she chatted amiably all the way to the Black Sea. The obligatory inspection en route of a collective farm did nothing to dampen our spirits. At Sochi we were invited to don trunks and take the plunge into the murky water of the Black Sea, so buoyant that swimming was almost impossible. The return journey was enlivened by a stop at a Russian champagne factory and it was dark when we got back to Krasnodar, very late for Raikin's first-night performance. The brightly lit theatre beckoned. As we hurried across the square the sound of laughter, waves of it, came rolling towards us like Atlantic surf. Ushered in through a side door we found ourselves part of a thousand-strong crowd, the like of which I never saw again until I attended one of Barry Humphries's Dame Edna Everage extravaganzas. Gone were Raikin's inhibitions when trying to sing in English. In came the sketches about Communist Russia, more teasing than satirical, which so endeared him to his public. After an avalanche of curtain calls we joined Raikin's troupe as they walked across the square through a line of applauding admirers to a restaurant where Tim and I found ourselves to be the guests of honour at what proved to be a genuine banquet. What a contrast with the miserable food at Soviet hotels in Moscow and Leningrad! The table was laden with grapes and figs, with watermelons ripe to burst and tasty pomegranates, with all manner of sweetmeats and any number of glasses to savour the good Georgian wines. The endless toasts we drank to Anglo-Soviet friendship were like something out of a feel-good theatre-folk story by Charles Dickens. As we left for our hotel, Irina presented me with a giant watermelon which I was to take home for my family. When I awoke next morning I discovered the ripe fruit had burst in the night, spattering pips all over the overheated hotel bedroom's walls – a gruesome sight which prompted me to check out rather hurriedly.

Tim and I left Krasnodar convinced that Arkady Raikin and his company would make a splendidly esoteric ingredient for the opening night of BBC2. The show was produced at the Television Theatre by Joe McGrath, a zany Scottish director in Light Entertainment who went on to do great things with Peter Sellers and The Goons. That the show didn't work out as well as it should have done may have been due to the depressed mood created by the power failure on the evening the new channel was due to be launched: the opening night had to be postponed by twenty-four hours. A more profound reason was that Raikin's show lived and breathed Russian-ness and the London audience gathered at the old variety theatre on Shepherd's Bush Green was no match for the good people of Krasnodar.

When we returned to Moscow, en route for the UK, I was happy for the genial Tim Holland Bennett to take charge of the tedious contract negotiations at Goskonsert, and it was with a colossal sense of relief that I left the Soviet Union. I managed to wangle a flight home via an overnight stay in Stockholm, where I arrived in time to catch my beloved Elisabeth Söderström in the last act of *La Traviata*; she had arranged for me to be slipped into the director's box, a joyful moment, and bliss compared with the hysteria of the theatre at Krasnodar a few nights earlier.

The most urgent production on my agenda back at Television Centre in October 1963 was the tribute I was preparing for Benjamin Britten's fiftieth birthday on 22 November: only six weeks remained to prepare a ninety-minute programme. When I originally wrote to Britten telling him that BBC Television was planning a birthday salute his first reaction, polite but quite firm, was 'no thanks'. His lack of interest in television was difficult to explain, given his history of composing for features and plays on BBC radio and the regular broadcasting of his compositions and recitals with Peter Pears.

He didn't even have a television set in his home. His letter to me was depressingly negative. 'It sounds rather as if you are preparing my obituary; can't you come back when I am 80?' Luckily, since he died when he was only sixty-three, I pressed more firmly and outlined my plans: the LSO would be in the studio under the exciting young Russian conductor Gennadi Rozhdestvensky to play sections from the *Sinfonia da Requiem* and the Frank Bridge Variations; Ronald Dowd, the craggy Australian tenor from Sadler's Wells, would sing a big scene from *Peter Grimes*; we would have clips featuring Britten's music from pre-war commercials for the Post Office and the evocative *Night Mail* with W.H. Auden's unforgettable poetic commentary. Finally I would spend several days filming in Aldeburgh to update the excellent festival footage John Schlesinger had shot five years earlier for *Monitor*.

I suspect that like T.E. Lawrence, Britten was not averse to backing into the limelight, because he eventually agreed to my proposal, even permitting me to film at his Red House home, though drawing the line at an interview: here again, his dislike of interviews was odd, since he spoke so well. I wonder whether there was a hint of vanity involved, an inferiority complex about his looks, particularly his receding chin? And yet since his childhood he had been happy to be photographed, and once our filming began in Aldeburgh he gave me all the time I needed and unrestricted access to his photograph albums – from which we constructed a telling portrait of a man at ease with himself, with his relationship with Peter Pears and with his place in the Aldeburgh community. He also allowed me to delve into the trunk containing his childhood music manuscripts, a real treasure trove, and for the camera I spread out dozens of those compositions, which up to this day have not been fully explored. The one request he declined point-blank came when I was filming him working on a Schubert song with Pears. 'Would you mind doing the song just once more?' I asked. 'I would so like to get a close-up of your right foot on the pedals.' I had been fascinated by the way Britten made incessant use of the middle *sostenuto* pedal, swivelling his foot to it after almost every chord. 'I'd rather not', he replied, very firmly. (No matter, the foot was clearly visible in the wide-angle I had already filmed.)

In the studio Huw Wheldon hosted *Britten at Fifty* with the right note of gravitas, admiring, enthusiastic, but well short of idolatry and with no suggestion of the obituary Britten had feared, quite the opposite: the composer was seen as an energetic leader in the musical world. Britten and Pears were described as 'friends and collaborators in music and in life for twenty-five years' – this despite the fact that homosexuality was still a criminal offence for which men went to gaol. By then Ben and Peter were friends of the royal family and consequently – one assumes – above the hateful law.

Britten's most significant creative collaborator in his youth was W.H. Auden, but they had fallen out and Auden was astounded when I asked him to participate. 'Does Mr Britten *know* you have invited me?' he asked in disbelief. (He didn't.) But Auden delivered a generous salute (on film, from New York) despite their earlier rupture. For me it was vital to have Auden's involvement: he had been part of my Britten mythology since I first sang their *Hymn to St Cecilia* back in 1943, at Long Dene. Michael Tippett and Hans Keller were in the studio to help define Britten's greatness. Gennadi Rozhdestvensky wished Ben many happy returns – in flawless English. His conducting was brilliant. This was his British television début and he made his mark, providing a passionate accompaniment for Ronald Dowd's heart-wrenching 'What harbour shelters peace?' from *Peter Grimes*. He then launched the orchestra into the Storm Interlude with a ferocity that was not easy to generate in a television studio. For my part I choreographed a camera movement for the end of the storm that had the camera swinging violently left and right over the serried ranks of the orchestra from the timpani at the top down to the violins and Rozhdestvensky on the studio floor: the switchback movement of the crane camera was intended to match the swirl of the storm music.

I decided to round off *Britten at Fifty* with his latest and for some his greatest composition, the *War Requiem*. Decca's sensational LP recording had sold a hundred thousand copies but not a note had been heard on television, eighteen months after the work's première in Coventry Cathedral. I settled on the 'Lacrimosa', in which the poetic Latin description of Mary weeping at the feet of Christ crucified on the cross is interwoven in Britten's masterly conception with *Futility*, the most moving of all Wilfred Owen's war poems, beginning 'Move him into the sun'. I thought I could match the contrast between Latin and English with a similar distinction between paintings and photographs. I knew from their use in our Elgar film that the Imperial War Museum archive had gruesome First World War photographs of soldier corpses in the mud ('Was it for this ...?') but I was stumped as to what visual counterpoint I should offer for the Latin passages. I plucked up my courage and telephoned Britten. I knew him well enough by then to share the problem. I told him I was aware that composers didn't normally write music with specific images in their minds but maybe on this occasion ...? He said I was absolutely right about the composing process in general, but it so happened that in the *War Requiem* there *was* a painting with which he associated his 'Lacrimosa'; it was the so-called *Grünewald Triptych*, painted for the altar at Isenheim near Colmar. We had only black-and-white television but even so the images by Mathias Grünewald (the very same 'Mathis der Maler' celebrated in Hindemith's banned opera) provided the perfect foil for the sombre photographic images of Flanders field. No words were possible at the end of this devastating sequence – the closing credit titles of the programme rolled instead over the sweet music of the Bourrée which I chose from Britten's *Frank Bridge Variations* and nobody said goodnight at the end.

It is a ghastly fact that Britten's fiftieth birthday, November 22nd 1963, was the day when Lee Harvey Oswald murdered President John F. Kennedy in Dallas. I was phoned at home just before seven with the dreadful news of the assassination and summoned to Television Centre's presentation suite. Horror of horrors, a Harry Worth comedy of singular banality was still being transmitted. An emergency schedule eventually replaced the advertised programmes. The distraught presentation boss, Rex Moorfoot, asked what our Britten tribute contained. Heads were shaking despondently as I read out the running order until I mentioned that the closing section was the 'Lacrimosa' from Britten's *War Requiem*. 'Did you say *Requiem*?' There was a collective sigh of relief. 'Your programme stays in the schedule.' Apart from the news, I think it was the only one that did.

I don't believe Britten ever watched the show, even though it was repeated, but he definitely warmed thereafter to the medium of television; that winter, at Fairfield Halls in Croydon, he conducted the Mozart G minor Symphony and his own *Nocturne*, and he and Pears came into the studio to take part in a television version of the popular radio series *Music in Miniature*. (This was another area of music-making I was exploring for the new channel: personally I love hearing and seeing 'room music' on television and do not understand why we cannot be given at least one quartet a week as a modest counterweight to all the cooking programmes.)

But concerning Britten I was proudest of the song recital I directed off the cuff in the spring of 1964; it serves as a pendant to *Britten at Fifty*. The deal Ben and Peter struck with my producer Walter Todds for the recital was that there should be no wearisome camera rehearsal, just a quick sound balance; what's more, the audience, Ben insisted, must consist exclusively of personal friends. Informality was the order of the day. Gone were the white tie and tails and the stilted introductions of conventional television recitals, to be replaced by cardigans and a conversational tone from Peter, who hosted the show as if he were at a party in Jubilee Hall, Aldeburgh, rather than Riverside Two studio

Peter Pears partnered by Benjamin Britten.

in Hammersmith. All the songs were in English: Purcell, Haydn and a clutch of Britten's marvellous folk-song arrangements including *The Plough Boy* (with dazzling piano playing from Britten) and the perfect encore: *Oliver Cromwell.*

> The saddle and bridle they lie on the shelf, Hee-haw, lie on the shelf;
> If you want any more you can sing it yourself;
> Hee-haw, sing it yourself!

It's a chastening thought that only a handful of the dozens of programmes I directed in my youth will ever be seen again. Many still exist but they are buried in the BBC vaults. Licence-fee money paid for them to be made but the licence *payers* have no way to access them. Of all my programmes, only my next big music documentary, entitled *The Golden Ring*, is still in wide circulation and that's mostly because it is on a DVD and serves as a pendant to probably the most significant classical *recording* of the twentieth century, Wagner's *Ring* cycle conducted by Georg Solti with the Vienna Philharmonic and a mostly splendid cast.

A little back history: I was still running *Monitor* when Decca's John Culshaw and Gordon Parry, respectively producer and senior engineer, first came to see me sometime in 1962. They were convinced that their *Ring* project, upon which they had already been working for five years, was of world-shaking importance and deserved to be the subject of a major documentary such as they thought I could make. Gordon Parry coupled his engineering know-how with a single-minded passion for Wagner. John Culshaw had a fine musical ear and was a superb negotiator, whose velvet-toned voice as he pitched the proposal to me concealed a penetrating mind and a will of steel. That much I could perceive immediately, indeed I was deeply impressed by the visionary fervour of the Decca Boys, as Culshaw's team became known. But how to make a programme for television about gramophone recording sessions taking place 750 miles away in Vienna, with troublesome prima donnas, an expensive orchestra and most of the working dialogue in German? Admittedly I had a taste for this type of project: I had seen the brilliant Canadian film about Glenn Gould taping Bach in New York and I had been backstage at the Decca studio when John Schlesinger directed *Hi-Fi-Fo-Fum*. But they were both film documentaries: the crucial new element which my television experience provided was the use of a five-camera outside broadcast unit. I first mixed film and television in our *Workshop* feature about Aaron Copland rehearsing the LSO in *Music for a Great City*. The best way to report on Decca's *Ring* in Vienna, I realised, would be to video-record the recording sessions and take one of our own BBC film units to fill in the location backgrounds, among them the airport for VIP greetings and swanky hotels for the interviews with Solti and his singers. But if I were successfully to turn their dream into reality I needed to sign up Austrian Television since the cost of hiring a freelance television unit would be prohibitive.

Fortunately I had Viennese credentials. I had been to the city of *The Third Man* twice in the late 1950s and loved the young people I met. In 1957, as I have already recorded, I attended a Jeunesses Musicales congress as Robert Mayer's personal representative; two years later I returned as manager of the British Students Orchestra (courtesy once more of Robert Mayer) and made friends with many young musicians, among them Wilfried Scheib, the future head of television music for Austrian Television (ORF). It was to Wilfried that I now turned for help for the *Ring* programme. I admired his enthusiasm and his positive approach, and he proved to be just the collaborator I needed: after sitting in on a Solti session he was as excited by the Decca project as I was and came up trumps with the offer of a camera crew which would be ORF's contribution to the production in return for transmission rights to the German-speaking countries. The BBC side of the deal was to take care of the talent and produce a version for ORF with German commentary. I thought

I was home and dry until Culshaw introduced me to Decca's *éminence grise*, Maurice Rosengarten. Said to be one of the original Gnomes of Zurich, Uncle Maurice's knowledge of money matters was matched by a love of music and musicians. Ostensibly Decca was run by the greatly respected Edward Lewis in London, but important decisions concerning classical music were channelled through this wily Swiss financier, who seemed to know everybody worth knowing in the music world and undoubtedly ruled the operatic roost at Decca. Culshaw, who was his star producer, went in awe of him, I guess because he was bankrolling the *Ring* project. Rosengarten had been Georg Solti's earliest supporter, initiating Solti's famous Decca contract which ran unbroken for half a century from 1946. But Maurice could not see the point of permitting a television documentary. The invasion of cameras was sure to disrupt the sessions and he certainly would not approve of letting the production go ahead without a substantial extra payment to the singers and orchestra, not to mention an equally substantial facility fee to Decca. But paying fees of any kind was not part of my plan. Culshaw joined me in explaining to Rosengarten the publicity value of a movie-length documentary. He was not impressed with our arguments. After a couple of meetings which got us nowhere, I told him I was negotiating with a rival company, EMI, to do something similar in Rome. He didn't believe me and called my bluff. 'Go ahead', he said, convinced I would fail. Miraculously, as it seems to me now, I managed to persuade David Bicknell, the amiable international artists boss at EMI, to let us loose on one of their prestige recordings of the year, *Il Trovatore*, which was shortly to be taped in Rome with Thomas Schippers conducting and no less a star than Franco Corelli in the title role. I scrounged the resources at short notice from Italian Television (RAI) and assigned the unflappable Francis Coleman to produce a BBC film about those sessions. The ensuing documentary, called *Modern Troubadours*, may not have been a classic but how I long to see it again: there is no sign of it in the BBC Archive. All I remember now is the gruff camaraderie of EMI's veteran record producer Victor Olof and how exceedingly hot it was in Rome that summer. But Maurice Rosengarten was impressed. Anything EMI could do, Decca must do better. The deal twixt Decca and the BBC was duly struck, and what a deal! We did not pay individual fees to the singers. Nor did we pay the Vienna Philharmonic, though we taped their sessions every day for a week. Those were innocent times indeed.

John Culshaw's book *Ring Resounding* (1967) is a lively and reliable account of Decca's entire recording of *Götterdämmerung*, but there are many differences between his book and my television film, highlights of which included the thrilling male-voice choral set piece in Act 2 when Hagen summons the vassals with his hunting horns; the Vengeance Trio at the end of that act; and from the final act the Death of Siegfried, the Funeral March and the Immolation Scene. I think above all of Georg Solti, a glamorous figure from the moment of his arrival at Schwechat airport with the film star Maria Schell on his arm – no matter that they had met for the first time on the plane: the celebrity image was perfect. But as soon as Solti gets into the limousine to

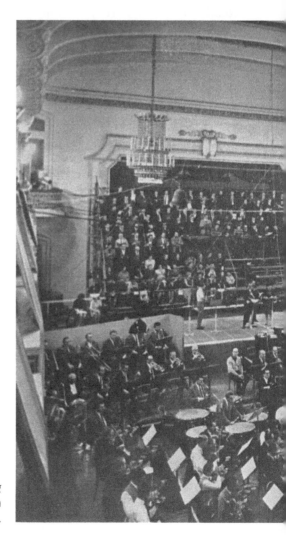

Recording *Götterdämmerung* in the Sofiensaal ballroom with Solti conducting.

be driven into Vienna he is talking work details with Culshaw, asking about retakes and a fluff in the horns from a session held months earlier. Next day on the podium Solti is astonishingly balletic, slim, dynamic, sexy: the image is of coiled energy ready to spring on the players like a panther. If he wants a more accurately accentuated rhythm he shouts it out demoniacally: 'ta-TA-ti-ta-TAA'. And in the electric silence between the stabbing bass notes that precede the Funeral March, Solti does not lose his cool when the clunking sound of a camera changing lenses breaks the mood. Those bars are a moment

of high drama and the camera noise ruins the take. Rashly I had promised there would be no noise from cameras – no buzz of lights being switched off or on, no hiss of cables slinking across the floor. But in the heat of the moment leading up to Siegfried's Death March I glimpsed Solti's transfigured face on the monitor screens and over the talkback I shouted for a close-up. The ORF cameras were old models with no zoom lens; to get a close-up the cameraman has to swing a 'turret' in which three different lenses are installed. My command for a close-up was expressed so imperiously that one hapless cameraman was galvanised into an instinctive but noisy lens change – an action that could be disastrous for relations between Decca and the BBC but thanks to Solti's diplomacy only a few seconds are lost. He puts down his baton. 'Unmusikalischer Kameramann' he says with a smile: 'unmusical cameraman'! Relieved laughter from the orchestra ensues and Culshaw swiftly announces another take.

Solti may have been the star but the singers come over equally well in *The Golden Ring*. The Brünnhilde, Birgit Nilsson, a major diva, was charming to us; she wore a very silly hat when we taped her at a piano rehearsal but I forgave her because on microphone she was the total professional, stepping back and forth for aural close-ups and switching from mic to mic as directed to achieve the different sound perspectives imagined in John Culshaw's stereophonic production script. Listening to the playbacks Nilsson would often complain to Solti that the orchestra was too loud, but in truth her steely soprano rode proudly over the grandest *fortissimo* the players could muster. At a drinks party in the cosy apartment which the Decca engineers had fitted out for themselves, she can be glimpsed through the party's cigarette smoke demanding royalties on the high Cs she had been singing. This 'in' joke referred to the famous session during Furtwängler's 1952 recording of *Tristan und Isolde* when Elisabeth Schwarzkopf (wife of the producer Walter Legge) obligingly sang the two top Cs in Act 2 for Kirsten Flagstad, with the great Wagnerian soprano's agreement. The circumstances are described in John Culshaw's *Ring Resounding*.

At the same party the great Dietrich Fischer-Dieskau can be seen happily smoking away on camera. (Regretfully I fear I had a cigarette between my fingers when I interviewed Culshaw at his recording desk.) Fischer-Dieskau had never sung Gunther on stage so it was inspired casting to give him the role; interviewing him I observed that he brought to the part a great sense of dignity. 'Of course,' he replied. 'Gunther is a king.' In his hands (and he was the greatest baritone of the age) Gunther the weak puppet took on a tragic

End of the day. Left to right: Gordon Parry, Roland Berger, Birgit Nilsson, Gottlob Frick, Dietrich Fischer-Dieskau, John Culshaw, Claire Watson, Dieter Warneck (F-D's assistant) and myself in the Decca apartment.

nobility worthy of Macbeth. The bass Gottlob Frick as Hagen was moody malevolence personified and his trio with Gunther and Brünnhilde was sensational, literally spine-tingling; their blood-curdling oath of revenge made the entire television project seem worthwhile in a single sequence. I was riveted to my director's chair and for minutes on end could not bring myself to vary the wide-angle three-shot of this transfigured, bloodthirsty trio, Fischer-Dieskau, Frick and Nilsson.

Decca's Siegfried, Wolfgang Windgassen, was a favourite of Solti's – he had sung Florestan in Solti's very first German opera production, in Stuttgart in the winter of 1946. Truth to tell, Windgassen was on the mature side to sing Wagner's young hero but everybody loved him and we had a film camera on hand to see him wave goodbye to the Decca Boys when he caught the night train out of Vienna a few hours after recording Siegfried's deathbed farewell; I believe it was his only studio recording of the role of Siegfried.

John Culshaw had assembled a close-knit team, not unlike the group of directors who were working with me at the BBC. None was afraid to get his hands dirty. The engineer Jimmy Lock, who was married and lived full-time in Vienna, was happy for me to film him and Gordon setting up the sophisticated stereo equipment using old-fashioned screwdrivers – 'hot to cold, Jimmy; red to red'. Neither Christopher Raeburn nor Erik Smith, John's producer colleagues, were Wagner buffs but it was all hands on the Decca deck for a massive project such as the *Ring* cycle. Christopher's first love was Mozart; he had lived in Vienna for several years researching *The Marriage of Figaro* and was the best-informed authority on operatic voices that I ever met, full of good advice and great stories. Pavarotti once observed that Christopher was a wise old man even when he was very young. Erik Smith was even younger, in fact he was exactly my age, born on the very same day in the same year, and for the rest of our lives we would celebrate our birthdays together, most notably our forty-sixth, when our mutual friend Leonard Bernstein was our guest of honour at a supper in the Garrick Club. Bernstein produced a two-part canon he had composed specially for the occasion. It received a lusty première rendition.

Erik and I played duets whenever we met. Indeed, one of the landmarks of my later life was the day he invited me to record the K19 duet sonata; it was to be the final sonata on an LP Erik was making of everything the boy Mozart wrote for keyboard while he was living in London. The two-manual harpsichord is not my instrument and more than once at our Kingsway Hall session we had to swap seats so that Erik could deal with the more demanding scales and arpeggios in the *secondo* part. There were seventy-two 'takes' in

A birthday round by Leonard Bernstein dedicated to two of his producer friends: Erik Smith of Decca and Humphrey Burton of the BBC.

The recording Erik Smith invited me to make on his harpsichord.

all, a blush-making total, many of them retakes to cover fluffs of mine. When I apologised to the recording producer he brushed my words aside: 'Don't worry; Rafael Puyana gives us much more trouble!' (Puyana was the top harpsichord player of the day.)

One of Erik's tasks for *Götterdämmerung* was to keep the weirdest log I ever saw: he ticked off on a big noticeboard all the screams that needed to be separately recorded in the course of the opera. Who screams at whom in the Ring, and when, would make a good quiz question. Erik also helped me follow the orchestral score when I was directing the cameras during the sessions. I was seriously ill-prepared: ideally one should know the score so well that one could step up to the rostrum and conduct it. One day while taping the Funeral March I had the embarrassment of cutting to the cymbals expecting a clash and seeing instead the percussionist busily counting the bars until his next entry. The duff shot is still there for all to see – in the early days of videotape there was no way of concealing one's mistakes. Truth to tell, I had jumped into this mammoth production without too much thought about how it could be achieved. Luckily I took John Drummond with me. He directed the film camera when I was tied up with the video; he was somebody to bounce structural ideas off and on, day and night; he was utterly charming with the stars; and he never stopped talking. I managed to capture him on film when he was debating with Jack Law, Decca's tape engineer, about which was the longest tram line in Europe. Jack opted for the link from Vienna to Wiener Neustadt; John countered with Aix to Marseille, which he claimed ran for twenty-six kilometres, though he added the bewildering information that it did not always *behave* like a tram.

Georg Solti and John
Culshaw – devoted
Wagnerians who
were deadly serious
behind the laughter.

Drummond played a vital role when we were back in London. I gave him the task of selecting the most effective sequences from the many hours of tape we had amassed over the sessions. Assembling that final version was a labour of love. To tighten the action, I still needed to make the occasional cut in the videotape, an excruciatingly slow process since every cut had to be carried out with a microscope, a razor blade and a superior brand of Sellotape. The programme's interlocking film sequences could be separately polished in the cutting room; it was videotape which was desperately unwieldy and I had no way of creating a rough cut with this mixed-media production: the transitions and commentary links all had to be rehearsed in my mind before we ran film and video through separate channels in the production gallery, adding pre-recorded commentary words and title captions as we went along. If ever I broke new ground it was with this production.

Of course it was not the technical side which caught the public's attention: it was the Wagner. My favourite revelation was the sight of John Culshaw dictating to Georg Solti the tempo to adopt for Siegfried's Funeral March. Our cameras eavesdropped on their conversation during a *Zigaretten-Pause*. Solti is hankering for something a little faster and says he will kill Culshaw if the Funeral March is too slow: Culshaw is adamant, reminding his conductor of a 2,000-schilling wager they have taken together. They laugh but the subject is deadly serious.

Next day came the taping of the Immolation Scene and with it one of the practical jokes for which the Decca team was justly famous in the record

198

business. In the final scene of the drama Brünnhilde commands that a funeral pyre for her slain husband Siegfried be built on the shore of the Rhine. Then she calls for her horse Grane and rides into the flames to be reunited with her hero. It's a grand concept that still defies even the most imaginative opera director. For starters, bringing a horse on stage is always a perilous business. Wagner employed one for the world première but since 1876 the challenge has usually been flunked: the horse remains offstage. Culshaw and his team thought otherwise. They arranged for a real horse to be delivered to the stage door. While the rehearsal continues upstairs under the flailing baton of Maestro Solti, with Birgit Nilsson in full flood and the orchestra in hot pursuit, our film camera observes a handsome steed being persuaded up the broad staircase of the Sofiensaal then led through the corridors to graze placidly in the empty Blue Ballroom. A surrealist vision: a thoroughbred racehorse quietly pacing the parquet floor under sparkling chandeliers. Exactly on cue – the point when Brünnhilde addresses her faithful Grane, 'Do you know, my

Birgit Nilsson singing Brünnhilde is presented with a real life 'Grane'.

199

friend, where I am leading you?' – the docile horse, trained for film work, is led on to the stage and shepherded around Birgit Nilsson, who stops singing, overcome by mirth. The orchestra grinds to a halt, even Solti shares the joke – for a few seconds. Then he tries to get back to work – deadlines are looming and the performance of the epic's final scene resumes.

The powerful, surging music after Brünnhilde has ridden into the flames was the passage I chose for the programme commentary's peroration. Solti is the obvious hero but my narration is equally concerned with the backroom boys. The closing montage is set to the last minute of the score. Slow pans across mixing desks, beautifully lit close-ups of microphones, tape recorders rotating, score pages being turned. Over it all presides a Sarastro-like John Culshaw at the control desk, flanked by his Armed Men Gordon Parry and

High Priests of Flawlessness. Left to right: James Lock,
John Culshaw, Gordon Parry at their recording desk.

THE GOLDEN RING
In this special double-length edition
of Workshop, film and television
cameras take you behind the scenes in
Vienna during the recording sessions
for Wagner's Götterdämmerung,
described by Alec Robertson as
'the greatest achievement in the
history of the gramophone'.
The singers:
Brünnhilde .... Birgit Nilsson
Siegfried .... Wolfgang Windgassen
Hagen ....Gottlob Frick
Gunther ....Dietrich Fischer-Dieskau
Gutrune....................... Claire Watson
The Vienna State Opera Chorus,
Chorus Master, Wilhelm Pitz
The Vienna Philharmonic Orchestra
The conductor, Georg Solti
The record producer, John Culshaw
Film cameraman, Peter Sargent
Film sound, Norman Allen
Film editor, Inman Hunter
Associate producers, John Drummond
and Walter Klapper
Narrated and produced by Humphrey
Burton
A BBC music documentary made as
a co-production with the Austrian
Television Service
Facilities by courtesy of the Decca
Record Company Ltd.

Radio Times billing for
The Golden Ring.

James Lock. My final words of commentary salute in reverent tones: 'the high priests of flawlessness, men who love Wagner, men who love music; men who are not afraid to harness machines to their endless search for perfection; men and machines coming to the end of an epic chapter in their quest for *The Golden Ring*.'

The orchestra has the last word, so to speak. Conducted, almost caressed, by a transfixed Georg Solti, the first violins play the redemption theme and in order to bring their instruments a significant degree closer to the microphones the players suddenly all stand like soloists. Their sound becomes stronger, sweeter. As the music ends, the image of Solti and his players dissolves (in my edit) to a recording deck, the tape still rolling on its spool; when it stops, the camera slowly pans in silence from the turntable to the vocal score where the pages are open on a portrait of Richard Wagner.

It was the end of a long programme. It was also a turning point in my life; *The Golden Ring* was still being edited when, on March 1st 1965, my name was announced as the head of a newly formed department at the BBC. Nobody had mentioned the plan to me in advance but I was now Head of BBC Television's Music and Arts Programmes Department. Ten years had elapsed since I first reported to Lime Grove reception on my way to join the *Monitor* team.

CHAPTER 11

HEAD OF MUSIC AND ARTS (HMAP Tel)

The newly announced Head of the BBC's Music and Arts Programmes
Department – telephone in hand, looking frightfully dynamic.

MARCH 1ST 1965. For the last time I was being promoted in the slipstream of
Huw Wheldon. He was now Controller of Programmes, a top dog at Television
Centre, sharing the bosses' kennel with Kenneth Adam. Adam was a very good
journalist, a broadcasting all-rounder, and close to obligatory retirement.
I was now what my children were later to mock me for being: an 'arts supremo',
running a department. A brand-new department at that, as Huw might have
said. I attended no appointments board for this promotion and was offered no

prior consultation about staff or spheres of influence. I should have said 'hang on a moment' but I didn't: I was highly chuffed. My elevation to television's peerage (that's what it felt like) was a by-product of the battle for power being waged at the top of BBC Television. In 1964, when Stuart Hood (brilliant brain but arguably short on people skills) suddenly resigned as Controller of Programmes – he was a rum choice in the first place – Donald Baverstock had been given the top job. As a departmental head, Huw Wheldon reported to him, not an easy situation for either Welshman. Now Huw was replacing him. Mike Peacock had been promoted to run BBC1, the senior service, even though he was not thought to have done all that well at BBC2. The loser in the shuffle was, of course, Baverstock, who was offered the compensation of BBC2, which not surprisingly he refused; he left in a huff, to be joined by his number two, Alasdair Milne. Alasdair was soon back in the BBC's higher echelons but Donald never returned to the top table. Who was to run BBC2? During the uneasy interregnum I mentioned to Huw the conversation I had had with David Attenborough a few weeks earlier while he was working for me as a freelance director (I hired him to make a documentary about the LSO's 1963 tour of Japan; he writes entertainingly about the film, *Orchestra to the Orient*, in his autobiography). David told me how much he was enjoying his freedom since resigning from his producer's job at the BBC. The only thing that would bring him back to the Corporation, he added, would be the opportunity to work closely with Huw. So I was not surprised when a few days later, to everybody else's astonishment, David was appointed controller of BBC2.

My own appointment came out of the blue, too. At the age of thirty-three I think I was the BBC's youngest departmental head and I was definitely rather wet behind the ears. I was given no choice as to who would be in this double department of Music and Arts. Some were former music department directors such as Patricia Foy, the redheaded Irish director currently in charge of *Music for You*, and Margaret Dale, a former dancer, who was bringing the Royal Ballet into the studio with great success. Others were members of the *Monitor* team and other arts producers from Huw's documentary department, among them Melvyn Bragg and John Read, son of the great art historian Herbert Read. Richard Cawston, another of Huw's top producers, was named head of a new pure film documentary department. Confusion was to reign for many years in this field since another non-fiction empire soon grew up around Aubrey Singer, a swashbuckling producer from Outside Broadcasts whose bailiwick was eventually entitled the Features Group; it comprised general features (documentaries by another name) as well as science features and for a time, after 1967, arts features, too – but that's a little too far ahead of my story.

Stephen Hearst was made my deputy (AHMA Tel). Like Dick Cawston, Stephen was a gifted film-maker who had been with the Talks Department since the mid-1950s. He was best known at the time for films about ancient Greece and Rome presented by two venerated establishment figures, Mortimer Wheeler and Compton Mackenzie. Personally I preferred Stephen's more vivid documentary *European Centre Forward* about Gerry Hitchens, the English footballer who played for Internazionale Milano; not for nothing had Stephen's dentist father been an Arsenal supporter in 1930s Vienna. Like me, Stephen had learnt a great deal from Huw but I doubt whether he was any happier than I was at the prospect of supervising other people's work rather than making his own programmes. He settled down loyally, however, and proved to be an admirably supportive colleague. He was a warm-hearted older and wiser man of broad European culture who later served the BBC well as Controller of Radio 3. In Music and Arts he encouraged bold experiment such as Christopher Burstall's *The First Freedom*, a studio reconstruction of the trial of the Soviet dissidents Daniel and Sinyavsky. Stephen also supported what I was trying to do with the *Workshop* music programmes we had been pioneering on BBC2. I received less understanding in that field from Desmond Osland, the music administrator I had inherited two years previously from Lionel Salter. Desmond made no secret of the fact that he would have preferred television music programmes to have stayed as they were in 1960. But at least his personal contact with Carlo Maria Giulini led to a handsome Mozart symphony cycle.

Stephen Hearst, a loyal colleague.

One of the new job's downsides was inheriting staff I didn't know what to do with. Christian Simpson was such a one: he was a legend among technicians because of his clever experiments with visual effects such as inlay, by which, through the wizardry of electronics, one image could be merged with another so that a fairy ballerina could appear to dance in the palm of a man's hand. But in my view Simpson's ambition to enlarge television's poetic vocabulary was not supported by a matching supply of good taste. He directed a competent edition of *Workshop* but my kind of exploratory programme was just not his game. Another 1950s survivor I inherited, Hal Burton, was no relation: he had been a prolific producer and director of television plays for many years. A charming gentleman of the old school, it was said that Hal had been a lover of the celebrated photographer Cecil Beaton; Beaton's oil portrait of Hal hangs in the Whitworth Gallery, Manchester to this day. Hal knew all the leading thespians of the 1940s and '50s, and he produced for Music and Arts a magnificent television series about the theatrical stars of my youth, among them John Gielgud, Laurence Olivier, Ralph Richardson and Edith Evans. *Great Acting* was the title of the book he spun out of the interviews and what his BBC2 programmes delivered in spades.

Hal Burton by Cecil Beaton. Our pay packets were easily confused.

One day I opened Hal Burton's pay packet in error – we were both H. Burton and the brown envelopes were identical. Opening it, I was a touch mortified to discover that he was earning more than I did as head of his department. To put this into perspective: Hal's salary was maybe £3,200 per annum and mine £3,000. When I grumbled about this to Huw Wheldon he rightly pointed out the length of Hal's service, not to mention his production track record. But I never did discover why he had been assigned to Music and Arts rather than Drama. Perhaps it was simply because he knew Cecil Beaton. Anyway, to be head of a BBC department employing more than a hundred men and women was, I discovered, emphatically not a bed of roses – indeed, there were times when I felt swamped by bureaucracy. Duty of care became a priority. I had to write annual reports and carry out annual interviews with dozens of senior producer colleagues, most of whom were older than I was; whether I liked it or not, I was turning into a father figure.

In those days the departmental head was also the commissioning editor. I had to assess programme proposals from colleagues and from the outside world. I also had to nurture new directors and smooth over professional jealousies. Every Wednesday at 10 a.m. I attended the senior staff meeting in the basement at Television Centre. Music and Arts was based in the Centre's newly commissioned East Tower, a soulless edifice in architectural terms and not a patch on the Centre itself. Programme Review, as the staff meeting was called, was a forum notorious for its inter-departmental sniping. As the chairman went through the *Radio Times* day by day, we were encouraged to say what we thought about other people's shows as well as our own; I would then report back to my producer colleagues the meeting's reactions, even if they were disparaging (as they often were). It was not such a battleground as the Talks Department meetings at Lime Grove had been earlier in the 1950s but no holds were barred or punches pulled, and sadly very few senior figures seemed to enjoy our Music and Arts pioneering productions. It was disappointing when such fascinating figures as Pierre Boulez, seen in *Workshop* discussing his own extremely contemporary music, were casually dismissed from serious discussion.

Forward planning was another preoccupation. I spent hours closeted with my 'organisers', as planning administrators were called, preparing budgets and estimates of the studio and film resources that future shows would need. I also developed a modicum of skill at the impromptu pitching of extra programmes to the planners of the schedule whenever I detected a vacant slot. There were no computers then; the advance schedule was chinagraphed on to a shiny wall

The Bartók film. Peter Brett and Rosalind Watkins as Bluebeard and Judith, with New Zealand House as Bluebeard's Castle.

chart. I made it my business to get on well with the forward planners since there were always a few 'one-off' programmes on my shelf which needed an unassigned transmission slot.

I fear I make the new job sound boring but of course there were many compensations. Within a few weeks of my promotion the annual British Academy of Film and Television Arts (BAFTA) awards saw me named winner of the Desmond Davis trophy, then as now the top prize of the year for innovative programme-making. I had no idea I would be receiving this award until I arrived at the Mayfair Hotel where the black-tie dinner was held. I couldn't believe it and neither could Tim Hewat, the maverick Australian producer of Granada's groundbreaking *World in Action*, then in its second year; on the way back to my table from collecting my bronze BAFTA, Mr Hewat stuck out a leg and tripped me, muttering as I stumbled past him: 'Well done, mate, but the wrong fella got it.' It was indeed an unexpected honour in that fiercely competitive world, but it served to measure the impact our new-style music programmes had made on the television landscape, particularly since the coming of BBC2.

Not everything about my life had changed: Ken Russell was still very much part of it. His first cinema feature, *French Dressing*, had been a box office flop, described by one reviewer as more Benny Hill than Buster Keaton, and Ken had returned to work for Music and Arts; his mid-1960s films for us included a biography of Béla Bartók which employed some spooky nature footage to illustrate the Third Piano Concerto's haunting 'night music' section. For Bartók's *Bluebeard's Castle* Ken used as background the modern landscape of New Zealand House, then the highest 'skyscraper' in central London.

The Debussy Film from 1965 was a much more ambitious Russell project. Ken teamed up with Melvyn Bragg to write the script; they used the convention of a film about the making of a film to create a lurid version of Debussy's life, with Oliver Reed playing the oversexed composer and Vladek Sheybal doubling the role of the film's slimy director with that of Debussy's associate, the avant-garde poet Pierre Louÿs. According to Ken, reminiscing many years

The Debussy Film starring Oliver Reed with Annette Robertson. The composer's family disapproved of the film and effectively prevented its overseas distribution.

later, Huw Wheldon objected to a lesbian scene included in the Debussy rough cut on the grounds that his mother-in-law, Mrs Stroud, would not understand what was going on. Huw was said to have demanded the offending scene's excision but I confess I never quite believed Ken's colourful account and the lesbian moment in the transmitted film was certainly quite raunchy for its time. The critic Peter Black, who had been rather hard on our Elgar film three years earlier, wrote that Russell's ideas had been 'carried out with superb boldness and certainty of technique … [they] worked marvellously in terms of pictures and music'. *The Debussy Film* was quickly repeated in the summer and was the obvious choice to represent the BBC that September in the music category of the prestigious Italia Prize. Then we ran into a brick wall. Responding to complaints from the composer's family, and from the Debussy expert Edward Lockspeiser, whom Ken had hired and then dropped, the publisher of Debussy's music refused to give the copyright clearance which was needed for foreign sales (but not for UK television), thus preventing the film from being seen anywhere else in the world. Prohibitive lawyers' letters were received. Ken's prizes and the substantial critical acclaim with which his work had previously been assessed were invoked, all in vain. Finally I went to Paris to plead personally with a member of Debussy's family, his niece. She was perfectly polite, as upper-crust French ladies usually are, but icy: Ken's film was not just a disservice to her uncle's memory, she declared, it was a gross misrepresentation of the facts and must be suppressed *tout de suite*. I mustered my best French (which a decade previously had been pretty fluent), but the lady was not for turning and *The Debussy Film* was not submitted for the Italia Prize or screened anywhere else for many decades. The same fate later befell Ken's controversial comic-strip biopic about Richard Strauss, *The Dance of the Seven Veils*. John Culshaw, my successor at the BBC, had to deal with that hot potato – which finished off Ken's BBC career for decades.

Following Debussy in the Russell *oeuvre* came a sympathetic portrait of Isadora Duncan, *The Biggest Dancer in the World*, to give the film its not very gracious full title. I loved this film for its zany humour and for its apocalyptic final vision of Isadora dancing down a Surrey hillside with five hundred schoolchildren in Greek tunics streaming out behind her to the music of Beethoven's 'Ode to Joy'. And I also loved it because my son Matthew, then three, had a cameo role in it: we see him having a dancing lesson with Isadora and later setting off in the doomed 1913 Rolls Royce (Isadora's lover Paris Singer was a millionaire), which, parking brake inadvertently left off, rolled

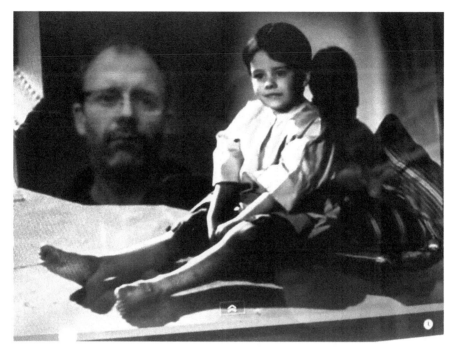

Fifty years later, Matthew peeps in on his former self.

gently down an embankment into the River Seine, drowning its precious occupants, Isadora's two children and the hapless chauffeur.

Back in *Monitor* days I had shown how music competitions provided good programme material. After conductors and tenors we turned now to pianists. I spent several weeks persuading Fanny Waterman, the celebrated Leeds-based teacher, and her chief ally, the pianist Marion Harewood, that the presence of cameras and lights would not affect the young performers in their international piano competition. The winner of the first event three years earlier, Michael Roll, had caused a stir, but patriotic delight was tempered by the news that he was actually one of Mrs Waterman's pupils. So she was keen to get television coverage in order to re-establish Leeds's credibility. I was impressed by the high calibre of the judges she was bringing to Yorkshire: William Glock was to preside – he had been a pupil of Schnabel's and played Mozart beautifully – and a phalanx of famous pianists would back him up, plus Hans Keller to add a dash of musical angostura. The fact that local people provided hospitality for the competitors was another point in its favour: there was surely the basis here, I thought, for an interesting documentary. But who was to direct it since I couldn't be out of the office for weeks on end? John Drummond was my obvious choice: he loved the piano, played it well himself and counted two superb soloists, Tamás Vásáry and Julius Katchen, among his personal friends. Moreover (as he never sought to hide), he spoke several European languages fluently – just the ticket for a film about an international event. We decided to videotape the finals in the magnificent Leeds Town Hall and take a film camera to cover the previous ten days of preliminary rounds at the university. John had worked with me on *The Golden Ring* so he knew what could be achieved with a mixed-media production. He filmed some lively informal conversations with the youngsters as well as getting a backstage tip-off about a scandal when Hans Keller, who loved to provoke, revealed publicly that the jury was hopelessly split between support for the Soviet competitor Viktoria Postnikova (later the wife of Gennadi Rozhdestvensky) and the Spaniard who eventually won, Rafael Orozco. The final round was effectively a competition between the Brahms D minor Concerto and Tchaikovsky's in B flat minor, with Orozco's Brahms winning by a short head.

I was never more impressed with John Drummond than during the editing of his Leeds film; his mother, whom he greatly loved, had fallen gravely ill and in fact did not live to see her son's best work on the screen. John divided his time between her bedside and his cutting room. We did what we could to press on without him but he was adamant on two counts: the transmission must not be postponed and he must personally see it through. The programme, which he narrated himself, made a hugely enjoyable hour and won the best director prize the following year at a competition in Prague. It blazed a trail for the BBC's own prestige-laden television competitions, *Young Musician of the Year* and *Cardiff Singer of the World*.

With hindsight I should have considered Drummond when the editorship of *Monitor* came up for discussion. If we are to trust John's own waspish account, Huw Wheldon could not be counted as a strong Drummond supporter. I don't recall Huw ever speaking out against him but it's true we spent many hours looking for somebody outside the White City bubble to revitalise *Monitor*, which was undoubtedly our arts flagship. To that end Huw and I took the young director John Boorman out to dinner at the Hilton; in those days Boorman was based in BBC Bristol and was making what I realise now were autobiographical drama documentaries to which I happily gave a network screening because they were so compelling. He was reluctant to move to London because he was off to Hollywood: he and Lee Marvin triumphed soon after with *Point Blank* and Boorman was lost to television's central path.

I also tiptoed gingerly round the subject of the *Monitor* editorship with the cartoonist Mark Boxer, an exact contemporary of mine at Cambridge. He was making waves in Fleet Street, as he had done on Cambridge's *Granta* magazine, but I felt he was too much of a dilettante. Boxer created a cartoon strip devoted to the String-Alongs of NW1 and it was to a real-life Gloucester Crescent resident, Jonathan Miller, that we finally gave the *Monitor* editorship. I had been aware of Jonathan ever since his Footlights appearances a decade previously in Cambridge. Now he was a celebrity in both London and New York thanks to his satirical show *Beyond the Fringe*, but his appointment as *Monitor*'s editor and presenter was a gamble since he was a television innocent who had never in his life directed a camera or headed up a production team. But Jonathan was a miraculous polymath; he could do anything. If one thinks of his *Monitor* successes such as the audacious Manhattan warehouse interview between Andy Warhol and Susan Sontag ('the egg-head's delight') or the revealing feature he built around Peter Brook directing Peter Weiss's *Marat/Sade* at the RSC, the gamble certainly paid off: these would be jewels in any arts editor's crown. Everybody at Lime Grove loved Jonathan: only Spike Milligan could reduce a studio or a cutting room to fits of laughter quicker or more convulsively than Jonathan. But the sad fact was that the new *Monitor* fell out of favour with the bulk of the viewers. *Monitor*'s ratings dropped to a depressing level. So did appreciation indices. We knew something had to be done.

Perhaps this was part of a general malaise. In-house directors, members of BBC staff, were tenured like university teachers. In theory they could be instructed as to what work they should do, but in practice the liveliest people were demanding the right (even though they didn't all have the talent) to emulate Ken Russell and make 'full-length' documentaries instead of the short film essays and studio interviews that had been the bread and butter of the television arts magazines. The parallel show on ITV (produced by Thames Television) was undergoing a similar upheaval. *Tempo* had been founded in 1961 by Ken Tynan and Lord Harewood (both only part-time television people) in direct opposition to *Monitor* and in 1965, the year when I was wrestling with the question of where *Monitor* should go next, the bosses of the commercial TV company ABC took a more radical step than I did by appointing an innovative programme-maker, Mike Hodges, who went on to direct the film *Get Carter*, as *Tempo*'s editor. His single-subject shows were only half an hour long and the strand disappeared after only two years when ITV was reorganised, but Hodges and his team did the sort of exciting things that Jonathan Miller had been exploring; the *Tempo* interviews with such luminaries as Harold Pinter and Jacques Tati are valuable documents of those times.

For a time I tried to have my cake and eat it: I tinkered with the idea of creating two complementary strands: *Monitor1* on BBC1 would be devoted to single-subject documentaries, and a new arts slot on BBC2 would be called *Monitor2* and would be more experimental. In the end, after much discussion with Huw and Stephen Hearst, we took a different route, concluding that longer single-subject documentaries were more often what the audience preferred to a miscellany and certainly what directors wanted to make. And so *Monitor*, our flagship, was dropped. Huw was not entirely sorry to see it go: the programme was primarily his creation, after all, and has remained so to this day in the consciousness of most older viewers. But *Panorama* is still going strong, nearly seventy years after its inception: maybe the BBC should have done without *Omnibus* and *Imagine* and kept faith with the title and expectation of *Monitor*.

BBC2 did well by the arts in the 1960s. You have to remember that the new network was far from being a national service; the first transmitters reached less than a quarter of the country and required the purchase of a new 625-line receiver. Meanwhile, on BBC1 the arts remained on the edge of the schedule, relegated to late-evening viewing. *Sunday Night*, the replacement for *Monitor*, was described in *Radio Times* as an arts feature strand. Despite the limp title, it flourished. Jonathan Miller was an early contributor: from the *Monitor* editorship he switched effortlessly (or so it seemed) to making films and almost overnight became a director of real quality, creating a charming filmed version of Plato's *Symposium* which he called *The Drinking Party*. What little I know of philosophy I gleaned from this film, shot outdoors between summer showers at Stowe school. Leo McKern played a grouchy classics master doubling as Socrates, surrounded by pupil acolytes of the quality of Alan Bennett, Michael Gough and John Fortune.

The programmes created for *Sunday Night* are almost all forgotten now, languishing in black-and-white archives when they could be screened regularly as part of our television heritage. Ken Russell delivered a witty portrait of Georges Delerue called *Don't Shoot the Composer*. In *Radio Times* the film was labelled 'highly personal', which was code for controversial if not outrageous – as was indeed the case in Ken's slanderous portrait of Richard Strauss a few years later – but there was no need for apology where Delerue was concerned: he had become everybody's favourite film composer since his score for *Jules et Jim* a couple of years earlier and went on to write the music for Ken's best feature film, *Women in Love*. On a loftier plane, the Finnish theatre director Caspar Wrede made a wonderfully evocative film about the young Jean Sibelius. Meanwhile, Stephen Hearst was buying in French and German art films. But equally important, he gave young programme-makers their first experience in the fifty-minute format. We recruited new directors. Peter Montagnon came in from BBC Schools. His first *Sunday Night* was *The Picasso Enigma*, scripted by John Berger. It's in black and white but I would love to see it again. His second show, just a few weeks later, was called *How to Stop Worrying and Love the Theatre*. Outreach was already a buzzword in the arts world and Peter's film reported on the RSC's efforts to attract a new audience in Paddington. The future head of arts on Channel 4, Michael Kustow, directed the play excerpts. Christopher Burstall had worked with Stephen Hearst at Lime Grove on the first regular programme about literature, *Bookmark*; he launched his Music and Arts career with *Poet of Disenchantment*, featuring W.H. Auden. Poetry can work well on television: Christopher had young Susannah York in his cast, speaking Auden's poems, not to mention a contributor I couldn't afford to approach when I filmed my *Monitor* interview with Auden in New York, a certain Igor Stravinsky.

In those expansive days there was enough cash in the kitty to look outside the BBC for promising film-makers. I was impressed by the Canadian *cinéma-vérité* director Allan King and bought for *Sunday Night* a new film called *Running Away Backwards*. This was King's ironic portrait of bohemian ex-pats living on Ibiza. King introduced me to Roger Graef, a young American film-maker who had been directing plays and even an opera at the Royal Court Theatre. With his beak nose, Roger could have played to perfection the young Aaron Copland in a biopic. An operator of soft-spoken eloquence, Roger went on to an important career in the field of crime and punishment; for Music and Arts in the 1960s he made illuminating fly-on-the-wall studies of Pierre Boulez, Jacques Lipchitz and, best of all, John Huston. I took a personal interest in two other young independent directors. Derrick Knight filmed a study of musical life among the enthusiastic amateur musicians of Harlow New Town. This post-war city was a dream come true for town planners: the population had ballooned to close on 50,000 in less than twenty years; choirs, orchestras and bands all flourished – so much so that we called Knight's film *The Pied Pipers of Harlow*; it was a good-news story if ever there was one. My other 'discovery' was the film-maker Robert Vas, who had left Hungary after the failure of the uprising in 1956. He was just a few weeks older than me and I felt great sympathy with him when we met at the National Coal Board's film unit, where he had been working out of the limelight for several years. *Master Singers* (screened in 1966) was an affectionate portrait of a Welsh mining village, built around rivalry between two male-voice choirs against the backdrop of a terrible pit disaster fifty years earlier. It was a strong story, finely narrated by the folk singer Ewan MacColl; one was immediately aware of the poetic sensibility for which Vas was to be greatly prized over the next decade at the BBC. As a colleague he could be infuriatingly stubborn but he was a true film-maker, greatly respected by his peers.

It took less than a season for Stephen and me to perceive that despite individual successes in *Sunday Night* we had probably swung too far away from the *Monitor* mould. To redress the balance we brought in a new lighter-weight arts magazine programme, which we called *The Look of the Week*. Robert Robinson was its acerbic host: his long interview with Mick Jagger (who only five years previously had been pursuing business studies at the London School of Economics) was one of the highlights of the first and only season. Another discovery was the compulsive art historian from Australia, Robert Hughes, whose dramatic report from the flooded city of Florence caused a stir. *The Look of the Week*'s editor, Lorna Pegram, had previously edited the *Wednesday Magazine* for BBC1's afternoon programmes; when that show was axed I was able to give Lorna a home in Music and Arts and she devised an ingenious art quiz for BBC2 in which competitors had to identify paintings from a tiny detail. In her spare time Lorna became a respected novelist, though never as fertile as Melvyn Bragg, who, post-*Monitor*, was keeping busy with the programmes he had devised for BBC2, among them *Writers' World* and *New Release*; best of all was his paperback review show, *Take It or Leave It*, which provided prejudice as well as preference and brought leading literary lights into our sitting rooms. It would be only a matter of time before Melvyn himself went on the screen regularly and played a more substantial role.

In the spring of 1967 I presided over another arts rethink, out of which the new flagship programme was born. I picked the title personally: *Omnibus*. It had been used by the Ford Foundation in America for a powerful strand of arts programmes networked, by government decree, on prime-time television. The show had clout. The downfall of the odious Senator McCarthy was hastened by an edition of *Omnibus*. It made Leonard Bernstein a household name before the series closed in 1961. For the British viewing public the title carried no baggage and it was adopted with enthusiasm. What did it signify? When

216

lawyers and journalists talked about 'The man on the Clapham omnibus' they meant anybody and everybody and that was the point: our new *Omnibus* series was to be inclusive in its choices rather than exclusive. Alastair Cooke had been the popular host of the American *Omnibus* but he was never its editor and for the BBC we made a similar decision, breaking away from the Wheldon tradition: there would be a host for the BBC's *Omnibus* with whom the public could identify but he (it was never a she) would be a spokesman and not the boss. The North Country playwright Henry Livings was the first 'anchor'; he was a gifted dramatist and a lovely man (by which I mean that he had an attractive personality).

Looking forward for a moment, the *Omnibus* strand on BBC1 ran for thirty-five years; there were over 800 editions. For a time it reverted to a magazine format. I hosted it myself for a couple of seasons in the 1970s and 1980s; Richard Baker and Barry Norman also did spells in front of the camera, but the presenter was always less important than the editor and his production team. Ironically the *coup de grâce* for *Omnibus* was delivered by Alan Yentob, by then long established as the top arts man in the BBC hierarchy, described as 'a towering figure' by no less than the director-general. In 2003 Alan replaced *Omnibus* with … guess what? A documentary arts series hosted by its editor, who called the new programme *Imagine* after the John Lennon lyric. At the time of writing Alan Yentob is still in charge. The wheel has thus turned full circle, right back to the Wheldon mould as exemplified by films such as *Elgar* and *Pop Goes the Easel*. But Alan has no Ken Russell in his creative team.

In the 1960s my East Tower empire also took in ballet and dance. The queen bee of television dance was a tough, no-nonsense lady from Gateshead named Margaret Dale. She had had a decent career as a soloist with the Royal Ballet and its wartime predecessor Sadler's Wells – she had even danced a few times on television at Alexandra Palace before the war – and in her thirties she bravely plunged into television, taking the directors' training course before working out the most effective way to transfer ballet to studios equipped with five or six cameras. Dance looked good on small screens even in black and white; the arrival of videotape prompted a long-term contract with the Royal Ballet to record at least one ballet a year for seven years. When I took over Maggie was only halfway through this project but was already exploring other ways of reflecting her passion for contemporary choreography. Huw had brought her into *Monitor* to direct a revealing film about her former boss, Ninette de Valois, a towering personality of the dance world. Then Maggie sold me the idea of taping *Ballet Class*, with another former Royal Ballet dancer, Peter Wright,

Margaret Dale (centre) with Dame Ninette de Valois and Sir David Webster
at the BBC Television Centre, 1961. She put dance for television on
the map and with my encouragement made *Ballet Class*.

serving as the ballet master. It was a beautiful programme and no ordinary
dance class. Peter came over on screen as a gentle giant, strict but poetic. His
ten dancers were put through their paces in one of the new studios at Television
Centre. They were the cream of the company, among them Anthony Dowell,
Christopher Gable, Merle Park, Lynn Seymour and my personal favourite,
Georgina Parkinson. The magical element in the edited programme was that
towards the end of the hour-long class Maggie introduced slow-motion video
and the rehearsal piano's tinkle gave way to full orchestra; the closing minutes
of the programme became the apotheosis of pure dance.

That same year, 1964, Maggie enlisted my support to persuade Harold
Pinter to write the storyline for a dance project she and the choreographer
Peter Darrell were developing, a new ballet, made for cameras, not the theatre,
danced to the witty, nostalgic music of Francis Poulenc's *Les Biches*. Maggie
wanted Pinter to develop a study of 1960s manners and morals as observed at a
chic house party: a meaningful glance here, a suppressed smile there; shadowy
gestures; a clink of ice cubes in a tumbler of Scotch; a flick of cigarette ash;
the touch of a slender, be-ringed hand ... all very Pinteresque. As a preliminary manoeuvre in our wooing process, I called on Pinter at his handsome
Regency house overlooking Regent's Park – his success with *The Caretaker*

218

had done wonders for his bank balance. I was ushered into a classic drawing room and given a somewhat chilly handshake by his somewhat chilly actress wife, the formidable Vivien Merchant. Harold was late. (Knowing now what nobody knew then, I wonder whether he had been detained by a daytime assignation with Joan Bakewell?) Eventually he arrived and I was able to make my pitch, to which he responded with one of his famous incredulous laughs. But he was intrigued enough to accept my invitation to meet us for tea and a chat at Television Centre. But when Maggie described to him her concept in more detail his response was courtesy personified but unmistakably negative: perhaps he was baffled by her notion of a play without words mimed to music. Fortunately another television dramatist, John Hopkins of *Z-Cars* fame, took up the challenge soon afterwards and helped to create a storyline for *House Party*, a minor masterpiece in black and white – one of the first fruits of BBC2, transmitted in June 1964. Almost forty years passed before Matthew Bourne choreographed *Play without Words* for the National Theatre. The publicity claimed it as a first in the field; some of us knew better.

House Party, a minor dance masterpiece by Peter Darrell
to Poulenc's major musical score.

With my encouragement, Margaret Dale became obsessed by an ambitious dance project (one might almost call it grandiose) entitled *Zodiac*. Each of the star signs would provide the themes for a monthly anthology of short ballets created for television by some of the world's leading choreographers. Lionel Radford's ambitious zodiac-inspired set in Studio 1 matched Dale's creative agenda and it was truly exciting to visit the show on a production day. Kenneth MacMillan, John Cranko and Birgit Cullberg were among Maggie's distinguished choreographers. But the grand project proved financially too problematic to sustain and although the intention had been to run for a year, *Zodiac* had to be cancelled after only six episodes. A great disappointment.

The days of televised studio dance were numbered when it became practical to film productions from theatres equipped with efficiently sprung dance floors – the dancer's *sine qua non*.

Opera was a different challenge. Since the pre-war days at Alexandra Palace, studio opera (in English) had been a regular part of BBC Television output. Menotti's *Amahl and the Night Visitors* was at the centre of the repertoire. When Lionel Salter left to run opera on the Third Programme in 1963 the responsibility for studio opera was handed not to me but to the Drama Group run by Sydney Newman, the ebullient Canadian who was the godfather of *Dr Who* and *The Wednesday Play*. It was a sensible decision: I had enough on my plate and Sidney had opera buffs in his team, directors and producers of the calibre of Basil Coleman, Herbert Wise, Philip Savile and Cedric Messina. And I managed to stay involved with opera as an adviser to Michael Peacock. With the launch of BBC2 in April 1964 came the opportunity to transmit full-length operas, with none of the awful cuts that had marred many previous productions of operatic classics – the most absurd being a BBC version of *Carmen* which totally cut the role of Micaëla. Peacock made a statement of intent as early as June 1964, when he scheduled the Sadler's Wells production of *Peter Grimes*, making it the first Britten opera to be transmitted by BBC Television. (Rediffusion had already screened *The Turn of the Screw* but ridiculously late at night and in two parts, over Christmas.) The BBC's Outside Broadcasts department produced the *Grimes* relay. Peter Dimmock, its chief, was one of the BBC's great player-managers, known to everybody because he hosted *Sports Report* every Saturday. Sport was the department's bread and butter but great occasions like Winston Churchill's funeral in 1965 also came under Dimmock's umbrella, not to mention live relays of classical concerts, ballets and operas. Between Outside Broadcasts (OBs) and Music and Arts there was a dotted line which a channel controller could join up when he wanted something special – he was the manager and we were all playing for the same team even if Antony Craxton, an aristocrat among the OB directors, remained a law unto himself. His younger colleagues John Vernon and Brian Large became friends as well as colleagues. And we were not short of opera and dance work away from the studio. Cameras were becoming more sensitive and lighting levels in halls and theatres could be lowered. Such relays were artistically preferable because the acoustic was greatly superior to the dry, boxy sound produced in studios. As early as October 1965, John Vernon directed a telecast from the Glyndebourne stage of *Dido and Aeneas* with Janet Baker marvellous as the vulnerable queen and Thomas Hemsley as the hapless Trojan. This was before the days of Glyndebourne Touring Opera. I had persuaded Moran Caplet at the opera house to stay open after the summer season specially for the BBC. The production was by Peter Ebert, the gifted son of Glyndebourne's Carl, and was taken into the house repertoire the following season, so everybody was happy.

Janet Baker singing Dido's Lament at Glyndebourne for BBC2.

John Vernon was a director of broad tastes but his younger colleague Brian Large did nothing but music: he was later transferred to the Music and Arts department, where he produced a string of studio operas which deserve to be revived (they are all in colour) and went on to become a world leader in the field of relays from opera houses, notably Bayreuth and New York's Metropolitan.

I got involved in studio opera production through the back door. After the success of *The Golden Ring*, the Austrians wanted to do another co-production. I introduced them to my versatile American opera-singer friends Evelyn Lear and Thomas Stewart, whom I had seen in *Figaro* at the Berlin Staatsoper when I was exploring modern opera house architecture. Evelyn Lear was a dazzling Cherubino, Tom a dashingly handsome Count. We settled on *Susanna's Secret* by Ermanno Wolf-Ferrari, a comedy concerning the perils of secret cigarette-smoking. Although composed to an Italian libretto, the première had taken place in Munich, sung in German. Tom and Evelyn had flawless German accents and were gifted actors. So on a single recording day they taped this witty opera in German and on the next they did it again in English – same sets, same music, same moves. The production never gets screened these days, I suppose because it was made in black and white, but it was a great success, for which the BBC supplied most of the creative talent. The director was the Austrian-born Herbert Wise, who had changed his name from Weiss and made a big name in British television drama; the producer was the genial South African Cedric Messina, who went on to produce the BBC's splendid *Billy Budd*, Kurt Weill's satirical *Mahagonny* and later, in the 1980s, the complete plays of William Shakespeare. Having negotiated the co-production with the Austrians, I was propositioned by Sydney Newman to join his department as the opera boss: I would have, he told me, the grand title of Assistant Head of Drama Group. But I declined. I was having too much fun being the boss of my own patch and in any case I have never been assistant head of anything. Assistant heads were often the ones that rolled in the BBC.

I was right to stay where I was. My unconscious should have been singing 'Something's coming, something good'. The 'Something' was an irresistible force named Leonard Bernstein. He was to transform my working life.

222

CHAPTER 12

WOOING THE GIANTS

Left to right: Leonard Bernstein, Glenn Gould and Igor Stravinsky.
Their CBS programme about the creative interpreter was an inspiration.

IN JULY 1965 Leonard Bernstein and his wife Felicia flew to England to attend the première of his *Chichester Psalms*, commissioned by Dean Walter Hussey and sung by the combined male choirs of the cathedrals of Chichester, Winchester and Salisbury. There had been a preview performance in New York a fortnight previously but I don't count that because it was with a small professional SATB chorus, lacking the unique tonal quality of an all-male ensemble featuring choirboys. When commissioning the *Psalms*, Walter

Hussey said he hoped Bernstein would include a flavour of *West Side Story*. The story of how Bernstein managed to work several numbers dropped from his Broadway shows into his most popular choral work is told in my Bernstein biography.

Meeting Bernstein at his Chichester première was a pivotal moment for me, the start of the second half of my working life. I went down to Sussex quite early and spent the day with the Bernsteins in Chichester Cathedral. During a coffee break they had me laughing out loud with their account of how the mattress at the deanery where they were staying was so lumpy that it was like sleeping on grapefruit. The music-making was less cheerful. I never found out why but although Bernstein had been invited to conduct his new score he had declined, so the performance was in the hands of the local man, Chichester's organist John Birch. I didn't know Bernstein well then but I could see he was worried by what he was hearing. The choirs had spent weeks mastering the tricky rhythms, the irregular bar lengths and the Hebrew pronunciation of the texts. They were excellent but the players of the Philomusica of London (famous before the war as the Boyd Neel Orchestra) were – to use Bernstein's phrase – 'all at sea'; it was evident as one watched the rehearsal that they had never seen the music before in their lives. The *Psalms* runs for only twenty minutes and British orchestras are renowned for their sight-reading skills but certain passages in that rehearsal made me acutely embarrassed. G.K. Chesterton famously opined that 'if a thing is worth doing it is worth doing badly'. How wrong he was. At the end of the session I heard Leonard mutter to Felicia: 'all we can do now is pray'. Yet for all the fluffs on the night (what the Austrians call 'fishes') it proved to be a grand performance: the jazzy syncopations of brass and bongos ricocheted around the cathedral's stone arcades and lofty galleries most excitingly; afterwards the bishop claimed to have had a vision of the Boy David dancing before the altar, the voices and harp uttering the joyful noise called for by the psalmist. My own vision was of a greatly relieved composer. 'Somehow', Bernstein wrote to his secretary next day, 'the glorious acoustics of Chichester Cathedral cushion everything so even mistakes sound pretty'.

I immediately began to make plans for a television performance worthy of the composition, but that project had to be deferred – for several decades, as it turned out, until 1986 at the Barbican. Instead, urged on by Ernest Fleischmann of the LSO, we decided to do something much grander with Bernstein the following spring, a performance of Mahler's Eighth, the 'Symphony of a Thousand', to be televised live from the Royal Albert Hall. The date was a few days before the second birthday of BBC2 so we could call it an anniversary celebration. Brian Large had learnt from Antony Craxton how to create on camera the sense of a grand musical occasion. And visually there is nothing grander in the classical repertoire than Mahler's Eighth (though it helps to be familiar with Goethe's *Faust*). It was thrilling to have Bernstein in our midst, galvanising the LSO players to heights of intensity such as only Mahler knew how to create. But a huge problem emerged on the day before the concert when the full forces were assembled for the first time at the Royal Albert Hall: the Leeds Festival Chorus was not living up to its reputation – it was claimed to be the best in the country but as a disappointed Bernstein described it backstage at the break there were too many ladies in hats who 'couldn't sing at all except in tea-time voices'. Emergency action was needed; extra money was found (from BBC coffers) and we hired a fixer (John Alldis) to spend the evening on the phone recruiting the best young professionals in town. Next day the show was not merely saved: it was a knock-out. Sydney Edwards, the *Evening Standard*'s arts reporter, painted a vivid portrait of Bernstein in action: 'arms outstretched, urging with demoniacal charm elderly grandmas in white from Leeds in front of him, schoolboys from Highgate and Finchley to the right and left, with brass from the LSO right behind'. It was an evening of elation. I had no inkling that in the decade to follow, Bernstein and Mahler would become central planks in my working life – but they did and I was glad.

Brian Large was as excited as I was at the prospect of making television with LB, as I shall call Bernstein for short, and we soon hatched a scheme with the LSO for LB to return in the winter and make three television programmes entitled *Symphonic Twilight* specially for the BBC. I easily persuaded Michael Peacock to support this for BBC1: he knew a star when he saw one. The three early twentieth-century masterpieces LB singled out were Stravinsky's *The Rite of Spring* and the fifth symphonies of Sibelius and Shostakovich. Did they really represent the *twilight* of the symphony as LB claimed? His pessimistic forecast has largely been proved right: few of the important composers of the past fifty years have written symphonies. But in 1966, under LB, his three symphonic choices came over as anything but twilight in mood: if the symphony was in decline it was definitely going out with a bang.

I managed to get BBC2 also to participate in the project: the LSO's first rehearsal for Shostakovich's Fifth Symphony was held at Television Centre. David Attenborough had recently been appointed the channel controller. I took him into the Studio 1 viewing gallery. On the monitor in TC1 we could see the director Herbert Chappell's wonderfully expressive close-ups of the orchestra (shots you could never achieve in a concert hall) and LB was tearing into the players with a maniacal energy that was so personal as to be almost indecent. Attenborough was riveted; he knew the orchestra well from filming them on tour in Japan, but he had never seen them stretched to breaking point as they were under LB. He went straight to his planners and cancelled an edition of *Late Night Line-Up* so our electrifying *Workshop* could run for two hours, double the regular length either side of the late news. It made an illuminating preview to the *Symphonic Twilight* series.

We chose the new Fairfield Halls in Croydon as the venue and gave away tickets so we could turn the place into a studio, but a studio with good acoustics. The result was phenomenal. *Symphonic Twilight* is quite simply one of the best-ever documents of a symphony concert conducted by a great maestro in full flood. In each performance Brian Large chose to stay on the conductor for minutes on end, showing how he moulded the paragraphs, living the symphony from moment to moment. I had myself directed a telecast of *The Rite of Spring* at the 1964 Proms with Colin Davis conducting. I have a comic memory of myself sitting on the floor in my office surrounded by scores and camera cards, distractedly counting the beats in the bar like a ballet master. Brian was a picture of calm.

Bernstein introduced each show. He was accustomed to the laborious process of writing every word of the lectures he delivered for his Young People's Concerts on American television; for the BBC he was making shows for adults and he was happy to speak off the cuff in the interviews. He enjoyed working with the BBC: it brought out the Harvard element in his make-up. After *Symphonic Twilight* we fixed a date for him to record a *Workshop* feature about his Symphony No. 2, lengthily described as being 'for Piano and Orchestra (After W.H. Auden), *The Age of Anxiety*'. Our conversation at the piano was eventually interwoven (by Brian Large) with a studio performance in which Leonard Pennario played the solo piano and André Previn conducted the LSO. It is a trailblazing programme: a living composer analysing his own composition.

Bernstein was now effectively part of the BBC stable of articulate conductors. In 1966 I undertook a more wide-ranging set of talks about music with another illustrious North American musician, the pianist Glenn Gould. Glenn and I had been corresponding since 1960. He was only a few months older than me and we were quite close friends: it was to me, in a letter, that he first announced his shock decision to give up playing public concerts. Since he was already a cult figure, I thought his retirement could only increase public interest and I made a successful pitch to Michael Peacock to bring

Preparing an interview for *Symphonic Twilight* at Fairfield Halls, 1966. The director Brian Large is at the left. For once it is the author who is smoking a cigarette, not the maestro.

him to BBC1. Plans progressed slowly – there was no email back then – but eventually we came up with a format which would preserve the high-spirited banter we had adopted for the radio programmes we made together back in the 1960s for CBC in Vancouver: the basic premise was that these would be conversations rather than interviews. I wanted to avoid the inquisitorial *Face to Face* style then much in vogue, preferring to create a relaxed mood which hopefully would capture Glenn's charm, his boyish enthusiasm, and best of all his readiness to leap to the piano to make a point. I flew to Toronto and we spent a stimulating week planning four shows, on Bach, Beethoven, Richard Strauss and Schoenberg. We chattered away in his big black Buick while he drove round Toronto, most evenings dining at a suburban hotel where he was warmly greeted by the maître d'hôtel. Glenn was as handsome as James Dean but appeared to have no amatory inclinations or social life; he told me quite proudly that he had never met the secretary he had employed for the previous six years. He spent an hour every morning on the phone to another person he had never met: his stockbroker. While in my company he never once removed his overcoat or his distinctive flat cap. Most of the time we did our planning in the spectacular mess that was his apartment on St Clair Avenue, piled high with books, magazines and long-playing records – records being his lifeblood: he was convinced they would replace concert halls as the best way to listen to music. He would have been as happy as a sandboy with today's technology but sadly he died just before the dawn of the digital age.

We worked out a structure for each programme but scripted not a word of dialogue: the clue to our endeavour was what I described to the CBC studio team as 'rehearsed spontaneity'. *Conversations with Glenn Gould* was another co-production – the BBC contributed me as producer and interviewer and no doubt we paid Glenn a fee of sorts, although the Corporation was notoriously stingy. The Canadians were happy to provide the bare-walled studio to which we imparted some atmosphere with a shadowy set consisting of camera dollies and sound booms. The grand piano was centre frame: it was the one Glenn always used and he was a CBC regular. He brought with him the low stool his father had built for him. What was unusual for my Toronto colleagues, who treated him ultra-deferentially, was that once we got talking I was prepared to argue the toss with Glenn about his crazy notions that future music-lovers would mix 'n' match their own interpretations: Klemperer's exposition, Toscanini's development section, Stokowski's recapitulation and so on. But Glenn's playing was phenomenal; he brought me round to Schoenberg and his transcription of Strauss's *Elektra* was sensational. The *Conversations* are also included in a massive twenty-eight-DVD set of Glenn's videos which is proof, were it needed, that the Gould mystique is still very much alive.

At the time I was only eighteen months into my new job but there was already gossip in the press concerning a promotion for me as part of forthcoming changes in the BBC hierarchy. Beavering away in Toronto I knew nothing about the rumours and was baffled to receive a cable from Huw Wheldon telling me to ignore the story. Get on with whatever it is you're doing was the gist of his telegram and that suited me fine. When I got back to London my most pressing concern proved to be Jonathan Miller's latest project: he had enjoyed another success in our *Sunday Night* series with his filmed version of *The Death of Socrates* (Leo McKern was magnificent as the philosopher) and while I was away he had persuaded Huw that he could be trusted to make a film version of *Alice in Wonderland* – as a feature for Music and Arts rather

Scenes from *Alice in Wonderland*.
Above: Peter Sellers,
Anne-Marie Mallik, Alison
Leggatt, Wilfrid Brambell.
Left: Michael Redgrave
and Anne-Marie Mallik.

than as an entertainment for the Drama Group – a decision that was ruffling a few feathers. But Jonathan's *Alice* was a wondrously fantastic production stuffed with stars. Some were Miller's friends from the satire world, among them Alan Bennett, Peter Cook and John Bird. Others were genuine A-list box-office names whom Jonathan had sweet-talked into cameo appearances: Peter Sellers was the King of Hearts, Malcolm Muggeridge and John Gielgud played Gryphon and Mock Turtle. Michael Redgrave was dream casting as Caterpillar.

Jonathan found a perfect girl to play his Victorian Alice and chose evocative locations in which to place her; he also had the inspiration, remembering the role of the Indian empire in the Victorian imagination, to commission incidental music from Ravi Shankar. Tony Palmer, working as his production assistant 'fixer', took Jonathan to a Festival Hall concert of Indian music. Dr Miller exclaimed that the sound of the sitar was perfect for his concept: he left the hall without hearing a single raga. All he had heard was Shankar tuning his sitar.

In retrospect, *Alice in Wonderland* was an unalloyed triumph, yet at the time it was a nightmare. The BBC Drama people were jealous. The Artists' Bookings people were up in arms because Jonathan was signing up stars without proper contracts, so we had no overseas rights in our own production. Publicity complained because without permission Tony Palmer had spent a night taking down the photo display in the wall showcases which lined the busy corridor leading to Television Centre's restaurants – a key display site – and substituting huge *Alice in Wonderland* production stills provided by the designer Julia Trevelyan Oman. For his part, Huw Wheldon was concerned that Jonathan was misinterpreting Lewis Carroll: Jonathan's concept was too dark, he thought, for general consumption and the show was eventually screened at five past nine, after the kiddies' viewing threshold. I thought this was an entirely unnecessary precaution.

I couldn't see what all the fuss was about: the film is as fresh today as ever it was. Marvellous photography by Dick Bush is part of the pleasure; Dick had shot Peter Watkins's mould-breaking *Culloden* and went on to make fine features for both Ken Russell and John Schlesinger. An additional private joke for me was that the actress Alison Leggatt in the role of the Queen of Hearts resembled the terror of Lime Grove, Grace Wyndham Goldie. Despite all his later success with opera and theatre, I believe *Alice in Wonderland* to be the most imaginative achievement of Jonathan Miller's entire career.

1966 had been a busy and a very fruitful year, and it also saw the beginning of an even grander project, Kenneth Clark's *Civilisation* series. David

Kenneth Clark introducing *Civilisation*: getting him to work with producer
Michael Gill was like persuading pandas to mate in a Chinese zoo.

Attenborough, the programme controller, was in search of something exceptional to showcase the introduction of colour television. The Americans had
upgraded to colour quicker than Europe and paid a price; cynics suggested
the letters of their system, NTSC, stood for Never The Same Colour. We had
to do better technically and we had to create programmes which would be
truly transformed by the introduction of colour. David asked Stephen Hearst
and me to come up with ideas for a series about painting. We immediately
thought of involving Kenneth Clark, the most experienced personality among
television art pundits. But there was a problem: Clark was deeply entrenched

231

in commercial television. He had been the first chairman of the ITA – the Independent Television Authority – the regulatory body of commercial television. And in the early 1960s, at the invitation of the flamboyant television mogul Lew Grade, Clark delivered on ITV no less than fifty talks and documentaries about art – all in black and white, of course – among them *Landscape into Art* and *Five Revolutionary Painters*. Clark had just finished a spectacular series about the world's great temples – all for ITV. But it emerged that he was not under contract, although he still took a retainer from Lew Grade, and he was happy to attend an exploratory lunch at Television Centre hosted by David Attenborough.

Stephen Hearst and I were there to represent the programme-makers and also present was Richard Cawston, the canny documentary-maker who had been named the BBC's troubleshooter on the use of colour film. His department was already working with Clark on a co-produced Christmas Day special on royal palaces which was screened during the hour before the Queen's annual broadcast. (The BBC served the House of Windsor well.)

We wanted Clark on board BBC2 for a colour-full *grand projet* but we had no idea what the urbane Sir Kenneth might suggest. Clark later wrote that Attenborough's mention of the word 'civilisation' in the conversation was the trigger that set him off: 'In a very few minutes', he wrote, 'while the lunch of persuasion went very cheerfully on around me, I had thought of a way the subject could be treated and from that first plan I departed very little.' I remember better the second lunch meeting a few weeks later when, even before we had sat down, he showed me the back of an envelope on which he had drafted thirteen titles – I suppose he knew that thirteen was a crucial number in the minds of BBC planners – BBC2's first epic, *The Great War*, shown in 1964 for the fiftieth anniversary of the First World War, actually ran to precisely twice that number. When I remarked cautiously that he seemed to have left out Spain and Venice from his overview, Clark brushed my objection aside; they were not central to the story he wanted to tell, he said, and the opening title of the series affirms that his is very much 'a personal view'. Admittedly Clark took the trouble to consult scholars of the calibre of E.H. Gombrich and John Hale, describing it to them as 'this ridiculous but fascinating project', but he stuck to his guns: Venice fairs poorly in *Civilisation*. True, the most prestigious Venetian artists Bellini and Titian are illustrated in the book of the series but there is no mention of my personal Venetian favourites, Giorgione and Carpaccio, and the eighteenth-century Tiepolo only scrapes in because he decorated Schloss Nymphenburg for the Habsburgs.

232

On the topic of his most admired Spaniard, Velázquez, there is only a tiny paragraph and not a single illustration.

But whatever my reservations, *Civilisation* was clearly what David wanted and we pressed ahead. To begin with, Clark played difficult to get. His first line of defence was that he was an old man (approaching seventy) and that he had specialist books on the stocks that he wanted to complete. Also, he wrote to David, he distrusted the wide generalisations which would be unavoidable in a project such as this. And yet he was obviously intrigued: in the same letter he described the BBC as a 'highly-skilled and intelligent organisation' and expressed great regret that he was denying himself the pleasure of working with us. We took this as a sign that he was susceptible to further negotiation. At this point David went away for several weeks to see for himself how colour television was working in the USA and elsewhere; negotiations passed to me and were sufficiently in our favour for me to be able to write (on 6 October, my daughter Clare's seventh birthday): 'we would like to have you as General Editor of this series. We would like you to lay down the principles upon which the series should be built, define the areas to be covered etc.'

We urgently needed to choose a producer to work alongside Clark; he should be experienced and disciplined but with flair and imagination: Stephen proposed Michael Gill, who had made some very good productions for BBC Schools, including films about cubism and Michelangelo's Sistine Chapel, before his recruitment to Music and Arts, where his films about Francis Bacon, co-written with David Sylvester, and Fernand Léger, script by John Berger, had made a strong impression. But an early meeting between Gill and Clark did not go well. Gill was in a BBC deputation led by me which had trooped in for tea at the Clarks's pleasant apartment in Albany, off Piccadilly. Lady Clark appeared on the scene late and slightly squiffy, making her entrance through what appeared to be a broom cupboard, though I suppose it might have been a back staircase. The room was overly warm and tension hung in the air, basically because Gill wanted to make proper films and was scared of having his creative wings clipped, while Clark (Gill feared) wanted to sit behind a desk and deliver the kind of lecture he had been doing so successfully for ATV. Clark wrote to me a few days later, giving me alternative dates for a 'longish discussion'. He was worried about Gill.

> It is a matter of mutual sympathy. It wouldn't do if we had a different idea about the kind of programmes to be produced. I fear that my kind of programme is rather old-fashioned – as is my approach to the subject. My style and content

might be a bit too square and stuffy. In that case better to get John Berger, who seems to have worked successfully with Michael Gill. I think this would really be more in keeping with current BBC policy.

It was satisfactory to have Clark worrying about 'current BBC policy' but I did not share his words with anyone at the time. Instead I put pen to paper (literally: it was to be another twenty years before I learnt to type properly) and wrote back as follows (28 November 1966):

We are not interested in a neo-Marxist approach. What we want is your view and with the greatest respect I don't believe there is anything old-fashioned about what you say or the way you say it … I wasn't surprised to learn that at first sight you hadn't 'taken' to Gill; I didn't think he spoke too well when we came to Albany. On the other hand he is gifted and anything but a whizz-kid or neo-Marxist! Which is why I thought we should go one stage further with him (and you) in the belief that in the long run he would provide the right kind of film expertise to interpret your script to its best advantage.

These were prophetic words. Our 'long discussion' took place at the St James's Club on Piccadilly; the institution has long since moved elsewhere but I give the building an affectionate nod every time I walk past because it was here that the Clark/Gill relationship was cemented. Getting them together had been, I observed, like supervising the mating of reluctant pandas (a procedure that was much in the news at that time) but Clark finally agreed to work with Gill – he particularly admired Gill's adventurous film about Francis Bacon – and the rest is history. Four months later, Clark wrote to me from his Saltwood home: he was, he reported, a month ahead of schedule:

When script number 6 is typed, perhaps you could spare the time to have a look at it, as it will probably be rather more representative than 4 or 5 [the programmes were to be shot out of sequence]. I do not wish to involve you in matters of detail, but I think that since you and David Attenborough gave me the commission you ought to be sure that it's being carried out in the way that you want.

It is only because I have been airbrushed out of the story that I have gone into the genesis of *Civilisation* in some detail. It is a little riling to hear David Attenborough say, as he does in the DVD feature accompanying the reissue of the *Civilisation* series, that the invitation to Clark came from him and Stephen Hearst, described as 'the head of music and arts' – a title which Stephen never held. Later in the same DVD interview David does mention me, describing me as 'head of arts', which was never my title. David is a lovely man and he was an excellent controller of BBC2, as I have already indicated, but I can't help but feel his memory of the period is occasionally a little rusty. To give another example, he writes in the first edition of his autobiography *Life on Air* about a Stravinsky concert screened 'live' on BBC2:

> I was a little put out to discover that Humphrey Burton, who had now left the BBC, was also trying to get the television rights to the concert for London Weekend Television. There was a battle – and BBC2 won.

But the Stravinsky concert was in September 1965, two years *before* my departure to LWT. At the time of the concert I was David's colleague, sitting in the Festival Hall audience as the head of BBC Television's Music and Arts department, which was producing the concert for television viewers on BBC2.

Enough said: there was no battle. However, there *was* a bit of a fracas concerning that concert. BBC2 was televising only the second half, in which Stravinsky himself would be conducting his *Firebird*. Unfortunately, nobody had told the lighting engineers that the public concert would be starting an hour earlier than their call. So in accordance with their work schedule the BBC riggers up in the gantry began testing their lamps sixty minutes before the start of the BBC transmission, which happened to be bang in the middle of the first half of the concert. The platform was suddenly flooded with extra light as the riggers shouted to each other across the rafters, apparently blissfully unaware that an audience of 3,000 was trying to listen to *The Rite of Spring* under the baton of Stravinsky's assistant Robert Craft. David Attenborough and I met on the staircase of the stalls, both hurriedly heading for the exit in order to alert the Outside Broadcast team that something had gone very wrong. The incident lasted only a couple of minutes but it seemed like a lifetime and what made it worse was that it occurred in the quietest section of Stravinsky's mostly raucous score.

The relay of *The Firebird* later in the evening was an historic occasion, sensitively directed for the cameras by Brian Large. There's a memorable moment when Stravinsky, who had the endearing habit of licking his first finger before turning the pages of the score he had composed fifty-five years earlier, gives a cue to the first horn to make his entry. Gasps in the control truck! The cue has been given two bars before it is due. Brian stays on Stravinsky. When the horn player Alan Civil enters unbidden at the correct point the smile of relief and gratitude on the old man's face, a smile tinged with glee, is a delight to behold. Thanks to television it has been preserved for posterity.

Igor Stravinsky, delighted he got away with it. Royal Festival Hall, 1965.

The BBC aspired to reflect the classical music scene in all its abundant variety so it was hardly surprising that in addition to Stravinsky another great composer, Benjamin Britten, should be on my priority list. I often wrote to him from the BBC's East Tower and excerpts from my letters are published in volume six of the massive Britten correspondence. What I hoped to achieve was for him to compose a new children's opera for Christmas; he expressed interest but the idea was eventually displaced by his charming 1967 composition for the Vienna Boys' Choir, *The Golden Vanity*, and two years later by another work for young singers, the infinitely bleak *Children's Crusade*. (I produced *The Golden Vanity* with London schoolboys a few years later; the *Crusade* has never been televised.) After the BBC's magnificent studio production of *Billy Budd*, hopes were ignited that Britten might compose something specially for television. Indeed, there's a letter from Gerald Savory, then the BBC's Head of Plays, offering Britten the stupendous sum of £10,000 (apparently more than £150,000 in today's money) for world rights to a new Britten opera. In the immediate future my drama colleagues wanted to follow up *Billy Budd* with a studio production of *Peter Grimes*, again to be directed by Britten's faithful friend and stage director Basil Coleman. But Britten's loyalties shifted drastically after the Snape Maltings concert hall was opened in 1967. He greatly preferred the Maltings acoustic and was persuaded that the hall could be turned into a makeshift television studio. Sadly, given the tremendous success of his *Billy Budd*, Basil Coleman's plan for a television *Grimes* never saw the light of day; instead the opera was taped at Snape Maltings, where two years later Britten's specific 'television' opera *Owen Wingrave* was also mounted. However, it has to be said that both *Grimes* and *Wingrave* would probably have received more sophisticated productions had they been mounted by Basil Coleman at Television Centre.

In this tremendously pro-Britten atmosphere, I concentrated on the field I knew best, documentary. The early months of 1967 saw the birth of two new Britten projects. One was a modest affair, a low-key version of my Wagner project *The Golden Ring*, again featuring John Culshaw but this time working in Orford church in Suffolk with his Decca team; we would tape a fly-on-the-wall account of the recording sessions for Britten's church parable, *The Burning Fiery Furnace*. This production duly went ahead at the end of May with my maverick protégé Tony Palmer sharing with me the direction of the outside broadcast cameras; he also directed the film crew which went off to watch Britten rehearsing his cast in the new library at the Red House in Aldeburgh. Tony also filmed the Decca Boys devouring lobster at Orford's Butley Oysterage. We were filming several years before Britten's health began to fail and in this production he comes over as happy, relaxed and totally in command. It is probably the most extensive coverage in existence of Britten the conductor at work on his own music.

The other Britten project was much more substantial, a portrait – in colour, ready for our colour launch – of the twentieth Aldeburgh Festival. Once I had obtained Britten's approval I had to spend time in America searching for a well-heeled co-production partner. I found one in the person of Henry Jaffe, the veteran producer of *The Bell Telephone Hour*, which in those days specialised in documentaries about stars of the classical music world. I returned with the promise of $100,000, close to half a million pounds, given inflation, in today's currency. How I persuaded Jaffe to cough up such a substantial sum I cannot recall; I guess it was a bargain for him, given the inflated cost of everything on American commercial television. For *The Bell Telephone Hour* we were obliged to film a separate opening sequence in which the Americans' regular host Willis Conover explained to his audience that he was speaking from 'the flat and stony shores' of a place he pronounced as Alder-burg. The extra cash meant we could offer sensible contracts to everybody appearing at the festival, including Sviatoslav Richter, Julian Bream, the Vienna Boys' Choir, Joyce Grenfell, the cast of *A Midsummer Night's Dream* and of course Pears and Britten, performing Schubert. And the festival received a hefty management fee. For me there was but one fly in the ointment: I had to quit the production when it had only just got under way.

Over the previous few months I had been experiencing a wave of antipathy towards the BBC ethos. I had recently attended a weekend conference of BBC Television's top management – bosses and department heads. The mood was relentlessly upbeat, not to say triumphalist. It's true the BBC had reason to be pleased with itself: it had fought back in the ratings war; its top show, *The Forsyte Saga*, was being watched by nearly everybody who possessed a 625-line receiver, even though it was shot in black and white. But I felt in my bones that the BBC was becoming smug and in some quarters philistine. In the bar I found a supportive spirit in Michael Bakewell, the Drama Group's current Head of Plays. I knew Michael distantly from our Cambridge days. An impressive mind, he loved Berlioz and wanted to televise *The Damnation of Faust*. His rooms at King's were opposite Philip Radcliffe's and when attending morning supervisions I would sometimes meet Michael's future wife Joan on the landing. Like me, Michael was a natural-born producer who had been pressed into administration and did not altogether like what he found. Not long after sharing our uneasiness about the way the BBC was going, Michael opted to return to production and as a freelance he went on to make many brilliant radio drama adaptations.

I am not seeking to blame Michael for the fact but I was in a vulnerable state. A few weeks later I found myself being propositioned out of the blue by no less an operator than David Frost. I was at Lime Grove reception waiting for a cab. Frost was there, too. He was already very famous thanks to his satirical weekend show *That Was the Week That Was* and we got talking at the kerbside. 'I'm glad I've bumped into you', he said, or words to that effect. I never knew whether Frost really had been intending to approach me or whether the idea popped into his head when he saw me – he was that kind of an impresario – but the impact of his utterance was unmistakable. It went like this: 'A few of us are thinking of putting together a group to bid for an ITV franchise when they come up for grabs in the summer. I'd like you to join us. Would you be interested?' As became my custom when major decisions were in the offing, I gave the matter maybe ten seconds thought before responding in the affirmative.

For the next few weeks I led a strange double life. I told not a soul in Music and Arts that I might be leaving. I convinced myself that the Frost consortium did not have a cat's chance in hell of winning the franchise but I can see now that the deep-seated reason for not breaking cover was because I was

The entrance to Lime Grove studios: the pavement
where I was propositioned by David Frost.

scared of incurring Huw Wheldon's wrath. My friend Michael Peacock had
announced that he was involved in the bid (he was to be managing director)
and he stood down from running BBC1; he actually left the Corporation.
By contrast, I kept mum. We had many secret meetings at Mike's house in
Barnes. Two very impressive ladies, Doreen Stephens (ex-*Woman's Hour*) and
Joy Whitby from children's drama programmes, were fellow conspirators; so
was the delightful Frank Muir, the BBC's Head of Comedy. Science, news
and current affairs were to be handled by two high-ranking *Sunday Times*
journalists who were friends of Frost: Tom Margerison and Clive Irving. It
all seemed unreal. Shortly before the bid had to be submitted it was perceived
that we had not included a Head of Drama in the application; I was quickly
invested with this extra portfolio and my proposed salary increased from
£8,000 to £8,500 – this was more than twice what I was currently earning.
To hand me drama was a preposterous proposition since I had never in my
life directed a play in the theatre, let alone on television, indeed had not even
acted in anything since my army days at Catterick. As I say, it was for me a
surrealist, fantasy world.

It transpired that the Independent Television Authority, the administrators of the bidding process, was still smarting from the hammering it had received about its philistinism five years earlier in the pages of the Pilkington Report, the government's white paper on the future of television. The ITA was particularly impressed by our group's plans (mine) to expand cultural programming. Basically our submission argued that it was possible to broaden the mix of programmes and still make money – to have your cake and eat it. I wasn't part of the delegation which attended the interview but my inclusion in LWT's application obviously helped to carry the day.

When the franchise decision was announced there was consternation and deep hurt at the BBC. With so many high-profile departures the whiff of treason was in the air. Huw refused to see me, and I understood why. When I went to say farewell to David Attenborough, I told him of the conversations I had recently been having with John Culshaw. In confidence I had mentioned to John that I might be leaving to join commercial television: I asked whether he would be interested in replacing me as head of television music? John had done everything he wanted to do as a recording producer, culminating in Wagner's *Ring*, so he was ready to try something new; he was duly recruited into the BBC at the end of the summer, thus ensuring the BBC's close collaboration with Benjamin Britten. Stephen Hearst took over arts with hardly a hiccup. Wounded by my defection, Huw Wheldon told David Attenborough that I had responded to the Three Cs: Challenge, Change and Cash. I couldn't

Card from Benjamin Britten: he made me feel less guilty about leaving the BBC.

have put it better myself. David said sympathetically that he could see why I had not confided in Huw: he would have talked me out of it.

It was a surprisingly reckless decision for me to throw in my lot with David Frost and his friends. Had I stayed at the BBC I might well have gone higher in the organisation. My friend Leslie Megahey, later the editor of *Omnibus*, told me recently that he and his colleagues had assumed I would be the next controller of BBC2. Maybe, and maybe I also would have risen to the position of, say, managing director by the age of fifty. Except that I did not have the slightest ambition to grasp power: all things considered, I conclude half a century later that I stepped off the BBC conveyor belt at the right time but for muddled motives. On the other hand, a case can be made that I was exhibiting the first signs of the midlife crisis which the following year would culminate in my leaving my wife and two children. So a critical point this decision to leave the BBC certainly was.

PART THREE

*Going It Alone,
1967–1975*

CHAPTER 13

LWT: NOT SUCH
A BRAVE NEW WORLD

Newly installed at London Weekend Television. Had I taken leave of my senses?

LEAVING THE BBC after ten years of intense activity as a producer was a tremendous wrench, an unparalleled shock to my system. I had not even begun to prepare myself for the reality of going to commercial television because I did not believe that David Frost's consortium had any chance of winning the franchise. When the news arrived that it had, I immediately experienced profound guilt feelings about the shoddy way I had kept my intention to quit a secret from everybody (except John Culshaw), though at least I had shown a sense of responsibility to my *alma mater* by recruiting such an outstanding figure to replace me. It was a twisted logic. There was no smooth transition: Huw Wheldon was angry as well as wounded and he struck back by decreeing I should not work out my three-month notice period as I had hoped but instead should pack up my papers and quit my East Tower office within a week. When I said goodbye to my colleagues in Music and Arts I got the impression they thought I had taken leave of my senses.

My crisis occurred in June 1967, the weekend that the Israelis emerged triumphant from the Six Days' War. Daniel Barenboim and Jacqueline du Pré were so caught up in the excitement that they got married in Jerusalem on the day Jackie was scheduled to be playing a concert at the Bath Festival; this I knew immediately because I was in Bath for a television relay of her concert and could observe the festival's director, Yehudi Menuhin, becoming quite cross with his young protégée for putting her personal life before her professional commitments – something he never did, even when his sister was dying.

Menuhin was one of several collaborators to whom I wrote letters over the next few days explaining as best I could why I had chosen to leave the BBC and withdraw from the projects we were working on together. Since

The newly engaged Jacqueline du Pré with Daniel Barenboim.

246

filming was already under way up in Suffolk, the first recipient was Benjamin Britten. 'My reasons', I wrote, 'are personal and complicated.' Happily Tony Palmer, who was never short of self-belief, seized the chance created by my defection and with Huw's blessing directed a very good film; his account of the twentieth Aldeburgh Festival was his first full-length programme (he has since made close on 130) and is one of his most enjoyable. Preparatory work for the other *grand projet* I had inaugurated, the thirteen films comprising Kenneth Clark's *Civilisation*, was well advanced and although my musical knowledge (and taste) might have helped the team in the occasional episode in which classical music figures prominently, my departure made very little difference to the series.

There was a year between LWT being awarded the franchise and the date of the actual on-air handover from Rediffusion, so the first few months of the company's existence felt as if we were fighting a phoney war. The reality of the challenge – to improve the range of commercial television without losing profitability – was undeniably high-minded but I refused to believe that it was pie in the sky: the example of equally high-minded Granada Television was there for all to see. The difference, I came to realise, was that Granada was run by the shrewd Sidney Bernstein and his chief lieutenant Denis Forman, both giants in our industry who contrived for decades to have their cake and eat it, whereas LWT's leadership was desperately short of show-business experience. Frost himself, then at the height of his screen career, had abundant flair but he was an absentee landlord, whizzing across the Atlantic every week to host chat shows. I personally knew hardly anybody in commercial television and I had watched very few ITV programmes: no plays or comedy, just the occasional edition of *This Week* and the arts programme *Tempo*. My new boss, Cyril Bennett, I liked very much; he was a canny political journalist who had only recently moved up to be programme controller at Rediffusion.

Our brave new company set up its temporary headquarters in swanky offices off Mayfair's Curzon Street provided by one of its investors, Arnold Weinstock of the General Electric Company, GEC. Lord Weinstock greatly admired the Italian conductor Riccardo Muti and every year attended the opening night of the La Scala season; I would have welcomed his participation in our plans but unfortunately he made no attempt to show any interest in my music projects and a few years later sold his LWT shares to Rupert Murdoch with alarming consequences. As his temporary tenants in Curzon Street, our happy band of pilgrims sat slightly uneasily at tables rather than desks placed around the edges of a large conference room. We were quite a bunch,

Department heads and drama chiefs at LWT. Left to right: Frank Muir,
Joy Whitby, Derek Granger, Kenith Trodd, Terry Hughes, Doreen Stephens,
Tony Garnett and myself, looking slightly uneasy.

headed by Doreen Stephens, who had previously been in charge of women's
programmes at BBC Television. When David Frost told her she would also
have to look after religion she was taken aback and reportedly exclaimed,
'Oh God!', to which Frost replied, 'Yes, you'll have to come to terms with
Him.' Doreen had brought her second-in-command, Joy Whitby, a wizard
producer of children's drama. Joy had a dazzling smile and was most ingenious
at making quality drama such as *Catweazle* with very little money. For BBC
Television she had invented *Play School* and she was also the first producer
to hire an African-American presenter. Joy's husband Tony Whitby was a
high-flying current affairs producer at Lime Grove, soon to be promoted to
Controller of Radio 4. Their pillow talk must have been interesting. (Alas,
Tony died in his forties in 1975.) LWT's own current affairs guru, Clive Irving,
popped in and out somewhat mysteriously. I suspect he knew very little about
television production but he was a great mate of Frost's: he wanted to create a
television news programme to rival the 'Insight' column at *The Sunday Times*:
our Sunday morning show called *Weekend World* was the eventual result. We
saw quite a bit of another *Sunday Times* recruit, the science writer Dr Tom
Margerison, who also delivered effective pieces to camera for the *Tonight*
programme. Tom was Michael Peacock's deputy and worked in the back room,
where unkindly he was said to have relied upon his slide rule a good deal.

The great excitement for me was sharing an office with Jimmy Hill, LWT's Head of Sport. Jimmy's was a household name: he was a top footballer who also, as head of the FPA (the players' association), negotiated the end of the £20 maximum weekly wage for professionals. (That's not a misprint: before 1960 £20 was the top whack, even for players of the calibre of Stanley Matthews.) Jimmy then turned manager and had just guided Coventry City to the top division when he surprised the sporting world by stepping down – to join us and become one of football's first television pundits. He was a great catch!

Apart from Jimmy, who had an excellent assistant in Veronica Hopcraft, we arrived without secretaries: a lively lady named Sheila Colvin looked after us all. Sheila had previously been assistant to John Calder, the enterprising publisher who mounted 'happenings' at the Edinburgh Festival. In a switchback of a career she later ran the Aldeburgh Festival for a decade: LWT must have been a quiet interlude.

My closest friend from BBC days was Frank Muir, our Head of Entertainment. He was immensely tall and debonair, soft-spoken and always cheerful, self-deprecating, witty and wise. He soon recruited Tanya Bruce Lockhart, LWT's original troubleshooter, to be his personal assistant: Tanya

Jimmy Hill and me by Barry Fantoni. In his book *The Media Mob*,
George Melly describes us as 'the cognoscenti of the idiot-box'.

was famously devoted to her huge dog Rikki, whom she had found, collar-less, on a Spanish beach; dogs were banned on LWT's office premises but Frank wrote a memo to the janitor explaining that Rikki was actually not a dog but 'an Andalusian, hornless, short-haired mountain goat'. The explanation did the trick.

Tanya helped me to recruit my own assistant, Elizabeth Queenan. Liz was fiercely loyal, well educated and passionate about the arts. We were all genuinely keen to do new things at LWT but I couldn't repress the occasional internal grin concerning the guilty knowledge that overnight we ex-BBC people had doubled our salaries and been given shares in the new company, shares which in the long run proved gratifyingly valuable.

LWT soon moved to more efficient offices in nearby Old Burlington Street. Mayfair replaced Shepherd's Bush as my daytime habitat. We lunched our prospective writers and producers in good restaurants, drank at famous bars, viewed programmes in West End screening theatres.

Late that autumn I met Christina Hansegård, a Swedish television journalist to whom I had been introduced the previous September in Palermo, at the Prix Italia. Her husband Lars was then serving on the radio jury but my own television jury duties didn't begin until the next day so Christina and I chatted pleasantly while sunbathing at the hotel swimming pool.

The following spring, just before I left the BBC, Christina had come to Television Centre to attend a planning meeting for an international satellite hook-up organised by the BBC called *Our World*. After reading about me in a gossip-press cutting pinned on an office noticeboard she impulsively phoned me on the internal switchboard. I happily showed her round the Centre and we kissed on the roof of the East Tower. But although the new Ingmar Bergman film *Persona* featured an actress who reminded me of Christina's disturbing beauty, I had done nothing about seeing her again since Palermo and my moving to LWT. The reason for Christina's visit to London was to write a report on British television journalism. She stayed at the Europa hotel and we started meeting for lunches at the Westbury: we fell in love very quickly. She became pregnant (although she had told me in good faith that she couldn't have children) and she went back to Sweden, where, determined to go it alone, she parted from her husband and worked as a television newsreader almost to the day when she gave birth to our daughter Helena. So within a year of leaving the BBC my personal midlife crisis was now in full flood. And my work was leading me into similarly dangerous uncharted waters.

My favourite picture
of Christina.

It did not take much discussion with Mike Peacock and Cyril Bennett to put flesh and blood on the three-pronged schedule we had promised for drama and the arts in our ITV application: frighteningly, I was required to create a new drama series for Friday evenings in the tradition of *The Avengers* and *The Prisoner*, the immensely popular and expensive film creations of the previous regime. Next I needed to fill a weekly slot on Saturday nights for one-off cultural 'Specials'. Finally we were committed to contributing single plays of quality to the ITV network on Sunday evenings. Drama was much more important than the arts for delivering ratings and building audience loyalties, and since I was an absolute beginner in this sophisticated field I needed help. We persuaded Derek Granger to join the LWT staff from Granada. Derek had begun professional life as a film critic in Brighton. In middle age his deeply lined face resembled the squashed lemon of a famous Idris advertising campaign but there was nothing either sour or comical about

Derek's experience, which at Granada ranged from producing *Coronation Street* and *World in Action* to low-budget situation comedy, which he enjoyed, he said, for the intellectual exercise it provided. 'How can I devise a situation where Arthur Lowe is upside down in a hammock with a toilet seat stuck on his head?'

Another early signing, Stella Richman, had previously been a successful producer on contract to ABC and Rediffusion. Stella had her finger on the pulse of new writers and clever directors, and she sold Cyril and me the idea of a television repertory theatre, the Company of Five. It was led by two especially fine actors, John Neville and Gwen Watford, and among her writers were Alun Owen and the young Dennis Potter. This repertory experiment was intriguing and worked reasonably well with audiences but was hardly going to set the Thames on fire. Looking for edge and innovation, I also negotiated a deal with Tony Garnett, producer of the BBC's disturbing homelessness drama *Cathy Come Home*. Like me, Tony was a BBC departee. Along with James MacTaggart, Ken Loach and Kenith Trodd – towering figures in television drama – he had created Kestrel Films, one of the first independent production companies in British television. LWT contracted Kestrel to make half a dozen dramas in our opening season, mostly on 16 mm film, although the first to be transmitted, amid howls of protest, was a studio show, a satire on the very process of how LWT had come to be awarded its operating licence. Called *The Franchise Trail*, it starred the actor David Battley as a dead ringer for David Frost and Willoughby Goddard as the syndicate's portly lawyer, who waddled down the corridors of power proclaiming his mantra 'one cannot be too large', a reminder that Frost had recruited twenty-four of the most powerful investors in London: Goddard's character was an unmistakable caricature of Arnold Goodman, the lawyer who seemed to have a finger in every 1960s theatrical pie. The script by Nemone Lethbridge, a former barrister, was coarse but funny and displayed our new company's healthy lack of concern for the ITV establishment. However, the management got cold feet and the play was shunted into a late-evening slot as a *Saturday Special*.

Among Kestrel's film dramas was *Bangelstein's Boys* by Colin Welland, a foray into the tough world of Rugby League that warranted comparison with Lindsay Anderson's *This Sporting Life*. Already famous for playing the role of a copper in the BBC's police drama *Z-Cars*, Welland went on to a second important career as a film writer, culminating in *Chariots of Fire*, which prompted his famous 'The British are coming!' speech at the Oscars awards ceremony of 1982. He and his wife Patricia became good friends.

In that long run-up year I devised a scheme for a television play competition that I fear was more of a public relations exercise than a genuine quest for new talent. I also produced a television play myself. I chose a one-acter by Strindberg as a test bed for our very first studio colour production. *Playing with Fire* is my only credit in the field of television drama, but when we were still working in black and white I also oversaw an exercise in *Grand Guignol* called *If There Weren't Any Blacks You'd Have to Invent Them*. The author was Johnny Speight, the cockney comedy writer whose great claim to fame was the invention of a racist bigot by the name of Alf Garnett. Warren Mitchell played this odious anti-hero in the enormously popular BBC series *Till Death Us Do Part*. Now Speight had turned playwright and to good purpose. Grimly funny, *If There Weren't Any Blacks* was an allegory that was way ahead of its time. It won a prize – LWT's first – at the Prague Television Festival and was remade in colour in 1974, but Charles Jarrott's original production, set in a cemetery, is powerful stuff, with Leslie Sands outstanding in a star-packed cast as a blind man who denounces a youngster for being black. The 1974 remake starring Leonard Rossiter and Richard Beckinsale is equally strong.

My personal passion at LWT was the *Saturday Special* strand. It has been cavalierly dismissed by more than one media historian as being out of touch with what the mass viewing public wanted on a Saturday night. I don't accept that for a moment. How can 'they' know what they want without sampling it first? The *Saturday Special* was high-octane performance territory, not documentary, and Derek Granger and I chose artists and shows which we thought exciting and different, among them Nina Simone singing soul and Leonard Bernstein conducting Berlioz. We included a popular hit of the 1720s, *The Beggar's Opera*, and Stravinsky's *Soldier's Tale* direct from the Bath Festival – with Yehudi Menuhin playing the devil's violin. Other shows were the *Private Eye* satire of *Mrs Wilson's Diary*, the LSO in *Mr Previn Comes to Town* and Britten's opera composed for the Vienna Boys' Choir, *The Golden Vanity*: it was an impressive list and I was proud of what we achieved.

I learnt a little humility too. LWT's new head of variety was the former bandleader Tito Burns, a lovely man who sported equally lovely jewellery on his shirtsleeves. Tito had been a household name as a jazz accordionist and later managed Cliff Richard and Bob Dylan. He called me into his office one day and trembling with pride revealed that he could negotiate exclusive rights for Simon and Garfunkel to appear on LWT's *Saturday Special*. I hung my head with shame: I had never heard of the most successful folk-rock duo of the 1960s. Tito was sweet but I knew I had been weighed in the balance and found wanting. Ironically it transpired that we could not afford the Americans' fee; wearing his managerial hat, Tito was a tough negotiator.

My most severe test at LWT came when Cyril Bennett told me I must cancel our new drama series, *The Inquisitors*, after three episodes had already been made. I had hired a freelance producer, John Bryce, who came to us trailing clouds of glory – he had worked on several series of *The Avengers*. One of his writers was Troy Kennedy Martin, who the following year scripted *The Italian Job*. Ken Wlaschin was the script editor; he became a noted film historian. On paper *The Inquisitors* boasted a strong team, but the end product was proving to be too clever by half for the 1960s mass audience. Personally I enjoyed the shows that were already in the can, but Cyril Bennett persuaded me that on commercial television at prime time they would go down like lead balloons. We must cut our losses, he decreed, and pay off the writers and directors. I was the one who had to pass on the decision to John Bryce and his closest director colleague Jimmy Goddard. Of course they were bitterly hurt by our lack of confidence in their project. Bryce retired soon afterwards to tend lobster pots in Cornwall, but happily Jimmy continued what proved to be a glittering career, which included the telecast of the RSC's *Nicholas Nickleby*. I can see now that I should have trusted their vision. This was 1968, the year of flower power – we might well have created a cult series. As it was, the most memorable thing to come out of this doomed show was probably the meeting on set of the lead actor Alan Lake and the guest actress of the current episode Diana Dors, a movie pin-up star nine years Lake's senior. They fell in love, married, squabbled and eventually divorced. In 1984 Lake shot himself, on the sixteenth anniversary of their first meeting at LWT. Dors had died of cancer five months earlier.

Faced with the crisis of an empty tape shelf where a thirteen-part series should have been accumulating, Derek Granger, ever the pro, dropped everything else and supervised the creation, in record time, of a substitute series called *The Inside Man*, about the work of a government criminologist combating international money laundering. What a far cry this all was from my previous work preoccupations at BBC Music and Arts, where my successor John Culshaw was now firmly established and Stephen Hearst was supervising Kenneth Clark's monumental *Civilisation*. But I had no pangs of regret: I had made my own bed and despite the setback I was still happy to lie on it. However, I did allow myself a brief excursion into Culshaw territory. My impresario friend Ian Hunter persuaded me that his most famous client, Herbert von Karajan, was prepared to consider allowing the Berlin Philharmonic to be televised (by me) on its next visit to London. Would I fly out to Salzburg, where Karajan lived and ran the festival, and show him my latest production to prove my competence? *Selbst-verständlich.* Of course!

I was met at the airport by the maestro's personal assistant, Lore Salzburger. Like her boss she drove a Porsche and as we whizzed into the city I rashly announced that I was thinking of buying a Porsche myself. Which was only vaguely true. Her interest perked up. Which Porsche model? she asked, obviously a connoisseur. A 928, said I, clutching at straws. 'Oh, that's not a *real* Porsche,' she pronounced condescendingly.

My session with Karajan was an equal disaster. The tape I had chosen as my visiting card could not have been more of a *faux pas*: Leonard Bernstein and the New York Philharmonic in the *Symphonie Fantastique,* taped at the Royal Festival Hall. Compared with the sophisticated orchestra films Karajan had recently been making in a Berlin studio, beautifully lit and not a hair out of place on the heads of the remotest desk of the Second Violins, my Bernstein telecast was crude, over-lit and visually pretty ordinary. And in my innocence I had forgotten that the two maestri, Bernstein and Karajan, were portrayed in the public prints as deadly rivals backed by the two most powerful record companies in the world. Karajan hadn't watched more than ten minutes of my video when he rose to his feet and haughtily declared that my type of (banal) camerawork was not appropriate for his orchestra, let alone for himself. After Frau Salzburger's gibe about the Porsche, I felt very small indeed.

A few months before the new station went on the air, LWT moved to Stonebridge Park. Our new open-plan offices were at the top of an ugly tower block on the North Circular Road, close to the old Rediffusion studios at Wembley, from where we would transmit our programmes until new studios were opened on the South Bank in 1972. The move was depressing: what a contrast with Mayfair! Frank Muir looked out of the unopenable weather-stained windows, high up in this soulless triangular edifice, took in the rows and rows of dull suburban streets spread out below and with arms uplifted uttered an immortal *cri de coeur*: 'Behold Stonebridge Park, the Florence of NW10.'

The lead-up to opening night was an awkward period. The ITA had devised a deeply clumsy system for the reallocation of television licences. LWT's studio staff had mostly come across from the disenfranchised Rediffusion company and were in truculent mood: not only did they resent being mucked about with professionally, some of them would now have to work at weekends, shock, horror! The Union, which was very powerful, was genuinely angry at management's disregard for its members. On Friday, August 2nd 1968, LWT started transmissions. Frank Muir kicked off with *We Have Ways of Making You Laugh*, a witty new stand-up and sketch show. At the end of the transmission, which had gone very well, his producer Humphrey Barclay had to tell him that the union representative had ordered the plugs to be pulled only seconds into the programme; nobody outside the studio had seen the show. Next day management staff like myself were called in to beat the strike by producing a makeshift version of the planned 'live' variety show. Joy Whitby was floor managing; David Frost was hosting the proceedings and Mike Peacock, in his shirtsleeves, was up in the gallery producing with all the authority of somebody whose last show had been the General Election of 1964. I was directing the cameras but during the afternoon rehearsal a message was sent in to me from the brothers encamped in the café across the road from Wembley Studios. 'If you continue to direct this bootleg show you will never

LWT had a penchant for tower blocks. Left: Stonebridge Park, 'the Florence of NW10'. Right: The South Bank Television Centre.

At the control desk in the Rediffusion Studios for a cameo with Barbara Ferris and John Cleese in the feature film *Interlude*, directed by Kevin Billington, 1968.

get your union ticket.' Mike took the threat seriously: the company would need my director's experience in the coming months. So I was sent home, feeling dreadful at having to desert the team. This nasty, ill-tempered dispute got the company off to a fractious start from which it took months to recover.

Two weeks later, the Russians sent tanks into Prague to put an end to Alexander Dubček's liberalisation policy. The enormous wave of sympathy for the Czechs resulted in a swiftly organised fundraising concert at the Royal Albert Hall in which Jacqueline du Pré played the Dvořák Cello Concerto, inspiring a remarkable example of ITV and the BBC pooling resources: Granada paid to televise the concert, LWT screened it and BBC Television provided the cameras. Because there was so little time to prepare the camera script, I shared the direction with Brian Large, he doing the second and third movements and I the much longer opener. A profoundly stirring occasion, the show went out live and what fun it was to be back in my natural habitat.

My personal life was equally stirring, but for very different reasons. I had heard from Swedish friends that Christina had given birth to a daughter on September 3rd. I was very anxious to see mother and child, and after weeks

257

With the choreographer Kenneth MacMillan.
A troubled time, contemplating a flight to Stockholm.

of fretting and indecision I flew to Berlin one late-October weekend to attend a performance of *Anastasia*, a new one-act ballet by Kenneth MacMillan starring Lynn Seymour. My hunch was that it would make an excellent edition of the *Saturday Special* (as it would have done had Kenneth not decided to expand the ballet to a full evening). I had arranged nothing in advance but from Berlin it was only a short flight to Stockholm and urged on from within by a profound need to act (at last) I rearranged my flight tickets and the very next morning found a Stockholm flight. By mid-morning I was introduced to my daughter Helena Gunilla. Sweden's women are famously independent and I found Christina preparing to combine single parenting (not a stigma in Sweden) with her professional life as a journalist. I promised nothing but flew home with my mind made up: I had to be with Christina and my new child. I arrived home in the early afternoon and told Gretel. She knew this disruptive move was a possibility (we had endured a stormy year) but still she was bitterly disappointed. When I drove off to pick up our son from his local infant school, William Walton's *Belshazzar's Feast* was playing on the radio:

'Thou art weighed in the balance and found wanting!' thundered the choir. I was both elated and terrified. Back home the family gathered in the sitting room. Gretel was icy calm as she explained to our children that I was leaving. Clare, then eight, was brave and bottled up her feelings. Matthew, only five, burst into tears. I was deeply miserable. I packed a bag and drove off from the Barnes house we had bought only a year previously, uncertain of what to do or where to go. I stopped to phone Tony Garnett and asked if I could sleep for a few nights in his spare room at Kestrel's HQ in Kensington. For weeks rather than days, as it turned out, I became a lodger in London's smartest commune, sharing meals and washing-up chores with committed left-wing playwrights and directors. Early in December, Christina flew in to London with our three-month-old baby and we took up residence in the smartest address I have ever known: Upper Phillimore Gardens in the Royal Borough of Kensington. The flat belonged to the actress Maria Aitken, whom I had met a few weeks earlier on the Brighton train when I was en route to tell my mother of the seismic changes in my life. Maria had just separated from her husband and taken up with David Jones, my friend and colleague from *Monitor*. He was now running the London end of the RSC: it was pure coincidence that we were all on the same train and sort of in the same boat. Maria's attic flat (at the top of her mother's spacious mansion) was momentarily free because of her marital estrangement and we were able to stay there the best part of a month: we particularly enjoyed our Christmas lunch of smoked salmon and scrambled eggs. Then I saw an advertisement in *The Times* for a house on Cheyne Walk which promised two grand pianos in a spacious music study. It turned out to be the former home of the Chinese pianist Fou Ts'ong and it was perfect for our needs: we took it on the spot. One of our first visitors was that wonderful musician André Previn, with whom I was producing a *Saturday Special* for LWT called *Mr Previn Comes To Town*. Sitting side by side at one of Ts'ong's gorgeous Steinways, I introduced him to the music I had been practising, Mozart's piano duet sonatas, which incredibly, he had never played before.

But our Cheyne Walk idyll was short-lived: one morning the lady who knocked angrily on the front door turned out to be Ts'ong's estranged wife, Zamira, daughter of Yehudi Menuhin. Her distemper was excusable: she had no idea her house was being let and didn't think much of our attempts to keep it clean: the dust and grime of the lorry-infested ring road outside the house penetrated every corner of the front rooms. So we had to move again and thanks to another tip-off from our friend Maria we once more fell on our feet, taking over the lease of a flat in Upper Harley Street from Ann Pennington, the actress with whom the film producer Sam Spiegel had just had a child, the future theatre producer Adam Spiegel. (I trust you are still with me.) Wonderfully placed just a few yards from Regent's Park, this new abode was our slightly cramped home for eighteen months until the prospect of a second child prompted us to look for something larger, and once again we were lucky: John Bryce, the producer I had been obliged to sack, had swapped the fleshpots of London for the lobster pots of Penzance and was forced to depart from his bijou house in St John's Wood Terrace. It came with a small garden and a garage where we could install a ping-pong table. My canny solicitor, Isador Caplan, a Fitzwilliam man who had long been Benjamin Britten's lawyer, conjured up a free lease for us with the Eyre Estate and we moved in with the new decade, in January 1970, at the same time as I was entering a new phase in my working life.

LWT had been on the air for only thirteen months when, without warning, the board sacked the managing director, Michael Peacock. I was in Mantua attending the annual Italia Prize as ITV's jury member. The heads of LWT's programme units, myself included, were incensed: our names had won the franchise for LWT but we had not been consulted about this major decision. A headline in the *Daily Mail* read: 'The Six wait for Number 7' – being the seventh man was my fleeting moment of front-page fame. I flew back that day and we achieved a stay of execution for Michael while the company took further soundings. But the facts couldn't be avoided: the investors were watching their money going down the drain. The spokesman of the old order, Lew Grade, grumbled that LWT was failing to produce programmes that the ITV public wanted to watch. In the middle of the crisis, LWT's chairman Aidan Crawley summoned the seven of us to his home in Chester Square, Belgravia. Crawley was a romantic figure: he had a matinée idol's good looks and before the war played cricket for Kent, later becoming chairman of the élite cricket club, the MCC. In the 1945 Attlee government he served as junior air minister, then in 1955 he created ITN, commercial television's mould-breaking news service. In the 1960s he switched to the Tory Party, serving as an MP for five years until he joined forces with David Frost to set up LWT. Despite his impressive pedigree, or perhaps because of it, we called him 'Creepy' Crawley. We sat all agog around his front-room table as he said he would like us to be the first to meet the company's new managing director, who was waiting in an anteroom. Like stout Cortez's men, we 'look'd at each other with a wild surmise', expecting a big figure from ITV or Fleet Street.

A troubled trio at LWT. Left to right: Michael Peacock, Aidan Crawley, David Frost.

When Crawley uttered the name Tom Margerison I'm afraid we fell about and laughed in his face. Tom was undoubtedly a gentle and sweet-natured man. But as we made it plain to Crawley, we did not rate him as a boss figure and with the exception of Jimmy Hill we all resigned that afternoon. Ironically Dr Tom survived for two years – rather longer than Mike Peacock. He then fell out with Rupert Murdoch, the investor he brought in to replace Arnold Weinstock of General Electric, who by then had had enough of television. *Sic transit gloria mundi.*

The dying months of the 1960s were days of great unease. I had a new partner and a new child to support, not to mention an estranged wife and two children whom I loved dearly and about whom I was feeling immensely guilty. By resigning from my managerial post at LWT I was saying goodbye to security and a guaranteed monthly pay packet. Only two years after quitting the BBC, I seemed to be cutting myself totally adrift. As usual, work was my salvation. Earlier in the year Cyril Bennett and I had concluded that our *Saturday Special* series was too expensive for the slot and I had suggested replacing it with a more modest magazine format which I would edit and produce, with Peter Hall, late of the RSC, as our persuasive frontman. Cyril had not resigned. He offered me a contract to stay at LWT and produce this new arts show. Only a few weeks had gone by when Peter Hall pulled out of the presenter role with the perfect excuse: he had teamed up with Colin Davis to run opera at Covent Garden. (Five years later, by then in charge at the National Theatre, Peter did make good his promise to present *Aquarius*. This was after I had moved back to the BBC, and he hosted the LWT arts show for three seasons in the mid-1970s, until Melvyn Bragg took it over. But that's another story.)

Faced with Peter's defection, Cyril was upbeat. He called me in to confirm my *Aquarius* posting. 'Bill', he said, brooking no argument, 'you're gonna have to present the show yerself. Get down to Duggie Hayward's in Mount Street and fix yourself up with some nice suits.' Duggie Hayward was already tailor *extraordinaire* to top showbiz actors such as Michael Caine. 'Go to Blades – that's at the top of the Burlington Arcade,' he continued, in his best Jewish uncle style, 'and come back with some striped shirts and kipper ties, maybe something different for every show.' (Huw Wheldon – I should have known – wore the same suit for every edition of *Monitor*.)

A new career loomed. But first I had a job to do in Los Angeles. As soon as I resigned from LWT my friend Ernest Fleischmann, formerly manager of the LSO, was on the phone within hours of my resignation. He was now established in California as the boss of the Los Angeles Philharmonic and on the spot he hired me to write the outline for a trendy project called *The Switched-On Symphony*. It was to be a very early example of pop–classical crossover which would feature the Los Angeles Philharmonic's conductor Zubin Mehta alongside such pop music luminaries as José Feliciano and Keith Emerson. When I arrived in Hollywood, curious and somewhat apprehensive, I was given no budgetary limit, just a desk and a yellow legal pad. I soon realised that Ernest's producers, Pierre Cossette and Burt Sugarman, were paying me to come up with ideas in a field about which they knew nothing. What they *did* know about was showbiz. Their office was a dream: leather sofas and armchairs; thick-pile carpet and a massive drinks cabinet. All day long I played records of Donovan and Jethro Tull and various rock groups with crossover aspirations who tended to perform in threesomes, like solicitors' firms, among them Crosby, Stills and Nash, Emerson, Lake and Palmer and Blood, Sweat & Tears, whose Anglo-Canadian vocalist David Clayton-Thomas made a huge impression on me. So did José Feliciano singing 'Light My Fire': Tito Burns would have been proud of my progress. My draft treatment served as the first-stage rocket essential to get the project successfully launched. It was, after all, the year of the moonwalk. *Switched-On Symphony* was brought to a sort of reality a few months later in a downtown Burbank studio under the experienced eye of another Englishman, a former *Six-Five Special* producer named Jack Good. Ironically the sponsor was *The Bell Telephone Hour*, which at my instigation had invested $100,000 in BBC2's documentary about Benjamin Britten's Aldeburgh.

Nothing could be more seductive than to be driven along a Californian freeway in Jack Good's Cadillac convertible listening to the blare of his eight-track cassette player. LA was lotus land and I would have liked to stay longer, but I had a pressing engagement in London, to set up my new arts show for LWT. My first priority was to find a title and I solved that conundrum while still in California. One evening the ebullient Jack Good took me to see the subversive rock musical *Hair*, which had already been running for a couple of seasons but was enjoying a new lease of life after a group of black musicians called Fifth Dimension recorded two vibrant songs from the show, 'Aquarius' and 'Let the Sunshine In'. I had a tenuous link with *Hair*: the show was originally mounted by Joseph Papp at the New York Public Theater, about which I had made a film for *Monitor* earlier in the decade. Backstage in LA I met *Hair*'s brilliant Canadian composer Galt MacDermott and the equally clever authors of the book and lyrics, Jimmy Ragni and Gerome Rado. We hit it off to such an extent that before the night was over they had given me permission to call my new ITV show *Aquarius*. They even gave me a set of beads which I wore around my neck for the next three years, day in and day out, no matter whether I was in shirtsleeves, birthday suit or dinner jacket. I never succumbed to drugs or flower power but I returned to London with high hopes for the new decade. They were fulfilled when at 10.30 p.m. on January 2nd 1970 I introduced the first of 186 editions of *Aquarius*.

CHAPTER 14

THE AGE OF *AQUARIUS*, 1970–1975

All fixed up in a nice suit and a kipper tie to host *Aquarius*.
The episode is 'Alfred The Great' (Hitchcock), directed by Derek Bailey.

AQUARIUS MAY HAVE been a promising title on paper but in the autumn months of 1969 I had nothing to support it: no production team, no programme projects, no studio dates or cutting rooms. And yet everything fell into place like a charm. One blessing was that for the first season at least we were to transmit fortnightly rather than every week. Friday nights at 10.30 was our slot. *Monitor* had also been fortnightly; it was a civilised tempo of programme-making. In 1970 the possibility of transmitting the new *Aquarius* show was merely an option for the other dozen companies which made up the ITV network and apart from Granada very few were willing to transmit culture, preferring to reach for their revolvers. But within the year, after we gained the confidence of the ITA, who declared the show mandatory, meaning every company had to screen it, we switched to a weekly schedule for thirty-nine weeks of the year, plus repeats on LWT in the summer months, so I was now a presenter, as well as an editor, regularly on the air hosting the show to audiences measured in millions rather than the meagre thousands with which arts programme producers have to pretend to be satisfied half a century later.

But in the autumn of 1969 I needed programmes and people to make them, and my cupboard was bare.

Having spent six years at the *Monitor* coalface, I guess I knew what was wanted. First I had to have a strong number two, a producer, somebody to keep an eye on everything, including me. It was in the videotape editing suite at Wembley that I got into conversation with Derek Bailey, who was then directing programmes for our adventurous education unit after previous work in Northern Island for Ulster Television. Derek had had a brilliant student career as an actor (Prince Hamlet) and stage director (*Tiger at the Gates*). Something told me on the spot that we could work well together and so we did, very happily, for five years. Derek was immensely proud of his Belfast heritage (the Troubles were just beginning), though politically he kept a neutral stance and it was years before I discovered that he was of Protestant stock – I'd never thought to ask him. His perceptive film about Seamus Heaney for our first series proved him to be a poet with a camera as well as a fine storyteller and a wry humorist. Astonishingly (to me), the fact that he had only one working eye had absolutely no effect on his acute powers of observation.

Nigel Miller was our first and most thoughtful researcher, and like most of the younger team players in *Aquarius* he eventually moved on to direction. His film about a modest barge-based theatre company which criss-crossed the country by canal was made special by his use on the soundtrack of *Tubular Bells*, Mike Oldfield's seminal album of pop music. Hilary Coote and Diane Milward were other level-headed researchers, and my final season was enlivened by the recruitment of Nigel Finch, who went on to co-edit the BBC's *Arena* with great distinction. In LWT's cutting rooms I found a brilliant film editor in Alan Ravenscroft, who shared his half-brother John Peel's love for the bizarre. When he, too, graduated to film-making we were lucky to recruit Paul Odell, in his way as inventive an editor as Allan Tyrer at *Monitor*. Paul made a significant contribution to my ninety-minute film about Venice's historic gondola race, as did Mike Humphreys, one of LWT's senior cameramen.

As the opening night approached, experienced PAs came on board. Trained by Rediffusion, the production assistants were capable women (it was not considered to be a man's job) who, thanks to generous perks, all seemed to be proud owners of soft-top sports cars. The PAs looked after vital elements in the programme-making process such as camera scripts, location reconnaissances and Equity contracts – the 'admin' stuff I had rather taken for granted at the BBC.

My embryonic *Aquarius* team was still in need of an extra dimension – the Ken Russell effect, I suppose you could call it, a film-maker who would provide a different slant on life from that possessed by university-educated chaps like me and Derek Bailey. My choice fell on Charlie Squires, a rough diamond of a director inherited from the Rediffusion company, who had been given his head as a film-maker by Cyril Bennett and was happy to find a welcoming home with me for his social commentaries. An early *Aquarius* Charlie Squires essay was about tattooing – body decoration. Challenged by a journalist as to what such a subject was doing in an arts programme, he replied (or so his faithful PA Frances Crossley reported): 'Tattooin'? Of course it's bleedin' art.' (Pause for thought.) 'Fuckin' *folk* art, innit?' His other films included *Derby Day* and a double profile of Raymond Mander and Joe Mitchenson, an eccentric overlapping couple, whose wondrous theatre archive (300,000 items) now belongs to the nation via Bristol University. Most of all I treasured Charlie's study of the cranky world of the occult, featuring a posse of middle-aged, middle-class lady-witches performing their midnight rituals in a wood prosaically sited near Effingham Junction in Surrey.

One of the earliest editions of *Aquarius* included another Squires gem entitled *Circus Hoffman: The Wildest Show on Earth*. The narrator and interviewer was Russell Harty, who proved to be the missing piece in my team jigsaw. Russell wrote to me out of the blue after a letter of mine in *The Listener* revealed that I was about to start an arts magazine on ITV. Russell had spent half a decade teaching in New York and at Giggleswick School, Yorkshire, before Philip French (who had been a contemporary of his at Exeter College, Oxford) recruited him to be assistant producer on *The Critics*, the BBC Third Programme's seminal arts review programme. Intrigued by his request to meet, I took Russell out to supper at a nearby Italian restaurant on Marylebone High Street. Christina and I were enchanted by his lively and sometimes outrageous opinions on all things quasi-cultural. At the end of the meal Russell brought

Russell Harty holds the 1972 Emmy Award for *Hello Dalí!*
I am next to director Bruce Gowers with the production team.

out an envelope and slipped it across the table with a conspiratorial whisper: 'Don't read it now,' he murmured, 'but I have written down the name of the man you should hire to introduce your new programme.' The hot tip was not himself but the stage director Ronald Eyre, then a big name in television drama, who like Russell had been a teacher at Giggleswick. They may perhaps have been close friends at some point and Russell certainly worshipped him. Eyre was a versatile man and would have done a good job for me but I wasn't looking for a presenter; what I *did* need was a quirky character who would contribute sharpness and wit to my own slightly solemn approach to cultural affairs. Within days I offered Russell a job on the *Aquarius* team – if he could extricate himself from his BBC contract, which, thanks to the kindness of Philip French, he did in double quick time.

Russell had three happy seasons with *Aquarius*, culminating in *Hello Dalí!*, a zany sequence of interviews with Salvador Dalí filmed for Bruce Gowers's hilarious location portrait. *Hello Dalí!* was a full-length documentary which won LWT and *Aquarius* an Emmy in 1972. Russell could have made a person-ality film career to match those of Malcolm Muggeridge or Louis Theroux, but he was drawn irresistibly (and, as it transpired, fatally) to the celebrity world: at Cyril Bennett's behest he moved office and studio in 1972 to host his own chat show, first for LWT and later for the BBC. Russell had a brilliance with words, in print as well as on air, and a curiosity about, indeed a *love* of people, that was unmatched by any of his contemporaries in the field of celebrity interview. That he should die aged only fifty-three was a tremendous sadness, and that he should have been hounded in his final weeks by grubby hacks intent on revealing his sexual preferences made his friends even sadder.

Returning to the opening edition of *Aquarius* in January 1970, I kicked the programme off with a short Charlie Squires film about the theatrical ladies who dress up as animals for the pantomime season – a fairly obvious declaration of my intent to give the arts a broad remit. A few weeks later came *Circus Hoffman*, featuring the two men who dressed up as the front and back of a circus horse. They hated each other and never spoke. Russell revelled in the fact that they spent their *Aquarius* appearance fee on a pub blow-out consisting of several pints and a big meal. Later, when they donned their horse costume for the evening circus performance, the man in the front was overtaken by a bilious attack from which he nevertheless derived the satisfaction known as *schadenfreude* (pleasure in another's discomfiture) when gales of wind were broken into the face of his partner supplying the back legs. Russell declared this to be a case of putting the fart before the horse.

For contrast we hired the satirist John Wells to create thumbnail lampoons of arts-world phonies; the first in the series was a hippy documentary director in love with jump-cuts and crash-zooms. There was a tenuous connection between this caricature and our main story that evening, which concerned the fate of a film called *British Sounds* directed by Jean-Luc Godard, which Tony Garnett's Kestrel company had made under its long-term contract with LWT. An hour-long documentary, it had been languishing on the shelf for months because, to be blunt, I thought it was too boring to screen as a *Saturday Special*. However, LWT was accused of censorship, perhaps because the film allegedly featured a sequence with mutinous assembly-line workers at the Ford car factory in Dagenham. *British Sounds* became a *cause célèbre*. We arranged a special screening at the Institute of Contemporary Arts, then a hotbed of radical thought, followed by what proved to be a boisterous audience debate from which we edited some pungent opinions. With an excerpt from the controversial film at the beginning, we assembled quite a lively package for our début programme. I had previously leaked to the popular press the fact that there was nudity in Godard's film: an attractive girl walks stark naked down a staircase – shades of Marcel Duchamp and his celebrated painting entitled *Nude descending a staircase*! What she was doing in a car factory I cannot recall, but I got what I needed, a protest from Mrs Mary Whitehouse, the guardian of the nation's morality: a public grumble from her was worth at least half a million extra viewers.

The edited programme was put to bed before supper on the evening of the transmission and the team went off, as one does, for a celebratory drink in the club bar. At 7 o'clock there was an anxious call from Granada, our partners in the north. 'There's nudity in your *Aquarius* programme. We can't show nudity if it hasn't been cleared with the ITA.' Shortly afterwards the Director General of the Independent Television Authority, Sir Robert Fraser, arrived at Wembley Studios. A testy, outspoken Australian who had earned his knighthood during the war, while running the Central Office of Information, Fraser had been in charge of commercial television since its inception in 1954. He was not best pleased to be called out on a Friday evening on such a footling errand. After viewing the nude sequence, he uttered, in my hearing, an unforgettable edict: 'I will not tolerate moving pussy on my network.' Everybody nodded in silent assent.

I proposed a compromise which involved a simple edit. But in 1970 videotape was still being cut, not copied, so nothing was truly simple. Out came the razor blade. One moment the nude girl was glimpsed at the top

Mrs Mary Whitehouse – an attack
from her was said to guarantee
improved audience ratings.

Sir Robert Fraser, Director
General of the ITA – 'no moving
pussy on my network'.

of the stairs. At the next she was at the bottom. It could have been a scene from *Breathless* (*À bout de Souffle*), Godard's 1961 *cinéma-vérité* masterpiece, famous for its jump-cuts. The revised tape was sent down the line to Granada and the other companies taking the show. Disaster was averted. The fact that Robert Fraser retired later that year has no connection with this incident whatsoever; he was already over sixty-five.

Fraser was succeeded in the top job by a former headmaster of Charterhouse school who was of great help to me in my final years with *Aquarius*. Brian Young was tall, handsome and mellifluous of voice; happily he was also blessed with the guts to stand up to Rupert Murdoch – a campaign in which he was supported by Colin Shaw, who came to the ITA from the core of the BBC's establishment, where he had been secretary of the whole caboodle. In the early 1970s it looked as if Murdoch, the Australian press mogul, was going to establish himself as the superman of the British media. Brian Young spear-headed the resistance. I had great support from him, the ITA insisting that all the commercial companies should screen *Aquarius*. Brian was keen on classical music (he later chaired the Arts Council's music panel) and enjoyed many of our programmes. Still, I fear I must have tested his patience more

Titbits magazine article. The *Aquarius* 'Oh! Calcutta!' controversy.

than once and looking back I note that I rashly persisted in seeking high ratings for *Aquarius* by sailing pretty close to the wind in terms of the subject matter I selected for the programme.

It was only a couple of years after Godard's *British Sounds* that I opted to include excerpts from a controversial show called *Oh! Calcutta!* This was a satirical revue which became famous for its nudity and frank discussion of sexuality. It was the brainchild of Ken Tynan, the much-admired theatre critic, chief henchman of Sir Laurence Olivier and notorious at the time as the first man to utter the F word on television. I gave a journalist from the magazine *Titbits* a shameful amount of quotable material, of which the following passage is particularly blush-making: 'I'm no fool ... a lot of people like to see naked flesh and there was a time when there wasn't much of it about'. I went on to claim stoutly that *Oh! Calcutta!* had 'real artistic purpose'. I survived, though perhaps I had upset John Birt (the new controller at LWT) too much for the *Aquarius* series to be continued when, two years later, Birt had brought on Melvyn Bragg to replace Derek Bailey.

In all I edited and presented nearly 200 editions of *Aquarius*. Derek Bailey succeeded me as editor in March 1975 and edited three more series before John Birt wrote *finis* in no uncertain terms by inviting Melvyn Bragg to revamp the slot. I can understand: Melvyn wanted to do his own show, not inherit mine. My five *Aquarius* years were a productive and immensely enjoyable period in my life so I am saddened when I read dismissive assessments of the programme in cultural histories of ITV which suggest that *Aquarius* did little more than pave the way for *The South Bank Show*. I yield to none in admiration for Melvyn Bragg: he did an excellent job at LWT for close on three decades. But if I had not decided to return to the BBC in 1975 I believe *Aquarius* would have survived through the John Birt era at LWT and might be in the ITV schedules to this day: I have only myself to blame. Melvyn had had a similar training to my own, serving on *Monitor* for a couple of years, then branching out into book programmes for BBC2. In the 1970s he presented *The Lively Arts* for BBC2 and edited as well as presented *Read All About It* for BBC1. When he joined LWT in 1978 he proposed a broad range of subject matter, just as *Aquarius* had done: the difference was that after a rather disastrous start with a multi-subject magazine format, Melvyn switched to a policy of one topic per programme and stuck to it for thirty years. The short film, one of *Aquarius*'s specialities, disappeared.

Working on the assumption that if I don't blow my own trumpet nobody else will, I offer a flavour of the original 1970s series, hopefully to make you wish you could view *Aquarius* programmes on some kind of ITV archival iPlayer. For example I would give several back teeth to see again our profile of Elton John, then in his mid-twenties and already a star. It was directed by the Scotsman David Bell, previously encountered by me at the Edinburgh Festival, whom I borrowed from LWT's entertainment department. David later made his name directing Stanley Baxter's brilliant shows. He used to treat us to lurid tales of his night-time adventures at the gay Turkish baths he frequented in the West End in the mid-1980s. He was one of the first victims of the Aids epidemic, dead at the age of fifty-three.

It was David who out of the blue urged me to make a programme marking Stravinsky's death in 1971. We did just that, and quite spectacularly, the following year, for the first anniversary of the composer's death. David put together eloquent newsreel of the Stravinsky funeral gondola being escorted to the cemetery island of San Michele. I teamed up with the English Bach Festival (Stravinsky had been its president), hired the Royal Albert Hall, installed a giant screen and invited Leonard Bernstein to deliver a eulogy (on film) and then conduct the LSO in three major Stravinsky works, the *Symphony of Psalms*, the Capriccio for Piano and Orchestra and *The Rite of Spring*. His performance – again with the LSO as in *Symphonic Twilight* – was breathtaking in its courage, marking the peak of LB's very substantial achievement as a Stravinsky interpreter. (This *Aquarius* Stravinsky Special has been commercially issued as a DVD by ICA.)

I enjoyed producing such grand classical music occasions. At Covent Garden we filmed the world's leading diva, Joan Sutherland, topping the bill at a fundraising opera gala. *Aquarius* was at the Royal Festival Hall when Mstislav Rostropovich and his wife Galina Vishnevskaya celebrated their departure from the Soviet Union. Their concert helped *Aquarius* to win BAFTA's award that year for the best specialised series. From St Paul's Cathedral I directed Carlo Maria Giulini conducting Beethoven's *Missa Solemnis*, part of a festival devised by Ted Heath, then prime minister, to mark the UK's entry into the Common Market. I invited Mr Heath to introduce the occasion from 10 Downing Street. Mr Heath would doubtless have enjoyed conducting something himself but my sycophancy wouldn't stretch that far, although I admired him, and still do, for bringing classical music to Number 10.

I also liked reporting on intimate music-making. Our camera team eavesdropped on the vivacious young Kiri Te Kanawa when she was being rehearsed in the 'Jewel Song' from Gounod's *Faust* for the Royal Opera with the wittiest of opera directors, John Copley. Derek Bailey also made a deeply sympathetic film about the Amadeus Quartet when they were in Vienna, home town for three of the members, celebrating their twenty-fifth anniversary. Derek took them up one by one on the Big Wheel, the *Riesenrad*, and got them to tell the story of how the quartet came together. The cross-cutting of their memories was akin to the delightful instrumental interplay in the Mozart G major Quartet (K387), which they played as the film's finale. I sigh nostalgically when I think of such affectionate half-hour films, which sadly have totally disappeared from today's schedules.

I even had the temerity to play the piano on air. Just the once. I invited the violinist Kyung-Wha Chung to perform a showpiece full of technical fireworks by Niccolò Paganini. Only she and I knew that the piano accompaniment was strictly plink-plonk, kid's stuff, and anyway all eyes and cameras would be on Kyung-Wha.

With Kyung-Wha Chung in the *Aquarius* studio.

There was nothing humdrum about *Aquarius*. Reporting on the theatre was always important. I had enormous fun filming a chunk of Alan Ayckbourn's latest comedy, *The Norman Conquests*, featuring Tom Courtenay and Felicity Kendal. I also relished the opportunity to work under the eye of a real film director when I shot a big scene from Clive Donner's stage production of *Kennedy's Children*, a touching lament for the hippy era. The production was at the King's Head in Islington, one of London's first pub theatres, whose landlord, the American Dan Crawford, had an uncanny knack of backing good unknown playwrights. I felt it was our job to highlight such pioneering work. For his part, Derek Bailey became close to the influential playwright Athol Fugard (*Sizwe Banzi Is Dead*) and was a fly on the wall when Harold Pinter discussed camera angles with Peter Hall for a scene they were filming from his latest play. We all liked working with Peter Hall; Derek filmed a day in his crowded life (this was after his plan to run Covent Garden had foundered and before he took on the National Theatre). We watched him at work making what I believe to be his best film, *Akenfield*, about his Suffolk *Heimat*. Cannily we also befriended Ken Tynan and paid court to his master, Sir Laurence Olivier, with the desired result that LWT won the rights to make a film about

Lord Olivier (left) with Peter Hall in front of the National Theatre.
It was being constructed at full volume right underneath my office window.

the building of Denys Lasdun's National Theatre complex next door to our headquarters on the Thames. Derek produced and directed the film.

When LWT moved in to its handsome new building on the South Bank in 1973 I was allocated a rather splendid corner office on the eleventh floor from where I could watch the sun setting over the Houses of Parliament and Westminster Bridge (what a change from Stonebridge Park!), while immediately below my window the National Theatre's foundations were being noisily excavated night and day. Incidentally, it was on the banks of the Thames that we did the principal photography for our fifty-minute portrait of Alfred Hitchcock, who was shooting the opening scene of *Frenzy*, his last masterpiece.

Americans figured substantially on *Aquarius*. We gave that great African-American soprano Jessye Norman her first outing on British television, and did a similar service for the choreographers Twyla Tharp and Paul Taylor. When Mary McCarthy arrived in London to promote her new book I was so much in awe of her piranha-toothed smile that I drafted in Russell Harty to share the conversation with me and divert her withering look. Of course, we also covered American movies. The director Joseph Losey, a fugitive from Hollywood's red-baiting era, gave me a very frank interview when his film *The Go-Between* appeared: his widow said later that it was the best thing he ever did on television. The Hollywood star Shirley MacLaine and Andy Warhol's superstar Candy Darling both made over-the-top appearances in the programme, and in 1971 I dealt with film again when I interviewed Dirk Bogarde about his role as Aschenbach in *Death in Venice*. I remember the date, March 1st, because that evening my son Lukas was born. He was the only child of mine whose birth I actually attended.

Russell Harty was in his element on film; one year he reported on the New Orleans carnival and flirted outrageously with dowager *grandes dames* at that colourful event. At the other end of the spectrum, the gifted Californian artist Ed Ruscha showed us how he used vegetable and fruit juices in his work. Ruscha had just produced a portfolio of screen-prints in which single words in Gothic typeface were printed in edible substances such as pie fillings,

My daughter Helena with her baby brother Lukas.

Kenneth Clark – as sweet as *La Gioconda* after a quick snifter.

bolognese sauce, caviar and chocolate syrup. It was indeed the dawning of the Age of Aquarius!

A more savage eye was turned on America by the British artist Ralph Steadman, whom we profiled at the time he was preoccupied with *Alice in Wonderland* – although echoes of another book he illustrated, Hunter Thompson's *Fear and Loathing in Las Vegas*, peeped out from almost every page. Other British artists whom we visited on location were Henry Moore and Elisabeth Frink (shades of *Monitor!*). On another day Frink brought her printing stone into the studio and peeled off an artist's proof before our marvelling eyes. I even arranged a personal postscript to *Civilisation* by inviting Kenneth Clark to repeat for a television audience his recent lecture at the Victoria & Albert Museum on the subject of Leonardo's *Mona Lisa* – ITV was after all Clark's original stomping ground.

Despite our lengthy negotiations in the 1960s, the noble lord's demeanour was very chilly when he came to the *Aquarius* studio, and he insisted on returning to his Albany flat between the rehearsal and the lecture, which meant the invited audience had to be kept waiting and I hadn't booked a warm-up artist. Luckily 'K' must have indulged in a snifter during his break because he returned all sweetness and light to deliver a fascinating talk.

We certainly liked to travel for the programme. In Cornwall we contrasted the lifestyles of a clutch of larger-than-life painters, among them Patrick Heron and Roger Hilton; in Israel a posse of pianist virtuosi, headed by Emanuel Ax, were filmed at the inaugural Arthur Rubinstein competition; in Teheran the Empress of Iran, the lovely Farah Diba, introduced us to ancient Persian art; in Munich we watched Bob Fosse filming Liza Minnelli in a spellbinding scene from *Cabaret*; in Paris, various style secrets were revealed by the fashion guru Pierre Cardin. On that Paris trip I also took the ex-pat actress Susan Hampshire (lately the beguiling Fleur in the BBC's epic version of *The Forsyte Saga*) on a rowing boat in the Bois de Boulogne; in another interview, an intellectual novelist named Claire Gallois had the nerve to ask me, on screen, why I posed such stupid questions. (She developed into one of France's most formidable intellectuals.)

Thanks to the astute bookkeeping of the *Aquarius* accountant Vijay Amarnani, there was usually enough cash in the production kitty for me to hire a freelance director once in a while. After Tony Palmer fell out – for the first of many times – with the BBC, I invited him to join us and for *Aquarius* he filmed John Lennon and Yoko Ono in New York; it was one in a slew of rather sad American films by Palmer, which he later reissued as a DVD under the title *The Pursuit of Happiness*. Another star director I hired was Jack Gold, one of the warmest human beings I ever met. He shared my admiration for the veteran film-maker Denis Mitchell (*Morning in the Streets* was probably his most poetic documentary), so I brought Jack in to make a Mitchell profile. At the time I didn't know that Mitchell's daughter Judith had quite recently married John Freeman of *Face to Face* fame. A man of many careers, Freeman had become LWT's chairman and managing director but he had nothing to do with my decision to make a programme about his new father-in-law: he told me he made a point of never interfering with the programme-makers.

We all had reason to be grateful to Freeman: he was LWT's saviour. In the early 1970s Rupert Murdoch started buying up shares in LWT. Since he had already acquired control of several UK newspapers, this move caused dismay in business circles and the ITA. With his customary acumen, David

Frost persuaded Freeman to steady the LWT ship by becoming chairman, even though he had no business experience whatsoever. Aidan Crawley was pensioned off with the title of president.

Any editor worth his or her salt is always on the lookout for talent. I'm rather proud that I gave director commissions to many other creative people, notably Barrie Gavin, Bryan Izzard, Nigel Finch and Mick Csaky. Csaky was a brash Anglo-Hungarian whose father later married Elisabeth Frink. Mick came to my office one day and pitched an improbable story about filming Berber tribes in Morocco, dancing fantastically and making wondrous music: I was so taken by his *chutzpah* that on impulse I offered him the *Aquarius* film crew and off he went. It was the beginning of an illustrious programme-making career.

Barrie Gavin was an obvious choice for me since we had worked together so easily at the BBC a decade earlier. Barrie has always been strong on musical subjects and I thought he would be ideal to pin down the essence of the somewhat obscure composer Havergal Brian. Born into a working-class family in Stoke-on-Trent, Havergal Brian was well into his nineties and had composed at least thirty symphonies, one of which he called *The Gothic*. I found Brian's music turgid stuff but nobody could deny the newsworthiness of this weird figure from a bygone age, and Barrie directed a touching documentary, filmed at the composer's home in Shoreham-by-Sea. The music was performed by the excellent Leicestershire Schools Symphony Orchestra. Gavin's second *Aquarius* assignment was to mount a studio production of Harrison Birtwistle's recent music theatre work *Down by the Greenwood Side*. Folk-tale ritual mixed with pantomime comedy, the piece made raw listening for the ITV audiences on a Sunday afternoon but was sufficiently successful in terms of brownie points for LWT's programme controller, still Cyril Bennett, to commission a longer opera from Harry, to be entitled *Yan Tan Tethera*. It was perhaps not entirely coincidental that the wives of Bennett and Birtwistle had been good friends since student days. Sadly Cyril died soon after and the opera, whose principal characters included two shepherds and a dozen sheep (I do not jest), was televised a decade later – but by BBC2.

Another musical creation for *Aquarius* was lighter in weight but undoubtedly provided more fun. Yehudi Menuhin frequently petitioned me to do something on television with his wife Diana, who never tired of reminding anybody who would listen that she had renounced the life of a star (ballerina and actress) to become Yehudi's wife. Whatever the truth of this claim, Diana definitely had a way with words and we eventually hit upon an appropriate vehicle for her, an entertainment entitled *How Pleasant to Know Mr Lear*, with music composed by Edwin Roxburgh, the oboist in Yehudi's Bath Festival Orchestra. Edward Lear's nonsense verse was accompanied by a small orchestra, conducted by Yehudi himself. Diana recruited the larger-than-life horror film actor Vincent Price to share the narration; Price turned out to be a lovely man and a true Anglophile; he had absolutely no side or self-importance despite his world fame. I needed a star director to mould this talent into a television show and I found one on my doorstep at LWT. Bryan Izzard was a large man with a flamboyant personality who came to work in a kaftan and had made his name producing big-time comedies and chat shows. Our affectionate salute to Edward Lear, delivered by two over-the-top performers and backed by Menuhin and his musicians, was a perfect fit for Izzard's camp temperament; he created a vivid and original show. Roxburgh's style was impeccable, indeed I enjoyed it so much that I persuaded Yehudi to commission him to compose another work for Diana combining speech and music, this time built around the poetry of Edward Estlin Cummings, who liked his name (and his verses) to appear in lower case type (thus, e.e. cummings). Izzard worked closely with LWT's clever graphic designer John Tribe, who found a host of unusual ways to lay out the text of Cummings's poems on the screen. It was an exciting experiment and I gave it the prominent transmission slot of our hundredth edition. Disappointingly the programme, which I thought a worthy successor to William Walton's *Façade*, did not receive a single review. I would love to see it again, but as is the case with so many shows from the early 1970s the programme has not been traced. Still I have a Cummings memento: in a second-hand bookshop in Manhattan I bought an oil sketch of Cummings, done by the poet himself, head and shoulders, very handsome in a lined, weary way, pipe in mouth and sporting a jauntily tilted hat. On the reverse it is dated 23 September 1947. It's unsigned but to judge from other Cummings self-portraits it is definitely painted by the poet himself; he was a dab hand, so to speak, as an artist.

Nigel Finch is the third director I want to mention. If you look him up on the internet he appears to have worked only for the BBC, ending up as co-editor of *Arena*. He was a passionate supporter of gay rights and was working on *Stonewall*, a full-length documentary, when he died of Aids in 1995. His career is said to have begun in 1978 with a famous *Arena* film about the popular song *My Way*. But when I selected Nigel to join the *Aquarius* team as a researcher four years earlier, it was his first job out of university. Nigel was a great personality. He rode a motorbike, wore a colourful leather

The poet e.e. cummings's self-portrait.

jacket and was passionate about the arts, bubbling with energy and ideas; he quickly became a first-rate visual storyteller. I put him together with Michael Holroyd and they made a revealing, deeply troubling film about biographer Holroyd's lifetime passion, the artist Augustus John. Nigel also directed a telling portrait of the Cookham painter Stanley Spencer and his dominating wives. I'm proud to have helped him on his way: for *Arena* and BBC2 he filmed Marschner's opera *The Vampyre*, declaring it to be the perfect soap opera, divisible into six parts.

When I left LWT the *Aquarius* team presented me with a vast photo-montage of programme highlights. I stole a glance at it just now and was mortified to discover that I had forgotten to include in this survey our film about that inimitable connoisseur and blues singer George Melly. (Derek Bailey's punning title for his film profile was *Thoroughly Modern Melly*.) There are dozens of other shows worth seeing again, but I am happy to rest my case that *Aquarius* made a significant mark on British television. The 1970s was a stimulating decade to be involved with the arts and what most surprises me now, writing nearly half a century later, is that I also had time for other LWT work, notably an educational series called *Music in the Round*, taped in 1971 at the tiny Cockpit Theatre in London. Derek and I chose the participants to emphasise that the music world was a very broad church. Gerald Moore, soon to retire, was urbanity personified. He spoke about his role as the perfect accompanist. The National Jazz Youth Orchestra (then only a few seasons old) made a striking appearance and so, famously, did the pop idol Marc Bolan, the prettiest person I ever interviewed. My grandchildren tell me that their friends (who watch the show on YouTube) laugh at my crass questions – but that was always the way to get interesting responses, which I did. Marc Bolan died tragically young: six years after our interview for *Music in the Round* his girlfriend drove his Mini off the road and through an iron fence, ending up embedded in a sycamore tree. When I take the road to the south coast or Glyndebourne I always pass the Bolan shrine in Barnes which his fans created at the side of the road.

The year 1973 saw the creation of commercial radio in the UK, the Tories thus fulfilling a 1970 manifesto promise. At one point I was recruited into a consortium applying for a London licence: there was much jockeying for position before the bids finally went in and instead of becoming a share-holder I found myself drafted by LWT (which had backed the successful new station) into the role of host and editor of Capital Radio's new weekly arts review programmes. Yes, here I was, already editing *Aquarius* and now charged additionally with creating independent radio's first-ever show in the same genre. I called it *Alternatives* and chose Malcolm Arnold's bright and breezy First Brass Quintet for the title music, played by the Philip Jones Brass Ensemble. We put the show together on Sunday mornings in Capital's new and mostly empty offices; I don't think we saw another soul on the site except for a couple of studio technicians and Richard Attenborough, who was obviously taking his position as Capital's driving force and major share-holder very seriously. I loved getting back to radio, where everything is so simple by comparison with television. I personally made the phone calls to invite guests; my devoted LWT assistant Jackie Warner (she took over from Liz Queenan) worked on the details with Susannah Simons, a bright young Capital producer fresh from university who went on to do major PR work for Radio 3. Of the programmes, I remember Tom Stoppard joshing with me as if we were members of the same creative community – didn't I wish! On the downside, Lillian Hellman, whom I worshipped because of her working with Bernstein on *Candide*, proved to be grumpiness personified when she came in to talk about her new memoir, *Pentimento*, which is not a patch on her plays. I thought involving young contributors might appeal to teenage listeners, so I invited my son Matthew, all of eleven years old, to do some reviewing. There was no way I could have guessed that he would give a new Bob Dylan release a bad notice. My daughter Clare, then thirteen, also proved to be no respecter of reputations, being embarrassingly dismissive of a successful group called 10CC.

I did a couple of seasons for Capital but 'the times they were a-changing' and I was soon to turn my back on the ITV fleshpots and return to the BBC. The first straw in the wind of change was when Christina and I, then living in our St John's Wood cottage with two small children, decided we needed more space and accepted an offer from my solicitor Isador Caplan to buy his classic Georgian town house on the crest of Richmond Hill. It was only a few yards from the park and bang next door to a hotel with which Isador had been feuding for several decades – such was his dislike of the owners that he inserted a clause into the title deeds forbidding me to sell the property *to* the hotel. The house spread over four storeys so there were many flights of stairs to keep us fit. Christina installed a darkroom in the basement: she had decided to quit Swedish journalism and retrain as a photographer. She studied for two years at the local technical college and was soon getting interesting portrait and reportage work with record companies and the opera houses, photographing the big names for publicity stills and LP record covers. Upstairs there were rooms for our children, Helena and Lukas, for the Swedish au pair girls and for overnight stays by my older children, who lived with my first wife in Wandsworth. The first-floor sitting room was an L-shaped *piano nobile* with a wrought-iron balcony and French windows looking out on the lovely curve of the Thames that artists from Reynolds and Turner to Oskar Kokoschka had memorialised in oil paintings. There was plenty of space for Christina's lovely Swedish furniture, inherited from her parents, and also – fulfilment of a dream – for the acquisition of a good grand piano. I bought it on the last day of a Harrods sale – it was long past closing time but the staff saw that I was serious and stayed in attendance while I tried out half a dozen pianos, eventually choosing a Model B Steinway made in Hamburg in the 1960s and previously owned by a school. I have had enormous pleasure from it ever since.

But the most significant thing about moving to Richmond was that our new house, number 144, was literally twelve Georgian doors away from number 120, the home of Huw Wheldon and his family. I had not seen Huw since what was widely thought of as my betrayal in 1967, but enough water had flowed under the bridge for a reconciliation. We met for lunch in a quiet floating restaurant near London Zoo. Inevitably I felt drawn to him once again and now that I had proved I could succeed on my own terms I found myself hankering for the larger canvas upon which the BBC made its mark every day of the week. At LWT I had been granted complete editorial freedom by Cyril Bennett but there would always be frustrations when one worked in the commercial world of 'independent' television. I often had to go cap in hand to our transmission controller Eric Flackfield if I needed so much as a two-minute overrun. True, we had televised Beethoven's *Missa Solemnis* for Ted Heath's common market festival but it was galling that the work had to be screened in two halves separated by a week! In the long hard light of hindsight I can see that I would have had a much easier life, and a better-paid one, had I stayed put at LWT. It would have meant thinking a little smaller, choosing musical works whose length didn't burst the schedule pattern and so on. But when an emissary from the BBC secretly met me on a Regent's Park bench to explore the possibility of my return to the Corporation's fold I was an easy target: I *wanted* to go back to the BBC and in April 1975 that was what I did. When I told Cyril Bennett my decision he was upset, disappointed and visibly saddened. So was I. But he did not seek to dissuade me.

The last four editions of the 1975 *Aquarius* winter season were all programmes I personally directed, leaving my successor Derek Bailey to get on with stockpiling for the future: *Aquarius* was to continue under his editorship, with Peter Hall taking my place as presenter, which (as already mentioned) he did with flair for the next three seasons. To bow myself out I decided to make two programmes about Venice and two with the pianist Alfred Brendel. The first Brendel programme was built around the preparations and sessions for a new recording of Mozart's last piano concerto, K595 in B flat. The framework was conventional: rehearsals with the Academy of St Martin in the Fields under Neville Marriner, control room conferences, Brendel practising at home in Hampstead flanked by his collection of *kitsch* objects, an interview with Marriner saying that he had to be flexible when working with such a perfectionist as Alfred; another interview with Brendel himself, conceding that when push came to shove he had to be the boss because having studied it for years he knew the piece better than anybody else. This relatively predictable material was enlivened by the secondary theme: the way this Mozart LP was marketed by Philips, then a major player in the classical world. We filmed a staff conference at which the sales director Quita Chavez – described by a colleague in the business as 'a true Boadicea' – instructed her sales force to go out into the field and get their boots stuck in to the opposition. 'Not only', she declared with thunderous conviction, 'do you have a regular winner with Brendel but there's also the marvellous B side, with the K456.'

This blatant piece of commercialism was intercut with Brendel playing the most soulful section of the slow movement cadenza. A secondary pleasure came from watching the give-and-take relationship between conductor and soloist, with Brendel sometimes going literally behind Marriner's back to show an individual player how he wanted a particular ornament to be performed. Marriner affected not to notice.

The companion programme to this documentary was a complete performance of K595 given to an invited audience in the LWT studio. I saw the video again recently: Brendel's immaculate performance compensates for the dry acoustic. And I imagine the sales of this particular LP did not suffer from the television exposure.

My final programme for *Aquarius* was *The Great Gondola Race*. This was planned to go out over two episodes, the first dealing with the run-up and the second with the day of the race itself, the famous Historical Regatta which for centuries has been raced up and down the Grand Canal by two-man racing gondolas on the first Sunday in September. It is second only to the Palio in

Venice in Peril. Left to right: myself with Sir Ashley Clarke, Contessa Anna Maria Cicogna, John Julius, Lord Norwich and Carla, Lady Thorneycroft on the roof terrace of the British Council palazzo on the Grand Canal.

The Great Gondola Race carried the
day at the 1975 BAFTAs. Christina
Burton's pictures spearheaded
the publicity campaign.

Siena as an historical spectacular. But for me as film-maker another race had to be counterpointed against the exciting exertions of the *gondolieri* and that was the race to save Venice itself: the city's palaces and churches were crumbling, with the floodwaters developing as an ever-present menace. In 1966 I had seen the appalling flood damage in Florence, upon which young Robert Hughes had reported most eloquently for *The Look of the Week*. Since then I had struck up a friendship with a music-loving BBC governor named Ashley Clarke, Britain's former ambassador to Italy, who with his devoted wife Frances had retired to Venice and was currently running a relief organisation called Venice in Peril.

Among its members were the delightful Renaissance scholar John Hale, the irrepressible *bon viveur* historian John Julius Norwich and the very effective lobbyist Carla Thorneycroft, wife of a prominent Tory politician. It was Venice in Peril's restoration work in churches and especially of the lovely sixteenth-century Loggetta del Sansovino on the Piazza San Marco which inspired me to go ahead with the film. And what a colourful affair it turned out to be. The *TV Times* made it the week's cover story, illustrating their feature with spectacular colour photos taken by Christina. The film helped us to win that year's BAFTA award for the best specialised series. If there had been specific awards for camerawork and editing they would surely have gone to Mike Humphreys and Paul Odell. Paul's use of music was brilliant. Vivaldi was an obvious choice for gondola shots but Paul often subverted the expectation. In the dawn sequence, for example, featuring glimpses of a racing gondola scything through the waters of the misty lagoon, he superimposed over a tranquil adagio a phrase of stabbing violin music, furiously agitated; both excerpts were taken from *The Seasons*. For the climax of the race, Odell switched from swirling Vivaldi, which works well when accompanying Canaletto's depiction of a 1740s *regatta storica*, to Bartók's thrilling fanfares from the finale of his Concerto for Orchestra – we used this music at the moment when our film cuts to the real-life struggle on the Grand Canal between the favourite gondola racer Ciaci, an Olympic oarsman, and his rivals, among them the contender we wrongly backed, an elegant gondolier from Murano, nicknamed Bufalo, the buffalo. Mike Humphreys had his camera everywhere. Two of his improvised sequences stand out. One is the pre-race briefing, which is observed only by eloquent close-ups of hands weaving patterns in the air, accompanied by the sound of high-pitched, incomprehensible Venetian voices – the racing oarsmen are arguing the toss about how they should move out of their starting lanes into the open lagoon.

The other revelation is a shot of the victor Ciaci borrowing an enormous bouquet of gladioli when he thinks nobody is looking. When he spots the camera filming him he launches into a bull's roar of guilt blended with victory.

LWT won seven awards at the 1975 BAFTA ceremony, more than the rest of ITV put together. *Aquarius* had beaten the BBC's *Face the Music* and *Omnibus*. It was a sweet triumph after the brickbats thrown at LWT in its early years. I did not have to leave LWT but I could not have chosen a better time to do so. It was time, I felt, to return to the reality of BBC Music and Arts.

CHAPTER 15

1970: BERNSTEIN'S *ANNUS MIRABILIS*

Leonard Bernstein and Gustav Mahler – a great adventure.

IN JANUARY 1970, a few weeks into the first season of *Aquarius*, the phone rang at home and when Christina answered a sonorous voice said: 'This is Gregory Peck. May I speak to Mr Humphrey Burton?' It was my third great adventure as the new decade began, along with marriage and *Aquarius*, and it affected the course of my working life even more deeply than the establishment of my own arts series on ITV. Mr Peck invited me to come over to the Dorchester Hotel; he had a project he wished to discuss. When we met later that day he told me he was the emissary of a new production partnership masterminded by Roger Stevens, the American impresario who had produced *West Side Story* back in the 1950s. Stevens was now in charge of the not yet completed Kennedy Center for the Performing Arts in Washington – but once a producer always a producer and he was currently backing Leonard Bernstein in a brand-new way. LB's inner circle consisted of his canny lawyer Abe Friedman, his literary agent Robert Lantz and his manager, previously an executive with CBS Records, Schuyler Chapin. Stevens joined them to form a new company called Amberson Productions, 'amber' being the English translation of the German word *Bernstein*, the much-prized gemstone derived from fossilised trees. Back in the 1940s when he first moved to New York and worked for a music publisher, LB had invented the *nom de plume* Lenny Amber for his transcriptions of jazz standards.

The witty and wily Robbie Lantz had his finger on the pulse of most important matters in the cultural world: Amberson, he insisted, must ensure that from now on LB's conducting performances would be recorded for distribution on domestic and educational videotapes. Home video was still several years in the future but these were visionary people and they wanted to be ahead of the curve. Their first project was to be a performance of the Verdi *Requiem* in St Paul's Cathedral given by four illustrious soloists and the LSO and Chorus, all under the baton of Maestro Bernstein.

Mr Peck came to the point: would I consent to be director of the telecast? I did not need to be asked twice. In theory I was fully occupied with *Aquarius* but this was that proverbial once-in-a-lifetime opportunity, and since the production could be televised by *Aquarius* for ITV (at Easter) there was no conflict of interest. With hindsight I realise that Amberson was making a leap in the dark by hiring me rather than the American colleagues who had directed the telecasts of LB's successful Young People's Concerts throughout the 1960s. I guess Amberson wanted to give the first-ever 'concert video' a different look, a musical film-maker's look (mine) rather than that of a gifted studio director. But there was no time to worry my head about the aesthetics of the project: the performance was less than a month away and nothing in the way of production resources had been booked. LB was already engaged by the LSO to conduct the *Requiem* at a concert in the Royal Albert Hall and to record it there with the American record company CBS. The Americans had recorded Mahler's Eighth Symphony under LB at that venue back in 1966 so as to avoid the enormous cost of hiring a unionised American chorus (see chapter 12). The LSO had since sacked their innovative manager Ernest

Fleischmann and recruited in his place a quiet American record producer named Harold Lawrence, who I liked a lot. It was probably Harold's idea to squeeze in an extra performance at St Paul's Cathedral and make it 'by invitation only' to avoid problems with the Musicians' Union television contract.

My first priority was to arrange a co-production with LWT. To his great credit, Vic Gardiner, LWT's acting managing director since the turmoil of the previous autumn's resignations, was quick to see the benefits of collaboration: LWT ended up supplying cameras and lighting in return for the British television rights to LB's Verdi performance.

It was an annoying fact of life that the USA and Europe used different television technologies and as a consequence there was a disconcerting loss of picture quality when programmes were transferred from one system to the other. A compromise involving an expensive tape converter was finally agreed and Vic Gardiner also negotiated a deal with the Musicians' Union. So the madcap idea was ready to go ahead and in no time at all the Bernstein caravan arrived in London.

Running the show was Schuyler Chapin, a tall and courteous old-style American who had known LB since the 1950s when he headed the Masterworks division at CBS. Schuyler's middle name was Garrison and his family had crossed the Atlantic on the *Mayflower*, or very soon afterwards. He had been wooed away from his most recent job at Lincoln Center to work full-time for LB. With him for the *Requiem* venture was Oliver Smith, the celebrated stage designer who had worked with LB since his first ballet, *Fancy Free*, twenty-six years earlier, most famously on *West Side Story*. The closing credits for our St Paul's concert should have read 'Designers: Sir Christopher Wren and Oliver Smith'. Oliver took one look at the lofty cupola, with its eight Victorian mosaic panels, and ordered up kilometres of electric cable and dozens of 10- and 20-kilowatt lamps: the cathedral was to be illuminated as never before. And he added a master stroke: the temporary wooden platform in front of the orchestra upon which the soloists and conductor were to perform was to be covered in a sumptuous carpet of royal blue. This splash of rich colour turned an already magnificent setting into something exceptionally beautiful. Incidentally, Oliver was the first person to call my wife 'Chrissie' (in a drawling voice) and I often think affectionately of him when I call her by that name.

This was my first meeting with LB since his retirement from a decade as music director of the New York Philharmonic and I sensed that he was still feeling his way as to how he should run his life now he was a free agent. In a

Left: LB's manager Schuyler G. Chapin. Right: Broadway designer Oliver Smith added a carpet of blue velvet to Sir Christopher Wren's masterpiece.

simpler world he would have stayed home and done nothing but compose: he had an enormous commission from Jackie Kennedy to write the opening work for the new Kennedy Center scheduled for 1971. But LB could not abandon conducting: he was an addict, craving the adrenalin flow that came from standing in front of a hundred musicians – as we were soon to see in his Verdi *Requiem* performance – and from the roar of the adoring public at its conclusion. He lived recklessly. Despite the Kennedy Center commission, he had taken on engagements with not only the LSO but also a raft of other equally high-profile music-makers. After London he was off to conduct orchestras in Paris, Rome and Vienna; at his side, Schuyler would be on hand to smooth his path.

I took a film team to LB's first rehearsal with the LSO Chorus. He was nervous. The debacle of the choir rehearsal for Mahler's Eighth in 1966 was still vivid in his memory. Readers will recall that the Yorkshire-based choir brought in for that performance was, to put it bluntly, overaged and under-powered; Ernest Fleischmann had been so shocked that he immediately set about creating the LSO's own chorus, and Arthur Oldham, one of the world's finest choral trainers, had recently taken command. LB was delighted with their youthful vitality. He urged them to shout out the separate syllables of the 'Dies Irae' like opposing crowds of supporters chanting at a big football match: 'DI-ES EE-RAY!' But the mood of elation was short-lived. There were gloomy faces in the maestro's dressing room. His tenor soloist Franco Corelli was out of sorts. A few weeks earlier Corelli had had a big success in *Cavalleria rusticana* at the Met, under LB's baton, but now he was being temperamental and hinting that vocal problems might force him to withdraw. Corelli was the great star among the four soloists in the *Requiem*, the others being Martina Arroyo, who described herself as 'the black soprano who isn't Leontyne Price', Josephine Veasey, the Royal Opera's reigning dramatic mezzo, and the young Ruggero Raimondi, who had sung Don Giovanni the previous year at Glyndebourne (and would sing it again later, for Joseph Losey's film) but was still a dark horse in London. Apart from LB himself, it was Corelli who would sell records and put bums on seats, so I was surprised at the calm with which Schuyler greeted the news next day that Corelli had pulled out, just forty-eight hours before the St Paul's performance. It transpired that before Chapin left

'The Lenny Leap': an elevated moment during the dress rehearsal of Verdi's *Requiem* at St Paul's Cathedral. Left to right: Martina Arroyo, Josephine Veasey, LB in mid-air, Plácido Domingo and Ruggero Raimondi with the London Symphony Orchestra.

for London he had arranged (suspecting the worst, which is a reasonable way to handle tenors) for a young Spanish tenor named Domingo to be on call to fly in from New York. Plácido was in the middle of his second season at the Metropolitan Opera but I think it would be fair to say that few music lovers in London had heard of him: his appearance in the Verdi *Requiem* was a genuine sensation.

The *Requiem* was one of the most reckless productions I have ever undertaken; happily there are only a few hints on screen of the panic mood in which the performance was captured on tape. I had precious little experience of directing a work of this stature: one learns on the job. The task began with an assessment of the location, walking round the cathedral (including the dizzying heights of the cupola) to choose positions for five cameras, a couple of which could be on wheels and consequently more versatile. I worked out a repertory of shots framing individual singers, groups of chorus, orchestral soloists and so on, and then wrote into the vocal score exactly what I wanted to see for each moment of music, making sure the cameraman (no women in 1970) had time to prepare the next number on his shot list. The production secretary prepares scripts for each camera. The vision-mixer copies my script into his (or more usually her) own copy of the score, complete with private signs warning of tempo changes and quick-cutting sequences. But trying to imagine in advance what shots the cameras could achieve in St Paul's was a great deal harder than I had bargained for. Over the years I developed a meticulous planning procedure; I always liked to have an afternoon between the dress rehearsal and the performance to give me time for a few script modifications that would improve the look of the thing. What you see on screen has to be in harmony with what you hear, something few of today's directors seem to understand. In later life a further luxury for me was to have two or even three performances of the same piece from which to build up the commercial master video. But in 1970 at St Paul's, conditions were primitive and I was seriously underprepared, just as I had been for *The Golden Ring*. Luckily I had a very helpful crew at LWT and during the all-too-brief rehearsal our cameramen found beautiful angles, some of which I had never dreamed of.

We could not start the run-through with the chorus and musicians until after Evensong. Then the orchestra needed time to change into their penguin suits and the lights needed resetting and the mics and cameras needed tweaking, so it was close to 8 p.m. before we could get started. Of course, a huge audience had turned up. Backstage LB was dying for a cigarette but

296

smoking in the cathedral was strictly forbidden, as the dean himself made very clear. Luckily Schuyler found a door at the back of the dressing room which led up via a creaky staircase to the very roof of the cathedral. At last a cigarette! It was mid-February and the cold soon drove the maestro back inside, but meanwhile the necessary nicotine had been ingested. The performance began with much pomp as Dean Martin Sullivan led soloists and conductor down the cathedral's central aisle and on to Oliver Smith's lovely blue carpet. Then the music began, that solemn invocation on the double basses and celli followed by the choir in hushed voice muttering 'Requiem'. Providence guided me that night. The shots reflected the pace of the music, slow and stately at the outset, dramatic when the chorus tenors burst in with 'Te decet hymnus'. Then comes the first entry of the soloists, a breathtaking moment which to this day makes me think of Atlantic waves surging majestically into Poldhu Cove in Cornwall. That night in St Paul's we were all inspired: chorus, the LSO, those magnificent soloists, cameramen, my team in the Outside Broadcast truck – all carried along on waves of emotion created by Giuseppe Verdi and given fresh impetus at every bar by LB. He was on fire but always totally in control. He even found a way of coping with the cathedral's unique acoustic, a reverberation time of seven or eight seconds. After the climactic chords he waited for the sound to drift away and dissolve high above in the cupola. Not for a moment did he let the tension sag. The crashing of the bass drum in the 'Dies Irae', the glitter of the trumpets in the 'Tuba mirum', the ecstasy of Domingo's 'Ingemisco', the black mood of the 'Lacrymosa', every great moment was given its due, and thus we proceeded all evening from mountain peak to mountain peak.

I remember with a blush how I spoiled a moment of serene musical beauty when on the spur of the moment I decided to cross-fade from the gilded cross above the altar to an image of LB in agonised close-up. (Only Giulini did agony with more intensity.) My score-reader in the OB van was the young music journalist Gillian Widdicombe. She looked up from the script, saw the mix take place and murmured disapprovingly, 'Oh, Humphrey, how vulgar!' I defend the right of the director to go with the flow on these grand occasions but she was probably right. A few minutes later, as Martina Arroyo delivered the prayerful opening lines of the final movement, *Libera me, domine, de morte aeterna*, we heard to our horror the solemn tones of St Paul's striking the hour. It was ten of the clock and all was decidedly *not* well. In an opera the addition of chimes might have seemed a master stroke, but in the *Requiem* they took away from the interior drama: the passage would have to be done again in a retake, a tall order for Arroyo to get herself back into that epic mood.

When the performance was over I hurried backstage to find LB dictating notes concerning the various retakes he had noted – the cathedral chimes was just one of many, and they all had to be done that evening with the audience still in place: the project had no tomorrow. LB was looking haggard. He had given his all for ninety minutes. 'I'd do anything for a cigarette,' he moaned as he sipped a consoling Scotch. The dean, God bless him, knew what to do. Invoking what he described as 'the incredible beauty' of the maestro's interpretation, he indicated that the smoking ban could be temporarily lifted without incurring the wrath of either the Lord or the fire brigade. He then reached inside the copious folds of his clerical garb and produced a cigarette lighter.

The retakes posed many problems: the hour was late and many members of the magnificent LSO Chorus had to slip away between takes to catch last trains to the suburbs. We had to close up the ranks of chorus singers as best we could to preserve visual continuity; several times I went out into the hall to urge the audience to stay with us since they were very much in vision behind the conductor. It was well after 11 p.m. before the retakes were completed and then, disconcertingly, when I should have been elated at the end of a tremendous session, I was instead assailed by a profound fear of failure: I was acutely aware of my recklessness in undertaking this project without the necessary experience: too many things, I felt, had gone wrong.

Our producer Roger Stevens had laid on a late-night supper at the Savoy and although I put on a brave front I attended with a definite dread of what the morrow would bring. I had scheduled a screening of the unedited videotapes for midday in a Soho viewing theatre. Except for LB himself, who didn't get up until the afternoon, the Americans were there in force, checking on their investment. Christina came along to provide moral support and Vic Gardiner, too, keeping an eye on his first US co-production. The tape rolled and there on the screen was St Paul's in all its majesty, illuminated as never before by Oliver Smith's lighting. The performance was spellbinding and the magnificent setting gave it an extra dimension of visual beauty without detracting from the intensity of the music. Very much thanks to the professionalism of my LWT colleagues, my fears proved to be baseless. At the end of the screening Oliver Smith turned to me and said: 'I think this is the proudest moment of my professional life.' In his memoir of working with Bernstein (*Notes from a Friend*), Schuyler Chapin wrote that tears came to his eyes when the house lights went up, 'partly from the emotion of the performance and partly from relief: for we clearly had something priceless before us'. Amen to that! When LWT screened the *Requiem* on Good Friday the London *Times* review confirmed that the programme 'conveyed much of the splendour of a very special occasion'.

The *Requiem* was for me an initiation ceremony: having survived, I was instantly offered by the Bernstein team an even grander project: to produce as well as direct a two-hour salute to Ludwig van Beethoven on the occasion of his bicentenary, which fell on 16 December 1970. Back in 1963 I had done ninety minutes on Benjamin Britten for his fiftieth, so two hours on Beethoven for prime-time American television didn't seem as crazy an idea as it would today. Soon I was having discussions in New York with LB, Chapin and Michael Dann, the head of programming at CBS. We hammered out a treatment: the starting point was LB's love affair with Vienna. Having endured a decade of sniping from the New York critics when he was music director of the Philharmonic, he was garlanded with ovations in Vienna for his *Falstaff* and *Rosenkavalier* at the Staatsoper, for his Mozart with the Vienna Philharmonic in the Musikvereinsaal and for his Mahler 'Resurrection' Symphony at the Konzerthaus. He just loved the fact that he was replacing Karajan in the affections of the Viennese music public (a substantial constituency) and he revelled in the chance to gossip away with the Philharmonic musicians in Viennese-accented German and to wear the snazzy green Austrian *tracht* jackets sported by the locals. For the filming in 1970, reflecting his status, LB would be conducting an important new production of *Fidelio* for the Vienna Festival. He had also agreed to play Beethoven's First Piano Concerto with the Vienna Philharmonic in a Musikverein concert. To those engagements, spread over a couple of months, we added a special fundraising spring concert of Beethoven's 'Choral' Symphony; this was to be mounted at the Konzerthaus, which was administered by Bernstein's friend Peter Weiser, and would feature a mouth-watering quartet of soloists in Gwyneth Jones, Shirley Verrett, Plácido Domingo and Martti Talvela.

How to squeeze all that music into a two-hour 'special'? I was flying by the seat of my pants but it was only a few months since I had written a treatment for the *Switched-on Symphony* project in Los Angeles so I guess I had learnt how to think big, American style. We would give the show a popular, unpompous title: *Beethoven's Birthday*. (It did not survive in America.) The first part, the shortest, would interweave passages from the First Piano Concerto with a biography of the composer, relying heavily on historical prints and paintings such as we used copiously in the *Workshop* programmes I had made for BBC2 in the 1960s. My friend H.C. 'Robbie' Landon, who contributed a marvellous show about Haydn in BBC2's first season, had since published a superbly researched history of Beethoven's life. With a local camera team I would film old Vienna and the woods near the suburb of Heiligenstadt where the composer took his inspirational walks.

Part Two would be a fly-on-the-wall documentary, narrated by LB, devoted entirely to rehearsals and performance highlights of the opera *Fidelio*. This was to be filmed at the Theater an der Wien, the venue of its première in 1805. The stage director was Otto Schenk, an experienced man of the theatre with whom LB had worked very happily on *Der Rosenkavalier* three years earlier. The excellent cast included Gwyneth Jones as Leonora, James King as Florestan, Theo Adam as Pizarro and Lucia Popp as Marzelline. The third part of this two-hundredth-birthday salute would be the 'Ode to Joy' from Beethoven's Ninth: impossible to imagine a more powerful climax.

It was good to be back working in Vienna, where I had had so much fun six years earlier shooting *The Golden Ring*. I loved our visits to my favourite restaurant, the White Chimney Sweep, and I also enjoyed slipping into the

Filming *Beethoven's Birthday* on location in Vienna. Left to right: the director, sound recordist John Jordan, cameraman Johnny Ray and LB.

casino upstairs in the Esterhazy Palace on Kärntner Strasse to enjoy an hour of late-night roulette. Our hotel, the Sacher, was just round the corner.

My Bernstein activity in Vienna – filming and videotaping over several months – had to be fitted into the *Aquarius* schedule of hosting and editing an hour-long show every fortnight back in London. Derek Bailey and Russell Harty were splendid in support. (Russell had worked wonders keeping the audience happy in St Paul's while we prepared the retakes.) In March 1970 Christina and I had flown to Rome to show LB the final edited version of the Verdi, complete with his introduction dedicating the performance to the cause of peace – this at a time when the US was fighting and losing the Vietnam war. The screening session in Rome went well, and afterwards Christina and I had dinner with LB and Elsa Respighi, the Italian composer's widow. LB entertained us with stories of his seasons at La Scala Milan, back in the 1950s, when he worked with Maria Callas. Opera journalists dubbed her 'the tigress' but apparently she was as gentle as a lamb when singing *Medea* and *La Sonnambula* for him and for the revered director Luchino Visconti.

Taping Beethoven's Ninth in Vienna's Konzerthaus was almost as risky an enterprise as mounting the Verdi *Requiem* in St Paul's. This was to be Amberson's second music video and it was decided that because the infant video cassette industry was Japanese the technology had to be Japanese/American even though the picture quality could be markedly inferior. At enormous expense, a 525-line camera unit was driven across Europe from London. Since the show was paid for by Amberson and CBS, I assumed I could choose optimum camera positions, but when I stationed a crane camera – an enormous beast – in the centre aisle of the stalls the Viennese press did not take kindly to what it dubbed 'the dictatorship of the cameras'. Nor did it approve of Oliver Smith's decision to hang light blue drapes between the gilded Corinthian columns which are the glory of the Sezession-period concert hall. I confess there was a hint of Busby Berkeley's Hollywood in my wide-angle shots, but I was proud of my idea of a specially constructed platform for the soloists jutting out high above the orchestra like the bridge of an ocean liner. One thing was certain: this concert looked *different* and that was what Amberson wanted for its new music videos. Looking ahead for a moment, I directed two more telecasts of Beethoven's Ninth with LB, the next being a glamorous affair at the Vienna State Opera and the last the Freedom Concert on 25 December 1989 after the fall of the odious Berlin Wall. That was the most emotional of the three performances, but if you want to see LB at the peak of his powers then the 1970 Vienna event is the production to choose.

301

A local critic, Rudolf Klein, agreed with me, writing that 'the perfection of this presentation will remain a standard, even in Vienna'.

Filming scenes from *Fidelio* at the Theater an der Wien with only two 16 mm film cameras was a different kind of headache, and eavesdropping on the stage rehearsals needed a particularly agile camera team. Luckily the opera people – singers, director Otto Schenk, Bernstein himself – all enjoyed showing off. Schenk was an enormously experienced man of the stage who generously allowed LB to chip in with production ideas at rehearsal, among them that the dreaded prison governor Pizarro should have a nervous tick and continually play with his glasses. Our cameras duly caught the moment. I was lucky enough to have Johnny Ray as my chief cameraman – he had shot several films for me at the BBC but was now, like me, a freelance. (I was on leave from LWT.) However, Johnny was technically the culprit when most unfortunately we set fire to the theatre. To get the light levels up to the intensity required for colour film, Johnny had arranged to install extra lighting up in the gods: it worked well, allowing us to follow the singers all over the stage. Next morning the stage manager called for the curtains to be closed preparatory to a full run-through. The 10 kilowatt lamps were where they had been placed by us the previous day, when the curtains were not required. And those lamps were switched on, ready for the filming. The stage rehearsal had not even begun when there was a loud shout of *Feuer!* (fire!). Heat and pressure had built up where a curtain rested on one of the lamps and eventually there was an almighty explosion; smoke billowed through a sizeable hole into the auditorium, where the orchestra was already rehearsing the overture. We caught all this on the camera because, blissfully unaware of the danger, we were waiting for the curtains to part and the rehearsal action to begin.

For centuries fire has been the dread of theatre managements, and there was pandemonium on stage as men wielding fire extinguishers rushed around. LB, unperturbed, was determined not to stand around wasting precious rehearsal time; he turned his back on the chaotic proceedings on stage and took the orchestra in the pit through the entire Leonora No. 3 overture. Then I was summoned to the house manager's office and given a dressing down. It turned out that the theatre's curtains were part of an expensive refurbishment programme and had been installed only a few days earlier, just in time for the festival. Quite understandably the theatre manager, Herr Kucerer, was very upset – in fact, he ordered the entire camera team out of his theatre. Fortunately Schuyler Chapin was on hand to negotiate on our behalf, and with the help of CBS's contingency funds we were allowed to return to our camera positions in time to capture the highlights of a gripping dress rehearsal.

I had a great time that summer filming around and above Vienna. Our helicopter flew right over the Staatsoper and St Stephen's Cathedral and then out to the Vienna Woods and down to Baden, where we filmed dramatic close-ups of the ruined castle of Rauhenstein, from whose walls Beethoven's nephew Karl had thrown himself in a botched attempt at suicide.

The last day of shooting involved the only statement to camera LB was to make in the entire film: I thought of it as Lenny's Peroration. It was to explain why Beethoven remained so powerfully significant two centuries after his birth and would lead us into the 'Ode to Joy', the final segment of the show. LB was seated at the piano, his pencilled notes on a yellow legal pad concealed among the piano music on the stand in front of him. But what he said was unconvincing. We had not worked on it together. I called a break after a couple of takes had faltered in midstream. I knew him to be acutely self-critical and I sensed he had a vision of what he wanted to express but was still searching for the right words. He asked us to come back in an hour. The crew sat out in the garden enjoying the Viennese summer while LB went upstairs to his bedroom with his faithful yellow pad. After the hour he duly emerged with a new script which we filmed in one take. I give it in full because so far as I'm aware it has never before been published and it is remarkably eloquent:

> Well, for the better part of three months now I've been living in terms of Beethoven, thinking about his life, visiting his houses, reading his letters, but most of all living with his music. I've studied it, and restudied it, rehearsed and performed it over and over again, and I may report that I've never tired of it for a single moment. The music remains endlessly satisfying, interesting and moving, and has remained so for almost two centuries and to all kinds of people. In other words, this music is not only infinitely durable but perhaps the closest music has ever come to universality. That dubious cliché about music being the universal language almost comes true with Beethoven. No composer ever lived who speaks so directly to so many people, young and old, educated and ignorant, amateur and professional, sophisticated, naive, and to all these people, of all classes, nationalities, and racial backgrounds, this music speaks a universality of thought, of human brotherhood, freedom, and love.
>
> In this Ninth Symphony, for example, where Beethoven has set Schiller's 'Ode to Joy' in the finale, the music goes so far beyond the poem. It gives far greater dimension and vital energy and artistic sparks to these quaint old lines of Schiller: Alle Menschen werden <u>Brüder</u> – all men become brothers; Seid

umschlungen Millionen – Oh, ye millions embrace ye; Ahnest du den <u>Schöpfer</u>, Welt? – O world, do you sense your creator? In other words, this music succeeds even with those people for whom organized religion fails because it conveys a spirit of godhead and sublimity in the freest and least doctrinaire way, which was typical of Beethoven. It has a purity and directness of communication which never becomes banal. It's accessible without being ordinary. This is the magic that no amount of talk can explain. But perhaps there was, in Beethoven the man, a child inside that never grew up and to the end of his life remained a creature of grace and innocence and trust even in his moments of greatest despair. And that innocent spirit speaks to us of hope and future and immortality, and it's for that reason that we love his music now more than ever before.

In this time of world agony and hopelessness and helplessness we love his music and we need it. As despairing as we may be we cannot listen to this Ninth Symphony without emerging from it changed, enriched, encouraged. And to the man who could give the world so precious a gift as this, no honor can be too great and no celebration joyful enough. It's almost like celebrating the birthday of music itself.

Here LB's image yielded to the performance of the 'Choral' Symphony we had taped back in September at the Konzerthaus, with LB in command at the rostrum. It was quite a coup de théâtre.

That I have such a great affection for *Beethoven's Birthday* is in part because it was so brilliantly edited by Mike Bradsell, like my cameraman John Ray a former star at the BBC Ealing film studios. Using montage to great effect (orchestral passages from Beethoven's Ninth and *Fidelio* make excellent backing tracks), Mike caught the high-octane spirit of those Viennese rehearsals and the excitement of the *Fidelio* first night. In the biographical section of the film, which explored the composer's hopeless love life and his restlessness, Mike used the fast-moving timpani blows in the Scherzo of the Ninth to accompany a vivid sequence of Beethoven's summer residences, dozens of them, a new image on every downbeat. It was virtuoso editing. Mike also slipped in a sardonic scene where LB complains to the Vienna Philharmonic management that he is getting different woodwind soloists at each rehearsal: 'Zey all want to play wiz you, Maestro' comes the oily reply.

On August 20th 1970 Christina and I flew to New York. LB had a weekend window before jetting off to Tokyo on the 25th, his birthday. For two days and a night we sat over the Moviola editing machine, writing commentary; it was my toughest assignment since the Elgar film with Huw Wheldon eight years previously. LB smoked incessantly and got me back on to the habit. And these New York sessions had an extra wrinkle: Schuyler Chapin was determined that

Far left: The wedding couple were locked outside the Unitarian Church, New York, while inside (right) LB rehearsed *Figaro*'s tricky Wedding March on the organ.

Christina and I should get married while we were in New York. He was already urging another friend, André Previn, to tie the knot with Mia Farrow and they did indeed get married two weeks later. We were even quicker to the altar. As a long-standing member of the Unitarian Church of All Souls on the Upper East Side (80th Street and Lexington), Schuyler was able to arrange a low-key ceremony for us. And as an old friend of New York's charismatic mayor, John Lindsay, he also helped Christina and me to pick up a marriage licence.

Both our divorces had come through, mine after a ludicrous scene in a Brighton hotel where a private investigator knocked politely on our bedroom door, noted that Christina and I were together (fully dressed) and departed with what the Law required as evidence. Only one problem remained: who would play the organ at the wedding? I rang my Canadian friend Glenn Gould; I knew he had been a regular church organist in his youth. He would have loved to do it, he told me, but I had forgotten that he had given up flying and there was no time to organise the rail trip from Toronto. I shared my disappointment with LB and to my delight he offered to play – the church is just around the corner from the Park Avenue duplex where the Bernstein family had lived for a decade. When Christina and I arrived at the church on the wedding afternoon we found the door barred and bolted. A churchwarden told us that the organist, whom he had not recognised, had insisted on thirty minutes' privacy while he rehearsed. We had chosen the sprightly wedding march from Act 3 of *The Marriage of Figaro* – the twiddly bits in the Fandango which follows the march definitely require practice. The performance was immaculate. After the ceremony and drinks back at his apartment, LB gave us his *Figaro* vocal score inscribed 'see page 199' with his familiar signature below. So far as I am aware he never conducted *Figaro* but inevitably he knew the score backwards.

We spent our honeymoon night in the famous Plaza Hotel. It boasted that it was the first New York hotel to install central heating. Unfortunately the radiators seemed never to have been refurbished and their clanking kept me awake long into the night. Christina was three months pregnant with our son Lukas and was not feeling particularly bright, though she had looked radiant at the ceremony. So it was early beds for us both and I whiled the evening away watching, of all things, a David Frost programme about the *Guinness Book of Records*. It was less than four years since Frost had changed my life by inviting me to join the LWT syndicate. Now he was on the screen so often that I could hardly bear to watch him. But that night I felt gratitude all the same.

LB with his wife Felicia.

At the end of the year *Beethoven's Birthday* was screened in many parts of Europe but not by our paymaster, CBS Television. Ignominiously, pathetically, deplorably, the Americans failed to find a sponsor so the show was shelved. Perhaps this had something to do with the ousting from the company that year of Michael Dann, whose pet project this was. Or perhaps the change of plan was a fallout from Tom Wolfe's devastating critique of the Bernsteins in his much-discussed 'Radical Chic' article, published that summer in the *New York* magazine. LB and his wife were mocked for their liberal gullibility and their alleged support of the Black Panthers. The Beethoven show, conceived as a centenary celebration, finally went out in the USA an entire year late, retitled rather tamely *Bernstein on Beethoven: A Celebration in Vienna*. But I ought not to grumble: the programme won a prime-time Emmy and cemented my working partnership with LB.

Later the same year, LB took the momentous step of signing a contract with Unitel, a subsidiary of Beta Films based in Munich. Unitel was a production and distribution company which made most of its money by dubbing Hollywood movies into German for the television market. The founder, Leo Kirch, was a shrewd businessman who also loved classical music and in the 1960s built up a catalogue of opera and concert films performed by top-class musicians headed by Herbert von Karajan. When I was still a boss at the BBC

I had been wooed by Unitel to buy Karajan's extraordinary films of Beethoven symphonies but I found them cold and unsympathetic concoctions, with far too many shots of the conductor, and I turned them down for BBC2, not unreasonably since we had our own Beethoven series conducted by Otto Klemperer, the bicentenary celebration cycle of 1970 which we televised from the Royal Festival Hall with the New Philharmonia Orchestra. (Alas it is a terribly sad document: Klemperer can hardly move a muscle.)

Kirch was wooing LB to replace his former superstar, Karajan, who meanwhile had set up his own company. As a prominent American Jew, LB had qualms at signing a long-term deal with a German company, but he took the plunge and committed to filming all Mahler's symphonies over the next few years with the Vienna Philharmonic. Would I be LB's film director for the first project, asked Schuyler Chapin. I did not think about it for longer than the few seconds it had taken to agree to David Frost's invitation to bid for the LWT contract four years previously. I could surely fit in a month's filming and editing around my *Aquarius* commitment. So I accepted and was soon back in Vienna getting to grips with the multi-camera technique Unitel had developed for filming concerts. Leo Kirch's vision was that every concert involving his star performers should be filmed in 35 mm colour and with stereophonic sound. It was to be top of the range, state of the art, allowing no compromises on quality. As a consequence, Unitel's films were very different from conventional television coverage, a fact that remains true half a century later: Unitel's films are pin sharp and in warm, faithful colour.

But why Mahler: allegedly long-winded stuff, nothing shorter than an hour, difficult to schedule on television? The answer is that LB was a proselytiser. In the 1960s he had conducted the entire Mahler cycle with the New York Philharmonic (apart from the LSO for the Sixth and Eighth). In Vienna, notorious for its anti-Semitism, LB detected in his players a lack of enthusiasm for the symphonies: they were not part of the mainstream repertoire, indeed four of them had not been performed there since before the *Anschluss* in 1938. So learning Mahler and then filming the concerts represented a mighty challenge for the Vienna Phil as well as for me. To make things worse, LB was obliged to begin with the last and most profound of the symphonies, the Ninth, which was already in the orchestra's plan for 1971. But the filming would be done not in the Musikverein in Vienna, the orchestra's home, where Mahler himself had frequently conducted, and where Unitel had been filming for many years. No, the venue for our 1971 filming would be the ultra-modern Philharmonie in Berlin.

It is a lovely hall but I couldn't believe my ears when I heard this news because the Philharmonie was Karajan's home base, where he had dominated the Berlin Philharmonic for fifteen years. I was convinced Leo Kirch intended to cock a snook at his former partner but I have been assured that it was a fluke that the hall was free for filming during the Vienna Philharmonic's tour; there was no need to consult with Karajan since it was not a Berlin Philharmonic booking. When I first visited the Philharmonie in the mid-1960s I heard Barbirolli and the Berlin orchestra making gloriously noble sounds in a Bruckner symphony, so I knew that musically the hall would be excellent for Mahler. I loved the look of the place too: I had met the architect Hans Scharoun and admired his vineyard-style audience terraces. But I had problems. I did not know the symphony. To be frank, I did not know *any* of Mahler's symphonies. And I was uncomfortable with the filming technique employed by Unitel to capture live concerts. Most film cameras use cassettes containing enough film for a maximum of four minutes, nowhere near adequate for filming the long lines of classical symphony movements. So Unitel fitted massive sound-immunising blimps to eliminate the noise of the

The mysteries of Unitel's blimped 35 mm Arriflex camera.

camera motor and modified its big Arriflex cameras to run for almost eleven minutes per reel. Film cassettes could be changed in two minutes during performances but the changes had to be staggered; without my stopwatch planning there was a risk, nay a certainty, that all six cameras would run out of film at the same time.

As a consequence, much of my Unitel work was technical rather than musical. It was a complicated process which I will attempt to explain, asking only for a modicum of patience. At the bottom of the pages of the orchestral score I wrote a timeline for each camera indicating when it was to be switched on, what it was to film, when it should be turned off to save film and at what moment in the score the assistant should change cassettes. I had a team of assistant directors who copied the directions for their specific camera into their own score and then, during the filming, called out these instructions on a headset which was linked only to their specific cameraman. The assistant directors had screens on which they could see the output of their film camera. From the multi-screen array I could see the output of all six and override where necessary. Not too easy a process! My copy of the orchestral score was the storyboard. I had imagined what the finished film would be showing at any given moment – choosing (as in a telecast) between the conductor, a variety of wide-angle orchestra shots, a group of instruments or a solo, according to the ebb and flow of the music.

The process had a safety net of sorts; this was a technique Karajan had developed in the 1960s whereby small groups from the orchestra went into a Vienna film studio weeks later (after a rough cut had been made) in order to repeat phrases we had not been able to film effectively in the live concert.

Before setting off on their European tour in February 1971, the Vienna Philharmonic rehearsed Mahler Nine in the Sofiensaal, Decca's ballroom studio where I had filmed Solti recording the *Ring*. The Unitel contract allowed me to film throughout the rehearsals, so we were able to make a substantial reportage for which I brought over my director colleague Tony Palmer to find unusual angles with a second camera team. At the rough-cut stage LB wrote and recorded a detailed commentary and gave us the film's evocative title: *Four Ways to Say Farewell*. I rate it as his most deeply felt documentary. The previous year he had perhaps seen a bit of himself in the centenary portrait we were making of Beethoven – I am thinking of his reference in the commentary to 'a child inside that never grew up' – but with Gustav Mahler the identification was total. He spoke, I felt, with complete confidence about Mahler's state of mind.

For the Berlin filming my right-hand man, in due course to become a firm friend, was Horant Hohlfeld, a tall and very correct Berliner with piercing blue eyes who had been with Unitel for a decade and had a sure grasp of how to operate this complicated equipment to the best advantage. I was alarmed, to put it mildly, when at the end of the orchestra's run-through of Mahler Nine, Horant collapsed. An emergency doctor talked of a heart attack as Horant lay in a dressing room, out for the count. Our amiably laid-back producer Fritz Buttenstedt took the news calmly. As a lad Fritz had worked on the anti-aircraft defence of Berlin during the war and LB misleadingly nicknamed him 'the brown-eyed bomber from Berlin'. Despite the doctor's dire forecast, Fritz assured me that Horant would be OK and greatly to my relief 'Herr Hohlfeld', as I always addressed him in public, took his place next to me at the backstage control desk just before the first of the two performances was due to begin. A few moments later LB stopped on his way to the platform and saluted my team. 'Fasten your seat belts,' he said, 'we're in for a bumpy ride.' Not perhaps the most original greeting but it helped break a tension which had been at breaking point.

Mahler became part of my life. 'Gloomy Gustav', my children called him, but I loved every movement of every symphony. And then in the late 1980s and '90s came Unitel cycles of other composers, of Beethoven and Brahms and Schumann, concertos as well as symphonies – I made films every year with LB from 1971 to 1990; about 180 different works were filmed. I never had a long-term contract and I never earned any royalties; instead Unitel paid handsomely up front and bought out all my residual rights. Early in the 1970s there was a complaint from a German television station that all the Bernstein films looked the same. Other directors were approached to take over but it seemed that nobody else had the patience to master the multi-camera technique. The point is that it is the music that is important, not the shooting style, which we thought should be efficient but self-effacing. Of course there are grand moments. I think of the panning shot along the wooden ceiling of Ely Cathedral's nave at the conclusion of the 'Resurrection' Symphony. I think of the mysterious posthorn shots in the Third Symphony and of the grandeur of the Konzerthaus architecture in the Eighth; I remember the abstract violin bows as life ebbs away in the Ninth.

I think, too, of the great singers who participated: Janet Baker in the 'Resurrection' Symphony at Ely, Christa Ludwig in the Third, Edith Mathis in the Fourth, giving their all in this sometimes soul-searing, sometimes radiant music. Admittedly there is a funeral march in every symphony but Mahler was not exclusively *gloomy* Gustav; after living with him for a decade I concluded he was Gustav the Genius, the composer who was all-encompassing.

Bernstein's 1970s Mahler cycle for Unitel is a reliable account of how a great conductor tackled the Mahler classics in his fifties. This was LB's middle period. In 1972 we spent most of April in Vienna filming three symphonies, one a week, each more glorious than the last. Symphony No. 3 had the Vienna Boys' Choir installed on the gilded balcony of the organ loft, flanked, a little precariously I couldn't help thinking, by members of the Staatsoper chorus, and downstage centre, as I mentioned, stood the eloquent Christa Ludwig solemnly intoning the Nietzsche poem 'O Mensch! Gib Acht' – Take heed O Man!

The third symphony is the longest of all Mahler's symphonies and I adored it. In the Fourth the soprano Edith Mathis gave us the child's view of heaven: innocence and fantasy personified. The Fifth has no soloist and is arguably the closest Mahler came to writing a concerto for conductor and orchestra. Nothing could have prepared me for the drama at the Sunday morning performance in the Golden Hall of the Musikverein. Earlier in the week I had sat in on the rehearsals and heard LB demanding a tremendous crescendo from the entire orchestra at the climax of the first movement. 'At this point', he said (I don't have the exact words), 'all hell should break loose. It must be as if an earthquake is shaking the very foundations of the hall.' We were not allowed to film the Sunday concert for fear of upsetting the Philharmonic's venerable subscribers with our cameras but I didn't want to miss it, so I found a seat on the platform, squeezed in behind the double basses, and this is how I described the event in my biography of LB:

> [When the climactic moment was reached] the double basses redoubled their efforts and the entire concert platform seemed to vibrate in sympathy with Mahler's anguish and Bernstein's passionate conducting. An onlooker [that's me] glanced up to discover the magnificent chandeliers of the Golden Hall swaying to and fro above Bernstein's head. In the body of the hall panicking members of the public rose from their chairs and ran to the doors. The tremors of a genuine earthquake were being felt all over eastern Austria. Bernstein kept conducting until the musicians let him know what had happened; then he spoke calmly to the audience urging them to take their seats so the music could resume. 'I actually didn't feel a thing', he said afterwards; 'not a tremor.'

If I had to choose just one movement from LB's entire Mahler film cycle it would probably be the Adagietto from this Fifth Symphony – what many people think of as the *Death in Venice* music, but which I always associate with the earthquake in Vienna.

Back in Britain the *Aquarius* season was in full swing, but only days later, in May 1971, I was off again with LB, this time to Israel. Christina and our two children joined the party; Lukas took his very first steps as a fourteen-month-old toddler in the corridors of the Sacher Hotel.

A little back history might be useful at this point. The Unitel contract did not tie LB exclusively to the Vienna Philharmonic. Harry Kraut had taken over the Amberson management when Schuyler Chapin jumped ship to fulfil a lifetime ambition (I didn't blame him) by accepting the number two job at the Metropolitan Opera. Harry had previously run Tanglewood for the Boston Symphony Orchestra and knew LB well. I think it would be fair to say that he was a more canny operator than Schuyler. One of his first negotiating coups was to persuade Leo Kirch to make a film of LB conducting the Israel Philharmonic Orchestra. The work chosen was Mahler's *Song of the Earth*, a six-movement song symphony for mezzo, tenor and large orchestra set to Chinese poems, in which one of LB's favourite artists, Christa Ludwig, was joined by the Wagner tenor René Kollo. Tel Aviv, where we were to make the film at the Frederick Mann auditorium, was one of the most exotic locations of my career. We stayed outside the city – it was very hot, even in May – at a lovely garden hotel in Ramat-Aviv. Guests were housed in cottages dotted around the gardens. Opposite ours was a small synagogue where we saw the local women sitting outside during the Saturday prayers. On Sunday afternoons scores of local people played bridge (or was it whist?) on the hotel lawn. There was a pool where our Swedish nanny Irene supervised the paddling of Helena and Lukas under the affectionate eyes of the Unitel camera crew.

The music of *Das Lied* was stunning, the rapport between LB, Ludwig and the orchestra electrifying, the filming more confident and relaxed than the previous month in Vienna. When we had three excellent performances in the can my producers, Herrn Hohlfeld und Buttenstedt, decided that we should film no more because we needed to save expensive 35 mm film stock for the production a few days later of a Brahms song recital, a *Liederabend*, with Christa Ludwig, at which LB would be playing the piano. Next night at the orchestra's farewell party following the final symphony concert, LB asked me how the filming had gone earlier in the evening. I explained that the cameras had not been rolling for this particular concert. LB was aghast. I turn once again to my biography of LB:

Scotch in hand, Bernstein insisted that every minute of every performance should have been filmed. The director [that's me] told him he was unrealistic and self-indulgent. The two men glowered at each other. Bernstein said 'well, if that's what you think you can just fuck off'. Matching expletive for expletive, the director turned on his heel to leave the Israel Philharmonic guest house. In his blind rage he marched straight into a plate glass window and knocked himself out. Bernstein was the first at his side. Next morning, friends again, they went surfing together in Tel Aviv harbour.

The cost of flying a Munich-based film unit to Israel was astronomical. The following year, 1973, I rashly agreed to direct an Israeli-based three-camera television unit for the taping of a pair of Brahms symphonies (the First and Third) in Jerusalem's enormous barn of a concert hall. This proved to be one of Harry Kraut's less good ideas, since although videotape is cheaper, its quality is not a patch on 35 mm film, and the Jerusalem-based television crew spoke only Hebrew with a smattering of German and Yiddish, not my most fluent languages (though I was learning). To obtain a wider selection of images I arranged a playback session for the entire orchestra. They mimed to the music they had recorded the previous evening. For the great finale of Brahms's First I placed a camera on the conductor's rostrum, providing LB's view of the players. The problem was that the violinists found it impossible to appear committed when they were playing not to the maestro but to a cameraman in shorts and sweatshirt. The first 'takes' were marred by giggles but eventually I got the shot I wanted – the massed violins playing the big C major tune. These retakes were being done on a Friday morning. Suddenly the orchestra rose *en masse* from its seats and trooped out of the hall. It was Shabbat and they had to return to Tel Aviv before sundown. Happily there is no sign of this exodus on the finished tape.

My other Bernstein projects in 1973 were closer to home. One was to produce his one-act opera *Trouble in Tahiti* at LWT's spanking new studio centre on the South Bank. I hired Bill Hays to direct and Eileen Diss to do the design, both top people in their field, which was as it should be since it was a coup to have a composer of LB's standing on LWT's home turf. I am very proud of the production, which was both witty and sad and blessed with brilliantly inventive graphics created by LWT's staff man, Pat Gavin. I lobbied successfully for the production to be chosen to represent ITV in that year's Italia Prize competition and you can imagine my fury when I learnt that the jury chairman (a disciple of the dodecaphonic school) had dismissed LB's opera from contention on the grounds that it was devoid of musical interest. *Tahiti* has since received dozens of productions around the world.

For 1973's dose of Gloomy Gustav I could also stay in England. Harry Kraut had emerged triumphantly from a power struggle with the committee of the Vienna Philharmonic: to prove he didn't need the Viennese as much as they needed him, he fixed it that the Mahler symphony that year was to be filmed at Ely Cathedral with the LSO and the Edinburgh Festival Chorus, the latter trained by Arthur Oldham, who had done such wonders with the LSO Chorus in the Verdi *Requiem* back in 1970. The excursion to Ely would follow a performance at the Edinburgh Festival. I was baffled as to why LB had chosen Ely until I discovered that back in the 1930s the cathedral had figured in his aesthetics course at Harvard. From a BBC2 telecast of *L'Enfance du Christ* directed by Brian Large in the black-and-white era I knew the cathedral looked marvellous on camera. However, the logistics of assembling in a tiny Fenland city a 150-strong chorus, a 100-piece symphony orchestra and a Munich film crew were daunting and my troubles were exacerbated when the crane camera we imported toppled over just minutes before the start of the dress rehearsal. Worse was to come: the Troubles in Northern Ireland were at their height and when the police received a telephoned bomb warning that afternoon the cathedral was swiftly evacuated. Groans all round at the loss of precious rehearsal time but the final film, with Janet Baker and Sheila Armstrong both in glorious voice, was made all the more powerful by the hugely atmospheric cathedral setting. The film of the closing bars of the 'Resurrection' – '*Aufersteh'n!*': 'Rise again!' – never fails to move me: it's the sequence I use in lectures to illustrate LB's tremendous inspirational power.

It was in the same year, 1973, that Professor Bernstein, as he briefly became, delivered his six Eliot Norton lectures at Harvard under the title *The Unanswered Question*. I was hired as an adviser and made several brief visits to Cambridge, Massachusetts. It was the period of the post-Watergate shaming of Richard Nixon. Exciting times, indeed.

Bernstein's lectures were of gargantuan proportions. My contribution was modest: to make better sense of the lengthy orchestral illustrations which the Boston Symphony Orchestra had videotaped many months in advance of the lectures: Wagner's *Tristan*, Berlioz's *Roméo et Juliette*, Stravinsky's *Oedipus Rex*, Mozart's G minor symphony. The director Harry Kraut had hired Michael Ritchie (a Harvard man), who had made a successful cinema feature, *Downhill Racer*, but the visualisation of classical music was not Ritchie's forte. Hence my assignment. I intercut frequent shots of the conductor's score in the hope of clarifying things, and for the performance of *Oedipus Rex* – LB's chosen work to illustrate the genius of Stravinsky – I added images of a stylised puppet version of the blinded Greek King Oedipus, complete with blood-red eye sockets; it sounds horrific but actually worked quite effectively. The lectures are a landmark in LB's career; they represent a powerful declaration of war against atonality and provide proof of the durability of the musical assumptions of LB's youth, essentially that tonality rules.

In 1974 I went back to Vienna for another triple Mahler whammy. The First Symphony and the first movement of the unfinished Tenth (the only movement of Deryck Cooke's performance sketch of which LB approved) were filmed at the Konzerthaus and the Seventh at the Musikvereinsaal. The following year it was Mahler Eight, the 'Symphony of a Thousand', and what a wonderful sight the soloists made in the Konzerthaus, strung across the front of the platform. The previous week LB conducted this straggling masterpiece in stuffy Salzburg and that gave me a little longer to write my camera script: it was a labour of love. Nothing I was to do in later life could ever be superior to the satisfaction of working on the music of Mahler. The cycle was concluded in September 1976 with the Sixth Symphony, subtitled 'The Tragic'. LB's personal tragedy had already begun: he separated from his wife that summer and set up a sort of home in Big Sur, California with his former research assistant Tom Cothran. In the autumn he came out publicly and grew a beard. My life had also changed drastically. Not my personal life but my work. In 1975, as I reported in the previous chapter, I returned to the BBC, but to a very different organisation from the one I had left eight years previously. I sometimes think the new move was the biggest mistake I made in my entire professional life, but move I did.

PART FOUR

In and Out at the BBC,
1975–1990

CHAPTER 16

IN MAKE-UP OR MUNICH

Trog's cartoon of me appeared in a perceptive *Punch* article, which described my
new job at the BBC as 'a wearisome mix of cultural sensibility and bureaucratic fog'.

ON MARCH 1ST 1975, ten years to the day from when I was made Head of
the new Music and Arts Department back in the 1960s, I resumed that post
at the BBC. After my somewhat precipitate exit in 1967, the Music and Arts
departments had been headed by separate bosses, John Culshaw and Stephen
Hearst. I was originally wooed back to run BBC's Arts Features department,
which was in disarray since the resignation of Stephen's successor in the post,
Norman Swallow. Plans changed early in 1975 when John Culshaw decided he

had had enough of being a BBC boss and would resign, so my old department combining Music and Arts could be restored to me in its entirety.

I selected John Drummond to be my overall deputy. Apparently he had applied to have the arts job himself but Huw Wheldon was not a fan (or so John felt) and what was worse (and unbeknown to me), a group of Kensington House producers had sent a round robin to management opposing John's appointment: nobody doubted his intellectual ability but in those days his man-management skills were still being polished. As a temporary measure Mike Wooller had been named Acting Head of Arts and my arrival did not go down well with him either: I was seen as the prodigal son receiving unduly favoured treatment when he came home. All things considered, it was important for me to establish my authority early on. My standing as a presenter was a known factor: I had been on the screen hosting *Aquarius* virtually every week for five years. But being a boss was a different ball game so I arranged to address the department a month before I took over. Inwardly I was terrified by the proceedings. About 120 producers, directors, researchers and PAs squeezed into the basement meeting room at Kensington House. I knew maybe a quarter of them from my first spell as departmental head back in the early 1960s. I asked in advance for everybody to write me a brief note about themselves, from which I learnt that the room was full of unhappy colleagues who distrusted the management, weren't getting the transmission slots they deserved and had wonderful programme ideas that were being ignored. The room was ridiculously small and toxic with cigarette smoke but there was nothing for it but to plough on. Not long into the meeting, when we were discussing recent programmes made by the two departments, Christopher Burstall (ex-King's College and one of the BBC's first general trainees) got into an angry dispute with a young *Omnibus* director I had not previously met named Alan Yentob (a Leeds graduate and one of the last general trainees). The subject was *Cracked Actor*, Yentob's disturbing film portrait of the singer David Bowie. The burden of Burstall's attack was that the BBC should not be condoning the use of recreational drugs. The criticism did not stop Yentob's film from gaining widespread support within the department; it eventually acquired iconic status. Another of Alan's directorial projects, about Heinrich Böll, became famous in the *Omnibus* office for never having been completed.

I managed to navigate my way through that particular minefield but even before taking up my post I perceived that I had exchanged the 'harmony and understanding' of the *Aquarius* office at LWT for a hotbed of discontent. But as Bertolt Brecht put it so succinctly, 'Wie man sich bettet, so liegt man'

– as you've made your bed, so you have to lie on it. So I hunkered down to the business of recreating a double department at the BBC where everybody could feel they had a meaningful role. This was not an enviable task and the physical surroundings did not help. Kensington House was a building utterly devoid of comfort or charm. Built over former railway sidings, it followed the curve of the Metropolitan Line as it heads south from Shepherd's Bush to Olympia. Internally it had the layout of a third-rate ocean liner, four storeys high, with interminable central corridors; doors opened on both sides of this corridor into offices no bigger than ship's cabins. Architecturally the place was a terrible comedown from the BBC's custom-built Television Centre, which boasted a rather splendid entrance hall and a statue in the courtyard of a golden-balled Mercury bestriding the central fountain. Television Centre was home to the programme departments who were heavy users of the seven studios placed around its big 'O', such as the groups dedicated to drama and light entertainment, the meat and potatoes of BBC Television's output. Design and scenery construction were also based at the Centre and inevitably, since it was the hub of the empire, it was home to the planners, led by the channel controllers, the director of television, Alasdair Milne, and the managing director (MD Tel), Huw Wheldon. Political programmes (current affairs) remained at Lime Grove until the 1980s. News eventually moved into a separate wing at the Centre. Departments like mine, specialising in film, were relegated (as I saw it) to Kensington House – a miserable substitute for the skyscraping East Tower of the Centre: this was where Music and Arts had been lodged in the late 1960s when I first became head. These geographical details were important because for videotape editing and any form of studio production we had to traipse over from Kensington House to the Centre, twenty minutes away on foot, on the other side of Shepherd's Bush Green. Apart from the Music and Arts producers, who constituted the largest group, the Ken House offices were filled with staff from General Features, Science Features and Man Alive Productions, which was the personal fiefdom of my colleague, the player-manager Desmond Wilcox. I'm told that Religion was also based at Ken House. Outside Broadcast production teams certainly occupied most of one floor and I used to enjoy swapping pleasantries with Cliff Morgan, the Welsh rugby star turned head of sport, as I passed his door. Down in the basement were upwards of a dozen cutting rooms. The BBC's Transcription Service was also to be found in the lower depths: it had its own sound studios and sold BBC radio programmes around the world. For a small fee I used to nip down to host their recordings of Prom concerts, pretending

I was actually in the Royal Albert Hall as I did the topping and tailing for another wonderful Prom. My own Music and Arts office had no view except, if you stood on tiptoe, the railway line, but at least it was bigger than most and to help give it some character I imported a comfy sofa from home and persuaded the art dealer Leslie Waddington to lend me some modern prints from his Cork Street gallery – they were duly acknowledged and changed every year.

My yearning to operate on a bigger canvas was one of the reasons that prompted my return to the BBC. I had departed in 1967 when *Civilisation* was just getting under way. Under Aubrey Singer's leadership, BBC Television had then mounted the *America* series with Alastair Cooke and the science block-buster *The Ascent of Man* with Jacob Bronowski. In 1975 I inherited nothing so grand but there was an arts blockbuster in preparation entitled *The Shock of the New*; it consisted of eight programmes about twentieth-century art, presented by *Time* magazine's colourful Australian critic, Robert Hughes. But it was a more modest type of programme that I felt to be missing from the current output: there was no regular commitment to the contemporary arts scene on either of the BBC's networks. So I persuaded Aubrey Singer, who was then running BBC2, to let me have a weekly slot for which I came up with the title *Arena*. Under its banner, I argued, we could rotate subject matter between theatre, design, art and feature films; music already had a regular place on Saturday evenings. I put Leslie Megahey in charge and he did a fine job: the *Radio Times* billings for the first hundred editions make impressive reading. *Arena* in those days offered short but distinctive films about pretty well everything that was happening on the cultural front. Three years into its run I promoted Leslie to edit *Omnibus*. Alan Yentob had shown so much flair as a producer that he was the obvious choice to take over *Arena*: he replaced the magazine format with single features, some conventional but others on the very edge of the arts spectrum, not unlike Charlie Squires's films for *Aquarius*. Among the oddball subjects in Alan's first seasons were studies of the Ford Cortina, the Chelsea Hotel in New York and the evergreen song *My Way*. This policy, which brought encouraging results in terms of audience size and critical appreciation, was a perfect demonstration of my long-held axiom, Burton's law if you like, that all arts programmes aspire to the condition of the fifty-minute documentary. *Arena* became a cult. I like to think there was a hint of *Aquarius* in the mix because of the creative presence at Alan's right hand of the madcap Nigel Finch, who had worked so well for me at LWT.

Alan created a fiefdom in an open-plan office at the far end of the top corridor in Kensington House. The *Arena* space boasted green plants rising

Arena's message in a bottle has opened every show since Alan Yentob's first makeover.

to the ceiling, armchairs, table games, coffee machines … And Alan gathered round him an *Arena* team of gifted directors and researchers. It is eternally to his credit and to that of his chief lieutenants Nigel Finch (who died of an Aids-related illness in 1995) and Antony Wall (still going strong) that more than forty years later *Arena* is still in production (with over 800 programmes to its name) and still ahead of the curve.

But back to 1975. Since I considered *Omnibus* to be the flagship of the department, I needed to bring in a lively new editor when Mike Wooller opted to follow Norman Swallow back to the more congenial corridors of Granadaland. Choosing a replacement from within the department proved problematical. Among the candidates, I thought Christopher Burstall a touch too pompous, Christopher Martin too brusque and John Drummond too arrogant. John's put-downs to colleagues were famous. 'I watched your programme last night: so good to see you back on form at last', was one of the best: another runs, 'Watched your programme last night: I've been defending it all morning.'

My choice to run *Omnibus* fell on an outsider, Barrie Gavin, who had been a stalwart of the department in the 1960s but was then working as head of productions at the British Film Institute. Barrie could be a bit of a barrack-room lawyer but he had taste, knowledge and enthusiasm.

At *Omnibus* Barrie enjoyed two good seasons while Bryan Cowgill was BBC1's controller but fell foul of Cowgill's successor, Bill Cotton Jr, and was happy to take advantage of a devolution policy at the BBC which enabled him while still producing *Omnibus* to exchange the London rat race for the

With Barrie Gavin. In his hands there was no danger of *Omnibus* going soft.

relative calm of the BBC's HQ in Bristol. The experiment involved two other gifted directors, Dennis Marks and Tony Staveacre; it ended precipitately in 1981 following another regime change in BBC management.

On the music front I inherited reliable colleagues with whom I had worked happily in the 1960s, notably Walter Todds, Herbert Chappell and Ken Corden. John Culshaw had recruited a lively handful of younger men including David Buckton, Ian Engelmann, Rodney Greenberg, Dennis Moriarty and Roy Tipping. They continued to produce *Workshops*, documentaries for *Omnibus* and the greatly loved *Face the Music* quiz with Joseph Cooper. One of the panellists, Robin Ray, promised to be an attractive host for classical music programmes. Naturally they included outstanding symphony concerts throughout the year; Robin's early death was a great sadness.

On the debit side, the production of studio ballet was moribund. Margaret Dale was still making films about dance for *Omnibus* but she never really recovered from the collapse of her *Zodiac* project in 1967. In her place John Vernon, whom I knew from the 1960s to be a sensitive Outside Broadcast director, was delivering beautiful telecasts of Royal Ballet classics from the stage at Covent Garden. John Drummond and his protégé Bob Lockyer turned in some challenging documentary programmes about contemporary dance, so all was not lost.

Melvyn Bragg was already one of the department's major players, hosting a range of shows made for BBC2 which shared a theme that lasted all evening under the title *Open House* (later *Second House*); these shows were masterminded by two colleagues, Tony Cash and Bill Morton, for whom I had great respect, although the shows were worthy rather than exciting. Melvyn also came up with a winning formula for a cheap and cheerful late-night book show on BBC1 called *Read All About It*. A key element in the format was that the books under discussion were paperbacks so it was reasonable to assume that the watching public would have some notion of what was being discussed by the panellists, who were a fun mix of celebrities and literary lions. Were it not for the fact that every generation feels it has to reinvent the wheel, this series would still be running. In *Paperback Writer* it had a marvellous signature tune.

I needed a new *big* idea and I found it in a competition. In September 1975 I took over the presentation of the Leeds Piano Competition. As usual,

Melvyn Bragg, presenter of *Read All About It* – a winning formula.

the quality of the performers was extraordinarily high: Mitsuko Uchida, Myung-whun Chung and András Schiff were all in contention and I was very excited that we were televising 'live' such an important occasion. In the interval I rang Huw Wheldon at his home to canvass his reaction, but it was soon clear that he had not been watching the programme. I was mortified. If he wasn't watching, who was? I realised we needed to jack up public interest in such occasions. The top prize that evening went to the Russian Dimitri Alexeyev and not one of the six finalists was British. At the post-concert party the Leeds competition's redoubtable organiser Fanny Waterman threw fat on the flames by thanking everybody involved down to the last washer-up but said nothing about the BBC's televising the event to the nation. At the back of the room I shared with my colleagues a blinding revelation: the BBC must mount its own competition! It should be open only to British musicians so we would be sure of a British winner! The age limit should be the same as the NYO's, under nineteen, and players already studying at a music college would not be eligible. It was the NYO that inspired me: from my own experience in the 1940s I knew about the tremendous quality of our young musicians. Walter Todds and Roy Tipping took my basic idea and over the following months fleshed it out most convincingly. From the outset I felt certain that the competition should take place on BBC1, so at an early stage I pitched the project to the controller, Bryan Cowgill. To his eternal credit he gave *Young Musician* the funding and the airtime the project deserved and (with some reluctance) a couple of seasons of preparation time for Walter and Roy to work out the logistics, which crucially included settling on the Royal Northern College of Music in Manchester as our production centre.

The College's principal was John Manduell, an ex-BBC radio man of true vision with whom I had worked in the 1960s. It was an enormously important factor in our success that he threw his weight behind us and gave *Young Musician* the run of the entire college for two weeks.

We created four categories: piano, strings, wind and brass. Percussion, about which I have never been convinced, was not added until the 1990s after I had left the BBC. Bryan allotted more airtime to the competition than I had dared to hope for: we kicked off in early February 1978 with eight weekly evening programmes at 6.55 (after *Nationwide*) reporting on the regional finals – nearly a thousand young musicians had applied. Then on the Saturday and Sunday afternoons a week before the concerto finale came highlights of the national semi-finals (all taped in Manchester) and lastly a daily screening of each category final, with every player's performances receiving a decent amount of airtime so that viewers could make their own assessments. In the finals, where competitors played a complete concerto, Bryden Thomson conducted the BBC Northern Orchestra with great care for the youngsters' inexperience; the specialist judges, all world class, were Tamás Vásáry, Yehudi Menuhin, Leon Goossens and Harry Mortimer. The show went out live and in 1978 it drew an audience of 11 million. We made the production a major BBC occasion: the Duchess of Kent presented the award and the BBC's colourful chairman, George Howard, turned up in his kaftan to preside over the evening.

I went on to host the first seven *Young Musician* competitions, which discovered such gifted soloists as the oboist Nicholas Daniel, the clarinettist Emma Johnson, the cellist Natalie Clein and the violinist Nicola Benedetti – all wonderful artists. I had to leave the show in the 1990s when I moved to New York to write my biography of Leonard Bernstein. I was saddened by the way *Young Musician* was thereafter deprived of its massive audience. The rot set in when the show was relegated to BBC2 by Michael Grade (then Controller of BBC1) in the mid-1980s. Eventually it was transferred to BBC4 and nowadays

HRH The Duchess of Kent, Patron of *Young Musician of the Year*, with Sir John Manduell at the Royal Northern College of Music.

– in my view a great mistake – there are only three young musicians in the concerto finale. The quality of Britain's young musicians has not deteriorated: the downgrading of *Young Musician* is entirely due to the lack of care – one might even call it philistinism – of those now running BBC Television.

Opera became a central preoccupation in my second term at the BBC. During John Culshaw's time as head of music (1967–74), BBC Television had built up even closer ties than in my day with Benjamin Britten. But to free up the necessary budgets to mount Britten's operas *Peter Grimes* and *Owen Wingrave*, John had dropped the BBC's Glyndebourne connection. Southern Television (whose board of directors included George Christie, the son of Glyndebourne's founder) had stepped smartly into the vacuum and from 1972 onwards, with LWT's blessing, I produced Southern's telecasts from Glyndebourne. The hard slog of direction was undertaken by David Heather, one of Southern's staff directors, who became a close friend. (I am godfather to his daughter but proved hopeless in the role.) Dave spent weeks sitting in on the cast rehearsals, in the process getting to know the productions and the singers as a member of the team, something the BBC directors had never had time for. We began with Verdi's *Macbeth*. The Greek baritone Kostas Paskalis was splendid in the title role but I told Southern's head of programmes, the debonair Berkeley Smith, that I feared Glyndebourne's casting of Lady Macbeth would not work on television; she was a competent soprano but visually unconvincing. Moran Caplat, Glyndebourne's amiable (and very able) administrator, understood the problem and proposed instead the American soprano who would be taking over the role later in the season. This lady had the spitfire feistiness needed for the part, and the vocal edge, but she was also physically challenged, being short and stubby with a very prominent corsage. Again I felt it crucial to risk a row with George Christie and turn her down for the telecast, at which point the Glyndebourne management caved in and produced their understudy, a much younger singer named Josephine Barstow. The future Dame Jo was an excellent Lady, a little reminiscent of Margaret Lockwood in *The Wicked Lady*; the chemistry with Paskalis was electrifying and Southern's reign at Glyndebourne was off to a good start.

Other televised operas from the 1970s, thankfully preserved on DVD, express the intimacy and charm of the old opera house at Glyndebourne. Mozart's *Idomeneo* and *Seraglio* in 1972 were followed in 1973 by a well-nigh perfect *Figaro* featuring Kiri Te Kanawa, Ileana Cotrubas and Frederica von Stade as the Countess, Susanna and Cherubino. Only my return to the BBC prevented me from working on Glyndebourne's famous *Rake's Progress* designed in 1975 by David Hockney. By then Benjamin Britten was seriously ill with heart disease and I found on my return to Music and Arts that the BBC's close association with him had inevitably faded. Surprisingly, the BBC had not televised Britten's final opera *Death in Venice* during the year of its première, 1973, perhaps because Britten held the BBC to be at fault for the relative failure of the television opera *Owen Wingrave*. Culshaw and Brian Large, the BBC's most ambitious studio director, had instead turned the spotlight on Richard Wagner, spending a great deal of money on a documentary portrait of Wagner's Bayreuth opera house to celebrate the centenary of the *Ring* cycle. Brian Large then made a return to studio production with *The Flying Dutchman*, but felt obliged, in the best ENO tradition, to have it performed in English. My return to the BBC came too late to reverse this decision, even though everybody in the cast could have delivered the original German. Despite the powerful presence of Norman Bailey and Gwyneth Jones I couldn't help feeling that studio opera in English had had its day. Relays from opera houses had more immediacy and the introduction of subtitles, which I had pioneered at Glyndebourne with Southern Television, did away with the need to sing mainstream works (except comedy) in English.

Within months of rejoining the BBC I found myself supervising a telecast of *Cavalleria rusticana* and *I Pagliacci* from the Royal Opera House. These were Franco Zeffirelli productions with Plácido Domingo singing the lead tenor role in both operas. *Cav* went well but in the interval John Tooley, the Royal Opera's boss, and I were summoned to Mr Domingo's dressing room. He greeted us with desperate news: he had developed a vocal infection and had just been advised by his doctor that unless he stopped singing immediately he would do irreparable damage to his voice: Mr Tooley would have to send the audience home. Mr Domingo's vocal cords would surely be fine in a few days so he would be happy for the BBC to tape the next show.

We were appalled, Tooley at the prospect of having to give a full house its money back, I because there was probably no hope of rescheduling such a massive outside broadcast. We pleaded with Domingo for the best part of an hour. The audience became understandably restless. Tooley argued most persuasively for the principle that the show must go on but Plácido was adamant. A possible solution crept into my head. I knew a little about recording industry practices, how busy singers such as Domingo would sometimes go into a studio late at night and sing their parts to a pre-recorded orchestra track which they heard on headphones. I told him the BBC was recording the sound on multi-track; if he was not satisfied with his performance we could take him to a studio to retrack any faulty passages again. That offer did the trick, he consented to get ready for *I Pagliacci* and I went back to the OB van to explain what had been going on. A voice came over the talkback: 'Did I hear you mention multi-track?' It was the sound supervisor. 'Yes, that'll be okay, won't it?', said I, cheerfully, still rather pleased with myself. 'Sorry, Humphrey, this truck doesn't have multi-track facilities,' came the chilling response. 'The stereo is just good old-fashioned left and right!'

Luckily the tenor gave the performance of his life as Canio that evening and John Vernon's cameras caught the drama beautifully. A few days later Plácido came round to my flat to listen to a playback; after only a few minutes he expressed himself happy and he spent the rest of the visit playing table tennis.

In those years I looked after opera planning personally and I was particularly keen to get Glyndebourne's recent production of *Capriccio* on to television. John Cox and his designer Martin Battersby had come up with

Plácido Domingo and my son Lukas after the successful playback of *I Pagliacci*.

an enchanting art deco concept and the cast was led by my idol, Elisabeth Söderström: the Countess was a perfect role for her in her forties. Other Swedish singers, Håkan Hagegård and Kerstin Meyer, were equally fine as the Countess's brother and the seductive actress Clairon. John Vernon did a beautiful job of transferring the action from the stage to the screen. He was inventive, too: for the opening scene he relocated the string sextet from the orchestra pit to the imposing Glyndebourne library. The musicians played Flamand's exquisite serenade to the Countess while outside on the sweeping drive leading to the house at Glyndebourne a Bugatti could be seen delivering the guest Italian singers to the front door. Later Monsieur Taupe the prompter (the evergreen Hugues Cuénod) staggered in, hot and sweaty, after a long walk from the railway station. Sadly the Richard Strauss Estate took a dim view of John Cox's updating from 1775 to the 1920s and never allowed the BBC to sell the finished product to other countries, but I was proud to share *Capriccio* with a large British audience and to re-establish the BBC's long-term relationship with Glyndebourne.

I helped finance the show through a co-production deal with Germany's second channel, ZDF. When their producer Rudolf Sailer came to our planning meeting he flourished a list of the cuts he proposed to make. He explained that *Capriccio* had a duration of two and a quarter hours, but audience research in Germany had proved that 'the clerks and the small working peoples' who made up the majority of ZDF's opera-viewing public would not tolerate an opera lasting any longer than one hour and forty-three minutes. Hence the need for cuts. My friend Dr Sailer was a musician, and the cuts, he assured us, were all musically feasible: he would be happy to go through the score with the conductor. General consternation! Luckily I remembered that Rudolf was also a choir trainer. I told him that any cuts would have to be made at the editing stage: meanwhile we urgently needed his help to coach the eight servants in idiomatic German for their short but crucial scene. Off he went, and once he had seen the Cox *Capriccio* he was happy to take every minute of it. It is my favourite of all the relays I worked on at the old Glyndebourne, where we went on to restore the BBC's link with Britten's operas, televising Peter Hall's productions of *A Midsummer Night's Dream*, *Death in Venice* and *Albert Herring*. I was furious with Peter for arbitrarily draining the colour out of the pictures when he was editing *Herring*: he should have told the engineers in advance that he wanted a black-and-white look, something akin to the sepia of a Victorian photograph. But I have to admit that Hall's Britten operas, conducted by Bernard Haitink, have made well-nigh perfect transfers to the screen.

The planning process at BBC Television was something of a mystery to me. Every year I had a day-long planning meeting with each of the two channel controllers. We would aim to renew regular strands and I would pitch a slew of new projects, sometimes bringing in the producer to make his or her own case. The annual plan would estimate the film and studio resources we would need. Then everything went into the hopper to be sorted out by the controllers' planning teams: there were no computers in those days.

The departmental head, I discovered, was also the commissioning editor. There had to be a considerable degree of trust between him, the controllers in top management and the producers. Sometimes things went spectacularly wrong. I recall a huge fuss when *Omnibus* opened its new season with a feature on Japanese art narrated by David Attenborough. Enterprisingly the *Omnibus* editor Barrie Gavin had made a successful bid for an illustration on the cover of *Radio Times*, which meant prestige and the likelihood of a larger audience. When an advance copy of *Radio Times* was delivered to the controller of BBC TV, Alasdair Milne, he blew his top and it was me who had to take the rap. Had we taken leave of our senses? Didn't we know about anti-Japanese feeling in this country? Gagaku? Bugaku? Bunraku? Yukaku! It did not calm the waters to point out that the war in the Pacific had been over for forty years.

Co-production was another thorny topic. It was fine when the BBC simply took the money and remained in editorial command. A decade earlier I had been happy to negotiate a deal with *The Bell Telephone Hour* for our Aldeburgh film. But after Aubrey Singer started raising funds from American big business to pay for major series such as Alistair Cooke's *America* and Jacob Bronowski's *Ascent of Man* it had become clear that in addition to being editor-in-chief of Music and Arts I was also *de facto* a major fundraiser for the Corporation's heavyweight series. But my heart was never in the business of sweet-talking American oil executives who had promotional funds to burn and I can point only to the historian John Roberts's *The Triumph of the West* as a successful co-produced series in which I played a modest part. The funding for *The Shock of the New*, a series I greatly admired, was already being negotiated as I returned to the BBC; Time-Life came on board, which was a great asset, reflecting Robert Hughes's growing reputation in the United States, but our creative partner was an old friend of mine from Munich, Reiner Moritz, who over the decades put money into literally hundreds of BBC arts and music features.

Reiner Moritz –
a vital figure in the
world of television
arts co-production.

Reiner deserves a separate chapter: he was more of an artistic partner than a commercial investor. Like his former boss Leo Kirch of Unitel, he has had his share of financial misfortune but the threat of bankruptcy never weakened Reiner's sense of adventure or his style: we last met a few years ago in Prague when he had the look and the overcoat of a distinguished former ambassador.

* * *

The cap-in-hand element in my personal workload was considerably lightened in the second half of my Kensington House tenure when John Drummond left to run the Edinburgh Festival at the end of 1977 and Richard Somerset-Ward, a clever planner over at Television Centre, was drafted in by Alasdair Milne to replace him. I was not consulted about Richard's appointment but Alasdair presumably thought I needed a minder. I should have insisted on an appointment board, since Richard, agreeable fellow though he was, had no specific arts or music production experience. However, he was a fan and he knew the inner workings of the BBC's planning process, which was a boon. With Ian Marshall serving as the department's loyal and devoted administrator, I think we made an effective management team.

There were grumbles that I was away too much. I certainly had a generous contract. John Drummond once referred (a touch enviously, I can't help feeling) to the 'highly unusual terms' by which I could be away for up to a month each year working with Leonard Bernstein. But that clause had been the bottom line for my return to the Corporation and Huw Wheldon confirmed that my close working relationship with one of the world's leading musicians was invaluable to the BBC. In his sometimes savage memoir *Tainted by Experience* Drummond wrote that I was so busy presenting *Omnibus* and making Bernstein music films for Unitel that I devolved most of the day-to-day running of the department on to him. 'He's in Make-Up or Munich' was a familiar taunt, invented without malice by Russell Harty some years earlier when we were both at LWT. I can only respond by saying that I worked very hard for the Music and Arts Department. I wrote honest annual reports by the dozen and oversaw the careers of a hundred directors. I also arranged for stimulating figures from the outside world to address the department every month and generally acted as a father figure to many of my colleagues. Sadly, there were two suicides on my seven-year watch and several nervous breakdowns. And I had to find ways of counselling a senior colleague, a married man, who had been caught cottaging at a motorway service station. Every week I defended the department's output to the best of my ability at the often hostile Programme Review meetings held over at Television Centre. Incidentally, I don't think John Drummond ever knew that I had played a part in his appointment to the Edinburgh Festival. I was telephoned one day by a city father who asked in broad Scots whether I would consider taking over the artistic directorship since Peter Diamand was planning to retire. I replied that although flattered, I could not imagine enjoying a job where all my 'kicks' would be squeezed into the single month of August, but that I did have a well-qualified colleague who certainly *would* be interested and what's more was a Scot – by the name of Drummond. A few weeks later John confided that he had just been appointed to the post. His farewell programme was one of his best and the kind of project we both loved and had been making for a decade and a half: it was a multi-layered account of the Stravinsky/ Nijinska/Diaghilev ballet *Les Noces*, narrated by John himself and featuring the Royal Ballet and LB conducting a starry quartet of pianists headed by Martha Argerich. It was a fine show but the department's farewell to John was even better: at the Christmas party three of his colleagues (Tony Staveacre, Dennis Marks and Bob Lockyer) dressed up in kilts, danced a reel and spouted a valedictory poem written in the mock-heroic style of William McGonagall. Brian Wenham, recently appointed Controller of BBC2, whispered in my ear, 'If only your programmes were half as amusing as your parties'.

Wenham was an important ally. He loved classical music, especially opera, and gave me the go-ahead for an Opera Month featuring performances, workshops, documentaries and master classes – all the things I had been encouraging since the first days of BBC2. (They have all disappeared from twenty-first-century television schedules, with the honourable exception of Sir Antonio Pappano's revelatory features about opera and voices.) A year later, 1980, BBC2 ran a similar month devoted to dance and ballet. It was edited for me by Julia Matheson, one of the many talented women in the Music and Arts department, and someone who shared my admiration for the choreographer Maurice Béjart. Bob Lockyer chipped in with programmes featuring Robert Cohan and London Contemporary Dance. After Maggie Dale, Bob was the most effective dance producer the BBC has ever had – not that the list is a long one.

In the autumn of the following year, Brian Wenham adopted my suggestion that, in Wagner's centenary year, 1983, his *Ring* cycle should be transmitted on BBC2 – not over a few days, as Wagner had imagined, but in ten weekly instalments. This was the *Ring* re-conceived by two Frenchmen, the director Patrice Chéreau and the conductor Pierre Boulez, by general consent the most striking concept since Wieland Wagner's productions in the early 1950s. Wenham scheduled the *Ring* act by act as a sort of *Upstairs, Downstairs* set in Valhalla, each episode preceded by a ten-minute talk from me that served as a transition from banal television time to the epic spaciousness of Wagnerian time. Radio 3 joined us with simultaneous stereo broadcasts; this was a great selling point since in the early 1980s the sound in new television sets was still provided by a tinny little mono loudspeaker. We negotiated long and hard with Radio 3 to develop such relays, known as simulcasts. They were no longer needed when, very late in the day, stereo sound became part of the television experience – the broadcasts were in stereo and new TV sets had stereo receivers.

Not all such simulcasts were unqualified successes. I remember being roundly rebuked next morning when I suggested on Radio 3 that a Horowitz performance in New York, hosted by me on a BBC2 simulcast, had been wonderful. 'We don't use adjectives on Radio 3' had been the burden of the complaint from Ian McIntyre, Radio 3's controller. Try telling that to the gushing presenters of today.

Brian Wenham, witty, laid-back and a realist, was my favourite among the BBC controllers with whom I worked, but Cyril Bennett at LWT was a closer friend and it was a terrible shock when in 1976 he was found dead on railings below his third-floor apartment. Eighteen months had passed since my return to the BBC and I had not seen much of Cyril except for a splendid night at BAFTA when LWT picked up seven awards, more than the rest of the

ITV companies combined. Cyril was separated from his wife and had been having a hard time negotiating access to his children. He had just returned from a two-day conference at which he had been roundly criticised by LWT colleagues for failing to match the BBC's challenge on Saturday nights. But can his death have been suicide? Cyril was an affirmative spirit, a man who loved life. I like to think rather that he had drunk too much and leaned too far out of the window when checking to see whether his devoted chauffeur Vic Calder had arrived to pick him up.

The ITV industry mounted a splendid farewell for Cyril. Isaac Stern and Leonard Bernstein were in London and they accepted my invitation to play Gershwin in Cyril's memory. Earlier in the decade I had told Bernstein about the Mahler festival Cyril had screened on LWT at my suggestion; when Bernstein was next in London he invited Cyril to dinner together with my wife and his date, Lauren Bacall. (I was away.) The two very Jewish gentlemen, both excellent storytellers, got on famously. Lauren Bacall is no slouch in the anecdote department but she and Christina were happy to sit back and listen. Backstage at the memorial, looking out at the hundreds of mourners, Stern turned to me and whispered, 'You must have loved this guy very much'.

* * *

The major flop of my seven-year stint at Music and Arts was a topical arts magazine on BBC1 which I called *Mainstream*. When *Arena* morphed from magazine into single-subject films, the department was once again without a strand reporting on the current arts scene. Our colleagues in *Late Night Line-Up* (produced by the Presentation department) did their best to fill the gap but by definition that show went out too late for most people. I pitched a new format to the new controller of BBC1, Bill Cotton Jr. It was to be a half-hour show, on a weekday, offering what it promised on the label: mainstream arts topics dealt with in a bright and breezy style. No item would be longer than five minutes. There would be graphics in plenty and youngish women presenters such as Susan Stranks and Jane Wellesley (famous for having said no to Prince Charles). The programme would provide good nursery slopes to train young directors such as Anthony Wall (the future editor of *Arena*), who had just joined the department.

I had the rather weird notion that I should stand down from being a boss for a few months and with Tony Palmer as co-editor run *Mainstream* myself – a disastrous decision. Tony and I issued contradictory missives about the aims of the show, and Tony managed to upset Joan Bakewell, who I had hoped would become our arts reporter. On the morning of the first transmission Palmer sent a telegram – not to me but to the studio director – instructing him to take his name off the credits. He was in Aldeburgh that morning filming establishing shots for his (excellent) *South Bank Show* documentary about Benjamin Britten. I vowed there and then never to work again with Palmer and no doubt because I have held to that resolve we are now good friends; indeed, I think his *Wagner* biopic, starring Richard Burton, is one of the greatest films ever produced by an English director. To replace Palmer I drafted in John Selwyn Gilbert, a clever producer I had recently recruited from further education. He had ideas somewhat above his station but I was in a fix: Gilbert would only take the job, he told me, if he had full editorial control. After a rough start I believe he would have pulled it off had it not been for a damaging strike at the BBC which knocked out most forms of studio and film production. We limped onto the screen. The only bright spark to emerge from the wreckage of what the *Sunday Times* called 'the worst television programme ever made' was the calm demeanour under fire of the replacement presenter Bruce Parker, recruited literally two days before the first transmission. He subsequently enjoyed a long career as the political correspondent for BBC South.

I still have a lapel button inscribed 'There is Life after Mainstream'. Not surprisingly, Bill Cotton did not agree. He failed to commission a second run.

Sometimes I was able to bring together my BBC life and my alternative persona who still worked every year with Leonard Bernstein. In August 1978, LB's sixtieth birthday was marked with a gala concert at Wolf Trap Park, the summer outdoor venue of the Washington Symphony Orchestra then conducted by Slava Rostropovich. It was to have been a celebration and the show had to go on but this was a desperate time in LB's life: his wife Felicia had died of cancer two months earlier and he was convinced (as were family friends such as Lillian Hellman, who said as much in her rather acid eulogy) that his decision to leave Felicia and live with his assistant Tommy Cothran had created the stress that fired up Felicia's final illness. The couple had been reconciled after less than a year of living apart but she then developed lung cancer and died aged only fifty-six. (A more likely reason for her illness was that she smoked incessantly. LB tried to give up many times but always failed: emphysema was one of the things that got him in the end.) The Wolf Trap concert, which I presented for the BBC, ran for over three hours. There were Broadway numbers, of course, and songs from his new cycle *Songfest*, but all I remember forty years on is LB's conducting of a radiant performance of Beethoven's Triple Concerto with Yehudi Menuhin, Mstislav Rostropovich and André Previn as the resplendent soloists: the work caught fire, which it doesn't always. It seemed to me that the only way LB could assuage his guilt was by making music in this impulsive, tumultuous, going-for-broke manner.

For the record, I had already experienced some wonderful music-making with LB since my return to the BBC. In New York with the Philharmonic, his former orchestra, I directed a telecast of his vivid reading of Tchaikovsky's Fourth Symphony (the show won an Emmy) and also a pair of the Haydn symphonies he loved so much, numbers 93 and 94. If you know the symphonies those numbers will probably make you smile with anticipatory pleasure.

In Paris in the late 1970s LB was wooed by French Radio's orchestra chief, Pierre Voslinsky (a witty intellectual who sadly took his own life a decade later)

Left to right: Harry Kraut, producer David Griffiths, me and LB at Wolf Trap Park, 1978.

Wolf Trap, Washington, 1978. Left to right: Yehudi Menuhin, Mstislav Rostropovich, LB and André Previn take a bow at the end of the Beethoven Triple Concerto.

to embark on a cycle devoted to Berlioz containing *Harold in Italy*, *Roméo et Juliette*, the *Symphonie fantastique* and most splendid of all, the *Requiem*, which was performed at Les Invalides in September 1975, the very place where the première had been given, although the building had been much altered since 1840. Still, there was a splendid atmosphere in this grand mausoleum as LB made his entry down the centre aisle accompanying President Giscard d'Estaing to his seat before peeling off to conduct an immense orchestra (eleven timpani!) and a choir that found it so difficult to stay in tune that a portable organ had to be smuggled into the serried vocal ranks to steady the intonation. The grandest moment in the *Requiem* is the 'Tuba mirum', for which Berlioz added four groups of trumpets and trombones. We could find no description of the composer's own layout for the orchestra but ours was dramatic enough, with the brass players stationed at four points high in the roof of the nave, offering visual contact with the conductor. This was my favourite Berlioz telecast. Not for nothing are my initials HB!

Paris, 1975. My week with LB filming the Berlioz *Requiem* was a
pleasant diversion from the humiliation of *Mainstream*.

At the first evening's recording, the sequence, indeed the entire Mass, went
very well. However, Berlioz's gorgeous music had hardly died away when there
was a furious pounding at the door of the French Television van. My German
colleagues from Unitel, our somewhat reluctant co-production partners,
were utterly distraught. 'We cannot possibly transmit this performance', they
announced with fury in their tone. 'Why ever not?' I replied. 'We thought it
was great.' 'Did you not see the *drapeau* in the background behind Maestro
Bernstein?' came the answer. 'A SWASTIKA! Impossible! Unmöglich.'

The walls of Les Invalides are festooned with flags representing French
battle honours from the time of Bonaparte onwards. In the Second World
War such honours were thin on the ground but in North Africa in 1942 the
Free French under General Leclerc had indeed scored a victory over Nazi
forces and had a battle flag to prove it. Of course, I only had eyes for the
conductor and had failed to spot the offending swastika behind him during
the concert. Fortunately we were able to rearrange the flags for the second
performance. The Welsh tenor Stuart Burrows again sang beautifully. It may

340

not be quite as fervent an interpretation of what I think of as the St Paul's Verdi *Requiem* seven years previously but in LB's hands Berlioz's score still takes the breath away.

Meanwhile, LB concluded his Mahler cycle in Vienna and in 1978 moved on to a Beethoven cycle with a powerful Ninth Symphony filmed at the Staatsoper. I remember it mostly because my wife fell ill and had to go to hospital, something one should never do in Vienna unless (like Christina) one has an exceptionally strong constitution.

Looking back on the 1970s I see it as my divided decade. I can make a good case for my position in the early 1970s when simultaneously I edited *Aquarius* and filmed Mahler symphonies with LB. But I can confess it now: running a big BBC department like Music and Arts should have been a full-time job. Other 'robber baron' bosses such as Peter Dimmock and Desmond Wilcox, familiar figures on screen, managed to keep several balls in the air, but they were, so to speak, BBC balls. Whereas when I went away from my Kensington House office it was to work for a foreign company.

By the end of the decade my directing portfolio was expanding in a way that was flattering to me but inevitably took up more of my time: as well as filming LB with the Viennese every September I had also been hired by the American branch of Unitel to spend a couple of weeks making videos with the Chicago Symphony, then America's top orchestra, under Georg Solti, while from Germany I was summoned to direct the televised New Year's Eve concerts with the Berlin Philharmonic under Herbert von Karajan. With Solti I honed the multi-camera technique to a fine art; he said himself that he couldn't imagine a more faithful transfer from concert platform to screen than the one we achieved with Mendelssohn's 'Italian' and 'Scottish' symphonies. My personal Chicago favourite was Solti's hour of Richard Strauss: two tone poems, *Tod und Verklärung* and *Till Eulenspiegel*, and between them the *Four Last Songs* with Lucia Popp as the deeply moving soloist. (She died of cancer in November 1993.)

With Karajan, my baptism of fire – a 'live' transmission – was Beethoven's Ninth, which looked stunning in Berlin's exceptional Philharmonie hall. Karajan was a perfectionist. He spent an hour rehearsing the double basses for the brief recitative which kicks off the 'Ode to Joy'. It was indeed a joy to work with an artist such as Karajan, who, whatever his arrogance and narcissism, cared as deeply as I did about the *look* of the music being televised. For the first rehearsal he hired a student orchestra to serve as stand-ins and spent the

Scenes from Unitel recordings 1977–1978. Top left: on the set for a recording of a Beethoven piano concerto. Bottom left: technical hitch – 'Maschine kaputt!'. Right: camera rehearsal for Beethoven's *Choral Fantasy*.

Lucia Popp and Georg Solti: an ecstatic moment from Strauss's *Four Last Songs*.

entire day on the concert platform setting the lights and choosing the best angles (mostly for his close-ups).

The 31st December 1984 Berlin Philharmonic concert was all Bach, which Karajan chose to conduct from the harpsichord, though the orchestra fielded a second harpsichordist for the bread-and-butter sections. Karajan was no baroque specialist but the *Magnificat* went with a tremendous swing and Anne-Sophie Mutter, then a pulchritudinous twenty-one-year-old, played a Bach violin concerto ravishingly. But the most sensational of my Karajan experiences in Berlin was his interpretation of Ravel's *Boléro* (concert of New Year's Eve 1985), the highlight in an evening of classical 'pops'. He deployed three drummers to intensify the crescendo but I devoted more camera time during the *Boléro*'s fifteen minutes to watching the maestro transform himself from a seemingly detached observer in the opening bars to a catatonic dervish at the climax; at that orgasmic moment in Ravel's score Karajan was truly a man possessed.

To work with these great conductors was a privilege, even an honour, as well as being good fun and lucrative, but by 1981 the writing was on the wall so far as my BBC career was concerned. The previous year Alasdair Milne had asked me to be a candidate for the vacant job of Controller BBC1. It proved to be a farcical procedure since I truly did not want the job. At the time Milne insisted I was controller material, and had I been offered the controllership of the alternative channel, BBC2, I suppose I would have accepted. But Milne changed his mind about me – he had a very short fuse – and in the spring of 1981 he called me in: he was unhappy, he told me, that I had been advising an American company about a possible cultural cable service. I had been given formal permission to do the consultancy in New York, but a British trade paper, *TV Today*, suggested, incorrectly, that there was a clash of interest. Milne was probably disappointed by something quite different: my handling of an important three-part series about the ancient Greeks, a project in which he had taken a personal interest. The classicist Kenneth Dover was the writer and presenter but the producer I had chosen, Christopher Burstall, seemed less concerned with Dover's ideas than with telling viewers about his own first impressions of Greece. I suspect that lurking in the background of Milne's thinking was a whiff of scandal in my private life. We agreed it was time for

At a rehearsal with Herbert von Karajan. He left nothing to chance.

me to move on, indeed Alasdair began our meeting by suggesting I made a swift departure. I pointed out that such a move would look as if I was indeed guilty of some misdemeanour, which I certainly wasn't, so it was decided that I would quit my office later in the summer, allowing for an orderly handover to my deputy, Richard Somerset-Ward. In the press release it was stressed that I was not leaving the Corporation but would step down to a less exposed position, editing the BBC's classical music performance programmes. It was a role that suited me so well that I was to perform it for the next seven years.

CHAPTER 17

DISCOVERING MY MÉTIER

Checking my script in Vienna's Golden Hall.

I KNOW IT'S no guarantee of happiness or even of well-being, but the fact is I earned more money and was better off in the 1980s (my fifties) than in any other decade in my life. I had a regular basic BBC salary for my various jobs as director, producer and strand editor; my work as host of *Omnibus* was paid on a separate contract. On top of that came my Unitel fees for directing Leonard Bernstein's music films, to which I was soon adding freelance gigs with Bavarian Television in Munich, with Sony in Hamburg, with Eric and Katya Abraham's Portobello Films – all this for productions I directed in Budapest with Georg Solti and in Berlin with Murray Perahia

Oakwood Court. The second floor apartment was to be our much-loved
sound-proofed home until we moved to Aldeburgh in 2001.

– and, most lucrative of the lot, because the concert is transmitted to dozens of countries, with Austrian Television for the New Year's Day concert from the Golden Hall, which I first directed in 1988, when Herbert von Karajan was conducting.

My personal life survived a very sticky patch during this exceptionally busy period. In March 1981 my daughter Clemency was born. I am very proud of her work as a broadcaster, writer and musician, and though I see her rarely, I count her as a good friend. In amicable consultation with her I have decided not to write at length about the affair with her mother which brought her into the world. It was a long and intense friendship and my marriage survived only thanks to my wife's tolerance and fortitude.

A new start began when the Burton family left Richmond Hill and moved back across the river to a solid ten-roomed Edwardian flat in Oakwood Court, just a few yards west of Holland Park. Its hall corridor was exactly 22 yards in length and was occasionally used by my son Matthew as an indoor cricket 'net'; at St Paul's School he developed into an excellent all-rounder, going on to play every summer with The Gaieties, Harold Pinter's touring club team. The flat's walls were so thick we could make music at any time without disturbing the neighbours – even if it were Gwyneth Jones giving us a post-prandial *Liebestod* or Barbara Bonney bringing in the new year with Strauss's *Morgen*. My piano playing was stretched to the limit and beyond on such occasions.

As in our Richmond house, there was space for two medium-sized grand pianos – the Steinway I acquired in my *Aquarius* years and the Bechstein Christina inherited from her mother. They were stationed head to toe at the far end of the dining room, which was used for playing and listening to music rather than eating. We took our meals in the kitchen, which looked south-west over St Barnabas Church, where my eldest daughter Clare got married in 1983. We had space for a dedicated television room but apart from football, television in the 1980s was more often for making than for watching.

Down the corridor Christina installed a darkroom – after studying photography at Richmond Technical College she had built an interesting new career specialising in portraits and action photos of opera singers, conductors and classical music soloists. Record covers were her forte until the mid-1980s, when 12-inch LPs were superseded by much smaller compact discs and the illustrations were shrunk accordingly. I used to love watching her photos coming to life in the developer bath. The apartment was large enough for us

Two pianos, eight hands, at Oakwood Court.

both to have studies and there was room in the main hall for a table-tennis table, though we took it down the year Erik Smith lent me his harpsichord. Just inside the door was a rocking horse, much appreciated by my son Lukas in his tender years.

As I have noted, *Thank You for the Music* could have been the title of this memoir, and it was to music that I returned, 100 per cent, in the 1980s. Within a few weeks of quitting my administrative job and the spacious Kensington House office I had occupied for the previous seven years, I was installed in a cubbyhole on the top floor of that dreary building and preparing to direct my first television Prom since 1964: Rossini's *Stabat Mater* – an uneven work, I concede, but for me the next best thing to Verdi's *Requiem* for dramatic intensity and thus the perfect work to entrust to Carlo Maria Giulini, the noblest artist with whom I ever worked. 'Stabat mater dolorosa' is how the Latin text begins and no conductor has ever appeared more *doloroso* than Giulini: a suffering expression was his default position but he could also assume a truly terrifying aspect. I loved his interpretation of the Verdi *Requiem* (it had been the first music to be televised on BBC2) and I had already taped for ITV Giulini's magisterial conducting of Beethoven's *Missa Solemnis* in St Paul's Cathedral. But nothing had prepared me for the emotion generated by Rossini's dramatic aria 'Inflammatus et accensus'. I saw enough at rehearsal to know that the soprano soloist, Katia Ricciarelli, was frightened out of her wits: the musical intensity would best be expressed, I felt, by close-ups. So out went the cooler script I had prepared and in came tight shots of the beautiful but terrified soprano, who on this occasion looked like Mary Pickford in the climax of a silent movie, tied to a railway line with an express train bearing down on her. Giulini himself resembled a martyr close to expiration.

To be in charge of the cameras, to be in at the death, so to speak, was an intoxicating sensation and I realised then and there, in the BBC's 'scanner' parked outside the Royal Albert Hall, that *this* was my true *métier*, finding

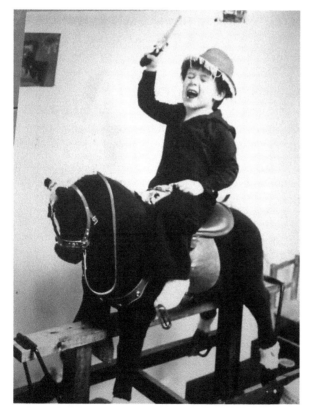

Lukas on his
rocking horse.

Rossini's *Stabat Mater* at The Proms. Left: Carlo Maria Giulini. Right: Katia Ricciarelli.

the best way for the cameras to express the high tension of marvellous music-making. It is as near as one can get to actually conducting without holding a baton between your fingers. I was gratified when next day Alan Blyth, the *Telegraph*'s music critic, wrote, reviewing the concert, that it was good to see me back in the director's chair after my long absence working as an administrator.

March 1982 saw the opening of the Barbican Centre. I had been hearing about this ambitious new arts centre in the City of London for a decade, often while sitting in Ernest Fleischmann's kitchen for post-concert suppers shared with one of the Barbican's architects, Peter Chamberlin. I knew about the limitations of the site: no room for a large choir, no organ, no sense of grandeur, either aural or visual. Still, after all the infighting and rancour it was an enormous achievement of the City Fathers to have got the Centre finished, to have the concept of a meeting place for all the arts actually up and running: galleries, library, cinemas, a splendid theatre for the RSC, all were in place in addition to the handsome and comfortable concert hall. I was genuinely impressed by the complex when a group of us wearing hard hats were shown around by the Canadian executive Henry Wrong, who had nursed the scheme for a decade and more. I first met Henry at the New York Metropolitan Opera when filming his then boss, Rudolf Bing, for my *Monitor* profile. It was surely from Mr Bing that Henry had learnt his showmanship. So the Barbican's opening ceremony was a night for him to celebrate. After Claudio Abbado had conducted the LSO at the royal gala the entire audience was invited to a lavish reception for which printed notices had been placed all over the hall reading: PLEASE WOULD YOU REFRAIN FROM STARTING THE PARTY UNTIL AFTER HER MAJESTY THE QUEEN HAS LEFT THE BUILDING. And then, in much smaller type: 'Thank You'. It was rather a dull party.

In the same month I produced three shows entitled *Live from the Barbican*. Incongruously, they were paid for by a betting-shop chain. The BBC was very concerned in those days with the delicate issue of sponsorship. We could not take money directly from business firms but under pressure from Lord Goodman and a posse of business leaders the BBC had backed itself into a squirm-making compromise whereby the Corporation agreed to carry two visual credits for the sponsors of events it was televising and another in the spoken presentation. It was an embarrassing procedure for old BBC hands like me who were born and bred in the ethos of public service. However, the LSO was quickly into this sponsorship field: they had done a deal with Ladbroke's Group and it was not for us to ask whether the betting firm's financial support was contingent upon the BBC's participation. The new

HM The Queen meeting Claudio Abbado with the LSO team and their wives after the LSO's opening concert at the Barbican Centre, 1982.

format, devised by me, envisaged live occasions with an unstuffy, relaxed atmosphere and the musicians in shirtsleeves; one of the aims was to persuade families to watch together at home. *Radio Times* trumpeted the dawn of a new era: 'From the Barbican's new concert hall, home of the LSO, comes a new style of presentation.' There would be rehearsal and performance – a mix I had been advocating since the earliest days of BBC2. 'With young people especially in mind', continues the *Radio Times* blurb, which I guess was written by me, 'John Amis talks about Beethoven's *Eroica* Symphony and interviews today's conductor, Yehudi Menuhin'. The violin virtuoso may have been no great shakes as a conductor but he was the most famous classical musician in the world, hence the casting. The host, my friend John Amis, had a lively mind and a broad following through his membership of the popular *My Music* quiz team. He spoke without using technical terms and I directed the music as effectively as I knew how. The afternoon passed pleasantly. On paper the other two programmes were equally enjoyable: in the first Rudolf Serkin played a Mozart piano concerto and to the last, on March 28th, William Walton, the featured composer, came in person, on the eve of his eightieth birthday, to hear Nobuko Imai play his lovely Viola Concerto. Walton was presented with a fine birthday cake by the orchestra, with whom he had a long and fruitful relationship, including my favourite recording of this concerto (the pre-war 78s, featuring Frederick Riddle, were one of my first schoolboy purchases). Eighty candles were blown out and there were many cheers. But the jollity did not translate into television audience figures. They were rather dismal. I had hoped these afternoon relays would become a seasonal fixture on BBC2 but the times were definitely a-changing; thereafter the BBC rarely visited the Barbican. I imagine Ladbroke's took their sponsorship money to a programme where the odds on winning audience ratings were more favourable.

There was no time to lick wounds. The next day, March 29th, was Walton's birthday and the Royal Festival Hall's celebration attracted a full house to salute music's grand old man. Truth to tell, Walton looked closer to ninety than eighty. Where once, back in the 1920s, his noble profile had suggested a Chelsea-based Adonis, Walton was now a gaunt, bony-faced figure in a wheelchair. His friend Gillian Widdicombe contributed a sharp-tongued biography for our interval feature, part of a live BBC2 relay shared with Radio 3 and sponsored by Ms Widdicombe's employer, the *Observer*.

André Previn conducted the Philharmonia Orchestra – an unusual pairing, explained by the fact that the LSO had double-booked itself, which was why they had made such a big fuss of Walton the previous afternoon at the Barbican.

Walton, musing on his youth, at the Royal Festival Hall exhibition, 1982.

Previn did as good a job with *Belshazzar's Feast* as is possible in the Festival Hall's clinical acoustic. Kyung-Wha Chung provided a passionate reading of Walton's Violin Concerto. This came after a suitably grand start with *Orb and Sceptre*, the coronation march Walton composed for Queen Elizabeth's Coronation in 1953; it was a pity (though typical of the House of Windsor's disdain for culture) that Her Majesty chose not to be there in person: at least Princess Alexandra, who came instead, actually likes classical music. I managed to inject a sense of history by adding colourful newsreel footage of the 1953 coronation – complete with a golden coach and an appearance in the rain by another popular monarch, the Queen of Tonga – making this telecast of Walton's regal overture rather more enjoyable than the conventional shots of orchestral musicians beavering away at their instruments.

I wish I had found a better way to salute my admiration for André Previn. I had loved his conducting since the days of his luscious LSO recording of Rachmaninov's Second Symphony, shamelessly used by my director friend Kevin Billington in his weepy feature film *Interlude* in which Oskar Werner

With André Previn in 1977 at the BBC for a recording of Walton's
Symphony No. 1. He was as big a fan of Walton's music as I still am.

of *Jules et Jim* fame plays a European maestro (heavily reminiscent of Georg
Solti) and Barbara Ferris is the reporter who falls in love with him, as did the
reporter Valerie Pitts in real life, or so it was rumoured, when she went to the
Savoy to interview Solti and not long afterwards became the second Mrs Solti.
I had been hired as musical adviser for that film, along with my friend Ernest
Fleischmann, who taught Oskar how to conduct.

The previous year I brokered a deal between Harry Kraut, Leonard
Bernstein's manager, and William Relton, the manager of the BBC Symphony
Orchestra, whereby LB would conduct a BBC concert at the Royal Festival Hall.
This event was now on hand and it did not go well. In part one of the concert
would be Elgar's *Enigma Variations*; part two, longer, would première LB's own
Songfest with an excellent sextet of British singers in this deeply American
orchestral song cycle. It would be LB's first meeting with the orchestra and
the first day's rehearsal – working on the Elgar – would be held at Television
Centre in the same studio where he had beaten the living daylights out of the
LSO fifteen years previously when preparing Shostakovich's Fifth Symphony
for his *Symphonic Twilight* series. The Falklands War had just broken out when
LB arrived in London to conduct this concert. His wife Felicia, now dead, had

been South American; his own liberal sympathies were anti-imperialist and sympathetic towards the Argentinian underdog (as he saw it). He seemed determined to get off on the wrong foot with our British orchestra. He was staying at the Savoy and when the BBC car was announced he told his new assistant Charlie Harmon that it was far too early to leave: the journey would take only a few minutes. Perhaps, as others have done before and since, LB was confusing Television Centre with Broadcasting House. The former is several miles further west, in Shepherd's Bush. Inevitably the maestro was late, desperately late, for the rehearsal. This was before the days of mobile phones and I, directing the televised rehearsal, was at my wits' end. Of course the BBC should have sent a PA to escort him but I was not to know that LB was entering his pampered-maestro period. In his dressing room we quickly fitted him up with the radio microphone we would need to catch his remarks during the rehearsal but this only added to the embarrassment: the mic was already switched on (unbeknown to him) so that when he went for a pee his grunts and groans could clearly be heard all over the studio. The orchestra had been twiddling its thumbs in frustration for at least twenty minutes when he finally arrived on the set, in cowboy boots. He made no apology for his lateness and brushed aside the gracious speech of welcome being delivered by the orchestra's leader, Rodney Friend, whom LB knew from the violinist's recent spell as concertmaster with the New York Philharmonic. Instead of making music he then launched into a rambling discourse about his affinity – through a love of puzzles and word games – with the composer of the *Enigma Variations*, whom he persisted in calling 'Eddie' Elgar, prompting sniggers from some of the players. LB meant well but his over-intimate style went down badly with these tough professionals. He even managed to complain about the way the orchestra was grouped around his rostrum. 'Why are you so far away?' he asked. 'Are you afraid I will contaminate you with some infectious disease such as conductoritis?'

Eventually he got down to the music and of course he knew the score backwards but in a personal, deeply affectionate and lingering style: the slow music such as the opening theme he took at an exceptionally deliberate tempo. LB saw Elgar as a late outcrop of the European symphonic tradition reaching back through Richard Strauss to Brahms and Schumann. To follow the rehearsal on television I had scripted the score in great detail, as for a complete performance, so I always had a camera ready on the individual player or instrumental section to whom LB was addressing his remarks. It was the most refined and efficient *Workshop* type of programme I ever directed and my vision-mixer Angela Wilson was in total command of the story we were telling. But there was no way we could conceal the lack of sympathy between players and conductor. For example, LB took what I can best describe as a very spacious view of the transition into the 'Nimrod' variation, spending an age getting what he wanted by way of changing string colour in a single bar, eventually prompting Rodney Friend to utter a 'you cannot be serious' objection that put me in mind of John McEnroe at Wimbledon. 'Of course I'm serious, Rodney', he shouted back. 'Now get on and lead your troops into the fray!' When a trumpeter dared to utter a criticism LB was momentarily thrown but the unfortunate player then muffed an entry and LB got a laugh from the other players: 'You talk big but you don't deliver.'

My schedule that April 1982 looks uncomfortably tight but I guess I must have liked it that way. The day after LB's somewhat calamitous studio rehearsal I travelled up to Manchester to join the production team of *Young Musician of the Year*. My Australian colleague (and friend) Peter Butler directed the telecast of LB's Festival Hall concert, which was received politely enough but quickly forgotten, except for the funereal tempo of 'Nimrod' (which I personally loved). LB was not best pleased with my apparent defection but luckily he and Peter Butler got on well and later in the decade Peter went out to Israel to direct one of LB's most ambitious film essays, *The Little Drummer Boy*, concerned with the Jewishness of Mahler's music.

Hosting the *Young Musician* competition was its customary whirl, each performance (fifty to sixty over the two weeks) being followed by an interview with the sometimes shell-shocked competitor. This was the year when I quizzed a teenage tuba player about the big instrument he had between his legs: the poor boy blushed deeply. For that sort of gaffe I was mercilessly teased by Roy Tipping and his colleagues: after I dared to suggest backstage that a piano was sounding uncomfortably clangorous I was presented with a certificate proclaiming me to be the Piano Tuner of the Year. In fact these were heady days, exciting and fulfilling because of the talent revealed. The BBC team was surrounded by fantastically talented young musicians from families of all walks of life, although inevitably pupils from the specialist music schools did especially well. It was only a few years since the Tory education minister, a certain Margaret Thatcher, had approved privileged status for institutions such as the Purcell School and Yehudi Menuhin's international school in Surrey. In 1982 the string finalists included the sixteen-year-old violinist Tasmin Little; she was one of several Menuhin pupils who made a strong impression but did not reach the concerto stage. That year, 1982, the grand finale was transferred from the Royal Northern College to Manchester's much larger and tradition-laden Free Trade Hall. The show started at the peak viewing time of 7.45 on a Sunday evening. Think of it: two hours of classical music in prime time. *O tempora, o mores!* The winner was a pianist named Anna Markland, who was studying close by at the excellent Chetham's School. She went on to Oxford, where she switched to vocal studies, becoming a founder member of I Fagiolini, one of the world's best early music vocal groups. A month after her Manchester triumph Anna represented Britain in a Eurovision version of *Young Musician*. I had created an informal working party of like-minded television music bosses across the continent and eventually obtained the blessing of the stiff-jointed European Broadcasting Union: our new competition did not have the same razzmatazz but it was the nearest classical music has ever come on television to the *Eurovision Song Contest*. Chairing the EBU music group was the last residue of my previous life as a bureaucrat. We met twice a year, sometimes during trade fairs such as MIDEM at Cannes, and sometimes, rather prosaically, at the EBU's Geneva headquarters. We arranged conferences and workshops on topics of shared interest such as the advent of television stereo sound, alternative ways of filming symphonic music and snags in the development of co-productions. It sounds dull as ditchwater but at the time it was important for me to make a reality of the European ideal of sharing programmes and experience.

It was therefore something of a paradox that the summer of 1982 also saw the renewal of close contacts for me in America. After Ernest Fleischmann was sacked by the LSO, he quickly established himself as a major player on the American orchestra scene. A dozen years after I worked on *Switched-On Symphony* he invited me to direct the telecast of an LA Philharmonic concert under Giulini, who had succeeded Zubin Mehta as its chief conductor. I had felt such a rapport with Giulini in Rossini's *Stabat Mater* that I jumped at the chance, especially as it also offered an opportunity to work with Murray Perahia, whom I had greatly admired ever since his victory at the Leeds Piano Competition. He played Beethoven's Second Piano Concerto, flawlessly. Working only a few miles from Hollywood, I felt an urge to introduce new dramatic camera angles in the hall. I requested that a camera be installed in the roof of the Dorothy Chandler Pavilion and I used the striking overhead shot of the orchestra just once, at the climax of the finale of Brahms's First Symphony. It worked tremendously well, all the better for being used so sparingly.

Christina and I had always enjoyed California. On previous trips we had sometimes stayed with the Fleischmanns but sadly their marriage had foundered and instead we moved in with our new friends Gordon and Judi Davidson, who had a lovely house in Maybery Road, in the coastal village of Santa Monica. Gordon was a theatre director of great drive and vision who since 1969 had created a strong theatre presence in LA as creative director of the Mark Taper Forum, part of an ambitious arts complex intended to rival New York's Lincoln Center. We had first met the Davidsons in London with David Jones of the RSC and felt an immediate 'elective affinity' with them both. They laid on lovely parties for us, inviting writers and composers and famous Hollywood movie friends: Christopher Isherwood lived close by. We loved swimming in the nearby Pacific Ocean – and also in their pint-sized pool, jokingly named after Leonard Bernstein because it was paid for out of the fee Gordon earned for directing LB's *Mass* at the inauguration of the Kennedy Center. (Not to be outdone, we eventually installed a Bernstein steam bath at our flat in Oakwood Court.)

Rest assured that I am not going to spend the remainder of this 1980s section reeling off a year-by-year list of my concert productions. Even if I wanted to, I couldn't: my appointment diaries are a grave disappointment. I discover to my shame that I was a decidedly sloppy note-maker, carrying what mattered in my head.

So I must rely on what I remember, and of the Verdi *Requiem* under Claudio Abbado at the 1982 Edinburgh Festival I do have a vivid image in sound and vision: it is of Margaret Price and Jessye Norman, two great divas, singing the 'Agnus Dei' in perfect unison at the octave. They were both statuesque sopranos. Margaret, who was so enchanting as Titania in Britten's *A Midsummer Night's Dream* at the outset of her career and such an impressive Isolde in Carlos Kleiber's 1980s recording, died in 2011, not yet seventy; Jessye passed on eight years later, universally acknowledged as one of the singing world's most impressive personalities. Her voice is categorised as a Falcon: close to a mezzo in timbre but with the range of a dramatic soprano. Although Verdi intended the lower line of the 'Agnus Dei' for a regular mezzo, the melody has never sounded more thrilling than in their duet.

During rehearsals Claudio Abbado and I had the first of several clashes concerning the placement of a camera actually on the concert platform. For Abbado to be watched at close quarters apparently gave him the willies. So at his urgent request (I put it mildly) we moved the offending cameraman behind the back desk of the violas, a few inches out of Abbado's line of vision; once the performance began, the cameraman discreetly moved back to get the

Clashing with Claudio Abbado. At the rostrum he was like a hawk about to pounce on its prey.

best angle. Studying Abbado at work was like observing a hawk preparing to pounce on its prey. He was both cool and volcanic.

It was at this performance that I conceived the idea of myself conducting the *Requiem* one day, a dream that became reality nineteen years later on my seventieth birthday.

In the autumn of 1982 I was preoccupied with producing and directing the nearest I ever got to good old-fashioned show business. I think it was Richard Somerset-Ward's idea to build a one-hour television 'Special' around Kiri Te Kanawa, who had become a huge star after singing at the wedding of Prince Charles and Diana Spencer. The show was billed as 'Christmas entertainment for all the family' and was screened on Boxing Day, on BBC1, though at the distinctly un-peak time of 10 p.m.

Highlights from the *Radio Times* billing give the flavour of the event. It was described as 'a Christmas entertainment for all the family, recorded by the popular New Zealand opera star at the Dominion Theatre, London. Her guests include Plácido Domingo, the famous Spanish tenor, who joins Kiri for a selection from Bernstein's *West Side Story*.' Another guest is the ballerina Doreen Wells, who *Radio Times* tells us 'dances The Dying Swan and tap dances her sparkling way through "Puttin' on the Ritz".' Norma Burrowes teams up with Kiri for Rossini's hilarious 'Cat duet'. Harry Secombe does a song and dance routine in 'We're a couple of swells' and puts on clown's garb for 'On with the motley'. Now comes the twist in this showbiz tale: 'The Maori Rugby Team gives Kiri powerful support in a New Zealand folk song "Pokarekare Ana"'. Also taking part: *West Side Story* girls Ursula Connors, Glenys Groves and Hilly Marshall; Tilly the dog; Children of the Eastcourt Independent School; also including the haunting 'Bailero' from *Songs of the Auvergne*; 'The ugly duckling', and 'Memory' from *Cats* (specially arranged by the composer Andrew Lloyd Webber). The conductor was the ever-patient Robin Stapleton.

This, I concede, looks like conventional, safe, middle-of-the-road stuff, designed to please at the end of the second day of Christmas feasting. However, the fact that there is not a carol in sight makes me wonder whether the Christmas placing was an afterthought. Maybe the preview was discovered to be so good that it merited a plum position on the holiday schedule.

Making *Call Me Kiri* was certainly a bumpy ride. Plácido Domingo was splendid at the dress rehearsal, singing with Kiri a suite of duets and solos from *West Side Story*. 'See you tomorrow', I said breezily as I thanked him on the Dominion stage after the run-through and bade him farewell: 'please be here by six pm'. 'What do you mean, tomorrow?' he replied. 'This was it. Tomorrow I shall be singing *Fanciulla* at Covent Garden.' Luckily we had taped the rehearsal but next day I had to explain to the invited audience, a full house of Domingo fans, that they would have to be content with watching their idol on a video. This did not go down well and Kiri cannot have been best pleased with the disruption to the show's running order. I remember my acute embarrassment at having to tell her that because we were running

Kiri Te Kanawa and Plácido Domingo singing 'Tonight' from LB's *West Side Story* in *Call Me Kiri*, 1982.

out of recording time we would have to drop her only aria. But Kiri is a great trouper and she did not complain.

A few months later, Kiri and Plácido were the stars of *Manon Lescaut*, the first opera relay I directed at Covent Garden. In truth it was the first opera relay I directed from *anywhere*. I had produced a dozen relays from the Royal Opera House and Glyndebourne during the 1970s but directing is a much more imaginative and lengthy procedure. I will describe it in a little detail since so much of my life over the next twenty years was to be taken up with recordings from opera houses. First and most obviously, you must attend rehearsals to discover the stage director's intentions and the potential for chemistry between the singers. You decide where you would like to position your five or six cameras in the auditorium, perhaps also in the pit and occasionally in the wings. You scribble hundreds of notes in the piano score. At the dress rehearsal you supervise a one-camera recording in order to know, in terms of the singers' positions on the stage and their interplay, exactly what is going on at every moment of the action. This precious video, a vital technical aid, is known as the scratch tape. I suppose 'scratch' because it is a visual aid which can be dumped (scratched) after use. With it you can freeze the frame or run backward and forward on a video cassette player plotting the action – I am describing the technique we were using in the 1980s. Supported by this precious video, you write the camera script for the entire opera, a thousand shots and more, all expressed in clear succinct language for the benefit of the cameramen who will be framing the shots. This script-writing period is like imagining an entire feature film in your head; every gesture, every reaction – all scripted in advance. In a cinema film the shots are assembled over many weeks in an editing suite and I was familiar with the cutting-room approach from a decade of film-making at the BBC's Ealing studios. But directing a television relay, especially if it is to be truly 'live', is a different ball game. Discipline and imagination are both needed – in spades. Working your way through the opera on the scratch tape, your script has to be unfolding in your mind's eye in an effective, harmonious way. You have a repertoire of images to tell the story. You cut between establishing shots and close-ups, large groups and tight two-shots. You can add zooms, tracks and pans – an endless range of possibilities is available to intensify the mood. Everything has to be assessed in advance and written into the score at the exact point you want to see it.

The scripting process ought to take a week or longer but sometimes has to be squashed into a few very long days and nights if the opera is to be televised early in its run, as was the case with *Manon Lescaut*. A dry-run read-through of the script will be scheduled to familiarise the cameramen with your intentions. The team may have been covering a football match the previous week or a church service; I always found cameramen and women to be marvellously flexible and keen to be involved.

In twentieth-century outside broadcast units the control room was known as the 'scanner'; it was the hub of the operation. In the digital era equipment has been miniaturised and techniques streamlined. In my day the director saw the output of each camera in front of him on a bank of monitors. As the music proceeded, the shot numbers were announced by the PA and punched up on the transmission monitor by the vision-mixer: 'Shot 5. Camera Six next'. The latter information prompts the director to check the incoming picture and maybe ask the cameraman to adjust the framing, talking quietly because the director's mic is open to the entire team; you had to speak clearly and concisely and always preface your remark by announcing to whom it was addressed. I never commanded a fighter squadron, indeed only once took the controls of an aeroplane (a friend's flying boat en route to the city of Victoria on Vancouver Island), but I imagine the experience of flying must be similar to multi-camera direction, very exhilarating just so long as everything falls into place as you planned it.

Unfortunately the new production of *Manon Lescaut* was accident-prone. Kiri Te Kanawa was making her début in the role and she was having difficulty in remembering every last detail of what is one of the longest parts in the soprano repertoire. There was a glitch in the second act and because the show was being taped for worldwide distribution by the National Video Corporation, my producer Robin Scott had to request a retake. Robin was an old friend and an extraordinary man: composer, linguist and civilised bureaucrat, he had been the BBC's man in Paris and later controller of Radio 2 (which he founded, along with Radio 1, as the BBC's answer to pirate radio; the two new channels replaced the old Light Programme). In 1968 Robin was appointed controller of BBC2. This was a job I might have had when David Attenborough was promoted, had I not defected to ITV. Robin did it better. Long-since retired from management, he revelled in the producer's role. He was an excellent diplomat who quickly called Plácido's bluff when the tenor, half in jest, suggested a retake after Act 3 on the grounds that he should have equal treatment with his co-star. We had technical troubles of our own in the final act when not one but two cameras went 'on the blink' in Kiri's powerful death aria 'Sola, perduta, abbandonata'; my script in ruins, I was close to despair when a voice from the end of the control panel calmly called out, 'I've got Kiri in close-up all the way'. It was Hazel Wright, then a rookie director and now a highly respected international television businesswoman. I had placed her in charge of a separate 'wild' camera, recording independently, giving her a roving commission to find significant details that caught her attention or that of her cameraman. They had chosen well; looking at the show now there is no sense of improvised camerawork, in fact one is simply not aware of changing camera angles, so strong is Kiri's performance – and that of Plácido when he joins her for the final despairing duet. The video of *Manon Lescaut* is one of the most satisfying in my archive. The razor-sharp stage director was the very experienced Götz Friedrich and the strong set designs were by Günther Schneider-Siemssen, but much of the opera's overpowering intensity was generated by the conductor Giuseppe Sinopoli; in his febrile hands Puccini's music drama really was a revelation.

Sinopoli intrigued me. He was born in Venice and studied music there as a teenager. Then he moved to Germany and became an avant-garde composer of the Darmstadt school, complete with a controversial opera, *Lou Salome*, to his name. Simultaneously, to please his father, he trained as a physician

NVC Arts DVD of The Royal Opera House, Covent Garden production of *Manon Lescaut*.

and surgeon. Later he went to Vienna to study conducting under arguably the world's best teacher, Hans Swarowsky. He was married with two young sons but was alone in London so Christina invited him to our flat, where he cooked us the most tasty pasta dish, flavoured with, of all things, vodka. He was then in his late thirties and making waves in many directions: later he studied architecture in Rome and ran an arts festival in Taormina. Like his eminent predecessor Ferruccio Busoni he gravitated to Berlin; he was briefly music director of the Deutsche Oper and he died there of a heart attack in 2001, in the middle of a performance of *Aida*, aged only fifty-four. Terribly young, but what a way to go!

Manon Lescaut was my first co-production for NVC Arts and I did well enough for Robin Scott to nominate me to direct virtually all the opera relays from Covent Garden over the next five years; they included *Die Fledermaus*, *Andrea Chénier*, *Prince Igor* and two by Mozart: *The Abduction from the Seraglio* and *Così fan tutte*. (I mix the languages because that is how I first learnt those Mozart titles at the Chelsea Opera Group under Colin Davis.)

My diary was filling up with freelance and BBC directing work but I was about to lurch in a very different direction: from May 30th to September 17th 1983, close on four months, I was to be based in Los Angeles, probably the longest time I ever spent in one place during my entire sixty-year career. I had accepted a surprise invitation from Ernest Fleischmann to be the guest artistic director of the 1983 season of the Hollywood Bowl. And as Sarastro sings in *Die Zauberflöte*, 'die Stunde schlägt' – the hour had come. Just a week after the transmission of *Manon Lescaut* on BBC2, Christina and I were flying to California, our children left in the capable hands of our super au pair from Australia, Ruth White. My diary of those hugely enjoyable Nights at the Bowl forms the basis of the next chapter.

CHAPTER 18

HOORAY FOR HOLLYWOOD

Impresario and sound supervisor. My training at Maida Vale
stood me in good stead at The Hollywood Bowl.

ERNEST FLEISCHMANN HAD been at the helm of the Los Angeles
Philharmonic since 1969. He had been a good friend with programme ideas
all through his 1960s LSO days and he turned up trumps again at the turn
of the decade. After I directed a video of his new orchestra in 1982, Ernest
confided that he wanted a rest: he no longer enjoyed running the crowded
summer season of concerts at the Hollywood Bowl. He asked whether I would
consider taking over for a year so he could enjoy a sabbatical; we would swap

houses, he and his partner Rebecca Rickman going to our little French *maison secondaire* in the village of La Garde-Freinet (half an hour from the beaches of St Tropez) and we to his house in the Hollywood Hills, close to the Bowl and not far from the downtown freeway. I was curious and eager for new experiences so I agreed, fondly believing that Ernest, who was famous for his abrasive interventionism, would be 7,000 miles away. In the event there was a financial crisis at the orchestra, or so Ernest claimed, and he and Rebecca were unhappy with our not very mod-con French cottage. So after only a few weeks they were back in LA. Meanwhile, the Burton family had installed itself in their house, which meant they had to spend the summer living with friends in far-off Pasadena, but Ernest's presence in town meant Big Brother was watching my every move.

Happily, the Bowl was a marvel. Once a park and picnic place in Bolton Canyon, off Highland Avenue, the Bowl's natural amphitheatre was transformed into an outdoor concert venue back in the 1920s. The eccentric Australian, Percy Grainger, was famously married on its stage. The Bowl was beautiful, and because of its seating capacity it was also a tremendous moneymaker. A record 26,000 had crowded in before the war to hear Lily Pons: in my year, 1983, the top attendance was close to 20,000 and that was for another diva, Sarah Vaughan, singing jazz with Michael Tilson Thomas at the piano; wherever one sat that night it was an electrifying experience. 'Music under the stars' was one of the Bowl's branding slogans. Amplification played a big part in how one heard that music. On stage there were microphones

Left: Ernest Fleischmann – he was famously abrasive and once left my stomach in knots with his criticisms.

everywhere, and dozens of hi-fi loudspeakers lined the site, organised electronically to micro-manage the sound by split seconds so that no matter how far back one sat the sound would still arrive simultaneously with the image. The Bowl had its own engineering team and one of my tasks each day was to attend the morning rehearsal and supervise the balance, much as I had done three decades previously for symphony broadcasts and recitals from the BBC's Maida Vale studio.

The ten-week season added up to over fifty concerts. The official opener was July 12th 1983 but I needed a month to settle in to my new life as an impresario and concert promoter. Much of the detailed planning had been done with Ernest on previous visits during the winter but I had stuck my neck out with a few unusual events, among them a concert of Andrew Lloyd Webber's show music that required local singers and these were still to be auditioned. And I needed to get to know the staff at the Philharmonic's downtown office and the people who ran the Bowl, half-an-hour's drive away. There were rich patrons from Old Hollywood to be charmed and local chat shows on radio and television upon which I had to display my curious British accent, not to mention frequent press conferences and photocalls – the routine was not so very different from my BBC life as head of Music and Arts but at least in LA many events took place outdoors in the sunshine. And everybody was laid back. To drive around LA's urban sprawl, which I learnt to love, I was allowed to use Ernest's turbo-charged Volvo, but eventually I persuaded the local Jaguar distributor to lend me a spiffing, brand-new car with Vanden Plas coachwork. It was a model of British craftsmanship which I gratefully returned without a scratch at the end of my stay. Driving around in a posh Jag I enjoyed a Californian status similar to that in England of owning a Rolls Royce: Isaac Stern was seriously impressed when I met him with it at the airport.

During the quiet period before the Bowl season's July opening, Christina and I were able to slip away to Mexico for a few days' holiday. After exploring the great Mayan site of Chichen Itza we drove south as far as Tulum and experienced for the first time the joys of swimming in the warm Caribbean Sea. Flying back to Los Angeles we stopped off in Houston, Texas to attend the world première of Leonard Bernstein's new full-length opera, *A Quiet Place*. This was a different Bernstein from the one I saw every year conducting the Vienna Philharmonic. At the rostrum in the Musikverein he was in total command. In 'Cow Town', as he tactlessly described Houston, he was on edge with nerves and making a great deal of noise to compensate, sporting a ten-gallon hat with cowboy boots to match. His opera house evening began with his jazzy 1952 one-acter *Trouble in Tahiti*, a forty-minute curtain-raiser about a suburban marriage on the rocks. After the interval came the new work, a thirty-years-later sequel to *Tahiti*. It was a portrait of a barren marriage and to me it came over as two hours of post-Alban Berg gloom performed without a break, employing a much larger orchestra and telling a much more intense tale. (I discuss the opera at some length in my Bernstein biography.) We saw two performances and on both occasions we spent long hours around the hotel pool afterwards discussing with LB's family and friends the opera's merits and problems. But my current worry was more practical: LB's next port of call was to be Los Angeles, where he and Michael Tilson Thomas were to inaugurate the Los Angeles Institute, a West Coast version of the conducting summer school at Tanglewood. LB had fallen out with the management at Tanglewood, where he had taught every summer for decades. Aided and abetted by Harry Kraut and Ernest Fleischmann, he decided to set up his own school out West, basically to deliver a rebuke to his *alma mater* – at least that's how I read the move. The Institute Orchestra would be playing at the Bowl. Young conductors would share concert programmes with LB. But a maestro depressed by the contentious reception of his opera was likely to be one more disturbing factor for me to cope with that summer; we would be walking on eggshells.

The Bowl's official opening is traditionally on the second Tuesday of July, when evenings are starting to draw in and music really can be enjoyed 'under the stars'. But the Los Angelinos have never been averse to making money in advance of the set date and my first test came on the morning of Independence Day, July 4th: the Bowl mounted a patriotic celebration and I had to balance the microphones for a phalanx of marching bands. A few days later came a visit from Helmut Rilling's Oregon Bach Festival for a small-scale but perfectly judged performance of the B minor Mass.

'Dusk falls during the Gloria,' I noted in my diary. 'One or two planes disturb the atmosphere but in general the mood is one of intense stillness and rapt attention – a wonderful contrast to yesterday's rather vulgar proceedings' [the marching bands].

For a flavour of my Hollywood summer I shall bring forward selected highlights from my sometimes indiscreet diary to take centre stage for the remainder of this chapter. (I cannot remember why I kept a diary but I guess I thought it might come in useful one day – which it has.)

July 12, 1983

The official opening of the Bowl ... expectancy is almost tangible, also nervousness. André Watts announces he will switch to a mellower Steinway [for Brahms One] but there's virtually no time to check the microphones – KUSC [the local university radio station] are broadcasting 'live' and insist (with my support) on a 15 minute spot-check. By this time (11.45) I have left for the Music Center and a live radio luncheon interview – half hour talk and half hour music and commercials plus delicious poached salmon ... The food for the opening night picnic was not so hot but the company was again delicious. [A feature of the Bowl, where it never rains, is that you arrive at least an hour before the concert and scoff picnics in your four-seat open-air box. Our picnics were made in-house and were unremarkable; others were of a Glyndebourne level of sophistication.] Chrissie and I wandered through the boxes talking to friends and press people. We met the John Greens, the Kirk Douglases and various other celebrities. [John Green had supervised the music for the film version of *West Side Story*.] 2000 balloons were released as the National Anthem played and spectacular lighting faded in and out: Ernest [Fleischmann] thought this was a great advance.

July 13

Went down to the Bowl for Jean-Pierre Rampal's flute recital – piano and harpsichord backing plus tuba and percussion, so plenty of choices to be made for microphone setting, which is one of my principal tasks, the others being the lighting and overall presentation, announcements introducing performers, warnings that the concert will soon be starting etc. – the human touch. Rampal told me Poulenc had strictly forbidden the orchestration of his flute sonata (since done by Lennox Berkeley). It's my choice for the evening!

July 14

MTT [Michael Tilson Thomas] has devised a French evening which was like the oeuf du curé, only good in parts. The duds were the two flute concertos played by Rampal – Devienne (1707) and Rivier (1963), both horribly boring. But Bizet's L'Arlésienne, Debussy's La Mer and Ravel's Daphnis were all gorgeous to hear at the Bowl. [MTT was Giulini's deputy as the conductor of the LA Philharmonic.]

Top left: Kirk and Ann Douglas with Olive Behrendt, *éminence grise* of the LA Phil. Bottom left: With John Green and his wife Bonnie. Right: Two thousand balloons at the Opening Night Picnic at the Hollywood Bowl, 1983.

Michael Tilson Thomas and Sarah Vaughan – their Gershwin was the Bowl at its best.

July 15

The pace of the Bowl is revealing itself – and it's a killer. Last night we were within a minute of an expensive over-run. Today, the first of two concerts featuring Sarah Vaughan and MTT in Gershwin … She is an amazing woman. When she arrived I just thought she was somebody from the office when she sat in the stalls listening to MTT rehearse … But when she sings she is transformed. The microphones help, of course. This is great jazz: never the same thing twice, nothing on the beat or square, her voice is a paint-box full of vocal colours; she has a sense of humour, too, and a relishing of the words … Robert Harth [Ernest's number two and already a good friend] is doing the sound balance so I can wander round the Bowl, which is good because I see the crowds pouring in, the restaurants, the first aid center, the ushers on the job and so on, all very satisfactory. Then I climb up to the back of the Bowl to look down on this totally sold-out performance: 17,800 people drinking in the jazz-singing of divine Sarah and marvelling at the fantastic jazz pianism of Michael T.T. This is the Bowl at its best: warm, good-humoured, democratic and beautiful.

July 19

Lunch in Beverley Hills with John Green and his wife Bonnie and his assistant Dennis – collective age 200 years at least. His guests were David Caddick [the English coach for the upcoming Lloyd Webber concert], Harry Rabinowitz [its conductor] and I feel we are walking into a museum. Johnny has won five Oscars and a million citations (Americans 'cite' easily) but he is sweet and charming as he shows us his work room, library and so on; good gossipy photographs on the wall from his time as music director at MGM.

July 20

11 a.m. I am participating in a seminar about the arts for 200 school teachers. Speaking on the same bill as Walter Mirisch [big-time film producer]. Had nothing prepared so lammed into American TV (quite convincingly) … Lunch afterwards with delegates; very rich food. Feel queasy and continue to do so during ghastly jazz concert at the Bowl. Guests in my box are Bill Kobin [head of the local public broadcasting station KCET] and Sue Weil of PBS – both jazz lovers. But Miles Davis shambles about aimlessly: his music has no forward drive. Leave before Gil Evans [unforgivable!] and retire to bed, terrified that I might fall ill on the eve of ALW concert. Am I experiencing a genuine psycho-somatic illness?

[In fact the Lloyd Webber concert next evening worked out well. Much to my annoyance, Andrew had vetoed my proposal for a full evening of his theatre music – the problem was something to do with grand rights, which I never understood – so we featured numbers from *My Fair Lady* before the interval and my director friend Alan Cooke (whom we had got to know in Richmond a decade earlier) coached the LA Doolittles in cockney accents.]

22 July (two days later)

By lunch time Harry Rab has completed (on time) his one and only rehearsal and it is not going to be a disaster. I spend most of the afternoon writing links for my presentation. I resolve to include a reading of the Jellicle Ball poem [T.S. Eliot]. My nerves and bad tummy are forgotten. My white tuxedo fits … The show begins at 8.40. My Fair Lady is terrific. Helena and Lukas are both working with Frank Supak [engineer and scientific wizard] in the sound booth. Helena is reading all the technical data and Lukas is passing on messages over the intercom. On stage I get laughs for my ALW introduction and attention during the links [quite an achievement with Bowl audiences]. Some of the orchestral playing is rough and ready (David Caddick has been allowed to join the orchestra as pianist and this helps) but the spirit of the show was – thank the Lord – OK.

23 July (next evening)

The second performance was better: all the loose ends tidied up and everybody (15,000 audience) had a good time. Regrettably I had a backstage row about scheduling Lloyd Webber's music at the Bowl with EF [Ernest Fleischmann] immediately after the show which literally left my stomach in knots for two hours. But finally unwound at cast party at our house – 30 people having a really nice time. Basically still a triumph-over-odds day. I've arrived!

25 July

The Bowl people saw the ALW show and loved it (so they said). My stock has now probably reached its summer peak [with seven weeks to run!] what with appearing on 'live' TV and reading poetry at the Bowl. It is nice to have orchestra players coming up to say bravo. So from now on it will be downhill, I suppose, helped on my way (unconsciously of course) by EF who called me in for an hour's 'tour d'horizon'. I am, it appears, criticised for my style by the orchestra and disliked by the staff for my authoritarian manner. Luckily I know myself tolerably well by now and am able to measure my impact, and I know the real situation is not so black as EF would have me believe … The children took delivery of their new tennis rackets and are playing many hours per diem.

28 July

Eric Leinsdorf's second concert tonight was again blandly efficient, pleasurable but without the intensity of great music-making. [Leinsdorf was in his seventies, Vienna-trained but a US citizen since 1942.] Brahms Double Concerto: soloists, James Buswell and Lynn Harrell; again adequate but with many passages of poor intonation, not a patch on Gidon Kremer and Mischa Maisky with whom I filmed the concerto in Vienna last autumn under LB's uninterested baton. LB uninterested is still more exciting than Leinsdorf. [A strange comment; my recollection is that LB was always a committed Brahmsian.] ... Afterwards we gave a party for Leinsdorf. Attending were MTT and [his partner] Josh Robison, James Buswell, Robert and Melanie Harth and Joe Nakelstein [a loudspeaker designer from whom I eventually purchased two enormous speakers for our Oakwood Court apartment]. The two maestros told good jokes; Buswell did an excellent imitation of Brenda Lucas and John Ogdon.

29 July

Off with the kids to Disneyland ... we went on the 1890 steam train, jungle expedition, pirates of the Caribbean, Haunted House, Monorail, chair-ride up Matterhorn, bobsleigh (terrifying), Sputniks, Autopia, America the Beautiful (film, 360-degree wrap-around) and lord knows what else. We ate popcorn, drank gallons of juice, saw fireworks and watched the parade and it was all v. good humoured and superbly organized by the Disney people. [Ernest, bless his stony heart, had arranged VIP treatment which cut out most of the queueing.]

August 2

We have a good balance with the children who are making friends across the board at the Bowl. Lukas works like a grown-up at the sound console and Helena has been accepted as an usher.

Rehearsal for tonight goes well. Mendelssohn Violin Concerto is done flawlessly by Young-Uck Kim ... he plays with passion as well as purity. Leinsdorf in the evening reveals why he is not among the true greats: he cannot lift Shostakovich 5 out of the accurate but uninspired. No flexibility, no emotion, no excitement, ungainly movement. Sad.

With my son Lukas and daughter Helena, willing helpers at the Bowl.

August 3

Jazz at the Bowl. Mind-crushingly boring. Rosemary Clooney. No interest. Concert had to start early (!) because she had a plane to catch.

… We saw a fox in Maravilla Drive [our home street] looking in the dustbins.

August 4

Beethoven Emperor Concerto. Alicia de Larrocha plays superbly at rehearsal – strange that such a diminutive lady can make such an impressively grand noise. Alas, in the evening there are a great many wrong notes (though these were not noticed by the L.A. Times which gave Larrocha and our sound system good reviews). Still a big house turned out for Beethoven and my innovation of putting a trumpet on a floodlit lighting tower for Leonora No. 3 worked nicely.

August 5

John Green plus wife and daughter and all the soloists came to supper at home [after his Bowl concert] – a gentle, laid-back occasion which Chrissie does so well with the help of pasta salads and savoury croissants. I sneakily enjoyed Green's programme [Kern, Rodgers and Cole Porter].

August 6

A very hot day indeed, the hottest August 6th ever recorded in LA; downtown it was 105 degrees. L, H and I made things worse by playing tennis at mid-day – talk about mad dogs and Englishmen. Then I defrosted the three trout Frank Supak caught for us a month ago and we had excellent trout and marrow, all cooked by me. Later I got my files in order downtown and then it was time to go back for more Bowl melodies with John Green, more relaxed than yesterday despite the heat and the larger crowd. Christina and I held hands under the stars as the band played 'I didn't know what time it was' and 'You're the tops, you're the Eiffel Tower' etc. Dreary supper afterwards at Scandia [a fading Old Hollywood favourite of EF's on Sunset Boulevard]. Talk is about duty-free purchases from China and foot doctors in Beverley Hills. Still, $154,000 at the Box Office was a small compensation. If I ever do this job again I will try to negotiate a contract with a bonus for increased box office revenue.

August 8

[Later] it took two hours to get to the Bowl from downtown on account of a brush fire on the hills near the Bowl. I detoured off the freeway – got hopelessly lost but enjoyed discovering new by-ways of Hollywood – lovely lanes and hillside villas.

August 10

Phone conversations with Peter Adam, Richard S-W and Jane [Tanner] bring BBC Ken House pleasantly close. Difficult to sort out my feelings – the unreality of Hollywood has many positive aspects but running a concert hall, even one as elaborate as the Bowl, is really nowhere near as satisfactory and fulfilling as making a good programme.

... At the Bowl a recital by Itzhak Perlman. I work hard to achieve a reasonably faithful sound for Bach and César Franck. In the evening these go reasonably well: the disappointment is with the encores by Sarasate and Kreisler which comprise the second half; not the right balance, a careless disregard for public taste, a sloppiness of presentation unworthy of somebody with such fantastic technique and musicianship.

August 11

Third day of Perlman – today is the Scandinavian concert and he will play the Sibelius. But he arrives out of sorts complaining of kidney pain, a recurring problem, and then goes out on stage to play a wonderful performance: tonal beauty to bring tears to the eyes even at a rehearsal. Real tears, not smog-induced eye-watering. We count ourselves privileged to be able to attend rehearsals. Scandinavian flags are delivered for tonight's festivities and then I go off to have a hot game of tennis. Home for lunch ... Rebecca [Ernest's partner] rings around 3.30 with a tale of major woe. Worth recounting as an indication of problems sometimes faced by incipient impresarios. Perlman has phoned to say his kidney stone is causing agony – he probably won't be able to play the concert. Pinky Zukerman is standing by but can't play Sibelius (could do Beethoven). Lucky he is in town but this concert is subsidised by 'Scandinavia Today' – if no Sibelius then no subsidy?? Touch and go till 8 p.m. Zukerman now at restaurant romancing Tuesday Weld. Rings to say he wants a drink badly. I can tell him to go ahead. Itzhak arrives, wants his cheque. There are Scandinavians galore at the concert, with me making a speech of welcome and an itinerant Danish fiddler entertaining the subscribers in their boxes. Blomstedt and two orchestral players come home for quiet supper at Maravilla.

August 12

James Loughran conducts Tchaikovsky as if it is the Last Night of the Proms. He looks like a conductor and in the evening the crowd responds. But disaster strikes concerto pianist Norman Krieger. [Tchaikovsky B flat minor.] Splashes of wrong notes. Then the wrong key. Then, in the finale, silence. Blackout. Breakdown of pianist. He picks up again after about 3 minutes of eternity in which the orchestra has played its part and there's been no response from the piano. He limps home for the final pages. Crisis talks follow at intermission.

James Loughran to the rescue.

I resolve that if Jimmy [Loughran] will agree to coach him we can rescue the Saturday performance. Part 2 is Romeo and Juliet followed by 1812 with fireworks. The customers go home happy and we go home for supper with EF and the Loughrans. A heavy day!

August 13

The atmosphere remains gloomy as we grapple with the Krieger Affair. At 11.15 he and Jimmy meet at the Bowl and the coaching begins. I am pleased I didn't panic and instead resolved to put this young man's career in front of the requirements of tonight's concert. To get another pianist – without rehearsal – would have been just as much a gamble as trying to bring Mr K up to concert pitch. Leaving Jimmy to be Svengali, Lukas and I play a brief and sweaty set of tennis (the weather remains desperately hot and humid). Fingers crossed for Krieger. He plays very much better, and actually listens to the orchestra. [Norman Krieger was a Los Angeles musician who happily went on to a substantial solo career.]

August 15

News from Harry Kraut [the Bernstein caravan had just rolled into town]: At the Beverly Hills Hotel Michael TT, Lennie Bernstein and others were held up at gun-point in Lennie's bungalow and robbed of all their cash ($350). Luckily Harry hadn't collected the $5000 to which he was contractually entitled. Nobody hurt, but nobody loves the Beverley Hills Hotel any more. Office all day. At 5 p.m. Leonard Slatkin rehearses Elgar, Tchaikovsky 4th and Panufnik's Tragic Overture. Glad Andrzej wasn't here for this rather perfunctory rehearsal. Slatkin is business-like – efficient, but short on romance in his soul or in his music-making.

August 18

Arrival of Rudi Buchbinder [Viennese pianist] to rehearse Brahms Two. Rather surprised by the wrong notes, trust things will improve this evening. But worse to come, much worse. By 10.30 a steady drizzle. The stage roof leaks,

LB – robbed at gunpoint at the Beverly Hills Hotel.

The concert that never was – washed out by torrential rain.

impossible to play. Rain doesn't let up but consensus is that it will be OK in the evening. Panufnik piece dropped – insufficient rehearsal time.

Meanwhile the rain doesn't stop and much too late in the day we cancel this evening's concert. Huge pools of water on the stage, every chair in the Bowl soaking wet. Attend dreary dinner in honour of Buchbinder – he gets his cheque from me for doing nix. We are all rather grumpy and depressed. The weather appears to be set foul – the mountains are wreathed in mist.

August 19

The rain continues but the orchestra is not that easily beaten. Rehearsal in the morning takes place in the warehouse, 100 yards up the hill and very very makeshift. Jimmy Loughran is a tower of strength.

By 5 the clouds are lifting and soon we are able to announce that the concert [a Beethoven evening] will take place. Fireworks [for the Battle Symphony] have been covered with plastic and are now unpacked. The soldiers don their uniforms – Bowl life can continue. The fireworks are much appreciated despite the occasional damp squib. Ilana Vered plays Beethoven with much sparkling finger work and the 8th Symphony and Egmont sound grand, despite the hectic and scratchy rehearsal. Loughran is now clearly established as my best importation of the season. He and his wife Lindi have become excellent friends.

Yesterday was the first ever August rain-out. This evening the sight of all the Bowl-goers turning up for their picnic and night out was most heart-warming.

August 20

We join the Loughrans for a trip to the Huntington in Pasadena. Huntington was an American railway magnate who built himself Kew Gardens, the Wallace Collection, a zen temple and the British Museum, all in one elegant Californian campus of good taste and learning. Then over to lily ponds [not the soprano] and a tropical garden, then into the house and the total contrast of English 18th century painting: Reynolds, Romney, Gainsborough's Blue Boy etc. etc.; wild nature turned into a backdrop for the English aristocracy.

… A terrible crash on the freeway holds up audience and Ilana Vered the piano soloist. I announce a reversal of programme order. Vered arrives, shocked: she'd seen a dead man at the wheel. Later, when she is playing, a cat runs across the stage (or was it a fox?) and there is much audience laughter which leaves Ilana and Loughran puzzled. A good performance is further spoilt by noisy planes. The Battle Symphony looks much better tonight with spruce lighting and troop movements and a clear sky for the fireworks. The effect of magic bullets zipping through the air in front of the orchestra and over the heads of the public in the pool area is quite spectacular.

August 21

Rehearsal for the last Institute concert, with Leonard Bernstein [the Institute's joint director] sitting in my box for the sound balances. The orchestra rehearses encores with LB himself and when he lifts his baton to start the last movement of Tchaikovsky Four they respond with his Candide Overture, all pre-rehearsed by MTT. Much laughter and pre-birthday jollity (LB will be 65 next Thursday).

August 23

Evening LB concert was a fine programme. Lamentation Symphony [i.e. the *Jeremiah*, LB's No. 1] preceded by Copland's Outdoor Overture, a much better piece than I first thought. Young Gail Dubinbaum sang Jeremiah with great fervour. LB did the Eroica as well as in Vienna. Afterwards a party at our house, (h)eroically organized by Chrissie – 35 people. Lennie left at 3.30. Good talk. Lukas met Danny Kaye and said he didn't look as good as the real thing.

August 24

In the morning Bowl rehearsal for tomorrow night's Hoffnung concert. [The late Gerard Hoffnung was an English humorist and cartoonist.] The two young violinists who have learnt the Wilfred Josephs Concerto d'Amore do well with their colleagues; the orchestra also love the piano concerto [Reisenstein's Concerto Popolare]. Possibly a success is on the way …

The evening concert is a 'Virtuoso Recital' by Ivo Pogorelic, a true virtuoso. He plays Haydn, Ravel and Prokofiev to 8000 people, an amazing number for a programme with no concessions to popularity. The legend about this rather effete-looking young man is completely justified. He played with effortless virtuosity and enormous dynamic range but little hint of intellectual capacity.

August 25. Bernstein's Birthday

Later in the day we wore his blue arm-bands to demonstrate musicians' fellow-hatred of nuclear armament … The Hoffnung rehearsal started and finished late but went very well: all the bottle-blowing and the vacuum cleaners had celebrity performers and a sense of a fancy dress New Year's Eve party quickly developed. My TV producer role, holding it all together via script, lighting cues etc. etc. was strongly needed: all I missed was a Jane Tanner to type out my own texts. My narrative was shamefully insecure on the night yet I had dallied late in the afternoon, going shopping and trying to get a tennis game with Lukas, when I should have been concentrating: my usual fault of needing to create a last-minute mental panic. And the concert in the evening was a triumph: VW, Grainger (splendid stuff) and Elgar [Cello Concerto with Ralph Kirshbaum]; then the Hoffnung high-jinks, including the placing of an additional sphere in the roof of the Bowl which popped and fell down.

385

Hoffnung's popped sphere.

August 26

We bid farewell to the Hoffnungs [Gerard Hoffnung's widow Annetta and her partner Tom Bergman, both devoted to the cause of comedy]. I play tennis after lunch with the kids and drive to the downtown office in my smashing new Vanden Plas in time for a little work and an office party in which we make up a High School kazoo band and serenade Stacey, Ann and Rebecca, all of whom have birthdays. The Friday office party is one of the most civilised aspects of the LA Phil organization. Race back to the house to change and get Lukas down to the Bowl for his nightly prowl among the lady ushers. … In my box – a memory of Long Dene days 40 years ago – is Lindis Guinness, daughter of my school headmaster. The dance programme goes off well. The dancers work on the front half of the stage with a special Marley floor. The orchestra plays in the gloom, but conductor Jack Lanchbery is spotlighted and turns to face the dancers and the audience. It looks a little silly. But the pas de deux from Fille, Romeo and Juliet and Le Corsaire all look good – young

Christopher Boatwright is outstanding. [This gifted dancer from the San Francisco Ballet died of Aids in 1997.]

August 27

Pleasant day: we dropped work for a few hours and headed south for Marineland ... On the way we saw a strange sight. Coming off the highlands behind Marineland the sea was nowhere to be seen. Instead there was a vast plain of cotton wool, out of which Catalina Island could be perceived, sticking out of the clouds, 10 miles or more off shore. The Pacific was covered, as far as the eye could see, by sea mist. We all enjoyed Marineland, the dolphins, the pilot whale, the killer whales, the high diver, the sharks in the aquarium, the seals off shore, the walrus and the pelicans, and the hamburgers. Helena fell in love with dolphins, stroking them with an affection not observed in her since she stopped loving ponies two years ago [after she was thrown in Richmond Park].

August 29

In the afternoon we have Wagner rehearsal and Linda Esther Gray sings her very first Brünnhilde's Immolation. I think it will sound exceptionally dramatic: she is a lovely bouncy Scottish lady, full of gossip and jokes. Not unlike her teacher Eva Turner. [Because of nerves (she mentions a 'life-threatening illness' in her memoirs), Linda had to abandon her stage career as a Wagnerian diva later that year. She was a great talent.]

September 1

The Bowl reaches a climax for Christina and me with the Wagner's Ring evening. At rehearsal we met William Johns the heldentenor, who turns out to have a remarkably fine voice, a little reminiscent of Jon Vickers, less character but more youthful. The microphones cope well with all the voices, including Thomas Stewart [Wotan] whom we heard in June in San Francisco. I had difficulty persuading Ernest Fleischmann that we should use Tom [with whom I had done a BBC2 *Workshop* in 1964] but he sounds good despite his age. Linda was nervous last Friday before her first read-through of the Immolation but this morning sounds fresh and radiant ... I spent the afternoon at the office refining my script for this evening – a combination of Wagner's stage directions and my own narrative. I'm convinced the public should have this kind of mood-setting – at the Bowl they can't read programme notes or translations of text because it's too dark.

... A smallish house; during the Immolation Scene I walked up to the top of the Bowl and was thrilled by the sight of close on 8000 people listening in rapt silence – spoilt only by the early leavers – I don't understand such people's totally insensitive attitude. The orchestra rose to magnificent heights before the end. Edo de Waart was an excellent conductor, very different between rehearsal and performance.

September 2

Morning rehearsal with John Williams – musically a dreadful anti-climax after the sublimity of Wagner last night. Williams's choice for solo violinist for the Tchaikovsky v.c. plays insensitively and frequently out of tune. The Hollywood show music is saccharine stuff.

September 3

The 15th birthday of Helena Burton ... LA Times has stinker review of the Ring concert – I remain unrepentant. Donna Perlmutter likes it better in the Herald. [My gamble of casting Linda Esther Gray – frowned on by Fleischmann – proved worthwhile.] We buy chicken and bangers and chips and thousands of barbecue accessories and are soon home preparing for the birthday party influx. First arrival is Olive Behrendt, the godmother of the orchestra [and a major arts patron]. She brings a present for Chrissie having got the birthdays wrong but Helena is enchanted with the gift, a Seiko travelling clock-alarm. Olive stays long enough to repeat her grumbles about this year's Bowl: too much talk and concerts too long, so that the President of the LA Phil had to leave before the end because of an important meeting next morning ... Thank goodness this is only a temporary job! Though she is no more fatuous than the Chairman of the BBC [George Howard] or Aubrey Singer [former chief of BBC2] on a bad day ... Soon it's time for the Bowl where we have a party in our box before the music starts. [Christina, Helena and Lukas will be flying home next day for the start of the autumn school term.] The box is decorated with balloons and at 8:15 we have a surprise visit from the Ushers

Orchestra. I am handed the baton and asked to conduct a George M. Cohan medley. Fun. All the ushers are in evening dress, by the way; it's their New Year's Day Party. There are more presents for Helena and for the family; then all the girls from the Picnic Department arrive with cakes and candles and a serenade for Helena.

The concert is a fearful anti-climax … Afterwards a party at Spagos – the food is nice but Christina feels lousy and I'm exhausted and not too intrigued by John Williams, a quiet charmer but not a great programme builder. (His applause at the end left no doubt, however, that the folk in Hollywood love him and his success!) The children arrive back from their ushers' party at 3.30 a.m. Great sadness, tears, so many goodbyes. Lukas topsy-turvy with love coming at him from so many different directions.

September 4

Frantic packing, everybody delivered safely to the airport but one suitcase has been forgotten at the house. After a madcap mid-day ride through LA I rescue it and get it back to the departure lounge just in time. In the evening a chorus rehearsal for Verdi Requiem, supper afterwards at home with [Giuseppe] Sinopoli – gossip about Muti and the Philharmonia.

September 5

Today was Sinopoli's first rehearsal day and he worked v. hard and v long. In the morning rehearsal for Tchaikovsky Pathétique and Dvořák Cello Concerto. [Later] we rehearse the Verdi trumpets on the lighting towers – very exciting effect. Sinopoli staggers through most of the Requiem. He is not Giulini or Abbado but he has plenty of nervous energy which the piece also needs. Rosalind Plowright is v. tall, nice-looking in an English-rose way, not Italianate enough for my taste. [The other soloists are Katherine Ciesinski, Neil Shicoff and Robert Lloyd.]

September 6

Full-scale rehearsal of Verdi Requiem. Roger Wagner [excellent choir trainer] joins me in the box. He has told Sinopoli there was no need to rehearse pianissimo because such effects could never be heard above the noise of the helicopters and the wine bottles. But today Wagner is attentive and constructive. We both dislike Sinopoli's tendency to slow things down without justification from the score. His leaden tempi also make life difficult for the soloists, as Tony Kaye points out. La Plowright's manager, Kaye will shortly become her husband. Supper at Spago with EF and Sinopoli. Most of the talk is again about orchestral politics. I wish Sinopoli took me more seriously. Since he is German-trained and an excellent composer it is v. sad to see him turning into a primo uomo conductor. He confesses on the way home that he only came to Hollywood Bowl out of friendship with me [following the *Manon Lescaut* I televised at Covent Garden].

Sinopoli thinks EF behaved v. badly over cancellation of LAPO concerts next year and was all set to retaliate by cancelling this visit to LA.

… I find myself musing as to whether I would want to do this kind of job regularly. My head says certainly not but my heart has to admit that I have enjoyed a lot of it very much indeed.

September 7

Dress rehearsal for the Verdi Requiem. It goes like a dream. Everybody singing superbly and Sinopoli has taken all the notes I gave him! I felt like John Culshaw must have done with the other and greater G.S. [Georg Solti] correcting the tempo of Siegfried's Funeral March.

September 8

I sit in the booth so that I can call cues but first there's an on-stage announcement to make, dedicating the performance of the Verdi Requiem to those who died in the Korean Air tragedy. [The Russians shot down a 747 with 269 dead.] … The performance is less good than the rehearsal. Plowright cracks once or twice and departs from her final top B flat very nervously.

September 9

Good to hear from Christina that the children have got back into school routine – they are very much missed here. Today was the second of John Williams's two weekends at the Bowl. This one is his own music entirely and the rehearsal is not very promising – tricky music but the only thing with real melody is Fiddler on the Roof (by Jerry Bock) for which John wrote variations, splendidly played today by [the LA concertmaster] Sidney Weiss – he got an enormous ovation from the orchestra in the morning and from the public at night.

The EWOKS ['mammaloid bipeds' from the *Star Wars* universe] appeared at the concert in the evening for the end of The Return of the Jedi and even better all their dwarf midget friends appeared after the show for a dressing room party, an astonishing and heart-warming sight. The audience for John Williams was quietly respectful for the music they didn't know (Jane Eyre etc.) and raucously rapturous for the stuff they did know, above all Star Wars and E.T. I felt it was like taking money from a blind man's plate – $159,000 of it!

With John Williams – then, as now, a hugely popular figure.

September 10

Ernest and Rebecca were in raptures about last night's concert [John Williams] when they arrived to collect clothes for Europe and inspect their property before leaving. It is mildly interesting to conjecture what might have happened if Ernest had actually stayed away on sabbatical as originally planned. I would have survived professionally but EF certainly helped me to avoid some mistakes.

September 12

Final week, but there is no letting up in musical activity. Today MTT is back and rehearsing The Rite of Spring, a wonderfully highly-strung and precise performance even though it lacks the excitement of Lennie. Balance tests proceed all morning because there is so much extra to cover with Sacre ... Isaac Stern enlivens proceedings by announcing (by phone) that he is bringing Pinky Zukerman to the Bowl on Thursday to play the Mozart Sinfonia Concertante [for violin and viola]. Even though I know it's because Pinky wants an excuse to see Tuesday (Weld), I welcome the development.

14 September

The arrival of Isaac Stern – the big burly Henry Kissinger of the violin ... To the Hillcrest Club in Beverley Hills, an exclusive Jewish club where Belle and Seymour Owens [Bowl patrons] are giving a fund-raising lunch for the Israel-America Society. Isaac and his wife Vera speak eloquently; I eat (silently) next to a man with the evocative name of Laemmle. He was very old. They were all v. old, including a producer named Henry Jaffe with whom I made a Benjamin Britten special in 1967!

Returning to Hollywood, Isaac makes the Jaguar smelly with his cigar but suggests I could do worse than make a career in music management.

15 September

The last classical concert is dedicated to Isaac and Pinky. The Bruch goes well and the Kreisler pieces, but even at rehearsal one senses that, like Yehudi Menuhin, Isaac is not in complete command of his fingers at all times;

Left to right: Isaac Stern in rehearsal with his surprise guest
Pinchas Zukerman and Michael Tilson Thomas.

intonation slips, there are moments of roughness. Pinky on the other hand produces a most eloquent tone from his Amati viola and flawless musicianship … After the concert I attend a party given for Isaac by the Gregory Pecks. The restaurant, Le Dôme, makes Spago seem quite homely. Also present: the Walter Matthaus, Mrs Danny Kaye and Peter Ustinov and his delightful daughter Pavla (on whom Ernest used to have a crush).

September 16

My last day and one of the busiest and most touching. At the rehearsal MTT narrates the Young Person's Guide but afterwards says I must do it tonite (he knows I would enjoy it but I had to be sure he will be OK tomorrow when I will have left!) … For lunch I go down town with Frank, Bob Socko and Paul Geller [Bowl staff] giving them a Mexican meal as a thank-you … The office party is enlivened by champagne, provided by me, and by speeches and presents. I get

Narrating *The Young Person's Guide to the Orchestra*, my final appearance at the Bowl.

a white Bowl sweater upon which loving messages have been inscribed [I still have it in a bottom drawer]. The concert proceeds most entertainingly except that I have not had time to check and rewrite the text of the Britten Guide [*to the Orchestra*]. Am doing so in the interval in my trailer when a delegation of security guards arrives with a farewell cake – actually a set of icing-coated buns with a message … Then comes the Benjamin Britten. I am on stage and performing – I even work in a joke about the piccolo (played by Miles Zentner, the orchestra shop steward) being 'miles' higher than the flute. The sensation of being up there next to MTT on one side and the concertmaster Sidney on the other is very intoxicating but events move too fast for me to be able to stop and relish them. The Britten music brings back my childhood – I played the piece with the National Youth Orchestra in 1949 in Leeds Town Hall … While the stage is being reset for the fireworks I go back out front for the highpoint of the season. With the help of Joe Coulombe (Trader Joe) I have acquired 20,000 matchbooks which have been distributed through the Bowl (attendance that night: 17,300) by Raoul and the ushers. I have prepared the audience for what I call the match-lighting ceremony. Already lots of people have lit matches but I call for them to be extinguished and then, in the blackness, I count down from 5 to zero and then BINGO the place is alive with teeny twinkling flames; it is very beautiful and everybody is very happy. The fireworks afterwards are a big success and Robert Harth comes back later and says he'd have given $10,000 to have had Ernest present. I am happy to have made things work at the Bowl and I am touched by the warmth generated around me and Chrissie and the kids ... I am also realistic enough to know

A fond farewell to The Hollywood Bowl.

that from a human relations point of view Ernest's is not a very tough act to follow but he was very important behind the scenes in planning the series. In my office party speech I told them all how lucky they were to have a leader like Ernesto ... No speeches backstage after the concert: lots of horse play with champagne and pizza. Michael TT played beautiful jazz piano and there was much mirth and high spirits.

September 19

No time for nostalgia – just packing and handing over the house to Martin [EF's son] and delivering the Jaguar to an airport garage (what a wonderful bonus that has been!) and checking in to PanAm Clipper Class and off to London.

CHAPTER 19

ON THE MUSICAL MERRY-GO-ROUND

With the Unitel production team in the Musikverein. I am leaning over my half-brother Jonathan and daughter Clare. Unitel's producer Horant Hohlfeld is on my left.

I SURELY DESERVED a break after my non-stop Hollywood summer but my diary (which I soon abandoned once I was back in Europe) tells me that Christina and I were on a plane to Naples within five hours of my touching down from Los Angeles. A quick hug from the children, a hand-over of Bowl party snaps and we were off to Capri, where the Italians were hosting the annual Premio Italia; my modest European TV music group was meeting in the margin of the annual television festival with myself as chairman. It seems incredible to me now that I was in that much of a hurry to return to the world of television and I confess that I made time, later in the week, to take my favourite sea trip: the catamaran hydrofoil across the Bay of Naples from Capri to the island of Ischia, where we could chill out around her pool with Susana Walton at La Mortella, the unforgettable home and garden she and her husband William had created out of the side of a hill back in the 1960s. We had become regular visitors after I filmed a big interview with him about his First Symphony for *Omnibus* (marking his seventy-fifth birthday).

Sir William had died in March 1983, aged eighty. I flew out to represent the BBC at his funeral. Walton had inherited from his mother a deep suspicion of the Catholic church ('Papists', she called them scornfully) and as a consequence stipulated that he should be cremated. It transpired there were only two crematoria in all Italy, the nearer to Ischia being located on a hillside in Fiesole, just north of Florence.

We were a very small group of mourners that morning. Susana, in black mink, had travelled up the previous day from the island. Tony Palmer drove from Rome at crack of dawn. Gillian Widdicombe, supposedly Walton's biographer, was there too. (She never finished her biography of Walton, her labour of love.)

Walton's corpse had been transported from Ischia in a tin coffin. Gillian asked to have it opened so we could have a glimpse of Walton and pay our last respects. She was a brave woman: given the tin coffin I would not have dared to make such a request. After a huddled conference of crematorium officials we were asked to leave the room and when invited back the coffin's lid had been rolled back exactly like a sardine tin, revealing Walton's head and shoulders in his best suit but – as it seemed to me – shrunken to half size and embalmed. Then we went outside. We heard a loud boom as the crematorium furnace was fired up; soon a heavy plume of smoke billowed out from the enormous chimney and drifted across the Tuscan sky. We had to wait while the ashes cooled and then Susana collected the funeral urn and we went back for lunch in Florence. When Susana was back at La Mortella she scattered the ashes around William's Rock, the monument she had created at the top of those lovely gardens. I thought that day of so many Italian moments in Walton's music, the soaring melody at the beginning of the Violin Concerto's first movement (composed across the bay at Amalfi), the excoriating wit of the *Scapino* overture, the throbbing melancholy of the Cello Concerto. All gone up in smoke and yet with me to this day.

My work in the autumn of 1983 suggests that my exposure to the impresario business in Hollywood was no more than a passing fancy: I was quickly back to what I most enjoyed – and what paid the school fees: directing television music shows. That season I really was more in Munich than in make-up. Leonard Bernstein had struck up a new relationship with the orchestra of Bavarian Radio, one of Europe's top-notch bands. After his regular stint with the Vienna Philharmonic, which that autumn included a glorious collaboration with Krystian Zimerman on the first of the two Brahms piano concertos (the second, even grander, was filmed a year later), LB moved to Munich for a rehearsal week and then took the Bavarians on a tour which included Budapest, the scene of his greatest success back in the 1940s: a Hungarian reviewer had dubbed him 'the man from another planet'. The programme included his quirky new *Divertimento*, Bartók's powerful *Music for Strings, Percussion and Celesta* and Schumann's Second Symphony, a work LB had learnt to love, he told me, at the feet of the Greek conductor Dimitri Mitropoulos, who may or may not have seduced the undergraduate Bernstein in 1938. It was undoubtedly a splendid programme but I personally had a miserable experience. The Hungarians are clever but if my television crew was anything to go by they are both proud and insular. They spoke not a word of English between them, and not much more of German, a language which I can manage at a pinch, at least in a television truck. An interpreter was assigned to the team but he was totally ignorant of our technical language: my script was much too ambitious for a one-day in-and-out operation with a crew accustomed to winging it like a football match, nothing prepared in advance. I have to assume that the absence of any VHS or DVD of this concert is because my video was beyond rescue. I remember only running out of the truck when the transmission was concluded and swearing very loudly in English – 'fuck, fuck, fuck'. That night I drowned my sorrows in Tokay wine, in the company of LB's dearest and oldest friend, Adolph Green, whose parents were Hungarian. At the Café Gerbeaud he caused a sensation by dancing a czárdás on a tabletop.

I made another visit to Budapest in 1987, when Georg Solti brought his great Chicago Symphony Orchestra to the country of his birth. The television went better this time but not without mishap: the finale of Bartók's *Concerto for Orchestra* has a fine fugue which begins with the second trumpet. Except that despite my warnings the cameraman gave me the *first* trumpeter, who at that point does not play. Luckily the show was not going out live and I had a separate recording of Solti which I was able to edit in to cover the gaffe, but it looked odd to be watching the maestro at such an obvious point to be on the solo instrument. Only Karajan did that kind of shot.

Later collaborations with Bavarian Television were much happier. For two seasons LB conducted their orchestra and chorus in great choral music by Haydn – his *Creation* and the *Mass in Time of War*. Then LB moved on to Mozart – the *Requiem* and the C minor Mass. All were performed in grand eighteenth-century monasteries, none of whose basilicas were more spectacular than Ottobeuren. A lovely custom of these summer afternoon performances was that there was never any applause. The music died away. Sunshine poured into the Ottobeuren basilica as the audience joined the musicians in a deeply felt two-minute silence. Our 1990 production, the last before Bernstein's death, was at the Cistercian abbey of Waldsassen at the very centre of Europe, a few miles from the Czech border, which, when we took a stroll, turned out to be marked by nothing more sinister than a wooden gate with not a frontier guard for kilometres. President Václav Havel, whom LB was to meet in Prague two months later, sent his personal cook to look after the maestro and his entourage. Although LB looked gaunt I had no presentiment that he was close to death; we were all under the impression that he was a permanent fixture in our lives.

Back in 1983, another Austro-Hungarian treat was in store: I was asked to direct *Die Fledermaus* from the Royal Opera House, a live transmission on New Year's Eve starring Kiri Te Kanawa as Rosalinde, the flighty Viennese lady who attends a ball disguised as a mysterious Hungarian countess. John Cox's production – mixing English dialogue with German lyrics for the songs – was really good fun no matter how peculiar the concept, and the cast was outstanding: Hermann Prey, Benjamin Luxon, Dennis O'Neill, Hildegarde Heichele, all consummate actors as well as excellent singers. To cap it all, the conductor was Plácido Domingo, my third encounter in a year. Eyebrows had been raised when his name was announced, making his UK début on the rostrum, but he proved to be attentive to the singers' needs, rhythmically ebullient and fully in the spirit of the show.

The drunken jail-keeper Frosch was played by a witty Austrian actor named Josef Meinrad. When a lady visitor to the prison tells him her name is Ada, Frosch mishears it on purpose as 'Aida' and in a deep baritone starts serenading her with the opening bars of 'Celeste Aida' – a reasonably good musical pun. Domingo taps his desk with his baton and sings solo the next line in perfect lyric tenor style: Frosch joins in and then comes downstage to

With LB at Waldsassen Abbey working on the C minor Mass, our last production with Bavarian TV, 1990. LB dedicated the performance to the memory of his late wife Felicia.

Covent Garden's *Die Fledermaus,* New Year's Eve 1983.
Left: Plácido Domingo conducting. Right: Josef Meinrad as Frosch the jailer.

confide to the audience: 'Once at least I have sung with Plácido Domingo!'
They shared a showstopping laugh.

As is customary, some of the casting details for the gala in Act 2 were
decided at the very last minute – the choice depends on who is in town and
ready to have a laugh. I hated being without a camera script, so I was franti-
cally scribbling away until half an hour before transmission. And what an
eclectic mix the gala provided: there was transvestite comedy from Hinge and
Bracket; intimate chamber music, two cellos and a piano, by Paul and Maud
Tortelier accompanied by their daughter; a romantic ballad from Charles
Aznavour; and a delightful new Frederick Ashton *pas de deux* danced by
Merle Park and Wayne Eagling. The whole starry evening can be watched on
YouTube, all 150 minutes of it. The *pas de deux* is first class, pedigree Ashton.

* * *

In the spring of 1984 Christina and I took the holiday we had missed the
previous year. We went halfway round the world on Pan American flights,
first class, using the air miles I had accrued during my stint at the Hollywood
Bowl. From California we flew on to South Korea, where we spent a morning
in Seoul en route for Tokyo. Christina had lived in Tokyo twenty years earlier
and enjoyed rediscovering the impossible city's vast department stores: I was
more impressed by the temples and Zen gardens of Kyoto. Travelling on a
bullet train was a fun thing to do once, like crossing the Atlantic by Concorde,
but it was Zen that caught my imagination.

After the exotic holiday we flew back over the north pole to Geneva, where
I had a date to host the second Eurovision *Young Musician* competition.

I thought our candidate, the delightful clarinettist Emma Johnson, had a good chance but she was eventually pipped at the post by Olli Mustonen, the brilliant Finnish musician, playing Ravel's G major Piano Concerto and by Isabelle van Keulen, who dazzled in one of Vieuxtemps's flashy violin concertos. Dear Yehudi Menuhin, who was chair of the jury, announced he wanted to give all seven participants first prize. I suspect the jury's deciding factor was the choice of composers: Emma, placed third, was playing a less character-full concerto, by the Swedish Finn Bernhard Crusell, which came over a little like watered-down Beethoven. But like Anna Markland before her, Emma has gone on to make a prominent career in music: she was also the first woman to be made an honorary fellow of her Cambridge college, Pembroke.

In September 1984 Munich gave way to make-up: working in front of the camera was back in my frame. When *Omnibus*'s editor Ian Squires invited me to present the next series my first reaction was of the incredulous 'you cannot be serious' variety. I had done the job with Barrie Gavin as my editor in the mid-1970s, combining it with running the department. A few seasons later the next editor, Leslie Megahey, dropped the in-vision host figure (me, and with my approval), preferring to mount single-subject, self-contained documentaries. And who can blame him? Leslie's own films about John Donne and the Dutch painter Schalcken are classics. Then the pendulum swung the other way and the film buff Barry Norman did a stint of hosting *Omnibus*. Now it was my turn again. But introducing stuff I had not selected (never the case with *Aquarius*) soon lost its appeal. *Omnibus* was the BBC's arts flagship but I was not interested in becoming a celebrity host and by mutual agreement I withdrew the following year.

However, the *Omnibus* series kicked off rather satisfactorily (as I saw it) in September 1984 with a film I had directed earlier in the year, *The Quest for Reginald Goodall*. 'Reggie' was a Wagner conductor revered by singers who studied with him but he was virtually unknown to the wider musical public until the 1970s, when his *Ring* cycles at ENO brought him belated recognition. The title I chose for my film paid homage to my favourite literary biography, *The Quest for Corvo*; I liked the process of digging in the past and Goodall certainly had a past, including a flirtation with the English fascists under Oswald Mosley in the late 1930s. When we filmed he had just turned eighty and was shyness personified: the central interview was a classic example of the theatre of the uncomfortable. For what seemed like eternity he hummed and hawed, his hand in front of his mouth, his head turned away, declining to reply in anything but mumbled monosyllables to my questions. After ten minutes I mentioned Benjamin Britten. 'Ah, dear Ben,' he said, smiling, no doubt remembering their work together on *Peter Grimes* almost forty years previously, and thereafter he was forthcoming about everything from Wagner to his love for his wife, recently deceased after forty-six years together.

The *Omnibus* programme has some revealing rehearsal sequences filmed in Cardiff at Welsh National Opera, especially notable for Reggie's coaching of the young Anne Evans in Brünnhilde's 'Ho-jo-to-ho' war cry. There are memorable cameos from the indomitable soprano Joan Cross, who was Reggie's boss at Sadler's Wells in 1945, and from the veteran tenor Peter Pears, who that year sang the title role in *Peter Grimes* under Goodall's baton. I was astonished when, in his interview, Pears declared that it was Goodall (not Britten) who conducted the greatest performances he had ever heard of that landmark opera.

In September 1984, *Omnibus* went to New York to film the recording sessions for Leonard Bernstein's *West Side Story*. This documentary was to be in the tradition of *The Golden Ring*, a fly-on-the-wall account of the intensive days of recording one of the most popular of all Broadway musicals under the baton of its composer – who had never before conducted it. The film was to be shot on 16 mm film rather than tape. It was funded as a co-production by Unitel, who still had LB under exclusive contract. In his wisdom my successor Richard Somerset-Ward insisted that while I produced, the director should be Christopher Swann. I had recruited Chris from Radio 4 some years earlier and quickly concluded he might become the next-but-one Head of Music and Arts (he was then thirty-five and ended up running his own production company). I was happy to take the overseeing role of producer, keeping the peace between the Bernstein camp, the Deutsche Grammophon sound-recording team led by my dear friend John McClure and the stars, headed by Kiri Te Kanawa, suffering from what she dubbed 'airconditioningitis' and José Carreras. He was apparently suffering from a more substantial problem – a lack of famil- iarity with LB's music. Swann did an excellent job covering the action; his film editor Howard Billingham assembled a show that breathed energy and exuberance in every frame. The entire film, all ninety minutes of it, is often shown on television. Some sneer at the casting of a mature-sounding operatic diva in the role of Maria, a virginal Puerto Rican girl. Others remember only what they think of as LB's maltreatment of Carreras in the role of Tony, when the tenor baulks at singing his top B flat in 'Maria'. Naturally this incident was highlighted in the editing. Carreras's Spanish expletive was picked up despite being off-mic and amplified in the dubbing theatre to match the

The Making of West Side Story. Morose LB and anxious Carreras during a playback review with the record producer John McClure.

explosive thump as the angry Spaniard shoved his vocal score into a briefcase and stormed out of the studio. The irony is that LB said nothing hostile to him although naturally he was disappointed not to complete the number: apparently LB had not been informed of the singer's plan to record the high note next day, when his voice would be fresh. (Nobody told me, either.) When the session came to an abrupt halt, one of Swann's cameras caught LB feeling very sorry for himself. Six years later, when LB died, Carreras spoke forgivingly about the episode; it revealed, he said, the tension underlying this kind of high-pressure musical work. Very true!

Was the concept of a *West Side Story* sung by opera singers a mistake from the beginning? Obviously I did not think so, having produced Kiri and Plácido Domingo in some of the show's best numbers for her *Call Me Kiri* special a few years earlier. I tackled this vexed question in an article I wrote for *Gramophone* magazine. Here, taken from a conversation we had during the recording, is LB's explanation. 'I'd always thought of *West Side Story* in terms of teenagers and there are no teenage opera singers, it's just a contradiction in terms. But this is a recording and people don't have to look sixteen, they don't have to be able to dance or act a difficult play eight times a week. And therefore we took this rather unorthodox step of casting number-one world-class opera singers. I suppose the only foreseeable problem was that they might sound too old – but they don't: they just sound marvellous.' LB thought Kiri sang Maria like a dream. 'There is a dark colour in Kiri's voice – coming, I suppose, from the Maori blood – that is deeply moving and just right for this part.' He also explained the much-criticised slow tempo he adopted for 'I feel pretty'.

405

'In the theatre', he said, 'it is always played as brightly as possible to dispel the dreadful shadows at the end of Act 1, which closes with two corpses on the floor. Ugh! "I feel pretty" is there to say to the audience: "don't despair: Act 2 is going to have some up moments". But for the recording we don't have to do that, and we can take the tempo at which I really dreamed it, which is rather elegant and lyrical.'

Chris Swann and I went back to New York to show the fine-cut to our American co-producers. 'How long is it?' they asked. 'Ninety minutes,' I replied. Pandemonium! 'Forget it! We can't take a minute over the sixty for which we've contracted because the additional fees for the musicians would be prohibitive.' I urged them to keep calm and watch the film. After the screening we heard no more about its length.

One of the reasons I enjoy *The Making of West Side Story* is because it shows LB in such a playful mood. Of course it has grand and sombre moments, above all the two operatic duets 'A boy like that' and 'One hand, one heart', but the essential child inside the grizzly old man doing the conducting comes out when LB, in a flamboyant red sweater, teases his producer John McClure – 'you haven't done your homework' – or chatters away in Spanish before launching into the Puerto Rican girls' ensemble 'I like to be in America'. He was enchanted by so many of the show's big set pieces: I lost count of how often he announced at the end of a take, 'That has to be my favourite number in the show.' I pressed him as to what pleased him the most about this exhilarating work. 'It's so funky,' he exclaimed. 'I'm so proud of the way my twenty-eight-year-old score seems to stay young.' (One could hardly blame him.)

At the 1985 BAFTA awards, the film won the Robert Flaherty prize for the year's best documentary. Six months later came the prestige-laden Italia Prize festival. As a former jury chairman I surveyed the competition and was pretty sure we would win, but I had not reckoned with a handful of puritanical middle-European broadcasters who tried to disqualify our film on the grounds that it was a commercial enterprise plugging a new recording. When the awards were announced the BBC was fobbed off with a consolation prize from the Region of Sardinia – the 1985 festival was held in Cagliari. Especially galling was the award of the top prize to PBS, America's well-respected public broadcasting service, for a *film* (not a television programme) which was produced in Hollywood under the guidance of the respected producer Francis Ford Coppola. The film's title, *Koyaanisquatsi*, was an American-Indian word from the Hopi tribe meaning 'Unbalanced Life'. I had seen *Koyaanisquatsi* in a movie theatre in Los Angeles two years previously: it is a fascinating hour of abstraction, mostly of slow-motion footage of car headlights travelling at night on American freeways accompanied by minimalist music composed by Philip Glass. My complaint was not that the film was bad, but I felt that it should have been disqualified from a competition dedicated to new music programmes made for television. For PBS it was a canny investment, not a creative act. I was angry and I have never been back to the Italia Prize.

Omnibus and I went back to New York, however, in February 1985 for a *Requiem*. In the 1970s, when I was running *Aquarius* with Belfast-born Derek Bailey at my side, I had suggested to Andrew Lloyd Webber that he should write a requiem for those on both sides who had fallen during the Ulster Troubles. Nothing came of the proposal then, but in *Evita* (1976) he did compose a 'Requiem for Evita'. In 1984 Lloyd Webber invited me to his festival at Sydmonton, near Watership Down. The visit was not to be forgotten. His extraordinary house was chock-a-block with Pre-Raphaelite paintings, while up in the attic there was an electric train layout to die for. Richard Somerset-Ward had tipped me off that the festival's featured music, presented as a work in progress, would be a setting of the Requiem Mass. I liked it. A deal was quickly struck. The world première, which *Omnibus* was to televise under my direction, was to be given in New York at the fashionable St Thomas's Church on Fifth Avenue and there was to be no concession to budgetary restriction: the tenor soloist, inevitably, was Plácido Domingo and the A-list conductor, adding gravitas with every downbeat, was Lorin Maazel, who to his credit revived the *Requiem* thirty years later at his own festival.

For *Omnibus* viewers I recorded my introduction from the church steps on Fifth Avenue and then stepped inside, passing pews packed with curious New Yorkers to deliver my producer's pre-concert welcome. Cell phones were just coming on to the market so it was thought to be a wise precaution for me to ask the well-heeled, gadget-conscious audience to make sure their mobiles were turned off. This got an unintended laugh in the church, which I fear did not go down well with the composer.

His *Requiem* looked good that evening, and sounded good too. It contains many moments of genuine musical inspiration: I suspect the reason it has not matched the popularity and longevity achieved by John Rutter and Karl Jenkins in similar large choral works is the *Requiem*'s elaborate and expensive orchestration: I remember devoting an hour of the dress rehearsal to shooting over eighty 'cut-aways' of orchestral details, which I would not be able to cover during the show; they were inserted at the editing stage (a lesson learnt from my Unitel film work).

The 'Pie Jesu' duet leaped into the charts and deservedly stayed there: it's a true earworm of a melody and was beautifully sung by Sarah Brightman (hailed later by the composer as 'my angel of music') and by young Paul Miles-Kingston, the head chorister at Winchester Cathedral. The chorus that evening, all in dazzling red robes, combined the choirs of St Thomas's and Winchester. The CD of the *Requiem* sold 400,000 copies. A VHS cassette followed shortly afterwards. But you cannot buy a DVD of the *Requiem* for love nor money because no transfer to DVD was ever made. Not even YouTube can show you the original St Thomas's video of the 'Pie Jesu', but at least there is a grainy print of the opening Kyrie, probably recorded off-air back in the 1980s.

My next big production in this very busy decade was in France, a crazy affair featuring scenes from Rossini operas performed in the jewel-like court opera house in Versailles. This was a dream-fantasy of a co-production, organised by the enterprising Andrea Andermann (who later created the splendid televised *Tosca*, shot on location in Rome) who produced it in tandem with a dynamic young American named Peter Gelb (who since 2006 has been head of the Metropolitan Opera). Frank Dunlop staged this homage to Rossini, built on the conceit that a magnificent concert has been arranged for the celebrated composer, who arrives late for his own party after dallying with his friends at a gargantuan picnic (Rossini was a famous gourmand), eaten and drunk in front of the spectacular fountains of Versailles. Everybody was dressed in Second Empire splendour: audience, orchestra, even the zesty maestro Claudio Abbado. The singers were the finest *bel canto* interpreters in the world: Monserrat Caballé, Marilyn Horne, Francisco Araiza, Samuel Ramey and Ruggero Raimondi, joined by a bunch of veterans for the comic ensembles. I had worked with Raimondi on the Verdi *Requiem* in St Paul's, before he became famous. At one fraught rehearsal in Versailles he took me to one side to tell me he was not to be trifled with because (in case I did not know) he was now a leading light in his profession. I heard myself replying that in my field I too was by way of being quite prominent. Boastful stuff but it did the trick: I received no more complaints. Raimondi was wonderfully funny in the comic aria from *Il viaggio a Reims*. Musically, the complete programme was an unalloyed pleasure, but working with a Paris camera team was less than joyful – their favourite directors preferred intuition and improvisation to analysis and preparation, so cameramen were unaccustomed to having scripts and following shot numbers.

The Versailles Court Theatre. The actor Paul Brook playing Rossini.

My production assistant Jane Tanner bore the brunt of liaising with the French camera crew. Jane was part of the BBC's co-production deal for the Rossini production. She was admirably cool and patient. In my years as a BBC boss I had done no typing and had two secretaries, a ludicrous, humiliating situation but still commonplace in the 1970s. My senior assistant in those days, when I was head of Music and Arts, Desirée Mills, was older than me and had been something high-up in the WAAF (the Women's Auxiliary Air Force) during the war. 'Dizzy' remained a friend for the rest of her long life but once free of administrative chores I no longer needed anybody of her calibre to look after my diary, correspondence and telephone calls. Producers' assistants such as Jane Tanner had secretarial training but basically they administered whichever production their boss was preparing, whether studio or film – I did both. Jane had worked on music shows at Radio 2 and then, being a trained dancer herself, she migrated to television to work as the PA on ballet productions with the department's star director in that field, Colin Nears; it was from Colin that I poached Jane in the early 1980s. We did such mammoth

With my PA Jane Tanner.

410

shows together as *Eurovision Young Dancer*, *Manon Lescaut* and *Call Me Kiri*. She also moonlighted with me for a week when I directed a telecast of Verdi's *Les Vêpres Siciliennes* at Nice Opera. Later Jane moved to the calmer and better-paid field of head-office administration. I worked with other dedicated PAs but nobody quite matched her commitment and musical sensitivity. Jane died of cancer when only in her fifties. Her devoted husband Nigel, who was a victim of motor neurone disease, followed her to the grave only nine weeks later: he had been determined to stay alive to nurse her through her final illness.

* * *

In March 1986 I was attending an EBU music meeting in Lisbon when news came that Huw Wheldon had died. Christina and I had seen much less of him since our move from Richmond Hill to Kensington but he had remained a sort of father figure, very much loved. In the late 1970s, when I was head of the department and he, having retired, was in name at least merely a contributor, I had travelled with him to Washington's Library of Congress, where over a very enjoyable lunch we persuaded Daniel Boorstin to allow us to make a film portrait of the noble institution of which he was the boss. Huw was good on nobility: he had recently made a *Royal Palaces* series for the BBC. Ann Turner, our colleague from *Monitor* years, directed the Library of Congress documentary, which was sober, unsensational and informative, though arguably less lively than Huw's Christmas parties on Richmond Hill, which were events to treasure. Huw's novelist wife Jay (Jacqueline), later the subject of a most touching memoir by their son Wynn, always created a feast. Their guests were a sympathetic crowd drawn from television, the London School of Economics, where Huw was chair of the governors, and the arts – the Welsh poet Dannie Abse was an old friend and Huw's sister Nans was harpist of the English National Opera Orchestra. I dedicated my Bernstein biography, my first book, to Huw in gratitude for all he had taught me.

* * *

To complete this account of what proved to be the final years of my directing decade, I must first spool back to May 1987. At the Royal Opera House I took on the direction of a cut-price telecast of *Turandot*. This was emphatically not a luxury co-production with NVC Arts: BBC Wales footed the bill, and booked me solely because of the persuasive powers of Wales's national treasure

Two Princess Turandots.
Left: Dame Eva Turner.
Right: Dame
Gwyneth Jones.

Dame Gwyneth Jones. She wanted her performance of the Ice Princess to be preserved on video but the Welsh money was only enough for a piano stagger-through the previous day (which she did not attend – we used a stand-in) and the taping of a single performance, where normally we had a full dress rehearsal and two recording sessions. My trusty vision-mixer Angela Wilson, who was as much a perfectionist as I was, had sat with me in a security caravan half the previous night revising the camera script: when she needed the loo she had to visit the police station next door in Bow Street. My chief worry, however, was neither script nor loo but the fear that the highly strung Italian tenor Franco Bonisolli would do something unexpected: a few seasons previously he had thrown his sword at Herbert von Karajan during a dress rehearsal of *Trovatore* and stomped off the stage. In the event he was disappointingly tame as Calaf, but delivered the goods in 'Nessun dorma'. Our relay of Andrei Serban's vivid production went out live, with Radio 3 providing vivid stereo sound, but there seems to be no record of the show on CD or DVD. So you will have to take my word for it that Cynthia Hayman's Liù proved a touching foil to the imperious Dame Gwyneth. In the interval Robert Lloyd, our sonorous Timur, interviewed Dame Eva Turner, who had sung the Ice Princess at La Scala sixty years previously. (Once when Christina and I drove her home after an evening at the opera, Dame Eva, then in her late eighties, insisted we come in with her to her Bayswater flat. When we had got her safely through the front door she explained she needed our assistance to take off her stays: the lady who 'did' for her had helped her to dress but had long since gone home.) Eva Turner was a very brave lady – and the same must be said of Dame Gwyneth, past eighty herself at the time of writing and still singing lustily. The 1989 revival of *Turandot* marked the twenty-fifth anniversary of Dame Gwyneth's first appearance in the role at Covent Garden: they rightly gave her a silver medal.

Much of the spring of 1987 was taken up with planning a *Salute to George Gershwin*, a project I put together with my colleague and friend, and eventual successor, Dennis Marks, and my American conductor inspiration, Michael Tilson Thomas, with whom I had grown close at the Hollywood Bowl, working in tandem with David Horn and John Walker, two producers on the staff of Channel 13 in New York. Their *Great Performances* series was masterminded by a canny ex-designer named Jac Venza. The channel had been transmitting my Unitel Bernstein Beethoven films for a decade.

It was fifty years since the death of George Gershwin: time for a celebration. When we came in on the planning, Michael Tilson Thomas had already been booked to be the star conductor of a fundraising Gershwin gala at the cavernous Brooklyn Academy of Music, Brooklyn being Gershwin's home town. The choreographer and stage director was a bright ex-dancer named Patricia Birch, who was working with her regular producer Arthur Whitelaw. They were an authentic Broadway team – Pat had danced with Martha Graham's company and played Anybodys in the original production of *West Side Story*; Arthur's credits included the endearing Peanuts musical, *You're a Good Man, Charlie Brown*. It was MTT and his partner and manager Joshua Robison who suggested making a twin-city salute: the LSO would perform some of Gershwin's big orchestral works at BBC Television Centre and these great compositions would be interwoven with a chronological account, taped at Brooklyn Town Hall, of George and Ira's showbiz progress from Tin Pan Alley to Hollywood. MTT would record linking commentary (to be filmed in the Ealing studio where I had started my television career twenty-nine years previously) against a vivid backdrop of coloured footlights, antiquated horn gramophones and equally ancient player pianos, all bathed in a romantic haze created by dry ice. In the editing sessions John Walker would add every evocative frame he could find of Gershwin himself.

It was a collaborative effort enjoyed by all – the most enjoyable show I ever worked on, resulting in two ninety-minute programmes transmitted on successive Sundays in the UK (and the US) with so many highlights that it would be exhausting to enumerate them all, though I have to mention MTT himself. As I knew from the Hollywood Bowl, Michael has a profound knowledge of the Gershwin repertoire and style, coupled with a dazzling piano technique: on stage in Brooklyn he played *Rhapsody in Blue* (in the original

BBC Television Centre Studio 1. The set for *Salute to George Gershwin*, 1987. Note the keyboard skyscrapers.

jazz orchestration) as if he were in a trance, seemingly inspired by the spirit of the composer; in London a few weeks later he tackled Gershwin's unjustly neglected *Second Rhapsody* with the LSO, preceded in our TV show by the scene from the forgotten 1930 film *Delicious* that inspired it. In the same salute, Mikhail Baryshnikov danced entrancingly in Gershwin's *Walking the Dog*, choreographed specially for the show by an unknown genius named Dan Siretta. Dan was a devotee of the less-is-more principle: at the last moment he

sacked all his male dancers. Baryshnikov's lazy charm came over even stronger when partnered solely by long-legged ladies. Elsewhere in the show Leonard Bernstein played one of Gershwin's bluesy Preludes with the poetic intensity pianists normally reserve for Chopin. Liza Minnelli, Rosemary Clooney, Larry Kert and Johnny Green were among the showbiz icons taking part: another figure of world fame, Bob Dylan, was so embarrassingly raw (and incomprehensible) when he performed a Gershwin song in Brooklyn that I felt obliged to drop him from the BBC version, although for the Americans such a cut would have been tantamount to treason.

CHAPTER 20

HITTING MY STRIDE

LB with Aled Jones, the boy soloist in his *Chichester Psalms*, 1986.

IN THE SPRING of 1986 the LSO mounted a festival at the Barbican Centre in honour of its president, Leonard Bernstein. The Queen and Prince Philip came to the final evening and heard Aled Jones sing the boy soprano solo in *Chichester Psalms*. At the reception afterwards the prince was in jocular mood. At the time Aled was the best-known boy soprano in the country. The prince looked him up and down. 'Well, you haven't got much of a career in front of you,' he observed cheerily, little dreaming that the adult Aled would become a much-loved presenter of *Songs of Praise* and a successful disc jockey for Classic FM. The Queen was more diplomatic. 'Do you do this sort of thing awften?' she asked LB. Rarely lost for words, LB was flummoxed: did she mean appear in London often, conduct an entire programme of his own music, preside over a Bernstein festival or what? By the time he was ready to respond, maybe three seconds, her majesty had moved on. I am not making this up; I was in the BBC Outside Broadcast van directing the cameras and surreptitiously listening in to the presentations. Earlier, at the concert, the BBC had taped Krystian Zimerman playing the jazzy passages in LB's *The Age of Anxiety* with phenomenal agility. He shared the soloist's platform with the violinist Gidon Kremer, who dug deep into LB's beautiful *Serenade*. It was a splendid evening of positive Bernstein.

In July 1986 I was in Bayreuth, not for Wagner but for the centenary of the death of Wagner's father-in-law, Franz Liszt. (Their relationship makes a good quiz question.) Bavarian Television hired me to direct their Liszt memorial concert which would be relayed all over Europe from the festival stage; it was only the second time that music by anybody but Wagner had been heard in those hallowed halls, the first being the post-war reopening of the festival in 1951, when Furtwängler conducted Beethoven's Ninth. It felt a privilege to be ushered into the presence of Wolfgang Wagner, the grandson who had been running the place since the death of his theatrically more gifted brother Wieland twenty years previously. The only problem was that Herr Wagner's Frankish accent was so thick I could not understand a word of his welcome to the television team. Still I appreciated his reconciliatory effort towards his great-grandfather, Franz Liszt, remembering that Richard Wagner's widow Cosima had been absolutely beastly to her own father when he was lying on his deathbed in Bayreuth a hundred years earlier.

Daniel Barenboim had been chosen to conduct the Bavarian Radio Orchestra and I confess to experiencing a measure of disappointment after his final dress rehearsal. I knew Liszt's *Faust* Symphony from a sizzling performance conducted by LB that I had taped in Boston in 1976. Barenboim seemed leaden by comparison – until the performance itself, when he moved up through several gears and inspired the orchestra to deliver a searing interpretation. The high point was the finale, when the men of the Bayreuth opera chorus, a massively impressive group, sang the ecstatic chorus Liszt composed for Goethe's words beginning 'Alles Vergängliche', the text set later by Mahler in his 'Symphony of a Thousand'. It was one of those rare moments when every element combined and one felt the House on the Green Hill, Wagner's venerated opera house, might very well take off and journey into the spheres with all aboard singing their souls out:

Alles Vergängliche
ist nur ein Gleichnis
das Unzulängliche
hier wird's Ereignis ...

'Everything is but a symbol. The incomplete is here fulfilled': a view of life's eternal mysteries made tangible through Liszt's creative genius. It was a sublime moment, inspired by Barenboim.

In the autumn of the same year I swapped the grandeur of Bayreuth for the banality of Elstree, the BBC's film studio outside London. I wanted to show my colleagues in Music and Arts (who were dwindling in numbers year by year as incoming controllers cut back on classical music programmes) that there was plenty of life left in the modest *Workshop* format – rehearse, discuss, perform. Elstree was the only available studio. My trump card was another conductor with tremendous sympathy for Gershwin's music, Michael Tilson Thomas. MTT was about to take over as the principal conductor of the LSO. We had become close during my season at the Hollywood Bowl, a period when he was the Los Angeles Philharmonic's principal guest conductor, master-minding two weeks of lively concerts, while all through the summer he also taught the young conductors and players assembled for the brand-new Los Angeles Philharmonic Institute. I see now that Michael was exploring a personal dream with the Institute: an exploration involving postgraduate music-making for the country's best young players. This was leading up to his creation of the enormously successful organisation he called the New World Symphony, which he based at Miami Beach and which nowadays boasts a fine concert hall with conservatoire facilities designed by another of his LA friends, the renowned architect Frank Gehry.

Michael has always talked brilliantly about music. I first met him in Leonard Bernstein's dressing room in 1971, when he was preparing to take over the Young People's concerts. With me he wanted to try out something new, based on a performance with 'his' orchestra, the LSO, of Strauss's virtuoso tone poem *Till Eulenspiegel*. In the editing I would interweave a detailed rehearsal with his lively analysis at the piano (of course, like Barenboim – and LB and Solti before them – Michael is a superb pianist) and the hour-long show would be rounded off by a concert performance of the entire work. With the San Francisco Orchestra (where he was in charge for twenty years)

The LSO recording of *Till Eulenspiegel* conducted by
Michael Tilson Thomas at Elstree Studios, 1986.

Michael developed the educational format into his *Discovery* series, which includes revelatory location filming and much fancier camerawork, but the groundwork was laid on that intense afternoon at Elstree: the subsequent video editing by Michael Williams – involving gadgetry galore – almost matches the quicksilver of MTT's brain.

One day during the previous summer I had been invited to take lunch outside Salzburg with the top brass of Austrian Television. I naively thought it was a social affair connected with my chairmanship of the EBU working party but over the brandy it emerged they had another mission in mind: they were working out how to fill the gap left by Lorin Maazel, who had been in charge of the famous New Year's Day concerts from the Golden Hall of the Musikverein for the previous seven years but had recently quit after a mighty falling out with the Austrian Ministry of Culture. With bated breath they told me that Herbert von Karajan, Salzburg's most famous son after Mozart, had agreed to conduct the next New Year's Day concert in 1987. And *mirabile dictu* he had asked for me to be the director. By then I had done four *Sylvesterabend* (New Year's Eve) concerts with Karajan in Berlin, commencing in 1977 with a Beethoven Ninth that was, as his biographer Richard Osborne kindly remarks, 'directed with great cogency and flair'. It had long been a Berlin tradition to mount a concert of popular classical music on New Year's Eve afternoon. Another of those Karajan *Sylvesterabend* concerts culminated in a staggering version of Ravel's *Boléro* (1985) which remains among my all-time favourite music videos: Karajan begins totally detached and caring not a jot – or so it seems – and ends up waving his arms like a dervish in a trance. I was gratified that he had confidence in me for the prestigious Vienna New Year's Day event, which was estimated (doubtless by an optimistic Austrian) to draw an audience of 700 million. If the ORF emissaries were disappointed that Karajan suggested the engagement of a foreign director for a very Austrian occasion they hid it well: after all, I had been a sort of colleague in Vienna since *The Golden Ring* back in the 1960s.

Karajan chose a brilliant programme for his big occasion, featuring most sensationally a group of beautiful white stallions from the Spanish Riding School, which were given their solo moment in the *Annen-Polka* (very good fun to film!), and a soprano singing a famous Strauss waltz, *Voices of Spring*, something Karajan remembered from a Strauss concert he had heard in his youth in Salzburg back in 1929! His choice of singer was controversial: Kathleen Battle. Richard Osborne in his biography gives us Karajan's shocking assessment of Battle: 'She's a complete bitch but, my God, what a voice!'.

On the day, Battle looked wonderful in a bright-red dress and despite her reputation I found her pleasant to work with, as I did a few years later when I directed her in a telecast from of all places the Temple of Dendur at the Metropolitan Museum in New York – her evening song recital on that occasion was televised 'live' by satellite for cultured breakfast-time viewers in Japan.

On the Vienna concert platform, Karajan himself was courage personified. He was evidently delighted to be back in Vienna, away from the bad feeling about his appointment of Sabine Meyer to the First Clarinet chair, a decision which poisoned the atmosphere during his last years with the Berlin Philharmonic. But physically he was in bad shape – he was seventy-eight and had already been seriously ill. Because of his weak legs it was difficult for him to walk, so he ordered that the cameras were to stay discreetly distant as he entered the hall and made his slow progress through the orchestra. Once at the rostrum he leaned back into an elaborate shooting-stick contraption which provided him with the stability of a saddle. Comfortably installed, his work with the orchestra was a joy to behold.

In the lunch break on the dress rehearsal day he announced that he wanted to look through the entire show with me on the video-player imported to the back of the control room. He spent half an hour on the opening works, first *The Gipsy Baron* overture and then the *Music of the Spheres* overture by Johann's brother Josef Strauss. At one point, matching a crescendo, I had directed the cameraman to make a slow zoom from a wide angle of the orchestra to a mid-shot of the conductor; I then cut to a responding instrument. 'Why do you leave me as soon as you have arrived?' he asked in his gravelly voice. 'You must stay with me: I am the expression of the musical line.' He was right and it was not a question of vanity: the musical line is paramount and I never forgot his simple observation. Soon afterwards he got bored and cut short his review. I have no idea whether he ever saw the finished show but after he died his wife Eliette told me that he always enjoyed working with me. (That should probably read: 'he always enjoyed my working for him.')

On the eve of the first of the three performances of the programme (on December 30th, reserved for Austrian army soldiers), Karajan's daughter Arabel reported that he looked in terrible shape, but the moment he came face-to-face with the public, she wrote, 'it was as though a mask had been peeled away from his face'. She was right. It is my impression that there are more smiles in this single New Year's Day video than in the rest of his enormous DVD collection put together. He was on splendid form throughout,

Herbert von Karajan at eighty – frighteningly honest.

eyes wide open and laughing at himself when having mixed up the order of the encores he gave the gentle downbeat for the *Blue Danube* when the orchestra was expecting to play the fast polka *Ohne Sorgen*. In the *Radetzky March* he conducts the audience with wit and gusto, *pianissimo* as well as *forte*, and he obtains the most delicate of effects in the *Perpetuum mobile*. In the television truck with my excellent script assistant Monika Fröhlich I felt we were capturing an indelible moment of musical history. Richard Osborne summed up the *Annen-Polka* with the horses as 'a performance of incomparable grace and nobility, tinged, as was the entire concert, with a profound sense of sadness and longing'. Karajan seemed human as never before.

I had one more encounter with Austria's musical supremo. My successor at Music and Arts, Dennis Marks, accepted my suggestion of an eightieth-birthday interview with Karajan which would be illustrated with two orchestral showpieces conducted by the maestro, *Also sprach Zarathustra* and *Boléro*. Dennis assigned Donald Sturrock to direct the interview. At his home in Anif, the old man was frighteningly honest about his troubled relationship with the Berlin Philharmonic. He said there were times when they exasperated him so much he felt like roping them all into a barrel, pouring molten oil over them and setting them on fire with a match. Donald was so upset by the shocking image of this outburst that he took himself off the programme, reporting back to Dennis that the interview was no good and could not be salvaged. I took a different view, hating to waste our time and our flights to Salzburg; Karajan's English was not as good as he thought it was but I edited a reasonably interesting conversation, leaving in the boiling-oil story. Karajan had finished that ghastly anecdote by reporting the orchestra's reaction: 'But without us, maestro, you would have no orchestra.' It was creepy stuff but it made good television, and the concert performances were most effective at showing what an orchestral magician he was.

Karajan died suddenly in the summer of 1989 while he was preparing to conduct Verdi's *Masked Ball* at the Salzburg Festival. It is said that his pet llama, tethered in the garden at his Anif home, dropped dead the same afternoon. I was in the city to direct a Mozart concert for New York's Channel 13, a lovely event at which James Levine conducted and played the piano for Jessye Norman in 'Ch'io mi scordi di te?', a divine piece of Mozart. Meanwhile, at the opera Georg Solti stood in for the deceased Karajan, conducting the Verdi at very short notice. So we were able to support Solti and also the opera's director John Schlesinger, for whom I had worked thirty years previously in my first year at *Monitor*. We all attended the Karajan memorial concert: the slow movement of Beethoven's *Eroica* symphony was the perfect choice with which to remember a departed hero, his flaws for the moment put on one side.

* * *

In 1988 I was faced with two roads and I chose the 'path less travelled', which turned out to be a mistake. Henry Wrong offered me a part-time job (a hundred days a year) at the Barbican Centre, which he had managed since it was a hole in the ground in the bomb-torn city of London. As usual I reflected for only a few seconds before accepting, when the briefest cautionary enquiry would have warned me to be careful. My role, at a time when the Barbican apparently lacked vital leadership, was to find ways of persuading everybody to pull together. The Centre's constituents included: the RSC, which under Peter Hall (before he went to the National) had helped to design the theatres; the art galleries; the City's biggest reference and lending library; and the conference halls. They all had their separate agendas and were largely going their own sweet ways. My problem, I soon discovered, was that I had no troops and no budget. Henry's planners were led by Antony Lewis-Crosby, a genial Irishman with encyclopaedic musical knowledge who headed the small team which co-ordinated concept concert programmes at the Barbican Centre. The use of the concert hall was their prime consideration since almost every day of the year involved a different booking. The proudly independent LSO, then run by the redoubtable Clive Gillinson, claimed pride of place for rehearsals as well as concerts, but the City Fathers rightly thought their Barbican ought independently to be a power in the land, not merely filling in behind the LSO by arranging low-key bookings for sundry concert managements and university degree ceremonies.

Barbican Hall had prestige. There was no denying that Claudio Abbado's concerts with the LSO had been memorable. The Leonard Bernstein season brought more glory, as did a clutch of festivals. But criticism of the hall's acoustics grew louder by the year and there was much hand-wringing (as there still is) over the fact that getting on for 20 per cent of the orchestral repertoire could not be tackled because the hall did not have an organ or a large enough space for a proper chorus. The hostile din over the difficulty of actually finding one's way around the Barbican's component spaces – despite the provision of yellow lines on the floor of every corridor and passageway – became deafening. I had many a tussle on the phone with carpers such as Brian Sewell, the acerbic art critic of the *Evening Standard*. (I found his other claim to fame more intriguing: he was said to be the natural son of the composer Peter Warlock.)

I have no intention of raking over the coals of daily life at the Barbican in Henry Wrong's final years – Henry had stamina and style and he was a gentleman, even if the details of orchestral programming no longer excited him. Nor will I dwell on the disastrous collapse of confidence which followed the Corporation's appointment of Detta O'Cathain as Henry's successor; she was a former chief of the Milk Marketing Board with no experience in arts management.

I was in my new post of artistic adviser for over three years but I have to concede that my only creative contribution to the Barbican was to dream up a month-long festival devoted to the arts of the Nordic countries, a special project eagerly taken up by Anthony Lewis-Crosby and his senior colleague Cecile Latham-Koenig; it helped that she was half Danish. The festival's title, *Tender is the North*, a quotation from Tennyson's *The Princess*, was vacuous but the festival's programmes had merit, taking in as they did all six Nielsen symphonies under the young Simon Rattle and eight rather than seven symphonies by Sibelius – this after Colin Davis yielded to my plea to include the rarely played *Kullervo* symphony, a tale of incest and rape which proved to be a rip-roaring success, due in large part to the lusty participation of a male-voice choir from Helsinki. For me, however, the high point of the festival was the reconstruction of the Drottningholm court opera house on the Barbican's concert platform. Transported from Sweden in numbered containers, the replica historic theatre was assembled like an Ikea super-kit and proved to be a perfect fit to the last centimetre of the Barbican's stage. My idol Elisabeth Söderström was then Drottningholm's artistic director: she presided over the candlelit evening, playing the part of the cultivated, stage-loving Queen Lovisa Ulrika, inspirer of the original rococo theatre back in 1766. She was mother of the Swedish king who was assassinated at Verdi's masked ball.

The Barbican's 1992 festival was reputedly the largest ever mounted in London; it won a prestigious international award and personal medals for several Barbican officials, myself *not* included. I returned for the festival and on the opening Gala night had the discreet pleasure in the green room of witnessing our Queen Elizabeth greeting her assembled cousins – the crowned heads of Denmark, Norway and Sweden and their consorts – plus the presidents of Iceland and Finland, with the memorable words, 'Oh, hello!'.

I can see now that working only part-time at the Barbican was a miscalculation but at least it allowed me to go on accepting freelance television work. In 1989 BBC Wales asked me to take over the television production of the singing competition they had devised entitled *Cardiff Singer of the World*. This was the dream-child of a well-liked BBC Wales producer named Mervyn Williams; in the 1970s I had been on the BBC board that appointed him over more obvious contenders to an important television producer post in Cardiff. Under his ambitious leadership the BBC's National Orchestra of Wales became the most frequently televised orchestra in the country: Mariss Jansons conducted a dazzling Tchaikovsky symphony cycle with them. Mervyn thought up the idea of an international singing competition: it would be a way of integrating BBC Wales with Cardiff's brand-new (and admirable) St David's Hall. This was in 1982. I had resigned from running Music and Arts the previous year but I was still chairing the EBU's music working party. Like my international *Young Musician* programme, Mervyn's scheme depended on collaboration with other European broadcasters. I invited 'Merve the Swerve' as he was known to make a pitch at our next meeting, in Venice. He wrote in a memoir:

> Only Finland and Belgium offered their support at that stage. BBC Two turned the idea down. I was dejectedly sipping a coffee in St Mark's Square when I was

approached by Humphrey Burton. 'It's a good idea,' he said: 'stick with it and I will see what I can do' ... Burton worked his magic with BBC Two. The dark clouds were lifting.

I don't know about magic, but I was glad to support a kindred spirit. Gratifyingly the first Cardiff Singer competition in 1983 discovered an outstanding winner in the Finnish dramatic soprano Karita Mattila. A couple of years later I was dismayed when, like so many talented producers in the Thatcher era, Mervyn left the BBC to set up his own production company. I have to say that even without him, BBC Wales remained committed to classical music like no other region in the kingdom. It was Mervyn's successor, Huw Tregelles Williams, who hired me to produce the next two Cardiff Singer telecasts, and what luck it was that the 1989 competition featured the so-called Battle of the Baritones, between Wales's own Bryn Terfel and the smooth Siberian Dmitri Hvorostovsky.

There was little to choose between them in the earlier rounds but on the final evening the Soviet competitor drew ahead. Both had lovely natural voices and big personalities, so once again it was the choice of repertoire that made the difference. Bryn staked everything on the Flying Dutchman's monologue in the first act of Wagner's opera. It showed off his command of the German text and his wonderfully luxuriant tone but the long haul left him no time to offer a contrasting aria, whereas Hvorostovsky rang the changes with a variety of showpieces: his best effort was by Verdi, Rodrigo's dying farewell to Don Carlos. The Russian's breath control was astonishing: phrases flowed

CARDIFF SINGER OF THE WORLD 1989
DMITRI HVOROSTOVSKY

Dmitri Hvorostovsky –
all *chutzpah* and honey.

The Battling Baritones: Bryn Terfel and Dmitri Hvorostovsky sign
a T-shirt backstage at *Cardiff Singer of the World*, 1989.

with unparalleled eloquence. At the end of the aria the arrogant Hvorostovsky stared out at the audience and at the judges as if defying them *not* to award him the prize. I learnt later that he had borrowed money to buy a new evening suit for the final, gambling that he would win the prize and the cheque that went with it. When, backstage, he heard Terfel's magnificent Wagner he thought for a moment that he was done for, but (as I have said and he said of himself later) he was an arrogant young man and in the end his honeyed voice (and his *chutzpah*) carried the day. But Terfel, who rightly took the consolation of Lieder Prize, made equally giant strides: a dozen years later, when Covent Garden reopened with a flourish after a major refit, I had the honour of televising his genial interpretation of *Falstaff*: a splendid occasion which proved that in the Cardiff 1989 battle there were no losers.

I was back in Cardiff the following April to introduce *Young Musician of the Year* – my last tour of duty as it turned out, though I did not know it at the time. The winner was a gifted violinist from North London named Nicola

428

Loud. She played Bruch's first and finest violin concerto, most sympathetically accompanied by Charles Groves conducting the BBC National Orchestra of Wales. In all those competitions I never saw a more committed performer – her evident passion for the surging romantic music was tempered by a deeply poetic sympathy and I was surprised that she did not proceed to an international career. Her outgoing personality still makes friends for music wherever she goes – I read that nowadays she sometimes plays on long-haul cruise liners.

Televising opera house productions, preferably 'live', had become one of my regular job satisfactions in the 1980s. Apart from the operas already mentioned, I directed a marvellous handful at Covent Garden: *Die Entführung aus dem Serail*, *Andrea Chénier*, *Prince Igor* and *Così fan tutte*. What an education! But the most significant of my Covent Garden productions actually took place in Leningrad. This was Mussorgsky's *Boris Godunov*, a wonderful production by the Russian film director Andrei Tarkovsky, first mounted at Covent Garden in 1983 under the intense musical inspiration of Claudio Abbado. I attended the première and knew instantly that it would translate splendidly to television. But Tarkovsky – a prominent dissident – died in exile in 1986 and no revival of this immensely long epic was planned. Dennis Marks, who I think of as my true successor at the BBC, had meanwhile forged a friendship with Valery Gergiev, the new music director of the Kirov in Leningrad: together they hatched an audacious plan to pay tribute to Tarkovsky by mounting his Covent Garden production of *Boris* on stage at what was then known as the Kirov Theatre in Leningrad.

Boris Godunov belonged in St Petersburg, as Leningrad was to be renamed the following year in 1991: Mussorgsky wrote and rewrote it there; it received its première at the Mariinsky Theatre. The Royal Opera team was led by Paul Findlay, a true friend and colleague; he backed the idea to the hilt. What made it extra-special for him was the casting of Robert Lloyd in the title role. Bob was then fifty and at the top of his game. He spoke no Russian and was to perform with a company that boasted three distinguished basses who specialised in the role of Boris. But Lloyd had premièred the Tarkovsky production in London and Lloyd it had to be: in the event he was overwhelmingly moving in a role I had always loved since hearing Chaliapin's unforgettable recording of the death scene.

The most dangerous element in the project was that the evening was to be relayed back to the UK as a live BBC2 transmission. Going live with a project of this magnitude was a 'first' for me and I welcomed the challenge, even

429

The BBC's satellite dish next to the Kirov Theatre in Theatre Square, Leningrad, 1990.

With Dennis Marks and members of the BBC team by the Outside Broadcasting truck.

Andrei Tarkovsky's production of *Boris Godunov* starring Robert Lloyd.
Designer: Nicolas Dvigoubsky. Triumphantly recreated by Stephen Lawless
and Irina Brown in Leningrad for the telecast on April 28th 1990.

Curtain call for the first night of *Boris Godunov* at the Kirov Theatre.
Left to right: Sergei Leiferkus (Rangoni), Olga Borodina (Marina),
Valery Borisov (Chorus Master), Alexei Steblyanko (Dmitry), Valery Gergiev
(Conductor), Robert Lloyd (Boris) and Alexander Morozov (Pimen).

431

though it involved a huge amount of painstaking detail; nothing could be left to chance or the spur of the moment.

Living conditions in Leningrad were appalling. Mikhail Gorbachev's *perestroika* was supposed to mean restructuring the Soviet Union towards a more democratic society. In practice it meant hardship for everybody in Leningrad; it sometimes felt as if there was a bankruptcy of hope as well as of cash. The canteen at the Kirov had virtually nothing edible on offer. Maestro Gergiev had to queue for this disappointing sustenance like everybody else and if he arrived late he was turned away by the officious *babushkas* who ran the theatre backstage and treated him like an obscure second violinist. And yet it was Gergiev who inspired the Kirov company to deliver a most beautiful and profound production. Stephen Lawless and Irina Brown, the Royal Opera stage directors, brought Tarkovsky's staging back to life. The sets and many of the costumes had been packed in vans and driven across Europe. The rehearsals were psychologically gripping, especially for the way Bob Lloyd won the admiration of his Russian colleagues for his committed interpretation.

The opera fascinated everybody. At a time when the Soviet Union was faltering, *Boris* asserted the indomitable spirit of the Russian people. The first scene had peasants stumbling around a pitch-dark stage in search of light and leadership; the closing scene had the Fool lamenting the fate of oppressed Russia. In the four hours between we had experienced the story of Boris, the

Dennis Marks (right)
with the Kirov stars
Sergei Leiferkus and
Olga Borodina.

haunted tsar, and of Princess Marina, the Polish heiress who is manipulated by the Jesuit priest Rangoni. (Productions that omit the Polish act in this opera, which Mussorgsky added in a major rethink, tell only half the story; it is as bad as leaving out the Fontainebleau act in Verdi's *Don Carlos*.)

Olga Borodina played the lustrous, calculating Marina and Sergei Leiferkus was the odious Rangoni. At the first-night party Leiferkus assured me that Borodina would soon be a world-ranking artist. I noticed that without stage make-up her skin was in a dreadful state because of the ghastly diet the singers had to endure, but he was right: La Borodina became Russia's leading mezzo in the 1990s. As Boris, the tsar with the guilty secret, Robert Lloyd was magnif-icent; even the Russians thought so. Behind the scenes the hero of the telecast was Dennis Marks, holding together a team of at least twenty BBC colleagues, as well as dealing with Stephen Lawless and Irina Brown of the Royal Opera, who felt their sacred task was to recreate Tarkovsky's vision in every detail. Dennis was tireless in negotiating with officials of the Kirov company; he was (for Dennis) amazingly diplomatic. In the middle of it all he found time and energy to interview Gergiev in his *loge* during the interval of the live relay televised back to the UK. Dennis also authorised the line producer (my eldest daughter Clare Dibble) to order pizzas for the entire crew – they were brought in forty miles from a pizzeria just inside the Finnish border and were most welcome after a week of scrawny chicken and fake caviar.

In 1991 the team returned to Leningrad for an equally crazy project: the televising live to BBC2 (starting at 4 p.m.!) of a brand-new production of Prokofiev's epic *War and Peace*. The stage designs were by Timothy O'Brien and Graham Vick was the producer: the idea was that the production would later be mounted at Covent Garden. Unfortunately the set – three electrically operated and totally independent ramps – proved to be so heavy that the show was abandoned after its first run and never seen in London. It is one of Vick's most powerful productions and proved that the opera, on which Prokofiev laboured for the last ten years of his life, is among the great works of the twentieth century.

Once again Valery Gergiev was the musical driving force. His was not an interpretation but a statement of how the work should unfold. Every tempo was perfectly judged and the Kirov's home-grown casting was sumptuous, with a standout performance by Elena Prokina as Natasha. The show was the highlight of a midsummer festival which after the breakdown of the Soviet Union was retitled White Nights of St Petersburg; the Kirov reverted

Tarkovsky's *War and Peace*, another memorable production televised 'live' from the stage of the Kirov Theatre in Leningrad. Top left: The entrance of Napoleon (Vasily Gerello). Bottom left: Graham Vick directing a rehearsal. Right: The Ballroom Scene from the first act (designer Timothy O'Brien).

to being the Mariinsky and the city of Leningrad reverted to its original name, bestowed by Peter the Great.

In July 1991 the theatre's working conditions were as bad as ever. A pack of Lucky Strike cigarettes paid for your airport taxi: a carton would buy you almost anything. This time the BBC equipment lorries had brought from London not only a complete camera unit but also an inexhaustible supply of tinned sardines. I had the same frantic task of preparing a camera script

which involved nightly revisions after the evening rehearsal. Some nights I would walk back to our hotel in the mysterious half-light that occurs just before the drawbridges are raised at 2 a.m. (to allow ships to pass through the city's canals). One night I worked exceptionally late and was still there when the male dancers arrived for their morning class – their practice hall was just across the corridor from where my video-cassette player had been installed. How they found the energy to dance on their miserable diet was a mystery only partly explained by the galvanising personality of Valery Gergiev. But the entire company was a marvel and working with them so intimately was one of the greatest experiences of my professional life.

Solti on Solti, a seventieth birthday conversation on BBC2. Left to right: Christina and me, Gloria and Michael Birkett, Valerie and Georg Solti. A reunion of friends.

Both productions are preserved on excellent DVDs. It was especially important to do honour to Tarkovsky and Prokofiev, both of whom had been hounded by the Soviet authorities.

A final satisfaction for me in the late 1980s was my work with my friends Eric and Katya Abraham and my duet partner Michael Birkett. A couple of years older than me, Michael had been Peter Hall's number two at the National Theatre when it opened in 1976. When economies had to be imposed he made himself redundant and got a job running the arts for the Greater London Council – until Margaret Thatcher abolished the GLC in 1986. By then we had been friends for a decade: his second wife, Gloria Taylor, a former model and friend of the writer Bruce Chatwin, had been press officer at the Royal Court in my *Aquarius* days; she and Christina became close friends, and Michael and I loved nothing better than playing Schubert and Mozart piano duets at our London flat or at their house near Petworth in Sussex. Our most significant joint operation was the creation of the annual Royal Philharmonic Society Awards. Over the years I had conspired to get involved with a champagne company which had cultural ambitions (the chairman's wife was a keen amateur pianist): in 1988 I produced a lavish awards ceremony for

Krug and Charles Heidsieck at the Banqueting Hall in Whitehall. Our guest list of the great and the good rivalled that of the *Evening Standard*'s drama awards and we persuaded a royal to grace the top table in the person of the very affable Princess Alexandra, who had the inestimable advantage among court personalities of actually liking classical music. The bill came to over £50,000, and my fee was paid with a case of Mouton Rothschild 1962. Lord Birkett and I then contrived to merge my solo prize-giving effort with a similar awards project which the Royal Philharmonic Society had been mulling over for some time. Michael was close to the Philharmonic's committee and knew that they badly needed a sponsor. For their part, the champagne people were not averse to supporting an organisation with a royal in its title. A marriage was arranged.

Most of the categories we defined in 1989 remained in place for decades, as does the actual award, which quickly developed into classical music's Oscars. The Heidsieck design people had come up with some crass suggestions but luckily the chairman took a fancy to a doodled sketch of a lyre by the RPS's Laurie Watt and that elegant piece of silverware has also stood the test of time.

The Royal Philharmonic Society's silver lyre designed by Laurie Watt.

Michael was then headhunted to work with Bob Scott, a prodigiously energetic man of the theatre, whose ambitious scheme was to mount an arts festival in Manchester in support of that fair city's bid to host the Olympic Games in 1996. What I brought to the table was the support of my friends Katya and Eric Abraham, who ran Portobello Productions and had already made a lively film with Georg Solti and Murray Perahia playing the Bartók sonata for two pianos. Michael was the son of the great lawyer Norman Birkett; he had inherited his father's negotiating skills and persuasive power to the extent that Solti agreed to conduct the BBC's Northern Orchestra, a fine ensemble but not in the very first rank of orchestras with which Solti was accustomed to appear. Moreover, Solti brought with him Kiri Te Kanawa, who would sing Strauss songs in the first half of the concert, with Solti at the piano, and perform the composer's *Four Last Songs* with the orchestra after the interval: it was a truly five-star festive occasion which duly sold out the Free Trade Hall. My television programme, *The Maestro and the Diva*, filmed these two superb musicians rehearsing the songs in Solti's sunny St John's Wood studio; the prevailing mood is playful and affectionate, even a little flirtatious, but it is underpinned by intense seriousness of purpose: Kiri has a creamy soprano which is well-nigh perfect for Strauss but at the rehearsal it is Solti who encourages her to bring out every nuance and inflection in the poetry of Hesse and Eichendorff.

Earlier in the summer of 1990 the Portobello team asked me to take over an equally enjoyable project, an exploration of two Mozart piano concertos played

With the Maestro and the Diva in Solti's London music room.

438

by the virtuoso Chamber Orchestra of Europe conducted from the keyboard by Murray Perahia. The venue was in Berlin, the newly opened small hall in the Philharmonie, at the heart of the recently reunited city. The additional spice in this production was the presence of Sir Denis Forman, whom Eric Abraham had wisely booked to interview Murray. For decades Forman had been the astute joint managing director of Granada Television. A few years earlier he had invited me to take charge of his ambitious *Music and Man* series but I baulked at being away from live transmissions for so long. However, I had enormous respect for Denis – not only for masterminding such drama epics as *The Jewel in the Crown* and (three years previously) *Brideshead Revisited* but also because he had written an entire book analysing the first movements of all the piano concertos of Mozart. I guess Denis was a role model: a successful operator with a cultural mission. He did a marvellous job talking to Murray Perahia. It was not an interview so much as a conversation between equals, a conversation about Mozart which I interwove with extracts from a spellbinding rehearsal recorded earlier in the day. Murray is wonderfully articulate when conducting. He got on perfectly with the young virtuoso players of the Chamber Orchestra of Europe who at the time included Stephanie Gonley, a future leader of the English Chamber Orchestra, and the oboist Douglas Boyd, who is better known nowadays as the conductor of Garsington Opera. The concertos were the C major, K467, and the B flat major, K595. The conversation was limited to K467 and the name Elvira Madigan was never mentioned. This was the most literate, civilised music programme I ever made. It was enhanced by the use of wide-screen television cameras and edited with considerable sophistication by Terry Bennell, who was making pioneering use of a gadget named AVID, a brand-new technology that provided instant access to any part of the entire recording session. In 1990 that was miraculous. Nowadays every personal computer can have an AVID. But nobody makes programmes like the one I made with Perahia and Forman. And – predictably – that makes me sad.

CHAPTER 21

BERNSTEIN'S ENDGAME, 1989–1990

With LB in Vienna, 1989, for the filming of Beethoven's last three piano
concertos. John McClure at left. Krystian Zimerman at right.

LEONARD BERNSTEIN DIED on October 14th 1990. Twenty years earlier
he changed the course of my life by signing me up to direct films and videos
of his concerts. From the start we also filmed documentaries which threw
light on the music he was conducting. In the 1980s I persuaded him to widen
the field by getting involved in autobiographical essays, although the first of
these was actually his own whim – and LB had a whim of iron: his notion was
nothing less than a session on Dr Freud's famous consulting couch, agonising

as to why a good Jewish boy such as himself should be conducting the music of the grossly anti-Semitic Richard Wagner.

In 1985 LB was in Vienna because, as a *quid pro quo* for the Staatsoper's decision to mount his own opera *A Quiet Place* the following season, he had agreed to conduct a concert performance of the second act of *Die Walküre* on stage at the Vienna State Opera. LB had long been aware of Viennese anti-Semitism – on his first visit as a maestro, in 1966, he walked up and down the city's main street, the Kärtnerstrasse, asking passers-by for directions to Mahlergasse, Mahler Street, knowing full well that the city had still not reinstated the street name that had been stripped away by the Nazis, because Mahler was a Jew, after the *Anschluss* in 1938. He loved conducting Wagner – indeed, had recently recorded a complete *Tristan* in Munich – but naturally, being Jewish, he felt uneasy about enjoying the music of such a rabid Jew-hater. His response was to propose that since he was in the cradle of psychoanalysis he should undertake a session in the most famous consulting room in Europe at Berggasse 19 in the Ninth district, the home for forty-seven years of Dr Sigmund Freud.

I was not free to direct the filming – I suspect for diplomatic reasons – so my regular Unitel producer Horant Hohlfeld took charge of the shoot. Lenny reclined on what was said to be the authentic couch (the Freud Museum in London boasts another) and poured out his soul to the camera. But after several hours he admitted that he could not find an answer to his own good-Jewish-boy question and the session was wrapped without a final reel. On LB's next visit to London I spent a frustrating afternoon in his Savoy suite, trying to help him square the circle, but this proved to be one of three important programmes LB never did finish. The last of these projects was an essay about his childhood; the second was a film of his 'Kaddish' Symphony. In 1985 he took the European Community Youth Orchestra on a Far East concert tour that included a concert in Hiroshima on the fortieth anniversary of its atomic bombing. He then travelled with the orchestra to Vienna, where he suddenly called for his concert to be filmed. There was time only for a single performance and absolutely no time to prepare a script: the project had to be abandoned after the cameras one by one ran out of film. What a disaster! Over the years I managed to film all LB's other major orchestral works so this was a real disappointment and one that could have been avoided.

As the decade rolled on with no sign of him working on a written autobiography I felt duty-bound to get some of LB's memories down on film. Not because I feared he was soon to leave us: it is true that he grew old very fast after the death of his wife, but we soon got used to Lenny the Patriarch and

I never doubted he would always be with us. Perhaps he was happy to talk about himself because he knew he was hastening his own departure: he never managed to give up smoking, he drank substantial draughts of Scotch, had gay relationships when Aids was a dreadful scourge and habitually used drugs to get himself going on the concert platform. It was only in the last months of his life when cancer was a real enemy that he wrote poems about death, but I believe the spectacular burst of activity he undertook in his last few years was an endgame: he knew in his heart that he could not go on much longer.

I filmed the first instalment of memoirs in my flat at Oakwood Court. I called the programme *The Love of Three Orchestras*. The title had nothing to do with Prokofiev but it had a ring to it and was factually correct; LB had grown up with the Boston Symphony and was president of the London Symphony but three other orchestras meant even more to him, the Philharmonics of Israel, New York and Vienna, and he reminisced happily about them all afternoon. He described conducting as being like making love, but with a hundred people simultaneously. When pressed he said the Austrians were his favourite orchestra because they lived for music and did not fuss about overtime. In his next essay, *Teachers and Teaching*, he remembered the most influential of his mentors. I rented a hotel room on Fifth Avenue and filmed him at the window against the background of the skyscrapers of Central Park West, among them the Dakota. That afternoon I abandoned the interview format and got him to talk directly into the camera. Normally he scripted everything he said, down to the last comma and exclamation mark, and read it off a teleprompter, so this was a new experience for him, akin to making a confession on the psychiatrist's couch. The stories poured out, highlighted by memories of his terrifying Russian piano teacher at the Curtis Institute, Isabella Vengerova, and his conducting masters Hungarian Fritz Reiner and the Russian Serge Koussevitzky, so different in their approach to music-making.

Bernstein himself went on teaching all his life. He rarely missed a year at Tanglewood and after the Los Angeles Institute experiment in 1983 he joined forces with the German pianist Justus Franz to create a music academy in Germany at the new Schleswig-Holstein music festival. Horant Hohlfeld and I took turns the first year to direct telecasts of his conducting classes working on *The Rite of Spring*; among his students was Marin Alsop. Other pupils were less talented so the theatre of embarrassment was never far away. The old maestro saw himself as a Socratic figure, surrounded by handsome youngsters with whom he could take supper and go skinny-dipping at sunset. The north German *Schloss* at Salzau was undoubtedly a magical setting for his Greek idylls.

The year before he died, 1989, I taped a long interview with LB entirely about his childhood. Optimistically I had intended in the same BBC studio session to survey his compositions – a dozen scores were displayed on the table – but he kept coming back to his formative years and in particular to the life-changing experience when he was ten of touching a piano keyboard for the first time. His Aunt Clara had bequeathed to the Bernstein family her upright piano when she moved from Boston to Brooklyn. Our studio time ran out before I could explore the mystery of how he turned himself in the space of only a few years from a clever schoolboy into a thoroughly professional composer. It was a subject we never broached. Those last Bernstein tapes were still on the 'work in progress' shelf when he died, although excerpts from the raw interview (directed by Peter Maniura) turn up all the time in Bernstein compilations, starting with the obituary Peter and I hastily put together for *Omnibus* after LB's death in October 1990.

Bernstein grew up in Boston and learnt his conducting trade at the Boston Symphony's summer home in Tanglewood, to which he returned every year to give a fortnight of coaching. In 1988 the Boston Symphony hired me to plan and produce a $3 million festival to celebrate LB's seventieth birthday (August 25th) with four days of concerts and jollifications – we called it the Bernstein Seventieth Birthday Bash. Co-chairs of the fundraising committee were A-list New York socialites Kitty Carlisle Hart and Ann Getty; the celebration birthday picnic proved to be the party of the season. So Christina and I enjoyed another American summer, this time at Tanglewood itself in the beautiful Berkshire Hills, an area roughly a hundred miles north of New York and west of Boston. The rolling country around Lenox and Great Barrington offers the loveliest conjunction of nature and man in the whole of the North American continent.

I knew Tanglewood's music centre quite well: I first worked there in 1974, taping Tchaikovsky's Fifth Symphony in a performance conducted by LB to mark the centenary of his inspirational teacher Serge Koussevitzky. At Tanglewood in 1988 life was easier than at the Hollywood Bowl; there was no Ernest Fleischmann figure to hassle me: I was firmly in charge and greatly supported by the Boston Symphony's team, led by Dan Gustin and Costa Pilavachi.

My Bernstein biography gives a reasonable flavour of the lavishly funded 'birthday bash' so I will mention here only Slava Rostropovich's whirlwind participation: he left Sicily for London early in the morning, flew the Atlantic by Concorde and arrived at Tanglewood in mid-afternoon, in time to rehearse

With LB at Tanglewood, 1974. He loved being surrounded by young people.

Tanglewood's Bernstein Seventieth Birthday Bash, 1988.
Three generations: LB with his daughter Jamie and mother Jenny.

Strauss's *Don Quixote*, chosen because LB had conducted it in his first concert with the New York Philharmonic back in 1943.

My most satisfying moment, apart from seeing Lenny hug his mother, was the performance of his *Mass* given by students from Bloomington, Indiana. They moved into the Music Shed (Tanglewood's concert space, designed by Eliel Saarinen) with an efficiency similar to that of the Swedes transporting Drottningholm to the Barbican, and their *Mass* performance was very impressive, indeed a knockout.

A month after the 'bash' LB and I were in Glasgow watching Scottish Opera's terrific new production of *Candide* conducted by John Mauceri and directed by Jonathan Miller supported by his fellow satirist John Wells. Wells knew his Voltaire and had craftily reinstated scenes cut from the original 1956 score of the musical. As usual I wrote my camera script from a video of the dress rehearsal but there was a problem: because of a faulty recorder there was absolutely no sound on the tape. I discovered I was a competent lip-reader and since I knew the music tolerably well all was not lost. It was in fact a delightful

Relief all round. Mstislav Rostropovich jets in on time for his afternoon rehearsal with conductor Seiji Ozawa.

Left to right: John Wells, John Mauceri, LB and Jonathan Miller in Glasgow
for the dress rehearsal of Scottish Opera's 1988 production of *Candide*.

show and having loved *Candide* since the day the London cast came to the *Monitor* studio in 1959 to perform the opening number I was on a 'high' to be involved in this landmark production. At the gala opening in Glasgow LB sat next to the Duchess of Gloucester, Scottish Opera's royal patron, and appeared to enjoy himself hugely: *Candide* was a work whose form had given him headaches for over thirty years and at last it all seemed to be working well. After the show he went backstage to congratulate the cast. 'I loved it', he began. 'Dr Jonathan loved it. Even the fucking duchess loved it.' I included this judgment, discreetly edited, in the closing credits of the television relay which, alas, has never been available as a DVD or sold overseas – apparently for no better reason than that Lenny's manager Harry Kraut took a dislike to the appearance of Marilyn Hill Smith, the vivacious Ulster soprano singing Cunegonde. I loved Harry but this ban was unforgivable. Of all my Bernstein productions (over two hundred in total) this is the one I most regret *not* being able to share with my audiences (although a video has recently been made available on YouTube).

* * *

The last thirteen months of Bernstein's life were intense, dramatic, joyful and at the end deeply saddening: I was involved in many of his musical projects. They began in Warsaw with an international concert on September 1st 1989 marking the fiftieth anniversary of the outbreak of the Second World War. LB shared the conducting with Berlin-born Lukas Foss and two Poles, Krzysztof Penderecki and Antoni Wit. Earlier in the summer I had had the devil's own job making my way to Warsaw for a planning meeting at the opera house. Communism was collapsing and Eastern Europe was in a ferment. Arriving in Berlin, I discovered the ticket I had pre-booked was for a train starting at the Zoo Station in West Berlin which was run by the East German Railway and guarded by East German security. Brandishing my booking receipt (from Thomas Cook, no less) I managed – with the help of a handful of Deutschmarks – to talk the guards at the checkpoint into letting me through to the ticket office to collect my pre-paid ticket. I then found my way up to a station platform crowded with African students carrying computers in cardboard boxes; when the Warsaw train finally arrived it proved to be bound for Moscow, stopping in Warsaw only to pick up new passengers, not to let anybody off. I was close to despair at this disastrous news but then found a sympathetic German train official who looked old enough to remember the war. He heard the English in my clumsy German plea for help and pricked up his ears. 'You British?' I nodded confirmation. 'Eighth Army, General Montgomery,' he said, bewilderingly. 'I like England. Bitte, warte! Wait here.' Five minutes later he was back. Follow me, he ordered. We walked past a dozen carriages crammed with African students bound for Moscow University and arrived at a sleeping car attached to the back of the express. He rapped on a curtained window. A *baboushka* opened the train door and ushered me into a first-class solo compartment – which I had certainly not booked with Thomas Cook. I had a good night's undisturbed sleep, delicious morning tea from a samovar and later in the morning a productive meeting in Warsaw with my friend Peter Pietkiewicz from Polish Television whom I knew from my EBU working party.

The Poles assembled a strong cast to mark the anniversary. Liv Ullman narrated Schoenberg's frightening melodrama *A Survivor from Warsaw*. Her grandfather, not a Jew, died at Dachau after imprisonment for helping Jews in Norway. Krzysztof Penderecki conducted movements from his *Requiem*. They included a haunting soprano solo sung by Barbara Hendricks – this was the 'Agnus Dei'. LB led the orchestra in two works that uphold the human spirit: Beethoven's third *Leonora* overture and his own *Chichester Psalms*. The concert was narrated by a Polish-American holocaust survivor named Samuel

Pisar who recounted key moments in his early life – he survived Auschwitz but his parents were murdered by the Nazis – interwoven with wartime archive film tellingly edited by Peter Maniura, head of the BBC production team on the project. He also has Polish blood. During the production Peter saved my bacon after I had failed to coax a coherent statement from LB with which to begin the programme for English-speaking viewers. Peter took LB away to a quiet corner lit only by a candle; the prepared script on which I had worked was jettisoned and LB spoke directly into the camera. Thanks to Peter's calm direction and LB's sense of occasion, the programme was launched with quiet eloquence. Equally moving was the ending, the closing page of LB's *Chichester Psalms*: three boys shared the top soprano line of the sweet G major cadence, with its perfect message from the psalmist for a time of hope:

> Behold how good and how pleasant it is
> For brethren to dwell together in unity.

Three months later the Berlin Wall had become a horror of the past and East and West Germany were close to reunification. Brethren dwelling together in unity: that was Friedrich Schiller's dream, and it was becoming a reality for LB. He flew from Warsaw to Vienna for his annual concerts with the Vienna Philharmonic. I joined him there to direct films of the last three Beethoven piano concertos. Krystian Zimerman was the pianist, reaffirming his special relationship with LB. The cycle had to be completed after LB's death; Krystian conducted the first and second concertos from the keyboard. Physically LB seemed in good shape – he always enjoyed his Viennese lifestyle – but by mid-December, when he came to London to conduct a concert version of *Candide*, he was fighting off influenza; he dubbed it the 'royal' flu because everybody in town from members of the House of Windsor downwards was succumbing to the dreaded bug. The LSO's grand *Candide* project involved two public concerts of the satirical operetta at the Barbican (which I staged, as well as directing the telecast) followed by recording sessions at the famous Abbey Road studios to make a CD. Of the two versions of *Candide* which LB then conducted, I would unreservedly recommend the DVD of the 'live' concert. LB is very visibly enjoying himself hugely at the helm: his oldest friend Adolph Green croaked his way through the singing role of Dr Pangloss but narrated the evening with immense charm and humour. Backstage drama came late in the day when Candide (Jerry Hadley) and Cunegonde (June Anderson) both rang in seriously sick the morning after the first concert performance. Harry Kraut and the LSO office sent up distress calls and the music business rallied round: the feisty American soprano Constance Hauman was already in London to audition for LB; she got the nod and proved to be a great trouper, bringing down the house with 'Glitter and be Gay'. The only Candide on the European horizon was also American, the tenor Donald George, but he was working in Berlin and had only performed the role on stage in German. LB's former assistant Charlie Harmon, now his music editor (he had spent the previous six months preparing the performing edition of *Candide*), met the tenor at Gatwick Airport and took him through the part line by line during the nail-biting ninety-minute drive to the Barbican, where they did not arrive until 7.20 p.m. There was no chance of an orchestral rehearsal: just a quick meeting with LB in the green room and on stage he went. And there was only one tiny flaw in his entire performance: when Dr Pangloss insists that 'all's for the best in the best of all possible worlds', Candide has to challenge his optimism: 'But what about war?' On Donald George's lips the question came out as 'What about *Krieg*?' In every other respect his contribution was heroically accurate.

By the time the CD was taped the royal flu had been vanquished but nothing can match the joy of *watching* the DVD for LB's hip-swaying body language in 'I am so easily assimilated', the Old Lady's Tango (Christa Ludwig, dazzling) or the *chutzpah* with which LB interrupts Adolph Green's narration to throw light on the birth of an especially ghastly *Candide* rhyme dreamed up by his wife Felicia. The Old Lady was born, claims the libretto, in Rovno Gubernya in what was then Poland and is now Ukraine (it was the actual birthplace of Bernstein's father, Sam). But what could possibly rhyme, LB asked, with Rovno Gubernya? Felicia came up with:

> Me muero, me sale una hernia
> [I'm dying; I'm growing a hernia]
> A long way from Rovno Gubernya.

The audience loved this backstage confidence.

The autumn of 1989 was the most convulsive in Central Europe since the end of the war. Restrictions on East Germans crossing over to the West were lifted on November 9th. It was the beginning of the end for the Berlin Wall. LB's pianist friend Justus Franz was in charge of music at Bavarian Television in Munich. He proposed that LB should conduct a celebration on Christmas Day morning which would be televised around the world from the Schauspielhaus in former East Berlin. Tactfully nobody commented on the incongruity of bringing a Bavarian orchestra to Berlin, a city with a well-known orchestra of its own.

'I'm Spanish. I'm suddenly Spanish. I am so easily assimilated.' Christa Ludwig singing the Old Lady in the LSO's Barbican production of *Candide*, London, 1989.

Instead much was made of the international nature of the event: the Munich-based Orchestra of Bavarian Radio was expanded to include high-ranking musicians from the Kirov, the New York Philharmonic, the London Symphony and the Orchestre de Paris, representing the four nations who had occupied Berlin since 1945. Choirs from Berlin and Munich combined forces and the soprano line was reinforced by children from behind the disappearing Iron Curtain, the Kinderchor of the Dresden Philharmonie. Among the soloists only the tenor Klaus König was *echt* German: the American soprano June Anderson switched effortlessly from Voltaire to Schiller to lead the vocal quartet; the gutsy mezzo Sarah Walker carried the flag for Britain; and Jan-Hendrik Rootering, who had a Dutch father but was trained in Germany, was the stentorian bass. LB's task was to mould this manifestation of international goodwill into a genuine musical force; my job was to capture the spirit of the day in images that on Christmas morning were to be transmitted around the world. I also recorded the introduction at the start of the satellite relay. 'The Wall is down',

451

I announced portentously. But I could be forgiven a degree of emotion – everybody in Berlin was lifted up by the mood of euphoria. 'And to mark the occasion', I went on, broadcasting round the world, 'Leonard Bernstein has felt empowered – for this one occasion only – to make a change to Friedrich Schiller's poem. Instead of the word "Freude", as in An die Freude, the Ode to Joy, the choir will sing "Freiheit", freedom.' DG, the German record company, later marketed the DVD and CD as *The Berlin Freedom Concert*.

They were history-making days. On our first evening in the city Christina and I were awoken by the sound of shouting; our hotel was close to the Wall and in the middle of the night excited Berliners were starting to knock it

The Berlin Freedom Concert, 1989. Left to right: June Anderson, Sarah Walker, Klaus König and Jan-Hendrik Rootering, with children from the Kinderchor of the Dresden Philharmonie conducted by LB at the Schauspielhaus, Berlin.

down. Next day we walked through the linden trees of the boulevard that bears their name, the Unter den Linden, and joined the ecstatic crowds at the Brandenburg Gate. After the splendid concert on Christmas Day morning, LB held court backstage surrounded by young men. Eight of them were said to have flown in from Cologne and slept on the floor in his hotel suite. When we bade him farewell he looked drained, but there was no denying that he had achieved something significant on the world stage, a demonstration of support that outstripped even his flying visit to Berlin with the New York Philharmonic at the height of the Berlin Blockade back in 1961. I was elated to have shared this historic moment in his endgame.

Of course, the euphoria did not last long. LB was still exhausted the following month when Christina and I met him on holiday at his favourite resort, Key West at the southernmost tip of Florida. He had wintered there almost fifty years previously, when he was in search of relief from hay fever; he had listened to Cuban music on the radio, he told me, including the 'Conch' tune that became 'I like to be in America' in *West Side Story*. I was in Key West with my dear friend John Evans, LB's devoted sound producer, to play him the edited version of the Barbican *Candide*. He didn't particularly care about the pictures in any of my films and videos but in this *Candide* performance a misplaced quaver in what was otherwise the master take of the captain's music at the end of Act 1 gave us endless trouble. There is usually a solution to that kind of technical problem and John Evans had found it, but in Key West LB was a sorry sight for other reasons: he was bedevilled by insomnia and would spend the short winter days trying to catch up on lost sleep. Work sessions would be held at the cocktail hour, a frustrating experience for John Wells, who had gamely volunteered to help LB to create a libretto for the opera he was determined to compose (but never did) about the Holocaust.

It was a relief to return to Vienna at the end of February 1990 for LB's second filming session of the season. For the Unitel team the repertoire was something completely different: the unfinished Ninth Symphony by Anton Bruckner. LB had previously recorded the symphony in New York (in 1969) but this was the only Bruckner he ever tackled on film and he had no plans to start a cycle. I suspect the choice was part of his endgame: it is a deeply contemplative work, dedicated to 'the Dear Lord'. Perhaps also it was LB's gesture towards the late Herbert von Karajan, an undisputed Bruckner interpreter. The rehearsals and filming passed without a hitch and to keep the mood sweet Austrian Television arranged a hi-fi preview screening of our Barbican *Candide*. It was fun to watch with a discerning audience of several dozen and the screening went down well with Lenny himself, much to my relief. In fact, LB was on good form all week. One evening I invited him and his assistant Mark Stringer to supper at the Sacher Hotel's cosy Red Bar. He was touched by the gesture: normally Harry Kraut would take care of all his entertainment. The talk was calm and affectionate: Mark was no world-beater as a conductor but he went on to become one of the world's leading teachers of the conducting art. A few days later, to celebrate Christina's birthday, we laid on a party in the basement of our local restaurant, the Müllerbeisl. Tommy Gayda brought in a wind-up 78 rpm gramophone and a pile of 1930s show tunes, among them the *Carioca* rumba and *Tea for Two* plus, at Harry Kraut's request, *The Varsity Drag*. Lenny was genuinely happy and relaxed. I learnt afterwards from his assistant Craig Urquhart that he had spent most of the day concocting an acrostic birthday sonnet for Christina, whom he often called Chrissie, which was, conveniently, an eight-letter word to precede the six letters of Burton. I reproduce it here:

> Carissima Chrissie: here's a sonnet
> Halfly rhyming, tetrametric,
> Roughly hewn, no gems upon it
> I submit a loving attempt:
> Short as I am in time, erratic,
> Short of poetic breath (asthmatic)
> Ich wunsch' dir wohl und ganz von Herzen
> Every joy, niente Schmerzen.
>
> Be happy in your birthday cheer –
> Until at least the one next year.
> Repeat for years and years thereafter
> The miracle of inner laughter.
> Oh yes, one other little thing:
> No more Swedish blues: it's Spring!

A month later, in April 1990, LB conducted Mozart's C minor Mass in the basilica of Waldsassen, a tiny North Bavarian village close to the Czech frontier. He looked haggard and his eyes gleamed unnaturally bright, almost feverish, but still I had no intuition of the illness that was soon to strike him down. When we met again at the Prague Spring Festival in June the atmosphere had totally changed: I did not know it then but in the intervening months, back in New York, LB had been receiving radiation treatment for cancer. He recovered and in Prague was well enough to pay a formal call on

Christina and LB at the Müllerbeisl in Vienna, 1990.

LB after the closing bars of Beethoven's Ninth Symphony in Prague, 1990.

President Havel, but his hotel suite was out of bounds and a sinister line of oxygen canisters, stacked outside in the corridor, told their own story.

He conducted the Czech Philharmonic Orchestra and Choir in Beethoven's Ninth. The television process was a treat for me personally because my interpreter was Inka Vostresova, the Inka with whom I had been a fellow pupil at Long Dene in 1943, my first girlfriend. After the war she had returned to Prague, risen to become artistic director of the national folk dance company and later worked for the Czech Foreign Office as an interpreter. We had a joyous reunion and my instructions were conveyed perfectly to the camera crew. Once again LB changed the word 'Freude' to 'Freiheit' – this time as a salute to the Czech people and their new president, who had seen them through the velvet revolution and was in the midst of the first democratic elections since the 1940s. Lucia Popp led the soloists in a performance so intense that for the closing pages I abandoned my camera script and became a reporter, concentrating on her marvellously expressive face. After the final chord LB stood stock-still on the rostrum for thirty seconds, totally drained, ignoring the ecstatic applause led from his box by Václav Havel himself. I kept my camera trained on LB. I suddenly had the insight that under the pressure of conducting Beethoven's stirring music he hoped he would collapse and die on the spot – the perfect way to go.

This concert proved to be my last 'take' on Leonard Bernstein: after that Prague concert Christina and I never saw him again.

But Bernstein's endgame was not yet over. In the ensuing three months he exchanged serious illness for intense music-making not once but twice. In July he flew to Japan to inaugurate a new festival at Sapporo. He rehearsed a new youth orchestra in Schumann's Second Symphony, but illness forced him to fly home after only a few days. In August he began his annual teaching fortnight at Tanglewood, conducting Beethoven's Seventh and Britten's *Sea Interludes* in the Music Shed, but then he had to pull out of a planned tour of Europe with the student orchestra and soon took to his bed at the Dakota. In London I remained in denial about the seriousness of his illness and was shocked when early in October Harry Kraut sent me advance news of the press statement announcing his retirement from conducting. I then arranged to fly over to New York: perhaps he would be well enough, I thought, to complete the programme he had begun in 1989 about his childhood. But only a week later the phone rang at home in the middle of the night. Leonard Bernstein was dead.

PART FIVE

Changing Course,
1990–2001

CHAPTER 22

A WRITER IN NEW YORK, 1990-1994

Outside the Dakota Building, New York.

THE DAYS AFTER Lenny's death were desperate, so crowded that I had no time to grieve. Monday, the first day, was full of television interviews in London and transatlantic phone calls. On Tuesday I caught the early morning Concorde to New York and at 10.40 a.m. was walking up Central Park West with Christina to the Dakota Building on 72nd Street. Christina had arrived the previous evening and was staying, as usual, at the Mayflower Hotel. The funeral began in the Bernstein apartment: my account forms the prologue to the biography I was to spend the next three years writing. Later, out at the Green-Wood Cemetery in Brooklyn, we heard the Kaddish again and threw earth into Bernstein's coffin. He was buried next to Felicia; his score of Mahler's Fifth Symphony was placed in the coffin with him. That afternoon our hotel suite was turned into a studio and we videotaped appreciations from many friends, among them the composer Oliver Knussen, who had been receiving encouragement from Lenny since the 1960s, when his father led the double bass section of the LSO; other tributes came from the choreographer and closest creative collaborator Jerome Robbins; and from his beloved lyric-writing friends Betty Comden and Adolph Green.

That night I flew back to London with the interview tapes and over the next two days Peter Maniura and I prepared the hour-long *Omnibus* tribute televised by BBC1.

Harry Kraut asked me to produce the New York Philharmonic's tribute concert to be held a month later in Carnegie Hall. The date was November 14th, forty-three years to the day since Bernstein had made his unexpected début with the NY Phil in the very same hall. No recording or video was made of the occasion so only the 2,000 people who were present can share the memories: supreme among them for me was that of Christa Ludwig singing through her tears Mahler's infinitely moving 'Ich bin der Welt abhanden gekommen' ('I am lost to the world') from his Rückert songs. Near the end of the morning the orchestra, led that day by Rainer Küchl of the Vienna Philharmonic, was

Jerome Robbins
and Bernstein's
son Alexander.

Betty Comden and
Adolph Green.

scheduled to play the *Candide* overture. The players had run the piece through at rehearsal the previous day under Michael Tilson Thomas. Before it began there was an intense silence in the hall as if the orchestra was awaiting its conductor (though none was named in the programme). A door opened behind the second violins: a maestro was surely about to enter – but nobody came in; the door closed as mysteriously as it had opened. On its own the orchestra delivered a scintillating performance of the overture. I am not a fanciful person but I would happily swear that the curious door-opening incident was the moment when the spirit of Leonard Bernstein slipped into Carnegie Hall.

After experiencing weeks of intense emotion while preparing the Bernstein tribute I resumed the life of a freelance director, taping the visit to Budapest of Georg Solti and the Chicago Symphony Orchestra. It was a joy to be working again with Solti and with András Schiff, who played Bartók's Third Piano Concerto with deep emotion. But I knew that at this point in my life (I was close on sixty) it was time to do something different. Since in the previous few years I had made five documentaries about various aspects of his life, it seemed only natural that now he was dead I should want to write Leonard Bernstein's biography. I was equally certain that I was the best qualified person in the world to undertake this task. I let this immodest ambition be known in

461

New York and quickly had the crucial support of Harry Kraut and of Robbie Lantz, Bernstein's literary agent, who had written me a very warm appreciation of my production of the Barbican *Candide* when it came out that winter as a DVD. Ambition is one thing but it is quite another to convince a hard-nosed American publisher that a British television director would be the best choice to write one of the most eagerly awaited biographies of the decade. To make things harder for myself I stipulated that I would only do the job if I had total freedom editorially and the exclusive run of the Bernstein archive until after publication.

Reader, I got the job. I spent four months preparing my 100-page proposal. With it Robbie Lantz's business partner Joy Harris swiftly found me a distinguished publisher, Stephen Rubin, who was then working for Doubleday. For a novice biographer the advance Joy and Robbie secured for me was astronomical – but it had to be, since if I was to be a full-time writer I would have to give up all other ways of earning a living and settle in New York, where most of the research would be carried out. For the British edition of the biography Robbie Lantz's London partner Abner Stein, the most genial of exiled Americans, soon had me signed up with Faber and Faber: I could not have asked for two more distinguished publishers than Faber and Doubleday – but now I had to write the book. And that meant establishing a new home. (Our children were both away at university.) We decided to move to New York, and for our first weeks in Manhattan we sub-let a tiny flat from our new friend Constance Hauman, the soprano who had so valiantly deputised for June Anderson at the second *Candide* performance at the Barbican. Her music room boasted a grand piano that had belonged to the pianist André Watts, a protégé of LB's, and looked out over a tiny triangular park situated at the intersection of Broadway and Columbus Avenue. It was named Richard Tucker Square, complete with a bronze bust of the great tenor. I took that as a good omen because Tucker was one of the stars in the *Monitor* film I had made with Rudolf Bing at the old Metropolitan Opera almost thirty years previously. Across the road from Constance's apartment was the Lincoln Center, home of the Met and also of the New York Philharmonic and its archive, where I was to spend many fruitful days researching concert reviews and official correspondence from Bernstein's years as the Philharmonic's music director. 60 West 66th Street was our choice for an apartment. For us it was an ideal location: six blocks south was the Amberson office, where Harry Kraut ran the Bernstein business. Six blocks north was the Dakota, where the Bernstein family had lived since 1965. So we rented an unfurnished one-bed apartment on the thirty-second floor of this terribly ordinary building: our windows looked out at nothing more inspiring than the offices of ABC Television, but just a block away was Central Park, which we loved. I took to running up to the reservoir most mornings before breakfast, a deeply enjoyable thirty-minute jog (it was longer if one went round the reservoir twice, as one was tempted to do on sunny mornings). I even joined the New York Road Runners club and still have a T-shirt to prove that I entered their annual Sheraton Bagel Run which was three miles up to the top of the park – on the edge of Harlem – and then back again to finish near the Tavern on the Green.

I could not have adapted to this life without Christina's total support. From the local Ikea she equipped a kitchen and bought the essential furniture. Crucially for my research, she spent many days with me at the archive which Karen Bernstein (LB's niece) had established in a warehouse on 20th Street opposite Andy Warhol's enormous archive, close to the Hudson River. Christina photocopied all the important letters and selected the vivid photographs which illustrate my LB biography, nearly two hundred of them.

Our routine was monastic in its simplicity. After my run I would buy coffee at the delicatessen downstairs, two low-cal blueberry muffins and the *New York Times*. Then it was on with our simple life as very mature postgraduate

Second from the front. Striding out in the annual
Sheraton Bagel Run in Central Park, NYC.

With LB's niece Karen Bernstein, who created the Bernstein Archive, now at the Library of Congress.

researchers. Over the next few months Karen Bernstein and I interviewed scores of witnesses, she for a substantial oral history which is now in the Library of Congress, I for first-hand material to put flesh and blood on my original outline of the biography.

Bernstein's formidable assistant Helen Coates had been an inveterate hoarder and there were mountains of documents to wade through, most notably the letters exchanged between LB, his family, his teachers, fellow musicians and friends (the letters to and from Aaron Copland are worth a book on their own). We travelled to Boston where LB grew up and where his mother still lived. One weekend Christina and I flew down to Cuernavaca in Mexico, where in 1946 LB first encountered the writer Martha Gellhorn and five years later spent three honeymoon months writing the libretto for and composing his one-act opera *Trouble in Tahiti*.

After about six months of note-taking, calendar-reconstructing and perusal of 120 scrapbooks, not to mention literally scores of those wonderful letters, I perceived that researching the biography of a major figure such as LB was a never-ending task. Paradoxically, through my reading and my interviewing, LB's early days had come into sharper focus than the final two decades of his life, though the latter was the period when our paths had been interlocked for several weeks at a time every year. One morning I decided it was time to start writing. I began at the beginning and a year and a half later I reached

464

the end – for the first time. Stubbornly old-fashioned, I had no computer skills whatsoever: every word was handwritten in ink on A4 paper. I felt a new kind of satisfaction, however, different from anything in my television life, when the typed version of each chapter was delivered a few days later, my manuscript scrupulously transcribed by Kelly Briney (a typist recruited for me by Harry Kraut) with every page neat and virginal – until the inevitable bout of revisions and rewrites. It was very late in the day, for example, when a vital change was thrust upon me: Shirley Bernstein, LB's sister, suddenly gave me permission to include a revelatory letter from her brother, sent from Israel, announcing his decision to marry Felicia Montealegre. An entire chapter had to be restructured as a consequence. Even more devastating were the wholesale cuts imposed on my original draft by Doubleday's senior editor Roger Scholl. At just over 600 pages the biography is still long, its weight making it difficult to read except in bed, but Roger chopped out half as much again from the original draft. I understood the need for brevity: Sir Arthur Quiller-Couch's oft-invoked injunction to 'murder your darlings' was my watchword for a year. But it was the work of months to bandage the wounds inflicted on my text (that is how I saw it) and to ensure that there were no unexplained gaps in the narrative.

I would not have wanted to miss the experience of living in New York for three years. We were made welcome by LB's family and friends. We went to parties with Adolph and Phyllis Green; I played indoor tennis with LB's elder daughter Jamie and piano duets with Lukas Foss, who lived with his painter wife Cornelia in a handsome apartment on Fifth Avenue up in the 90s. Our children came over for holidays. In 1992 we rented a beach house on Water Island, a quiet hamlet of sixty homes just north of the allegedly riotous Fire Island, although the gay life we observed was reassuringly sedate. We flew to and from Manhattan in a little flying boat; this was a great adventure for my daughter Clare when she and her husband joined us with their young son Tom. He liked running up and down the beach shouting, 'Watch this, Grandpa Humph'. I did my best to hush him up: in this sophisticated corner of Manhattan-on-Sea I was less than totally happy at being identified as a grandfather.

Living in New York I could still direct the annual television concert from the United Nations General Assembly, something I had done every year since 1971. The 1971 assignment had originally come my way through Ernest Fleischmann. A South African friend of his who ran the media department at the UN, George Movshon, was looking for a director to cover what proved

The author with the composer Lukas Foss in his Fifth Avenue apartment.
Foss had known LB since their student days at Tanglewood and the Curtis Institute.

to be the most famous classical concert ever given in the hall. Pablo Casals, aged ninety-four, was to appear in public for the first time in nearly forty years – he had forsworn public performances in the wake of the establishment of General Franco's oppressive regime in Spain. A passionate humanist, he had composed, like fellow cellist Paul Tortelier before him, a UN Hymn – his to a poem by W.H. Auden.

I was taken to the suburban house in Queen's where Casals was staying and could not believe that this frail old man would ever be strong enough to conduct an orchestra as was planned for the following day. I had reckoned without the presence of his young Puerto Rican wife Marta – they had married fourteen years earlier when she was twenty and he was eighty. At next morning's rehearsal in the imposing General Assembly hall, Casals was conducting his new hymn when he stumbled and collapsed. Pandemonium ensued. Dozens of choristers, his wife included, surrounded him and the officials were distraught: would the concert have to be cancelled? Marta sent a message: he will soon be okay, she said, just give him some air. A cameraman found me a shot of a piano keyboard glimpsed through the crowd of well-wishers surrounding the ailing maestro. The sound supervisor wound up the volume so that one could just recognise the music of Bach being played ever more firmly on a grand piano, to which the great cellist had retreated. It was Casals himself playing a Bach prelude, as he did every morning (Marta told me) before breakfast. Life was being restored by the administration of a dose of JSB.

The concert in the evening was a huge success, culminating in the Secretary-General, U Thant, presenting the exiled Spaniard with the UN peace prize and Casals playing to a spellbound audience of diplomats and music lovers his signature work, *The Song of the Birds*. The venerable Catalan musician created a moment of grand emotion.

That was my first UN concert, in October 1971, and I had found it a thrilling experience every subsequent year to be back working in these famous surroundings, quickly meshing in with the UN's television crew, peeping in at meetings of the Security Council and, most fun of all, eating in the staff restaurant on adjacent tables to diplomats from exotic parts of the world – I had the irreverent thought that the UN's café was a super-version of the

Left to right: UN Secretary-General U Thant, a frail Pablo Casals and violinist Alexander Schneider at the United Nations Day concert, 1971.

467

multilingual canteen at Bush House, which had the best menus of any BBC eating place; but instead of the windowless basement at the Aldwych, UN staff members could enjoy the magnificent view over the East River.

I directed my last UN Day concert in 1993. Kurt Masur conducted the Leipzig Gewandhaus Orchestra. Masur was then also in charge of the New York Philharmonic and celebrated as the unlikely hero who had defied the communists at the beginning of the collapse of the Soviet Union. The UN always found top orchestras for their concerts: I vividly recall Yehudi Menuhin playing the Bach Double Concerto with one of his Chinese pupils and Joan Sutherland celebrating Australia's bicentenary in 1988 with of all things 'Sempre libera' from *La Traviata*, hardly the most tactful choice for a diva in her sixties. (I could swear she wore the same green ball dress at her Covent Garden farewell appearance a couple of years later, again with her husband, the excellent Richard Bonynge, conducting. That televised *Fledermaus* in 1990 was another night to remember, if only for the Act 2 party at which Dame Joan sang with Luciano Pavarotti and Marilyn Horne as her supporting act.)

Kurt Masur conducting the United Nations Day concert, 1993, with violinist Sarah Chang playing the Mendelssohn Violin Concerto.

At Leonard Bernstein
Place on Broadway.

A few weeks before the UN Day concert, on August 25th 1993, there was much pomp and palaver outside our building when the city of New York celebrated what would have been LB's seventy-fifth birthday.

The stretch of 65th Street adjacent to the Lincoln Center and Broadway was renamed Leonard Bernstein Place. Taking our cue from this happy event, Harry Kraut and I produced a one-night-only fundraising show entitled *Leonard Bernstein Place*; the venue was the Alice Tully Hall on Broadway, at the junction with 65th Street, so our show could not have been more site-specific. Furniture was borrowed from the Bernstein apartment at the Dakota (soon to be sold), so the concert hall setting had an authentic Bernstein look to it, while the cast we assembled would have graced one of the Bernsteins' celebrated Dakota parties. Jamie Bernstein was on hand to host the occasion and Lauren Bacall read the vivid and touching letters exchanged between Lenny and his wife Felicia during the Washington try-outs for *West Side Story*; Isaac Stern

469

and Lukas Foss led the choruses of Jets and Sharks in the famous 'Tonight' quintet; Michael Tilson Thomas and Christoph Eschenbach played piano duets; Mischa Maisky contributed a meltingly beautiful cello arrangement of LB's curiously neglected song 'Dream with Me'. Betty Comden and Adolph Green sat and sang on one of the Dakota sofas; a good time was had by all – but disappointingly the show went out on cable television and has not been sighted since. As a footnote I should add that I put the event together under the aegis of the Lincoln Center's producer John Goberman, who ran *Live from Lincoln Center* for thirty years. John's father, Max Goberman, was very close to LB in his early days; he conducted the world première of *On the Town* in 1944 and of *West Side Story* in 1957. Max was a feisty character who died young; to have his son, a pipe-smoking ex-cellist famous for his unflappability, sitting in the back of the television truck was like being supervised by a member of the Bernstein family circle.

Thanks to Jamie Bernstein's enthusiastic introduction, Christina and I became supporters of NYFOS, the New York Festival of Song, a concert-giving society not dissimilar to the Songmakers' Almanac in the UK. It was run by two remarkable musicians, Steven Blier and Michael Barrett. Blier was already suffering from muscular dystrophy and walked with a cane: nowadays

Stephen Blier (left), the inspirational director of the New York Festival of Song, with keen supporter Jamie Bernstein (right).

he is confined to a wheelchair but his piano playing remains as beautiful as ever (the best I have ever heard for Broadway song accompaniments) and he coaches eager young art-song singers morning, noon and night. I already knew Michael Barrett from his sterling work as LB's conducting assistant in the 1980s: you can catch him playing jazz piano in the Vienna Philharmonic's performance of *Prelude, Fugue and Riffs*. As a temporary American resident I was caught up in his work as an impresario: in September 1993 Christina and I flew out to Utah to be part of Michael's second season as director of a chamber music festival in the high desert township of Moab, which is four hours' drive south of Salt Lake City and set among the spectacular rock formations that abound in the Arches National Park.

I participated in a wild chamber piece for violin, cello and piano by a clever young American composer named Aaron Jay Kernis. (Michael specialised in promoting new music, as he still does.) Kernis's inspiration came from the Italian futurist poet and writer Filippo Tommaso Marinetti, who in 1930 wrote a manifesto about modern cooking, linking it in an arcane way with both fascism and futurism. The work's title tells it all: *Le Quattro Stagioni dalla Cucina Futurismo* (The Four Seasons of Futurist Cuisine). As the narrator I was first among equals in the ensemble and after three years before the mast as a self-effacing, solitary biographer I enjoyed myself hugely declaiming this pungent ABC mélange of the absurd, the banal and the culinary. We performed in a moonscape setting outside Moab, where one of the impressive geodesic domes designed by the visionary architect Buckminster Fuller had been erected for the festival; acoustically the space was dead as a doornail but visually it provided a mind-blowing experience.

A few days later, in stark contrast, I narrated Poulenc's enchanting *Babar the Elephant* at a free concert in Old City Park. It was a sunny afternoon, Moab families were out in force and Michael Barrett was in top form at the piano. I myself was in seventh heaven. I have always loved the Jean de Brunhoff text of *Babar*, and on this occasion I dropped into French from time to time to create the authentic Poulenc voice-and-piano sound.

We were back in New York to experience the worst winter in decades: in the space of three months there were thirteen separate snowstorms; the worst, in mid-March, was given the title Storm of the Century. Nevertheless I had to be out and about daily for meetings about the Bernstein book now it was close to publication. Doubleday assigned to us an excellent designer, Maryanne Quinn, who accepted our unconventional choice of cover photographs: on the front was a forty-ish Lenny, baton in hand looking vulnerable as well as

471

With Michael Barrett at the Moab Music Festival.

Inside the geodesic dome, narrating *The Four Seasons of Futurist Cuisine*.

persuasive; on the back an offbeat moment at a recording playback when LB is laughing his head off. So many of the portraits on record and CD covers are triumphalist in tone but our book covers suggested a sensitive man full of fun. Maryanne came up with a handsome design which had LB's elegant signature embossed in gold across front and back covers.

I made the book itself very simple for the reader to navigate. Each of the six parts had a title; each chapter within the part had its separate title, and all were prefaced by captioned photographs and pithy quotations. In addition, there were thirty-two pages of glossy black-and-white photographs which are still fun in their own right. Finding lively images of LB was not difficult, but making the right choice and then negotiating the publishing clearances needed all Christina's taste and diplomacy.

Eventually publication day arrived. Thanks to the kindness of the Bernstein children, who still used the Dakota as their base and daily meeting ground, the launch party was held at number 23, the former Bernstein apartment. I remember the occasion only for the late entry of Shirley Bernstein. 'Lovely book,' she called out to me across the very crowded room, 'BUT SO MANY MISTAKES!' She was referring specifically to page 532, an account of her brother's death which in the first edition concludes as follows: 'then he slumped in Wagner's arms, dead'. Of course, that should have read 'Wager's arms'. I had shown my account of the death to LB's actor friend Michael Wager, who visited him every day during his final illness. He corrected me as to what exactly had transpired after Dr Cahill had administered what proved to be the final injection, and although my biography was already at the printer's I rushed a handwritten addendum to Doubleday asking them to make the necessary addition. Foolishly I did not insist on checking the revised page and unfortunately the printer decided I meant Wagner when I wrote Wager.

The error no doubt prompted a few cocktail party guffaws that summer. However, the book's critical reception on both sides of the Atlantic was extremely positive.

I was only disappointed that the *New Yorker*, where Leonard's younger brother Burton Bernstein had been a staff writer since 1960, made no mention of the book whatsoever. (I sometimes wondered whether the omission was connected in some way with the fact that it was Humphrey Burton not Burton Bernstein who had been entrusted with the biography.) In 2008, the year of what would have been LB's ninetieth birthday, the magazine's music critic Alec Ross made amends with a particularly thoughtful Bernstein profile. (Burtie Bernstein died in 2017.)

Book signing on the American publicity circuit for my Bernstein biography.

I was soon on the road again with LB – but this time on a book tour. There followed a flurry of book signings, of which I never tired. Doubleday sent me all over the USA from Denver and San Francisco to Boston and Tanglewood. In Florida I signed five hundred copies in one morning: every delegate at an international IBM conference was given the book after I lectured them about the parallels between the role of the conductor and that of a top business leader – both dependent upon leadership skills and the ability to think simultaneously about the present and the future. At the University of Texas in Austin (Christina's *alma mater*) I talked to an audience of precisely four people: apparently the date clashed with two dress rehearsals (ironically both were of Bernstein works) involving all the faculty's music and drama students. Next day in Pittsburgh there were six hundred in the audience. You lose some and you win some …

CHAPTER 23

RETURN TO EUROPE

Flying to Paris as the guest of Yehudi Menuhin. He wanted me to see
Bruno Monsaingeon's new film documentary at a special ceremony in Paris.

BY THE TIME we moved back to our London home at Oakwood Court in 1994 our children had become adults. Helena had finished her degree studies in art history and was working in a nursery school with young children while studying art therapy; she lived in a Notting Dale flat we bought with the proceeds of selling our little terrace cottage in La Garde-Freinet. Lukas had achieved a Cambridge degree in classics but was intent on a career as a music producer – he was already working in the world of pop and 'garage' rock, for which I could summon up no sympathy though I admired his determination, and still do now that he is running his own company in Los Angeles, making trailers for major movies. I had just turned sixty-three, which is close to the conventional age for 'retirement', but I had no desire to stop working (nor indeed sufficient accumulated income) so I was intrigued when Revel Guest, a friend from BBC days, offered me a job as consultant for her new venture, a production company called Covent Garden Pioneer; with Japanese support, she was challenging the National Video Corporation's sphere of interest in opera and ballet but specialising in the brand-new format of LaserDiscs.

To the casual eye these 12-inch discs resembled long-playing records but they performed like CDs and needed a special player. Revel Guest is just a few months younger than me. She had been in Current Affairs at Lime Grove in the 1960s, directing films for *Panorama*, and soon after I left for ITV she also jumped ship and became an independent, founding an international production company called Transatlantic Films. I admired her independence and got on well with her ebullient Bostonian husband Rob Albert, a lawyer. Rob's sister Joy was married to a London dentist named Lionel Bryer. Together they created the much-admired European Community Youth Orchestra. I commissioned an *Aquarius* documentary about the orchestra, shot in Aberdeen by Tony Palmer in 1972. This gave the first hint on television of the musical excitements to come from that excellent initiative, notably when Claudio Abbado was its music director. (In 2018 the European *Union* Youth Orchestra, as it had been renamed, shifted its base from London to Ferrara; it is doing its best to survive in troubled Brexitian waters.)

Back in the 1990s the LaserDisc turned out, like the U-matic cassette and the quadraphonic sound system before it, to be a superior product which simply did not catch on with ordinary families. The Japanese firm Pioneer invested in it heavily and the list of LaserDisc productions was impressive: their technical quality seemed greatly superior to VHS cassettes and they were much simpler to navigate. But the disc-players were more expensive and when the smaller, lighter and cheaper DVD system arrived in the mid-1990s the fate of the LaserDisc was sealed. Still, during my first winters back in London I had a good run with Covent Garden Pioneer – thanks mostly to our involvement with Richard Eyre's supercharged new production of *La Traviata* at the Royal Opera House.

Thanks to a tip from Georg Solti, I was at Covent Garden for the dress rehearsal of *La Traviata*. Solti's intense conducting of the Act 1 Prelude was already stunning and from the opening scene it was clear that Angela

With Angela Gheorghiu
backstage at the Royal
Opera House after the
last-minute taping of
La Traviata, 1994.

Gheorghiu, the beautiful young Romanian soprano singing Violetta, was something very special; her 'Sempre libera' created riotous applause. Two years earlier, when I was living in New York, I had missed Gheorghiu's Covent Garden débuts as Zerlina and Mimì. But so had everybody else, it seemed, except the Royal Opera's canny casting director Peter Katona. That morning, as Solti predicted, a star was being born before our eyes and ears. In the interval I phoned my successor at the BBC, Avril MacRory. 'This *Traviata* is sensational,' I told her. 'Why aren't you filming it?' 'Oh, but we are,' she replied. 'We're planning to do it at the first revival next July when (she named a famous American diva) will be singing Violetta.' I did not conceal my disappointment and although I no longer had any official clout at the BBC, my admiration of Gheorghiu did not fall on deaf ears. A posse of BBC bosses attended the production's first performance two days later (last-minute seats were found by the wily Paul Findlay, still the head of Opera) and in the interval Paul took us backstage to the holy of holies, Solti's dressing room. 'When are you coming with your cameras?' was virtually his first question, to which there was only one answer: as soon as possible. Everybody was hooked by Gheorghiu. Surely she was the most impressive young diva since Maria Callas and her gifts were admirably showcased in Richard Eyre's powerful production. After the show I took the BBC brass to the nearby Garrick Club for a late-night conference. Being modern executives, neither Dennis Marks nor controller Michael Jackson was wearing a tie: in order for them to be allowed in, the Garrick's porter had to lend them the nondescript neckwear he kept in his booth for this peculiarly British purpose.

The remaining *Traviata* performances were all in the next couple of weeks, for which *Radio Times* had already been put to bed, so if the nation was to be given the opportunity to enjoy this historic production, as we had resolved in Solti's dressing room, there was nothing for it but to rip up the existing BBC2 schedule one evening in order to go 'live' from Covent Garden. This caused quite a stir in media circles. The following Tuesday was chosen for trans-mission, leaving us precious little time to write and rehearse a script worthy of the occasion. In fact, time was so short that two directorial teams were assembled: Peter Maniura took the first and last acts; I scripted the two scenes of the second act, which suited me because I felt it was here that Gheorghiu, the consummate actress, was at her most powerful. In the first scene she reveals the nobility of Violetta's spirit when yielding to old Germont's demand that she end her affair with his son; in the second we are moved by her pride and dignity when she is humiliated by her lover Alfredo at the gambling table. Peter Maniura would be directing the overwhelming deathbed scene so it was a fair distribution of the directorial spoils, but I was deeply excited by my assignment and worked as hard as I have ever done on anything to capture on video the essence of Richard Eyre's impressive concept.

It was a special excitement to be collaborating with Richard Eyre, an assignment only once renewed (after almost a decade, in 2003), when for the only time in my life I worked on the transfer of a full-length play from the theatre to the screen. Richard Eyre had directed *Vincent in Brixton* by Nicholas Wright, a moving and unusual piece about the passionate young Van Gogh's sojourn in London, a time when he was more concerned with faith than with oil paint. When the play transferred to a West End theatre I was hired by my friend Simon Flind to televise a live performance – it was my first experience of working with actors since my filming of excerpts of plays by David Hare and Alan Ayckbourn for *Aquarius* two decades earlier. I loved it.

In the 1990s transmissions from theatres were a rarity. I wish I could have done more of this work but by the time the excellent satellite relays from the

Jochum Ten Haaf as Vincent van Gogh and Clare Higgins as his landlady in
Richard Eyre's production of *Vincent in Brixton* by Nicholas Wright.

National and the RSC began I was in my late seventies and inevitably passed
over in favour of younger colleagues with sharper eyes. Or so it seemed to
me. However, the 1990s were for me every bit as stimulating in the opera field
as were the years before I went to New York. Backtracking for a moment on
this continuous whirl of activity, my return to the UK coincided with the
reopening of Glyndebourne after its major rebuild and I was asked to direct
a live relay for Channel 4 of one of the new productions, *Eugene Onegin*. I was
intrigued to learn that the director Graham Vick had cast Elena Prokina in the
role of Tatiana. She had sung Natasha in the Kirov's wonderful *War and Peace*
which I had directed for BBC2. Playing opposite her as Onegin now was the
gifted Polish baritone Wojtek Drabowicz, equally youthful and convincing;
it is sad to recall that in 2007, when he was only forty-one, Drabowicz died
in a car crash following a heart attack. In all aspects, including the brilliant
stylised dance numbers devised by Graham's sympathetic life-partner Ron
Howell, this *Onegin* was a very fine production, the standout of the season,
some would say of the decade. Andrew Davis conducted. Channel 4 was the
transmitting station and Simon Flind had taken over from Robin Scott at
National Video Corporation so I had a new set of masters, and it was a great

479

thrill to be working again at Glyndebourne, where I had been a punter for forty years and a documentary director since 1959; the beauty and efficiency of Michael and Patty Hopkins's new opera house was like the very best icing on what was already a splendid cake.

Simon Flind was my favourite producer. He looked faintly like Ronnie Barker and was almost as funny: we hit it off from the word go. It was an added delight that he was married to George Christie's high-spirited daughter Louise and was as a consequence exceedingly well connected with the opera world. Over the next five years Channel 4, to its eternal credit, televised two Glyndebourne opera productions each summer and I was involved with half a dozen of them. After *Eugene Onegin* came Rossini's unfamiliar *Ermione* with the formidable Italian soprano Anna Caterina Antonacci in the title role. In 1996 the tough nut to crack was Vick's illuminating production of *Lulu*, with the eminently cool Christine Schäfer as the *femme fatale* and Andrew Davis in the pit making Alban Berg's twelve-tone score powerfully lyrical. In 1997 the Glyndebourne production of Puccini's *Manon Lescaut* turned out to be something of a damp squib: the choice of John Eliot Gardiner as conductor was a little odd since he was operating well out of his baroque comfort zone. Additionally, the choice of a slightly chubby soprano in the title role was a

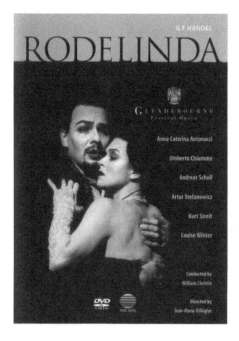

Handel's *Rodelinda* at Glyndebourne. Jean-Marie Villégier's silent movie-style production starred Anna Caterina Antonacci in the title role and Andreas Scholl as Bertarido.

questionable piece of casting since she was arguably less than charismatic on stage (and camera). But spirits were restored in 1998 with Jean-Marie Villégier's transposition of Handel's opera *Rodelinda* into a sort of art deco, black-and-white movie setting, turning into an early fascist morality tale; it worked a treat on television. One of the soloists sang a complete aria while puffing a cigarette clamped between his lips – quite a feat!

Rodelinda was my first chance to study at close quarters the inspiring art of the American conductor William Christie. I had loved the staging of his earlier Handel at Glyndebourne, *Theodora*, although I was appalled by the way the director Peter Sellars misdirected his cameras in the telecast of his own production: his speciality (or should that be vice?) was fast cutting between three or four different close-ups of the same singer during a single long-held note. Excruciating!

It turned out that 1999 was the end of the Channel 4 era in Sussex. I directed both the telecasts from that season. A mysterious gloom was created in *Pelléas et Mélisande* – this was another fine Graham Vick show, in which Debussy's hyper-sensitive music was underlined by Paul Brown's atmospheric Edwardian set. *Pelléas* was balanced that season by *Flight*, a witty new opera by Jonathan Dove, set in a weird airport departure lounge. *Flight* has never achieved DVD status despite its popularity with audiences: I treasure all the more my VHS off-air copy, even though we had a run-in with *Flight*'s enormously gifted stage director Richard Jones concerning the use of subtitles. He and the librettist April de Angelis thought it was disrespectful to the singers to put up the text as subtitles on screen of an opera sung in English. But for much of the time I could not understand what was being sung and in the end the telecast was indeed discreetly subtitled; I take the view that anything that helps comprehension is worth trying. (The surtitle battle has long since gone my way in most opera houses: even Brett Dean's operatic version of *Hamlet* was surtitled when it was premièred at Glyndebourne in 2017; the libretto text was exclusively by Shakespeare but in the opera the words did not always appear in the order you might expect if you were familiar with the play.)

With the new millennium came a change of policy at Channel 4. A new commissioning editor favoured quitting Glyndebourne as a production centre in order to make original films of such Glyndebourne operas as *The Death of Klinghoffer* and *Owen Wingrave* – a commendable decision, no doubt, given the creative role it implied for the art of television filming, but what a jolt for opera lovers deprived of their Glyndebourne 'fix'.

Those summer weeks at Glyndebourne were among the happiest of my working life. They are dead and gone decades ago so I shall try to evoke them here, for the record. They would begin for me with a few days getting to know the new production, attending rehearsals, meeting the director and eventually taping a single-camera 'snoop' of the dress rehearsal. Then came a solitary week at home scriptwriting, broken up by attendance at early performances. I knew the camera positions, so I could throw a net over the entire action, allocating camera shots to cover every bar of the action. After the scripting, in which one is playing chess with oneself on every page, come a couple of days at home with my PA Judy Chesterman, who prepares each cameraman's script from my master, and with our vision-mixer Sonia Lovett, who diligently copies all my shots and precise cutting points into her own vocal score. Then we head off down to Glyndebourne, where we start with a run-through of the 'snoop' scratch tape recording; this is attended by the cameramen, most of whom will also have been at the previous evening's performance. It is a tortuous process, stopping and starting the tape over and over again, but by the end of the day we are all familiar with the project and pulling in the same direction.

We have a full-scale production run at the next theatre performance. I review the new video next day with Judy and Sonia; we make some adjustments, occasionally switching cameras to get a better angle or taking out shots to achieve a more seamless flow. And I absorb the comments of the stage director (usually Graham Vick), who has been sent his own copy of our first recording. On the afternoon of the final recording day (the live transmission for Channel 4) we hold another review session with the camera crew, checking fine points of framing and running through scenes for which I have scripted quick shot changes. My half-brother Jonathan has been sitting in on these sessions and planning exactly when he will superimpose the subtitles. Jonathan does his own translations and has an uncanny feel both for text and timing. In the late afternoon comes the live transmission. It is preceded by a visit to the dressing rooms to wish the singers the traditional 'toi, toi, toi'. (The Italians say 'in bocca al lupo'; the Americans 'Break a leg!') Simon Flind ensures that we mesh in with the separate production team providing the introductions and live interval features which are an integral part of these Channel 4 relays.

The business of putting the show on-air has these days become a calmer process than had been my style in previous decades. In fact, I used to say very little during the transmission: nearly everything had been planned. How I miss this work in my old age!

My brilliant post production team. Left: graphics wizard Josef d'Bache Kane; and right: tape editor Steve Eveleigh.

In the truck, Sonia and Judy are voices of calm unflappability. When the live show is over, the unwinding takes time: there are countless hugs backstage and post-mortems with cameramen, all rounded off with drinks in the staff bar or a celebratory pub meal for the crew. Next day it was customary to head back to London for videotape editing sessions with the incredibly resourceful editor Steve Eveleigh and his laid-back assistant Josef d'Bache Kane in their Soho editing suite, which becomes a second home to me. Californian by background, Josef is a new member of the family. He designs all the credit sequences for the National Video Corporation.

* * *

In 1992, while I was working in New York on my Bernstein biography, the Classic FM commercial radio station opened in London. It was a national network, soon attracting an impressive weekly audience of over four million. I had met Classic's managing director Michael Bukht in 1972 when he was the very young programme controller at Capital Radio, for whom I made *Alternatives*, a weekly hour-long arts show. With LB in mind, I got in touch with Michael at Classic and successfully pitched the idea of making a documentary radio series – eventually seventeen episodes – about LB's life

483

and music. (Although I had a great LB ally and supporter in the BBC's John Evans, I knew I would never be given that much airtime at the BBC.) Michael Bukht took me on and Classic's lively young Irish producer Declan McGovern quickly brought me up to date with modern production techniques, the main difference from the BBC being that there were no studio managers: producers did it all, multitasking was the name of the game. Microphones and recording facilities were all in the same room: Declan didn't talk at me through a glass wall over a loudspeaker, he was literally on the other side of my mic, insisting that I keep my voice light and conversational, eradicating any hint of the schoolmaster I never was but sometimes resembled.

Classic FM's Bernstein shows went out on Saturdays at 5 p.m. They were totally ignored by the press but were for me a matter of considerable pride because no twentieth-century composer had ever been explored in such detail over so many months of broadcasting. The following year, 1995, when Classic FM launched a magazine, I was hired to write a regular column about anything that caught my eye or my ear; it was a pleasant chore though I confess I was chuffed when a couple of years later I was poached by the magazine's better-selling rival in the field, the *BBC Music Magazine*. Not that written journalism was ever going to displace my affection for broadcasting. Michael Bukht added to the fun I had at Classic FM by inviting me to stand in for their star host Henry Kelly. For a fortnight at a time, while Henry took a break, I did a daily three-hour stint as host of Classic FM's morning music and chat show. One of the daily routines had the station boss switching personalities. Michael Bukht became Michael Barry the Crafty Cook from the BBC's immensely popular *Food and Drink* series. Michael had become a household name in the 1980s. He was undoubtedly an imaginative cook and he was an interesting man too, who had made programmes for *Panorama* before switching to radio. He was also extremely devout. We were driving together one afternoon in south London when he suddenly stopped his car, ran to a nearby wall and started praying. After a few minutes he got back in and drove on as if nothing had happened.

I managed a couple of seasons in the unlikely role of a chat show presenter – very much helped by Jane Jones, Classic's veteran producer. But I came a cropper when talking about the performance of *Swan Lake* I had attended the previous night at Sadler's Wells. This was the historic Matthew Bourne concept of the ballet, in which the twenty-four swans of the *corps de ballet* are all danced by men: I loved it and before playing some of Tchaikovsky's music I told my listeners how beautiful the show had been in the theatre. 'And it's not just for poofters,' I continued with mounting enthusiasm; 'there's something here for everybody to enjoy.' The politically incorrect reference did not go unnoticed by the gay community. Complaints were made, the Independent Broadcasting Authority apparently rapped Classic FM over the knuckles and I certainly did no more live broadcasting on commercial radio.

In 1996 I had a new project for Classic FM, an even longer musical documentary series than the Bernstein to mark the eightieth birthday of another world figure in music – Yehudi Menuhin. I successfully pitched to produce twenty hour-long programmes with the title 'Menuhin: Master Musician' and again Declan was to be my producer. This time we had a subject who unlike LB was still very much alive and happy to collaborate. Every few weeks that winter I would collect Menuhin from his beautiful Chester Square house after yoga (his) and breakfast (mine) and drive him to the Classic FM studios in Camden Town, where he would reminisce with total frankness about any topic I introduced, for instance his virginal innocence as a twenty-year-old which led to him proposing marriage to his Australian sweetheart on the phone from an Amsterdam hotel bedroom, hiding under the bedclothes so his parents in the next room would not hear him. He spoke affectionately of his unofficial wartime flights across the Atlantic in an RAF bomber, his violin wrapped in a flying jacket; his playing for the inauguration of the United Nations in his home city, San Francisco; the parlous state of his finances following his expensive divorce – they were vivid memories engagingly retold and skilfully interwoven by Declan with striking musical passages from the innumerable concertos and sonatas to be found in Menuhin's recording catalogue, which is even larger than Bernstein's. On the documentary front, we made a radio portrait of the Menuhin School in Surrey and reported on a concert given by players from Live Music Now in a residential home for the elderly in north London, reflecting the two most important institutions created by Menuhin – they were already up and running very successfully (and still are). The final episode of the 'Menuhin: Master Musician' series was recorded in the Swiss resort town of Gstaad, where Menuhin had built both a festival and a lovely family chalet called 'Chankly Bore', named by his sometimes outrageous wife Diana after a line in Edward Lear's famous nonsense verse: 'To the hills of the Chankly Bore!'. When the Menuhin centenary arrived in 2016 I did some judicious re-editing and Classic FM was good enough to rerun the entire series in Yehudi's honour.

I sensed there was the raw material in those interviews for a book but Yehudi's advisers said a biography would not be appropriate when their man's own memoir, *Unfinished Journey*, was being republished to mark his eightieth birthday. So I parked the project in the long grass for a couple of years and then, recognising in myself the desire to achieve something less ephemeral than the programmes I was making for radio and television, I broached the subject again with Yehudi and received his blessing. Faber was again my publisher: American book people were less interested, perhaps because New York-born Yehudi had so clearly demonstrated his preference for living in London. Abner Stein eventually secured a modest deal with a minor American university publisher whom I never met. Diana confided that she was glad Yehudi would be seeing a lot of me: he had, she said, so few men friends. I suspect she knew about what she called her husband's *amitié amoureuse* in Brussels (where Yehudi presided over a foundation bearing his name) and rather wished she could enjoy something similar herself.

After the experience gained from researching Bernstein's life I was better prepared for the immense but unavoidable slog required to trawl through the thousands of Menuhin press cuttings pasted into scrapbooks by his devoted father Moshe. The Menuhin papers were kept in a sizeable and airy office (a welcome improvement on the Bernstein archives) in a business building in Upper Regent Street, close to Broadcasting House. (The papers have since gone to the Royal Academy of Music.) They were looked after by Suzanne Baumgarten, who had worked in Yehudi's office with his manager Eleanor Hope. Suzi was positive and immensely helpful to me for months on end.

I also did basic research in San Francisco, the city of Yehudi's childhood in the 1920s, but to explain my presence in California I need to open up a parenthesis and backtrack a year to 1997, when I discovered (following a bog-standard health check) that I was suffering from prostate cancer – except I was *not* suffering: left to itself the body provides no warning signs until too late, as my friend Andrzej Panufnik had learnt a few years earlier – he died after a painful final illness aged only seventy-seven. Months of tests followed my initial diagnosis, the most disagreeably invasive being the process by which tiny slices of the prostate gland are manually shaved off to check for cancer cells. I was within days of undergoing surgery in London when I read about an alternative prostate treatment called brachytherapy which had recently been developed in Seattle. As it happened I was due to visit San Francisco that month to meet Glenn Gould's biographer so I arranged to make the short detour to Seattle to consult Dr Haakon Ragde, the prostate pioneer.

Dr Haakon Ragde. His prostate treatment saved my life.

I proved to be a suitable case for the new treatment because the cancer cells were still restricted to the gland (to use the jargon, they had not 'metastasised') and the cancer could be nullified in most cases by the injection of tiny radioactive pellets into the poisoned area of the prostate gland. Three weeks later I was back in Seattle with Christina for the operation; a spinal epidural meant I could not feel a thing in my lower regions but instead could become an amused observer as the medics went about their business. On their screen they could see an image of the prostate with targets indicating its cancerous areas. To launch the radioactive pellets they used a sophisticated crossbow which reminded me of 'Bernie the Bolt' in the popular 1960s ITV series *The Golden Shot*: 'Up a bit ... left a bit ... hold it: fire!'. Over a hundred pellets were dispatched by this method and within a couple of hours I was being packed off back to my hotel; that evening we attended a lively party at the Ragdes' (most of the guests were oncologists) where I spotted my anaesthetist sporting a sous-chef's hat and slicing a giant ham. Next morning I gave a talk to students about my experiences as target practice. The procedure was wonderfully un-invasive: I felt well, was allowed to travel and was in Wales the following Monday, commentating for Radio 3 on the *Cardiff Singer of the World* competition. Over the next year I counselled scores of prostate victims who had read a letter I sent to *The Times* after the newspaper's esteemed medical correspondent published an article about various new treatments for prostate cancer without even mentioning brachytherapy.

There was, however, a sting in the tail of this success story: nearly twenty years later the sludge from the innards of the prostate gland (they call it scar tissue) had slowly oozed into my urethra, eventually causing a blockage – but that is part of another story, a tale I label my unfinished organ recital.

It was en route for a check-up with Dr Ragde the year after my 'procedure' that I had the opportunity to research Yehudi Menuhin topics in the city where he grew up. I photographed the Menuhin house on one of San Francisco's famous hilly streets. I inspected the Civic Auditorium (since renamed for Billy Graham) where Yehudi, the boy virtuoso, played a concerto to an audience of 15,000. And I solved a mystery that had been troubling me since the start of my researches. Menuhin wrote that his first teacher, Sigmund Anker, was an unsympathetic Svengali-like character with whom he studied for only a few weeks. But the dates did not tally. It was clear that Yehudi must have spent longer with Anker than he suggested in his own autobiography. I looked up Anker in the San Francisco phone book (they still had such things in those days) and struck lucky with the first of the three listed Anker entries. It needed a long taxi ride to a modest suburban villa but there to greet me was the granddaughter of the Austrian-born violinist Sigmund Anker, still nursing the family grievance. I discovered that Anker had taught Yehudi for two full years from the age of five. With forgivable pride he advertised the connection in his brochures and later wrote letters to the San Francisco press justifiably claiming to have been the teacher who laid the basis of young Yehudi's phenomenal technique. Sigmund Anker's unhappy descendant had the yellowed press cuttings to prove her point and in my biography I was able to set the record straight. Yehudi was still alive but when I taxed him with the discrepancy he could offer no explanation. After all, seventy years had elapsed; he had written what he remembered about Anker, which only goes to show that even the sharpest memory cannot always be trusted.

Sorting out the chronology of those childhood years required much spadework. I also had to deal with the bias against Yehudi's first wife, Nola, which had been injected into the earliest Menuhin biography (1956) by the *second* wife, Diana. My own book, close on six hundred pages, was published in 2000, a year after Menuhin's sudden death in Berlin at the age of eighty-two. Writing it had been, as with my Bernstein book, a labour of great affection and admiration. It is curious that a non-believer such as myself should have been so drawn to two of the world's most famous Jewish musicians; presumably the fact that they were both prominent humanitarians, movers and shakers had something to do with it. It came as a welcome vote of confidence when Faber republished my Menuhin biography for his centenary in 2016; that was followed in 2018 by the republication of my Bernstein biography – I wrote new chapters for both books, charting developments in the intervening years, such as Yehudi's creation of the Live Music Now organisation supervised by Ian Stoutzker.

My third biography was published in 2002. The subject, a more worldly figure and one whose music I had adored since childhood, was William Walton. There was already an excellent biography by Michael Kennedy, so this was to be a picture book divided into eight chapters, each with an essay and sixteen pages of photographs and press cuttings, dealing with the eight decades of Walton's life. The inspiration came from Maureen Murray, whom I knew from her work as producer with Ken Russell. Maureen had grown close to Walton's formidable widow Susana and was sometimes in residence at La Mortella when Christina and I attended the opera summer schools which Susana organised on the island of Ischia. I enjoyed those visits enormously,

At the launch of the Walton Centenary celebrations, 2002. My co-author Maureen Murray (left) and Walton's indomitable widow Susana (right).

as who would not, with such figures as Colin Graham and Jonathan Miller directing the young singers (and Susana in charge of the cooking)? I served happily as an adviser to the Walton Trust for over a decade, quitting only when Susana had us spending what I felt was too much time talking about fundraising rather than the propagation of her late husband's wonderful music. Maureen worked then (and still does) as curator of the substantial Walton archive, so she knew the photographic and written material intimately. In 2001 I was looking for a new literary project to follow my Menuhin book and we both saw Walton's forthcoming centenary in 2002 as an opportunity for a different type of biography, dominated by images. We took the project to Oxford University Press since they had been Walton's music publisher for over half a century. The Press was in the midst of a managerial shake-up and seemed less than overwhelmed with our project: our advance was minimal but we had secured a respected publisher and with the help of a gifted designer named George Hammond we created a visually rich and eminently readable document. (Apologies if that reads like a publisher's blurb: I am just so sorry that the book, of which I am very proud, sold fewer than 3,000 copies and is now out of print.) *The Romantic Loner* was, like my other biographies, essentially a labour of love. I probably earned more from the handful of radio programmes about Walton I made for Classic FM in parallel with the book.

The respectable income I earned in my sixties still came from the televising of operas and concerts. I have already mentioned my work at Glyndebourne. For ITV I directed three Christmas shows from splendid locations: St Paul's Cathedral, which was celebrating its three-hundredth anniversary, St George's Chapel, Windsor and the Queen's Chapel in St James's, close to Buckingham Palace. The shows were put together by a clever independent producer named Tim Woolford, who had the *chutzpah* to enrol Prince Charles and Princess Anne in his cast lists, along with Lord Carrington, Patricia Routledge, Richard Griffiths and such world-class singers as Kiri Te Kanawa (delightful, backed by the choirboys of St Paul's) and José Carreras, who came, sang and departed without saying a word to anybody. Woolford brought in Patrick Garland (a good friend since the days of *Monitor*) to supply intelligent literary material and genuine stars to deliver it, such as a poem by Betjeman, a Christmassy reading from Charles Dickens and seasonal Welsh nostalgia from Dylan Thomas. These were civilised programmes which I would be happy to watch on any Christmastide.

In 1998 I directed the telecast of a delightful new production of *Hansel and Gretel* at Welsh National Opera in the New Theatre, Cardiff; Richard Jones

490

was the effervescent director and in the pit was the exceptionally dynamic and thoughtful young Russian maestro, Vladimir Jurowski, making his first appearance in Britain. He was a major 'find' for WNO. I adored this music in his hands and was equally struck by John Macfarlane's designs, one of which hangs, in sketch form, in our kitchen to this day. Abroad I prepared to televise Giorgio Strehler's new production of *Fidelio* from the Châtelet theatre in Paris. Because I was working with a new employer I took the precaution of insisting on being paid a third of my fee on delivery of the camera script. I duly attended the final rehearsals and made a scratch tape of the dress rehearsal but the show was so absurdly under-lit that I had to guess which singer was standing where. Despite this Stygian gloom I persevered in writing a camera script which for the contractual reasons already mentioned I duly delivered, only to be told that the production had been postponed because Strehler was ill. Sadly he was forced to quit Paris for treatment at a seaside spa and died soon afterwards. I was disappointed: Strehler had an enviable reputation. My new director contract with the National Video Corporation was a consolation.

CHAPTER 24

END OF THE CENTURY: MORE BANGS THAN WHIMPERS

New Year's Day Concert in Vienna, 1994. In homage to Johann Strauss, Lorin Maazel borrows a violin from a player in the Vienna Philharmonic and leads from the front.

VIENNA, EVEN WITHOUT Bernstein, continued to be my happiest overseas location. On the bicentenary of Mozart's death, December 7th 1991, I directed a telecast of his *Requiem* from St Stephen's Cathedral. It was a colossal occasion. The Archbishop of Vienna celebrated the Mass and a Jew, Georg Solti, conducted the music: he was replacing another Jew, the recently departed Leonard Bernstein. In advance the event was surrounded in controversy because the Austrian president would be attending. Kurt Waldheim (whom I had met several times when he was Secretary-General of the United Nations) was still embroiled in accusations that he had committed war crimes while serving in the Wehrmacht during the Second World War; he had even been declared *persona non grata* in the USA, where the *Requiem* would be relayed by public service television (PBS). We solved the dilemma by shooting the entry of the dignitaries at a great distance, in a discreet 'long shot'. But our production had its own problem: the great American soprano Arleen Auger called in sick after the previous day's dress rehearsal and as a precaution the British singer Judith Howarth was flown out from London as a standby: she sat close to the performers throughout the Mass but as often happens on these tense occasions, Auger sang flawlessly. Only two months later, however, she was forced to retire; she died soon afterwards of a brain tumour. I count myself lucky to have had the joy of filming Arleen Auger in Mozart's *Exsultate, jubilate* a few years earlier for Bavarian TV: she was an artist on a par with Lucia Popp, another fine soprano who died terribly young.

At the end of 1993 I was back in Vienna when Austrian Television invited me to direct the New Year's Day Concert, which that year was to be conducted by Lorin Maazel. Decades earlier, in my *Monitor* years, I had taken Lorin and his young kids to a puppet show in London. I knew him to be an exceptionally gifted musician, a composer and a brilliant solo violinist in addition to his enormous talents as a conductor. I had most recently filmed him at St Thomas's on Fifth Avenue in New York, when he conducted with calm efficiency the première of the Lloyd Webber *Requiem*. Even so, I was not prepared for the virtuoso display he put on for the billion spectators of the New Year's Day event. His technique with the Vienna Philharmonic was dazzling. He knew every nuance of these waltzes and polkas. In midstream of one number he commandeered a violin from one of the Vienna Philharmonic violinists and proceeded to lead the orchestra from the rostrum, fiddle under his chin, in the style of Johann Strauss himself. Had there been time to change into a leotard he would doubtless have joined the elegant dancers who are always part of the New Year show. Instead he provided some slapstick comedy in the polka *Ohne Sorgen*, arguing the toss (by gesture) with the timpanist as to how loud his offbeat bangs should be. He then revealed a glockenspiel on which he tapped out the tinkly tune, eventually striking a single silver note where previously the drum had drowned the rest of the orchestra. There were lots of laughs for a routine that was surely more amusing in close-up on camera than for the audience in the hall.

A couple of years later when the Austrians teamed me up again with Maazel for another New Year's Day Concert, there was similar comic byplay, this time between the maestro and a supposedly recalcitrant percussionist – this one with a warble whistle imitating a cuckoo. I enjoyed working with Maazel and was disappointed, to put it mildly, when I was dropped from directing his next New Year concert in 1999. I blush to explain why. In the intervening years I had directed several rather gaudy Viennese Christmas shows for Austrian Television; one was held in the cavernous mock-Gothic city hall, the Rathaus, another in the new UN Centre to the east of the Danube canal. These were commercial productions: the first paired the pop singer Michael Bolton (very long hair and earrings, 75 million records sold) with Plácido Domingo, who is undoubtedly a quick learner but had his head in the unfamiliar score for much of the concert. Each year I did my best to create a frothy video which would match the populist spirit of the show but at one point in my third season, I scripted the wrong camera, focusing on a singer who at that moment was not actually singing – an error which put my reputation as a reliable 'live' director on the line. Maazel went with the flow and so far as I know did not question my disappearance from the New Year's Day team. I was too proud to appeal to him directly. As a consolation prize the Austrians gave me a very agreeable directorial chore with which to bow out from Vienna: Gregory Peck narrating Copland's *Lincoln Portrait*. This was for a Greek-Canadian producer named Attila Glatz who had developed a profitable line screening Viennese New Year concerts in cinemas all over Canada and the US.

Gregory Peck was then in his eighties and approached his speaking role with perhaps too much reverence: not to mince words, his narration of Lincoln's sonorous speeches was a touch tedious. Fortunately there was cheerful music by Strauss and Gershwin to enliven the proceedings.

I must not leave Vienna without mentioning the wonderful support I always had from my German friend and assistant Monika Fröhlich. She was a singer by training who had gravitated into more lucrative part-time work on the scripting of television operas and concerts. We first met in 1980 at the Hercules Hall in Munich when she was freelancing as the production assistant on LB's misbegotten project to film concert performances of the three acts of *Tristan und Isolde*. They spread over the best part of a year and were dogged by the illnesses of the tenor Peter Hofmann and the soprano Hildegarde Behrens. My producer Horant Hohlfeld was also impressed with Monika's work and she became a fixture in the Unitel filming team throughout the 1980s. I booked her elsewhere whenever I could because she understood the way my brain worked.

Monika liked nothing better than to sing so we rehearsed a brief *Lieder* recital with which we entertained the Austrian TV camera crew at the end of the New Year's Day Concert. This is one of the things that made working in Vienna so enjoyable: these tough super-professional cameramen who had been concentrating on their camera angles during a two-hour concert with well over a thousand shot numbers to cope with were happy to pause as they were packing up their equipment and listen to Monika singing Mozart ('Das Veilchen'), Gershwin ('The man I love') and best of all the *Gipsy Songs* by Brahms. We all knew that Monika was a different kind of animal from the general run of production assistants.

Viewed through the rose-coloured spectacles of old age, the closing years of the twentieth century seem to have consisted of one exciting assignment after another. In fact there were disappointments, apart from Maazel's desertion: my Bernstein biography did not do as well as I had hoped: it was one of the final four titles in the running for a major literary award in London but the chairman of the judges was Alan Clark (son of *Civilisation*), who apparently declared that from the start he would rule out the Bernstein biography on three counts: he was (a) a Jew, (b) an American and (c) a homosexual. True or not (and, as with so much about Clark junior, much tends to be apocryphal), the non-fiction prize went not to me, nor to Nelson Mandela for his ghosted autobiography, as one might have expected, but to a slender volume, since forgotten, about a mining community in County Durham. My consolation

Monika Fröhlich singing a Brahms Gypsy Song at the Austrian TV crew party, the conclusion of the New Year's Day Concert with Lorin Maazel, 1994. Note my suit, a genuine Austrian *Trachtenjacke*.

prize was a sleek laptop computer worth – I was told – over two grand: the downside was that I had no idea how to use it. I was on to my second biography before I acquired any computer skill. Perhaps foolishly, I gave the gadget away.

After *La Traviata* in 1994 I televised only two other operas from London opera stages, both gripping productions. In the mid-1990s my friend and former colleague Dennis Marks was in what proved to be his last beleaguered year running ENO; he had been no more successful than our mutual friend Jeremy Isaacs at making the perilous leap from broadcaster to opera administrator. I often thanked my lucky stars that I had been turned down as John Tooley's successor when Jeremy Isaacs got the job. Dennis persuaded Channel 4 to televise David Alden's surreal ENO production of *The Damnation of Faust*. I loved its craziness and felt sure Berlioz would have approved of Alden's vision of hell as men in straitjackets singing gibberish. I have already described how, thirty years earlier at the BBC, I had discussed with Michael Bakewell, head of television plays and a fellow Berlioz enthusiast, the idea of doing *La Damnation de Faust* as a television film fantasy. It was ruled then that the concept was too expensive but Alden's ENO version was a sophisticated realisation of my dream, with Willard White outstanding as Mephistopheles. Sadly there is no DVD other than a pirate of miserable quality which must have been taped off-air when the opera was televised. Dennis quit the Coliseum later that year, his plan unfulfilled for a new opera house away from the West End. He found a new outlet for his creative energy in broadcasting and writing, before cancer chopped him down in 2015. It was a great pity that he was never given full command of Music and Arts at the BBC.

My final foray into London opera was *Falstaff* at Covent Garden, the historic occasion when the new theatre was finally inaugurated after years of rebuilding. The beautiful auditorium was virtually unchanged but the backstage working areas had been transformed. Graham Vick was chosen to put the new theatre through its paces and he brought me in to do the television – we had been working together every year since *Onegin* in 1994.

In the 1999 production Bryn Terfel took the title part and the merry Windsor wives were led by the delightful Barbara Frittoli as Alice Ford. *Falstaff* had been my favourite operatic comedy (with *Figaro*) since Chelsea Opera Group days under Colin Davis in 1964, and with Bernard Haitink conducting this was another stimulating assignment, despite the long list of tedious new Health and Safety restrictions that obstructed our progress. Vick and his designer Paul Brown had devised six elaborate sets in bright basic colours: the meadow in the second scene contained a witty allusion to the then universally popular

Treasured Royal
Opera moments.
Above: Luciano Pavarotti,
Marilyn Horne and
Dame Joan Sutherland
in the party scene from
Die Fledermaus (1990).
Right: Bryn Terfel in
Falstaff (1999).

Teletubbies, while the finale climaxed in the spreading out before our eyes of a marvellous human tree (created by acrobats) to represent Hermes's Oak in Windsor Forest. This was a live transmission so every quicksilver movement (such as the *commedia dell'arte* tumblers who join in the riotous search for the fat knight at Ford's house in Act 2, Scene 2) had to be plotted down to the last semiquaver.

Looking back on my involvement in opera at Covent Garden, it is difficult to decide which I treasure more: this vivid *Falstaff* or the historic party scene in *Die Fledermaus* I had directed a decade earlier when Luciano Pavarotti and Marilyn Horne joined Joan Sutherland for her poignant farewell to the opera stage.

If television work was the icing on the cake in my late sixties, then radio was my bread and butter. I was still writing my biography of Bernstein when John Evans came out to New York to produce a 'Leonard Bernstein Day' for Radio 3. We had a whale of a time jumping into Yellow Cabs to visit locations and personalities connected with the maestro. Microphone at the ready, we penetrated the upper reaches of Carnegie Hall, where in 1943 young Leonard had resided in a tiny studio apartment while working as the New York Philharmonic's assistant conductor. It was a sign of the times that the space had been converted into an office occupied by no less than four ladies from Carnegie Hall's marketing department. They giggled when informed that they were working where LB had occasionally slept.

For Radio 3 I also presented a thirteen-part season devoted to Bernstein's teacher Serge Koussevitzky. After I resettled in London I was host on Radio 3 for a *Composer of the Week* dedicated to Bernstein's Broadway compositions, including the ill-fated *1600 Pennsylvania Avenue*, memorably assessed by Patricia Routledge, who played a succession of White House first ladies, as 'a diamond-studded dinosaur'. John Evans also created for Radio 3 a Tanglewood Weekend on a scale that would be unthinkable in today's austerity climate. A BBC team of eighteen engineers, studio managers, producers and presenters flew to Boston and then drove across Massachusetts to Tanglewood, in the Berkshires, to mount a broadcast weekend consisting of live concerts and conversations, documentaries and archive features, all reflecting Tanglewood's diversity and strength as a musical institution. We had our own satellite transmitter and converted the centre's music library into a continuity suite; the presenters working round the clock were the jazz buff Geoff Smith, the conductor Robert Ziegler and myself, joined by New Yorker Jamie Bernstein, who twenty years previously had worked at Tanglewood as an usher when her father ran the conducting school. She hosted a special edition of *Private Passions* with Frederica von Stade. These Radio 3 weekends had been founded by John Drummond in the 1980s but John Evans's vision outstripped all previous excursions and he quite rightly won that year's Sony Radio Gold Award for *Live from Tanglewood* (1996).

Two summers later, Dr John masterminded a Danube Week for Radio 3. For this radio-river journey we set sail in Linz and headed downstream past Melk Abbey to Vienna, where the opera was *Ariadne auf Naxos* with the Slovak soprano Edita Gruberova as Zerbinetta – in theory much too old for the part but defying her fifty-one years to deliver her stupendous coloratura aria; the applause lasted almost as long as the aria. We took in a pair of Haydn concerts at Eisenstadt en route and ended up in Budapest, first at the Liszt Conservatoire's art deco jewel of a concert hall, where Tamás Vásáry conducted Liszt's tremendous *Faust* Symphony, and finally at the Budapest Opera for Verdi's *Masked Ball*, which was sung in less than idiomatic Italian by a 100 per cent Hungarian cast under the American conductor Rico Saccani. He really knew his Verdi. I confess, however, that my highlights were more personal: a dinner with Vásáry in a genuine old-fashioned non-tourist Buda

With my dear friend John Evans, holding the Sony Radio Gold Award, and his BBC team.

restaurant and the playing of Brahms's Hungarian Dances (as piano duets) with my co-presenter Stephanie Hughes. This performance took place in a nearby bar at the farewell party after the opera relay. I still miss Stephanie's Belfast accent on the radio: her way of pronouncing Johannes 'Bramms' was very endearing.

I was more stretched in a documentary series I made for Radio 3 in 1997 about the Philharmonia Orchestra, six programmes tracing the 'vintage years' since the orchestra's foundation in 1945 by Walter Legge, a hero of mine although my first impression had been unfavourable. We met in the 1960s when he chaired the Philharmonia's conducting competition in the *Monitor* studio. After dinner we sat gossiping at the table about musical life in Vienna, where Legge had worked after the war producing recordings with many of the great figures of the opera world, including Herbert von Karajan. I told him about my happy stay in Vienna when I had seen *Figaro* in the Redoutensaal (the space where the Spanish horses are exercised) conducted by Karl Böhm and featuring a wonderfully lively interpretation of Cherubino given by Christa Ludwig.

He had been able to create the myth of the German conductor Karajan by bringing him together with the dream orchestra he had created in England, the Philharmonia. And that evening we were sitting with the supreme triumph of his fantasy world: Mme Elisabeth Schwarzkopf, his trophy wife. The son of a Jewish tailor from Hammersmith, Legge had been an impoverished pupil at my father's old school, Latymer Upper, who taught himself German and had become a leading expert in the songs of Hugo Wolf, creating for himself a niche at HMV Records as the much-admired architect of the Hugo Wolf Society, an immensely successful record club which raised funds by selling subscriptions for handsome record albums in such numbers that production costs for the song recordings were reputed to be comfortably covered.

Legge had become a powerful figure in the European music world, being the friend and assistant at Covent Garden to Sir Thomas Beecham – and to top it all he had eventually married the soprano who was said to be the world's most beautiful opera singer, Elisabeth Schwarzkopf. He had coached her in Hugo Wolf songs at a Vienna audition session, caring not a whit for the fact that he was keeping the impatient Karajan waiting to proceed with the task of casting their new recording project.

A little later, when I was head of Music and Arts, Walter invited me to dinner with Elisabeth Schwarzkopf. He and I talked first alone in his study and I noticed he was forever taking a cigarette from a silver box, lighting it,

Addicted and expensive.
Walter Legge, the
impresario, and his wife
Elisabeth Schwarzkopf.

inhaling for a single drag and then vigorously stubbing it out, only to immediately take another cigarette from the box. This was my introduction to the curse of nicotine addiction. The BBC wanted Schwarzkopf to appear on our new *Gala Performance* series – successor to *Music for You* – but Walter quoted the to my mind outrageous fee of £1,500 and the negotiations foundered. My Radio 3 programmes about the Philharmonia were rich with anecdote and lovingly assembled by another excellent Radio 3 producer, Adam Gatehouse. To give an idea of their enormous range, here is the *Radio Times* billing for the first episode, Saturday, January 4th 1997:

Vintage Years: The Philharmonia
Six programmes in which Humphrey Burton traces the history of the Philharmonia Orchestra.
1: Beginnings
In 1945, Walter Legge set out to form a London orchestra to equal any of the famous European or American orchestras.
With contributions from Elisabeth Schwarzkopf, Susana Walton and past members, including Hugh Bean and Gareth Morris.
Hugo Wolf: Italian Serenade (1st mvt) Conductor, Walter Susskind
Walton, arr. Muir Mathieson: Suite: Henry V (excerpts) conducted by the composer
Brahms Violin Concerto in D (1st mvt) Ginette Neveu, conductor, Issay Dobrowen
Ravel: Piano Concerto in G (Finale) conducted from the keyboard by Leonard Bernstein

Strauss: Horn Concerto No. 1 Dennis Brain, conductor, Alceo Galliera
Dvořák: Symphony No. 8 in G (1st mvt) conductor, Rafael Kubelík
Mozart: In Quali Eccessi ... Mi Tradi (Don Giovanni) Elisabeth Schwarzkopf
(soprano), conductor, Josef Krips
Schumann: Piano Concerto in A minor (1st mvt) Dinu Lipatti, conductor,
Herbert von Karajan
Producer Adam Gatehouse

My professional partnership with Adam Gatehouse was forged in
Amsterdam; he knew the city well, having worked as a conductor in Holland
for many years before opting for a career in broadcasting. At Radio 3, Adam's
enduring contribution to the musical world was the creation of the BBC
New Generation Artists scheme in 1999. In the spring of that year, Adam
chose me to host, for Radio 3, the Mahler symphony cycle performed at the
Concertgebouw's *Mahler Feest*. Three great orchestras, the Philharmonics of
Vienna and Berlin and the Concertgebouw, shared the cycle; the conductors
were Abbado, Chailly, Haitink, Muti and Rattle. This sensational assembly
of Mahlerian talent was inspired by a similar event organised by Willem
Mengelberg in 1920. To the symphonic works were added the orchestral song
cycles and recitals of Mahler's *Lieder*. The festival ran for two revelatory weeks
and I was actually being paid to attend! I was rarely more fortunate.

At the beginning of the new century (2001–4) Adam Gatehouse was in
charge of Radio 3's *Morning Performance* strand which ran from 11.30 until
1 p.m. He invited me to host literally dozens of programmes under the
banner of *Artist in Focus*. The musical performances all came from the BBC
archive but they were repeats with a personal focus – over a five-day span the
programmes often turned into career retrospectives. The musicians featured
included Julian Bream, Alfred Brendel, Charles Mackerras and the Takács
Quartet. Many were interviewed in the studio and their musical contributions later niftily edited by Adam. Occasionally we went on location: down to
Dorset to see John Eliot Gardiner on his farm, and most memorably to Paris
to interview Mstislav Rostropovich in his handsome Paris apartment close
to the Arc de Triomphe. He and his wife Galina Vishnevskaya had created a
little corner of Czarist Russia in the 16th arrondissement: we drank tea out
of fine porcelain cups, the interview was carried out as we perched on gilded
chairs and we were watched over by dozens of Russian Orthodox icons which
occupied every inch of wall space. In a break in what had been a riveting
set of reminiscences I reminded Slava of a less happy BBC moment back in
the 1970s, soon after their defection to the West. BBC Television invited the

Russian couple to give a recital at St John's, Smith Square – in addition to his cello-playing Slava was a fine pianist who often partnered his wife. He wanted her to open the recital with Mussorgsky's *Songs and Dances of Death*. Walter Todds, producing, suggested as tactfully as he could that for a television audience it would perhaps be better to begin on a lighter note. Slava would have none of it: 'BBC ne kulturny', he declared, wagging a finger at Walter and me: 'the BBC is uncultured'. There was no arguing with such a denunciation. The recital went ahead. The audience may not have been very large but Slava got his way, as he usually did.

In 2004 *Artist in Focus* was a casualty of drastic budget cuts. I was assured that there was nothing wrong with the programmes: they were simply too expensive. So they stopped and the schedule was redrawn to provide a virtually non-stop stream of recorded classics from nine until noon. That same year I made the last and probably the best of my radio documentaries, four hour-long programmes entitled *The Decca Boys*. The series was produced by Clive Portbury, another Radio 3 luminary who has done a lifetime of sterling work for the Corporation. *The Decca Boys* was the label given by Valerie Solti to the team which John Culshaw built up in the 1950s to make stereo opera recordings; my radio feature was a companion piece to the earlier series about the Philharmonia, this time telling the story of post-war music-making from the angle of Walter Legge's great rival. Forty years earlier, in *The Golden Ring* on BBC2, I had paid tribute to John for his epic Wagner recording; now I provided an overview of what he and his 'boys' had achieved in great opera from Mozart to Britten. The underlying message was that this grand chapter in the history of recorded sound was closed: Culshaw had died in 1980 and his sound art had largely been superseded by the live satellite relays from opera houses which began – all praise to Peter Gelb at the Metropolitan Opera – soon after my Decca series was broadcast. We no longer need the stereo-in-the-mind that Culshaw perfected. Stereo LPs and the CDs that followed seemed almost miraculously perfect at the time but they were a hybrid, only half the story: today many of us prefer to experience opera in the way our forebears did, with our eyes as well as our ears, through the medium of the high-definition relays into cinemas direct from opera stages such as the Met and Covent Garden, a process which had begun with the television relays I worked on in the second half of the twentieth century. Opera can once again be experienced as *Gesamtkunstwerk*, an entertainment involving all the arts. But who would deny the pleasure and the enlightenment still to be gained from listening to a good opera recording in sound alone? Broadcast engineers continue to perform prodigies of balance in opera relays from Covent Garden and the Proms. But CDs of opera remain treasured possessions. Solti and Karajan did not labour in vain.

* * *

In the summer of 1995 I went down to Cornwall to spend a few days with my daughter Clare and her family, who were staying at a hotel in the village of Mullion where I had spent many teenage holidays back in the 1940s (in chapter 3 I wrote about my love affair with Brenda and the birth of our son Nicholas in November 1949). I'd heard that Brenda was still living in the area and one evening I asked the barman if he knew of her whereabouts: he told me she owned a cottage half a mile inland. Next morning on my daily jog I slipped a card under the locked door explaining I was in the village and asking if we could meet. No answer came and I was about to check out and drive home when she telephoned the hotel. She no longer lived in Mullion but her tenant had stuck on a stamp and forwarded my card to her new home in Truro. 'What a shame,' I exclaimed. 'I'm just setting off back to London.' 'Wait,' said she. 'I'll see you in an hour at the Old Inn.' I walked over to the pub and sat down in the booth where we used to hang out after our cliff walks.

I had not seen Brenda since the early 1960s. Then she had rung me one day at the BBC to say she would like to meet. She had a disturbing tale to tell. Our son Nicholas was dead. How could she know this, I asked; Nicholas had been adopted in December 1949 and blood parents are not allowed to know the identity of the adopting family. Her explanation was that on a beach holiday in Somerset she had met the hospital sister who had supervised her confinement in Minehead. It was against the rules to do so but this nurse had confided to Brenda that very sadly Nicholas had died of a rare illness. Brenda said she thought I should know this. I thanked her. We were both married; we both had children; the wounds were healed. I don't recall feeling any grief. We said goodbye and had not met again until this morning in Mullion.

When she arrived, a little flustered and with the same gipsy bohemian look she had had when a girl, we sat together with a couple of beers in the nook well away from the other drinkers. I had not thought consciously about the matter in thirty years but I had a premonition and I blurted it out: 'Nicholas is not dead, is he?' 'How did you know?' she asked, the pupils in her eyes wide with amazement. 'I just did,' was my answer and then she told me her story. She had not told me the truth at Lime Grove because she was seeking closure of the Nicholas episode. But recently, she continued, she had wanted to know the fate of her first son. She knew from the nurse that his adopted family name was Hockey and she scoured the telephone books to find him. Fortunately there were only three Hockeys in the entire West of England telephone directories, or so she said, and she struck lucky with the first number she rang. 'Can I speak to Nicholas Hockey?' she asked the man who answered. 'I'll go and find him,' came the answer. And then after a long wait: 'He doesn't want to speak to you.'

I was intrigued and keen to get involved. At last I might have the chance to assuage some of the guilt I had felt back in 1949–50 when I was eighteen and, as I saw it, a helpless bystander. Before we said goodbye I urged Brenda to renew her efforts, offering to help in any way I could. Fortunately the law was changed that year to allow natural parents to make contact – if their child gave permission. Brenda rang the Hockey number again and after a few minutes established that she was speaking to Nicholas. Except his name was not Nicholas but Christopher. It turned out that the Hockeys already had an adopted son whom they had named Nicholas so they had changed their

At Oakwood Court with my three sons. Left to right: Matthew, Chris and Lukas.

second son's name to Christopher. It also emerged that the Hockey parents, whom Christopher loved, had both died recently, making it easier for him to accept the call from his real mother. They met soon afterwards and she wrote from Truro urging me not to dally in making my own contact. I sent Chris a CV of sorts and a few days later was greeting him at Paddington station. I drove him back to my Holland Park flat where my other sons Matthew and Lukas were waiting to greet him. We ate a delicious lunch, cooked by Matthew, and thus began a friendship which has not wavered from that day to this.

On his Christmas cards and emails Chris signs himself 'Son of Somerset', having lived all his life in the West Country. Like all my other children he is musical but his interest was more in Country and Western than classical and in singing songs to the guitar. He left school at sixteen, worked for many years in a bank but was now a respected independent financial adviser and a pillar of local society. Like me he had two children with his first wife and like me he had a *coup de foudre* which led to his marriage to his very sympathetic second wife Carol.

I dream of one day driving down to Cornwall with Chris to visit his mother in Truro. But now I must turn to the biggest dream of my life, a dream that was to come true in March 2001, on my seventieth birthday.

CHAPTER 25

'THE VIRGIN MAESTRO': CONDUCTING VERDI'S *REQUIEM* AT THE ROYAL ALBERT HALL

Rehearsing for the most intensely lived moments of my entire life.

I SPENT MUCH of my late sixties planning a concert I would conduct of the Verdi *Requiem*. It was an event I had dreamed of since hearing the *Requiem* in the Royal Albert Hall in the early 1950s. That key performance was conducted by the immensely tall Italian maestro Alberto Erede. Another inspiring performance I treasured (and televised) was Claudio Abbado's in the 1960s at the Edinburgh Festival with Margaret Price and Jessye Norman. What attracted me to Verdi's *Requiem*? The thrill of the four soloists entering the opening 'Kyrie' one by one, which I described earlier as resembling Atlantic waves rolling in to a Cornish cove. To that I would add the whiff of fire and brimstone in the 'Dies Irae'; the distant trumpets calling across the depths in the 'Tuba mirum'; the heart-turning melody of the 'Agnus Dei', sung in unison; the raw drama of the soprano's final, hushed, imploring 'deliver me from eternal death': *Libera me de morte aeterna*. It is a long list.

I wanted to conduct this magnificent work before I died. It would need stamina and untried conducting skills, the latter a risky assumption since I had last conducted a choir when I was still an undergraduate and had never conducted an orchestra in anything longer than a ten-minute Beethoven overture: my Turkish conductor friend Cem Mansur had invited me to try my hand at conducting the *Egmont* overture. That was with his Oxford orchestra in the Sheldonian. I followed that up on June 22, 1997 at St John's, Smith Square with the overture to Mozart's *The Impresario*. The main attraction of this latter concert, a fundraiser, was Claus Moser playing a Mozart piano concerto. We had enlisted as our principal conductor that evening a Cambridge undergraduate named Daniel Harding, only nineteen at the time and rightly considered the best conducting hope to have appeared in this country since Simon Rattle. His Haydn symphony that evening was very stylish. I still have a recording of the entire concert on a miserable little sound cassette.

To get my Verdi project under way I would also need money, a great deal of it, in order to reserve a concert date. From the start I had no alternative venue in mind: it had to be the Royal Albert Hall. I made enquiries and was assured that anybody could make a booking so long as their credit was good. However, to deter pranksters the hall insisted on a huge deposit, some of it non-returnable in the event of cancellation. I paid up with my customary thoughtlessness: I just knew this was something I had to do. (The event was still four years in the future.) Then came the question of the musical forces. First I approached my old friends at the LSO but sadly they already had a booking (or so they said), so I turned to David Whelton, the manager of the Philharmonia, for whom I had recently hosted a Bernstein concert at the Henley Festival conducted by John Wilson. He did not seem unduly perturbed by my lack of experience. Another friend, John Berry, then in charge of casting at ENO, kindly nominated four soloists who were members of his young artists programme and all highly promising. Claire Weston was already singing big Verdi soprano roles at the Coliseum; mezzo Susan Parry had a very special timbre and was probably the best Brangäne of her generation; the tenor Rhys Meirion possessed all the ardour needed for the great solo

With my Verdi *Requiem* soloists. Left to right: Susan Parry, Claire Weston, Rhys Meirion and Iain Paterson.

tenor moments in the *Requiem* such as the 'Ingemisco'; finally the bass Iain Paterson had the necessary gravitas and has since developed into a leading international Wagnerian.

I undoubtedly had a 'top' team. But what about a chorus? In my dreams I had imagined a really big choir, upwards of five hundred voices; I felt that nothing smaller would properly fill out the Albert Hall's noble acoustic. I had no idea then that Verdi himself had a choir of over a thousand voices when he conducted the London première of his *Requiem* in 1875. My friend Hilary Davan Wetton (then head of music at St Paul's Girls' School) was by happy chance director of no less than three splendid choral societies, those of Leicester, Guildford and the City of London, to all of which he introduced me. Each group generally provided a hundred singers and their participation guaranteed a truly powerful vocal mass – to which I added another hundred voices each from two other groups I contacted, the London Symphony Chorus and Ronald Corp's London Chorus (formerly the London Choral Society). So I was getting closer to Verdi's proportions and I had created a choir so large that every inch of space around the Royal Albert Hall organ could be employed: it took an hour just to marshal the singers into position on the day, but what a splendid sight and sound my five hundred-strong chorus provided! In the previous weeks I had visited each choir in its natural habitat and put the singers through their paces.

On the concert day itself the coach carrying the choir from Leicester broke down on the motorway and failed to arrive for the seating rehearsal or indeed for the pre-lunch run-through, for which I had persuaded my concert-pianist friend Ronan Magill to provide a rock-solid accompaniment – not a simple matter when coping with the intricacies of such a fiendishly tricky fugal movement as the 'Sanctus'.

Happily the Leicester coach made it in the end, so all hands were on deck for the afternoon run-through. At full force, *tutta forza*, as in the 'Dies Irae' and the 'Rex tremenda', my chorus sounded fearsome. But what was even more exciting was the sound of five hundred voices singing *pianissimo*: from the opening 'Kyrie' onwards it was miraculous. I could hardly believe my luck.

But I must get back to my earlier preparations. The centenary year of Verdi's death was 2001. The precise date was January 27th so I concluded that my seventieth birthday in March would be a not inappropriate date for me to mount my Verdi performance – except that when I stood back from it for a reality check, the entire project had a self-congratulatory aspect which I did not find attractive. Then fate took a hand, linked to my prostate cancer. After my successful treatment in Seattle, about which I wrote in the previous chapter, I became involved in counselling and in fundraising for prostate research, which was then in its infancy. I decided to turn the Verdi concert into a charity gala on the centenary of Verdi's death, and secured the promise of a £10,000 sponsorship from Nycomed Amersham, a major pharmaceutical company involved with treatments for prostate problems. Even grander support was to come. Eric and Katya Abraham of Portobello Films had introduced me to their friend John Studzinski, then a star financier at Morgan Stanley. Already a noted philanthropist, 'Studs' had just created his Genesis Foundation, with the intention of helping artists at the outset of their careers. I guess I just slipped under that qualifying wire (so far as my conducting career was concerned) and the £25,000 which Genesis donated towards the production costs made it possible to confirm the Albert Hall booking and set the tickets at a reasonable top price of £35. What a blessing the Genesis support proved to be!

Victor and Lilian Hochhauser, the very experienced concert promoters, had been good friends in my television days and for the *Requiem* Lilian advised me on where to advertise (the *Telegraph* was apparently the most effective national newspaper for arts advertising). A former PA of mine, Sue Johnson, helped with the mountains of administration, in particular negotiating with the box office as to which seats could be released to us – this was after we had been told that nearly 1,300 boxes and many individual stalls are privately owned and always will be.

Fitness was another issue. I had been jogging as a form of daily exercise since my fifties, inspired by Huw Wheldon and his son Wynn, who used to canter round Richmond Park. I joined them for one outing when we were

Left: Advertisement for my Royal Albert Hall début. Above: John Studzinski, founder of the Genesis Foundation, my most generous sponsor.

neighbours on Richmond Hill and was left humiliatingly out of puff before we had reached the Isabella Plantation. Later, when my family moved to West Kensington, the sloping cricket field in Holland Park provided a reasonable quarter-mile lap – I still remember every yard of it – and most days I would trot round half a dozen times before breakfast. Preparing for the Verdi required a much more rigorous programme. From Holland Park I jogged through some of the most handsome streets of Kensington into the Gardens and, on a good day, I would run as far as Hyde Park, having skirted the Serpentine lake with, to spur me on, a glimpse through the trees of the dome of my eventual goal, the Royal Albert Hall. I knew I had to build up my stamina and in the last few weeks before the performance I ran five or six miles a day, several times defying the traffic at Hyde Park Corner to cross into St James's Park and run all the way down to the Thames at Westminster. I was probably fitter than at any time since my officer cadet days at Aldershot half a century previously.

As the big day came nearer the crucial thing for me, not surprisingly, was to learn *how* to conduct Verdi's *Requiem*. As a television director I had observed Giulini, Bernstein and Abbado conducting the work in close-up; I had also made a *Monitor* documentary about training a great choir to sing Verdi. But watching other people, even geniuses, was no substitute for learning basic baton technique. For this I enlisted the help of the American conductor Robert Mandell. I knew Bob to be a passionate enthusiast for LB because since the publication of my Bernstein biography he had often written to me to compare notes: back in the 1950s he had worked as LB's assistant on his *Omnibus* television series but had then fallen out with him over the coveted post of assistant conductor at the New York Philharmonic, which Bob thought he had been promised but did not get. (Among LB's assistants during his years as boss of the Philharmonic were Zubin Mehta, Seiji Ozawa and Claudio Abbado, so the competition was hot!) Although he was a New Yorker by birth and training, Bob Mandell eventually moved to the UK, where he worked as the music director of several West End shows before settling in Leicester, in which city he was for decades music director of the Haymarket Theatre. He also carved out a niche for himself in the music world as the conductor and promoter of light classical music concerts based on the vast music library of the 'easy listening' maestro George Melachrino, a collection which he had been given after Melachrino's death. But I turned to him primarily because of his early conducting studies at the Juilliard School. Bob is a pugnacious man, maybe exaggeratedly so because vertically he is a little challenged. Only two years my senior, he behaved more like my father than my brother. He came to my Kensington flat for study sessions and sometimes I would visit him in Leicester – we must have had a dozen meetings in the months preceding the concert.

As a boy I had received a few conducting lessons at school from Mrs Anna Garfield Howe and in 1949 from Ruth Railton, when I was in the NYO. She had been taught by Sir Malcolm Sargent so I was already imbued with businesslike basics: make big gestures – always be clear – be ahead of the music – put a bounce at the end of each beat! With Bob Mandell I also practised dividing the basic beats in order to achieve flexibility, since in Verdi's music *ritardandi* (slowings down and occasionally the opposite, accelerations) are a basic element in the musical discourse. It's what LB told me he had learnt from Dr Koussevitzky: how to conduct the space *between* the beats of the bar.

Bob was at his best on the evening before the concert, when I had my first rehearsal with the Philharmonia Orchestra and the four soloists at the Henry Wood Hall. At the outset I was a little disconcerted to discover that the regular concertmaster Christopher Warren-Greene, whom I knew and admired, had taken the weekend off, his place filled by Maya Iwabuchi. (I need not have worried: Maya was extremely helpful and sympathetic.) We started at the top and read through every movement. Orchestral players can be awkward cusses, just going through the motions if they do not respect the conductor: I remember how shocked I had been at a Prom rehearsal when I saw the cavalier way the BBC Symphony Orchestra treated Raymond Leppard, a musician I revered; they were openly talking among themselves while he was giving notes. The Philharmonia players were not so disrespectful but they were definitely taking things easy. At the break Bob Mandell took me on one side, like a trainer talking to his boxer. 'Don't let the bastards get you down' was the gist of his advice, and I vividly remember his final injunction: 'Take no prisoners!'. I stepped up my authority quotient and by the end of the rehearsal was feeling quietly confident. From my concert scriptwriting days I had learnt about the *Requiem*'s peaks and troughs. I know how the work unfolds and now I was putting that knowledge into practice.

The performance next evening started very late. I was alone in my dressing room doing what LB always did before a performance, studying the score. Actually I was looking at the yellow Post-it Notes I had stuck in on almost

Before the performance. In my dressing room coping with the yellow Post-it Notes.

every page with messages such as 'Travel with the second beat' or 'Cue tenors' or simply 'Forward!'. At 7 p.m. the hall manager came in to tell me there would have to be a delay because literally dozens of people were still queueing to buy tickets. I suspect the box office was less than fully manned because they were not expecting much activity. They had not taken into account the impact of a filmed rehearsal and interview with me which Thames Television's local news had screened earlier in the weekend. The resultant last-minute walk-up was gratifying even if it created a 'Why are we waiting?' mood among the audience already in the hall. I heard later that there had been some slow handclapping until a conciliatory announcement was made over the PA system.

We eventually began nearly twenty minutes late and dammit I then got off to a bad start on the rostrum, entirely caused by my own forgetfulness: after the applause for my entrance on the platform I turned and gave the downbeat. There has to be something intensely sorrowful about the cellos' opening theme. They were playing as we had rehearsed it, ultra-sensitive and *pianissimo*, but after only a couple of seconds there was a rumbling noise like a herd of elephants on the move as the five hundred singers in the chorus got to their feet – as quietly as possible, bless their hearts! I had simply forgotten to give them the gesture to stand before I began conducting. I had thrown away the yellow reminder sticker only moments earlier! But there is no way to make an apology when one has just launched the performers on an epic musical journey. 'Forward' is indeed the only direction one can take.

Halfway through the *Requiem*, after the vast fresco of the 'Dies Irae', with its eight dramatic movements piling intensity upon intensity, I felt an urgent need to pause for a couple of minutes so that we all, performers and audience alike, could catch our breath. I sat down on the side of the rostrum and as I was taking a swig of water, the tenor soloist Rhys Meirion leaned forward and whispered, for all the world as if he were the manager of a Welsh rugby team: 'Keep it up: it's going bloody well, boyo.'

There was no time to feel emotion once I launched into the 'Offertorium'; the conductor is simultaneously living the moment with the musicians and also thinking ahead of the game, instinctively preparing by the use of body language and the look in one's eye for what comes next. Conducting can be an elating experience and those ninety minutes with Verdi were undoubtedly the most intensely lived moments of my entire life.

When it was over I sensed that the performance had gone well from the warmth of the applause with which it was greeted. After curtain calls and flowers presented to me by my daughter Helena, I made a short speech acknowledging the presence in the hall of the pioneer prostate surgeon Haakon Ragde, who had flown in from Seattle. In the programme book he had written: 'You were our first patient from Great Britain to be treated with brachytherapy for your prostate cancer. It is a privilege to be present at this memorable event to celebrate your cure from the hideous disease.'

The evening raised over £75,000 for prostate cancer research. There is absolutely no record of the concert on video or sound, except for a few photographs and a host of memories. Inevitably my life has been going downhill ever since. But I do have a couple of reviews to remind me of what went on that evening at the Royal Albert Hall. Rob Cowan in the *Independent* wrote, 'fully expecting to take a charitable stand … In the event the only charity worth speaking of is the Prostate Research Charity.' Cowan was quite generous about me: 'there was plenty of power: his beat was clear; his baton longer than most. He shaped a phrase much as any seasoned maestro might, and his choice of speeds showed consideration for his singers.' (My baton – I'm glad he noticed it – had once belonged to LB.)

The Times's critic Hilary Finch was also generous: the performance, she wrote, was 'well worthy of the composer's centenary celebration in a packed Albert Hall … It was a lifetime's ambition fulfilled for the television presenter, editor, director and writer. And it was also a rather fascinating performance.' She liked my soloists. 'Claire Weston's soprano excelled at spinning the finest, quintessentially Verdian line of sound; and tenor Rhys Meirion brought a rapt quality to his quietest supplications.' I would like to add that Susan Parry and Iain Paterson were every bit as committed and the choirs were magnificent.

Afterwards my family and friends crammed into my dressing room – I may have been a tyro conductor but I was a relatively experienced producer, so I had laid on an ample sufficiency of champagne. Among the crowd, to name-drop for a moment, were Harold and Antonia Pinter, John Julius and Mollie Norwich, Jeremy and Gillian Isaacs, Alan and Philippa Yentob, William and Jane Mostyn Owen. From Ischia had come Susana Walton. From Vienna Christl Lieben, a friend for over forty years. From Japan, in full kimono rig, Kazuko Amano, part of the worldwide Bernstein family. I will never know an evening like it, I thought to myself, but 'Basta' with the social column and let my account of the long decline of the rest of my life begin without more self-promotion.

However, a month later I was back in the Albert Hall. When my friend the philanthropist Jackie Rosenfeld came to my dressing room after the *Requiem* she invited me on the spot (and I accepted without a moment's consideration)

Applauding the Philharmonia Orchestra and my five hundred voices.

to conduct Verdi's *Forza del Destino* overture at the big charity gala *she* was organising with the London Philharmonic. Robert Mandell put in another spell of coaching (there must be at least a dozen tempo changes in the course of the eight-minute 'Force of Destiny' curtain-raiser) and I had a decent but frighteningly brief rehearsal. On the night I was handed an additional task: at the very top of the show, before the overture, I was to conduct orchestra and audience in the National Anthem. To walk out into the hall, take a bow, turn to the orchestra (with whom I had of course *not* rehearsed the anthem), give the sign to the timpani for a drum roll, bring down my baton for the first stately orchestral bar and then turn to the hall, crammed to the rafters again, urge the audience in a peremptory gesture to stand and sing their hearts out in 'God save the Queen' – all this high-drama activity coalesced into what was a slightly coarse and vulgar experience by comparison with conducting the Verdi *Requiem* but I confess it was not without its sense of fun. I remembered what Sir Malcolm Sargent did at the Proms: I threw my arms around a great deal. After the concert I was presented to Jackie's patron Prince Charles (who

With my conducting coach Robert Mandell and HRH The Prince of Wales.

520

At the piano with Claus Moser, one of my favourite duet partners.

very decently had also written a gracious foreword for the programme book of my own charity gala). 'Do you know Mr Burton, our associate conductor?' asked Jackie. 'But of course,' Charles replied, without missing a beat. 'No musical occasion in London is complete without his presence.' Delivered with only the ghost of a smile.

It seemed wise for me to leave London and retire while on such a high. My outings with the LPO and Philharmonia proved to be not only the beginning but also the end of my career as an orchestral conductor. Within three months I had moved from the metropolis to Aldeburgh, a seaside town in Suffolk. Ten years later, on my eightieth birthday, I emerged from obscurity to conduct our local amateur orchestra in Schubert's 'Unfinished' Symphony at the Snape Maltings concert hall. I had organised a five-concert Schubert weekend as a personal birthday treat, and many friends attended, among them no less a judge than the music critic and Berlioz biographer David Cairns, best man at my first wedding fifty-four years earlier, who told me after my concert that he found my Schubert interpretation personal and convincing. At the formal lunch next day another guest, Claus Moser, asked if he could say a few unscheduled words. 'If Franz Schubert had known that one day Humphrey Burton would conduct his B minor symphony he would surely have finished it.' Laughter and applause. Pause. 'On the other hand', Claus concluded, with superb timing, 'he might never have begun it.'

PART SIX

Coda:
The Twenty-First Century

CHAPTER 26

A LIFE ON THE OCEAN WAVE

Enjoying the ocean air with Igor Levit and Alison Balsom.

CONDUCTING THE VERDI *Requiem* for my seventieth birthday was a sort of last hurrah. I had achieved my biblical three score years and ten. Life-changes were afoot. Within a few days of the Verdi *Requiem*, on April 1st 2001 to be exact, Christina and I signed the rental agreement on a handsome 1930s house on the outskirts of Aldeburgh in Suffolk. Christina found it while I was working in Britten's archive at the Red House, exploring the composer's shaky friendship with William Walton. Our new home came with almost an acre of garden. Soon afterwards we managed to sell our Oakwood Court flat in Kensington for about nine times what we had paid for it nineteen years earlier, and in July we quit London. Christina and I definitely wanted this move to the country: we had had enough of traffic jams and permanent roadworks in Kensington High Street, not to mention intrusive year-round building work under our noses in Oakwood Court as wealthy foreigners with black Mercedes limousines manned by twenty-four-hour chauffeurs blighted the Edwardian charm of our much-loved apartment block.

Retirement has never for me been an attractive option but in the early years of the new century it became clear that the people running my stretch of television and radio had concluded that I did not fit into their forward strategy. When Radio 3 had to make financial cutbacks it dispensed with my programme, the enlightening *Artist in Focus* series, and replaced it with a bland classical music disc-jockey programme running from nine to noon. Verdi's *Falstaff* with Bryn Terfel in 2001 proved to be the last opera relay I was asked to direct for BBC Television. I had shown them how it was done at the turn of the century with my script for Graham Vick's elaborate production and quite sensibly the BBC then brought in staff directors to replace me (among whom Jonathan Haswell was outstanding). To be fair, I should add that the BBC's director general, Mark Thompson, laid on a very handsome luncheon at which to bid me farewell: I was very touched by the gesture.

On the radio, Classic FM gave me just four shows when my book about William Walton came out in 2002 (compared with seventeen for Bernstein and twenty for Menuhin). I persuaded Classic FM to commission a four-programme personal retrospective on my seventy-fifth birthday in 2006; this was taped in Aldeburgh by Classic FM's tireless producer Tim Lihoreau, but thereafter silence reigned at Classic FM until the centenary of Yehudi Menuhin a decade later in 2016.

My career as a director was also over. Unitel was a shadow of its former strength following the bankruptcy of its presiding genius Leo Kirch, and it suspended producing music films on its unique but super-expensive 35 mm film system, which only Horant Hohlfeld and I understood. Horant retired to a lovely farmhouse close to the Chiemsee in Bavaria. He went on to make some memorable music videos with his friend, the great conductor Carlos Kleiber, the best being a sizzling *Rosenkavalier* from the stage of the Vienna State Opera. A French company entrusted me with what proved to be my final video-directing assignment: it was in my beloved festival city of Aix-en-Provence and what a production Monteverdi's powerful *Il Ritorno d'Ulisse in Patria* proved to be, performed by Les Arts Florissants under William Christie, who is a true genius of a music director. With the help of my faithful colleagues Sonia Lovett and Judy Chesterman I believe I did full justice to Adrian Noble's strong and spare production and we did so in double quick time: we were recording only four days after we moved in! The video won a prize in Paris but I never worked again for BelAir Classiques.

This withering away of my customary production work did not trouble me unduly because out of the blue a totally new career had opened up: I became a tour director on land and a music lecturer afloat, mostly on cruises either at sea or on great European rivers.

Until my late sixties I had been totally resistant to the idea of going on any type of cruise. But as early as the year 2000, I had been signed up to lecture on a week-long Danube cruise: Christina accompanied me and to our surprise we had a good time. There would be concerts every day given by first-class

Testing my sea legs
as cruise lecturer
and musical MC.

artists, some coming on board to perform, others playing in churches and cloisters en route as we journeyed down the Danube or the Rhine, for which voyages I had been hired to give talks and video lectures.

Also on these cruises I would put the travellers' musical knowledge to the test in light-hearted team quizzes and on some trips we even discovered talent among the punters: I remember an uncomfortable postprandial occasion when an uninhibited guest sang a complete Gilbert and Sullivan patter song with acres of verses, and without accompaniment. That certainly broke the ice: the same concert concluded with the entire audience humming the 'Vilja' chorus from *The Merry Widow* before linking arms for the encore: 'You'll Never Walk Alone'.

Over the next couple of decades I worked for a mind-boggling selection of upmarket travel companies.

On land I began my tour director life modestly enough by guiding small groups around the Malvern Hills in search of the essence of Edward Elgar. In the evening I would screen the Ken Russell classic which I had helped to make. Then I was recruited by Richard Baker's manager, Stephannie Williams – a lovely lady with organisational flair and good musical taste – to take over some of Richard's further-flung cruises on P&O ocean liners; the vacancy arose

Home from home: the P&O *Arcadia*, a luxurious floating hotel.

because Richard and his wife Margaret no longer enjoyed air travel, preferring to start and finish in Southampton. Happily Christina and I inherited from the Bakers the tradition on P&O that the guest speaker occupied the best suite on the ship, complete with a personal butler who served tea and cucumber sandwiches punctually at four every afternoon.

Stephannie called her excellent operation The P&O Music Festival at Sea and she organised three or four of them a year. Her music team usually included a quartet of experienced freelance opera singers, a concert pianist, a string group, a woodwind soloist, a harpist or a guitarist – plenty of variety, therefore, which was essential because on days at sea I would be on duty to present morning recitals, afternoon tea concerts and gala opera evenings. Talks and quizzes also had their place and I always enjoyed playing a selection of piano duets with our inspirational Welsh accompanist Ingrid Surgenor.

It was far from being a conventional holiday but we certainly saw the world. Admittedly our very first sea cruise was almost a disaster. We were on a beautiful liner called the SS *Norway* – beautiful but old: the ship had started life in 1962 as the French Line's flagship, the SS *France*. The old lady's engine broke down outside Bergen and we limped home at quarter speed, forced to abandon the planned sea journey around the Hebrides and Land's End. I was so nervous I slept with my passport under my pillow for three nights.

In subsequent years conditions improved mightily on P&O's giant liners, which boasted as many as ten or eleven decks featuring outdoor swimming pools and half a dozen restaurants; we sailed all around the Caribbean and through the Panama Canal.

One cruise took us a thousand miles up the Amazon to the old rubber city of Manaus, where we laid on a gala opera concert in the beautiful *belle époque* opera house, Il Teatro Amazonas, whose acoustics are excellent; the passengers were persuaded to think of it as the equivalent of a night out at Glyndebourne (!) and they dressed up accordingly and partook of amazing picnics before and after the music.

One of P&O's Pacific cruises took us north as far as San Francisco; en route I was one of a small group of travellers who flew a hundred miles in a tiny plane to visit the Mayan temples of Tikal, hidden in the rainforest of northern Guatemala: I have never seen a more exciting archaeological site – except perhaps Knossos on Crete, which we explored on a Mediterranean voyage. On another trip, this one to the Black Sea, we were deeply touched by the massive war memorials erected on the clifftops to commemorate the ghastly, botched invasion of Gallipoli. In Libya we were fortunate to visit its two great

A glamorous evening for my cruise guests at Manaus Opera House.

Roman cities – this was before the toppling of Colonel Gaddafi and the war that devastated the country and thereby crippled the tourist industry. Ancient Libya boasted Roman glory but the Libya we visited was drowning in the banality of plastic bags, dumped in ugly piles at every crossroads.

On one P&O trip we sailed from Barcelona to the Black Sea, taking in Chopin's gloomy monastery on Majorca and Chekhov's sun-soaked Yalta estate in the Crimea: the great playwright's handsome villa was closed but we trespassed in the gardens and were admiring the splendid trees Chekhov had imported from around the world when a self-important Soviet-style gardener officiously insisted we leave the estate. It was not my finest hour. Further west at our next landfall we climbed the famous Odessa Steps, keeping a wary eye open for the careering pram immortalised by Eisenstein in *Battleship Potemkin*.

By 2002 I had published three biographies of great musicians and could provide examples of their work from the dozens of old television programmes which I had recorded on VHS cassettes and stored in my Aldeburgh garage, so wherever we sailed I came equipped with video clips to give illustrated talks and do book-signings *ad libitum*. However, I was encouraged to undertake more ambitious activity by another travel company named ACE Cultural Tours. ACE had been founded in the 1950s by Cambridge idealists and was a not-for-profit organisation. I liked the people who ran it and I liked the size of the operation, no tourist group being larger than twenty-five and most of the participants being Cambridge graduates. I designed three tours for ACE, in St Petersburg, Vienna and Cuba.

Christina and I first visited Cuba as tourists on a quaint little ship, fitted out like a country hotel, called *Hebridean Spirit*. We loved our first Cuban port of call, Santiago de Cuba, where Columbus had made landfall before us and where Graham Greene set a crucial espionage scene in his witty novel *Our Man in Havana*. The cruise on which I was lecturing ended in Havana but we signed up for four extra days and enjoyed what we then saw of Cuba so much that I persuaded ACE's management to reinstate a Cuba tour they had abandoned several years previously because of the burdensome bureaucracy involved.

Thanks to an introduction from the Royal Ballet's director Kevin O'Hare, whom I met on the plane when I did a planning reconnaissance, I was able to negotiate a deal with the Cuban national ballet company – the institution where Carlos Acosta had started his illustrious dancing career. I obtained permission for my ACE group to attend a rehearsal and also to visit the famous ballet school inaugurated by Alicia Alonso as long ago as 1948. (After the 1959 revolution Fidel Castro had doubled Alonso's funding and she was now an untouchably powerful figure on Cuba's dance landscape.) Apart perhaps from Martha Graham, Alonso was the most terrifying ballet personality I ever met: she was almost blind but attended every performance at the Gran Teatro de Habana, where her word carried more weight than the Almighty's. The theatre, in the heart of the city, is a grandiose venue which reminded me of the ornate but decaying Camden Theatre.

Tickets were cheap by European standards, but ten times cheaper for local people, who paid in the national currency. (Cuba's two-tier currency is one of the worst blights on its daily life.)

The focus on dance broke new ground for my revised ACE itinerary of Cuba, but music remained the most important element. To our tour plan I added my recommendations from the best of the delightful foot-tapping music to be heard in almost every Havana café and bar. Sampling local music groups is a highlight activity in every Cuban city, especially in the bars known as Casas de la Trova. (That's the word 'trova' as in *Il Trovatore*, the troubadour.)

531

Cuba's tourist circuit is pathetically restricted but Havana itself has been magnificently restored and boasts dozens of memorable sights, ranging from art deco hotels with mobster back-history such as the Hotel Nacional, to its museums, galleries and handsome city squares (some of them featuring micro-breweries), not to mention the attraction of the gorgeous 1950s Buick and Oldsmobile saloon cars which still adorned the city's wide avenues, sixty years after the Castro revolution.

With Carlos Acosta's teacher, Ramona de Saa, at the Cuban National Ballet Company.

Further afield, the Cuban tourist circuit takes in the southern shore towns of Cienfuegos and Trinidad. I especially enjoyed our annual excursion to a tiny lake in the state park outside Trinidad where after a long hike we could swim in a secret grotto under a delightful waterfall.

I added to the itinerary a visit to the impressive mausoleum outside Santa Clara dedicated to the revolution's romantic hero, Ché Guevara. My favourite city, Santiago, is too far for a coach journey from Havana and instead I scheduled a trip to Pinar del Rio with its Viñales Valley in the west of the island – it's an area which boasts a weird landscape of mini-mountains rising out of the plain. When planning the tour it seemed logical to start there, at the most westerly point. This proved a huge mistake: the group I led was delayed at the airport by the nightmare loss of a punter's suitcase and we then had to endure a three-hour motorway drive on top of the ten-hour flight from the UK, with the result that we arrived at our destination in pitch darkness, drained and with not a single hotel porter to help with suitcases. We survived but my standing as a tour leader dipped significantly and subsequent tours planned by me all began in Havana, close to the airport.

I rounded off my Cuban itinerary with a couple of relaxing days in the art deco splendour of the north coast hotel resort of Varadero. But four years of dealing with Cuban red tape was enough, after which I happily opted out, handing over my tour-leader responsibilities to ACE's effervescent art historian Peter Higginson.

Touring in St Petersburg was child's play by comparison. ACE already had strong connections in the Czarist capital, having for several years funded an annual scholarship for a promising Western dancer to attend the famous Vaganova Ballet Academy. ACE's intriguing local agent, Olga, knew everybody in the Leningrad dance world and that was a great advantage when it came to obtaining a permit to watch the final-year students being put through their paces – the class took place in the very studio where Rudolf Nureyev had practised his art before defecting to the West.

I had a useful card of my own to play when touring the vast city of Leningrad, now renamed St Petersburg: I brought with me a film featuring the famous mechanical clock at the Hermitage Museum: in it a clockwork peacock strikes the hour with the whirrings of a thousand perfectly aligned cogs. I extracted a video of the performance from the documentary Derek Bailey had directed for NBC and the BBC – a deal I had negotiated back in 1979 when I was with Music and Arts. The peacock clock was still on show at the museum but frustratingly it no longer sprang into life every hour. So

The famous Peacock Clock in the Hermitage Museum.
It only came to life in Derek Bailey's film.

the only way to see it was in Derek's film. The clock has since been restored
and preens beautifully. In St Petersburg I also had the advantage of knowing
the Mariinsky Theatre – formerly the Kirov – from the inside because of
the television relays I had directed for BBC2 (*Boris Godunov* and *War and
Peace*) in the heady days of *perestroika*. From our one-day P&O visits earlier
in the decade we knew that St Petersburg in the summer is as uncomfortably
crowded as Venice, but the new ACE tours took place in deepest winter so
there were no tourist hordes around the Hermitage's famous collection of
Rembrandts – or anywhere else. The streets and *prospekts* were mushy with
dirty old snow but the temperature was only a little below freezing, even when
we went for a troika ride (straight out of Prokofiev!).

We were in St Petersburg at the time of the Maslenitsa (Shrovetide) Festival,
when entire families of local people attend every ballet performance and
the shows' intervals are as stimulating as the operas and ballets themselves,
featuring balalaika bands and dancing schoolchildren. In those days the

Mariinsky management (in effect, Valery Gergiev himself) did not decide on repertoire until the last minute, which suited us well: all we needed to know was that the companies were at full strength and that they would be performing one of the Tchaikovsky classics (Pushkin-based operas and Petipa-choreographed ballets) side by side with other great Czarist-era operas by Rimsky and Borodin. The best days were when they also programmed the latest creations of Alexei Ratmansky, the foremost Russian choreographer of our own time. Over several seasons we saw *The Bright Stream*, *Cinderella* and *Anna Karenina* – three of Ratmansky's most satisfying ballets.

The third ACE tour I masterminded in my seventies was to Vienna, in the spring. To Vienna's obvious musical destinations I added the Kunsthistorisches Museum, where I would immediately lead my flock to my favourite gallery, the Breughel room, which I had first visited fifty years previously when attending the Youth and Music congress in 1957. I greatly loved Breughel's *Tower of Babel* and *Hunters Returning in the Snow*. I also took my pilgrims to marvel at the Sezession temple known as the Haus der Kunst and to the Papageno Gate at the Theater an der Wien, where I had filmed LB's *Fidelio* production in 1970 for *Beethoven's Birthday*. In the old city a visit to the awesome Kapuzinergruft, the imperial crypt where 138 members of the Habsburg dynasty are assembled in tomb after tomb, was balanced by sampling the domestic charm of the Figarohaus, close to the cathedral. This is where Mozart comes to life in his own apartment – much more fun than the Habsburg crypt. On another day my group would drive out to the Vienna Woods to stroll where Beethoven had walked two centuries before, jotting down themes for his 'Pastoral' symphony. A trip like this would cheer us up after we had visited the tiny chapel at Mayerling, which commemorates the strange deaths at his hunting lodge of Crown Prince Rudolf and his mistress Baroness Mary Vetsera, immortalised in *Mayerling*, Kenneth MacMillan's ballet. Apparently the thirty-year-old heir to the Austrian throne waited three hours after killing his seventeen-year-old mistress before turning a gun on himself. Or did she also commit suicide? The decadent atmosphere of that extremely disagreeable incident was frightening. Later we visited the abbey of Heiligenkreuz, where Schubert had once played the organ; every day the abbey's monks sing a service in Gregorian chant and sing it most beautifully. I enjoyed those Vienna Woods outings.

I had an equally pleasurable experience working for the English Chamber Orchestra: I hosted four of their fabulously luxurious music cruises, on which I got to play duets with the pianist Igor Levit (then an extravagantly gifted teenager); I also introduced English Chamber Orchestra concerts performed

Wind Star, a thrilling sailing vessel chartered by the English Chamber Orchestra for its very enjoyable music cruises. One voyage featured the Shostakovich piano concerto played by Igor Levit with Alison Balsom contributing the joyous trumpet solo.

in exotic temples, mosques and fortresses with such soloists as Maxim Vengerov, Grace Bumbry and Alison Balsom. Eventually I was dropped as host by the orchestra in favour of the much younger Stephen Johnson, a writer I greatly admire. But my Indian summer as a music lecturer continued when another company, Noble Caledonia, issued an invitation for me to be a guest speaker, this time on European rivers, mostly in the company of their unflappable Spanish-born cruise director César Perez. Live music onboard was supplied by an experienced ensemble of British opera singers recruited by the baritone Philip Blake-Jones for his London Festival Opera. My lectures were now about Mozart and Brahms and Bartók, delivered on the Danube as we sailed from Regensburg past Vienna and Bratislava and on to Budapest. We passed through the impressive Iron Gate and once sailed all the way to the Black Sea. On the Rhine we sailed from Amsterdam past the famous Lorelei Rock to Basel; on the Rhône we sailed from Lyon to Arles, glimpsing the white horses of the Camargue; we also spent time on the River Guadalquivir, where our cruise ship was anchored all week in Seville. As the Gershwin song suggests, this was nice work if you can get it – and get it, happily, I did.

Undoubtedly the purest musical pleasure I have had in the twenty-first century came during my visits to festivals of Schubert's music, the so-called Schubertiades; these take place in the Tirol and were with ACE, for whom I regularly led groups to the Schubert concerts given in Schwarzenberg, a small mountain village in western Austria. We lodged in what had been a monastery cloister in the nearby village of Bezau, run by a sweet family who were devoted to us eccentric Brits, probably because we were a welcome change from the serious religious folk who rented the place for sermons, seminars and the like. Our group occupied every one of the austere cell-sized bedrooms and the tour quickly morphed into a week-long house party. A grand piano was installed in the central hall where each morning we would listen to the Schubert songs to be heard later in the day at the recitals, and read through the song lyrics, poetry by Goethe, Heine and the like, and their English translations: I never came closer to being a teacher. Or happier. The smell of the harvested hay

Tour guide in the Tirol –
with my flock en route
to a Schubertiade.

being brought in from the Alpine pastures was intoxicating and the view of the Vorarlberg mountains from the summit of the nearby cable car lift really did take the breath away. Schubertiades are unique in their atmosphere. The intensity and seriousness of the Austrian and German concertgoers was admirable. I loved every moment of those expeditions.

But most good things have to have an end: when I passed my eightieth birthday ACE told me they could no longer arrange insurance for me to continue as a tour director. Luckily my very last ACE assignment was to the Scottish Highlands, enabling me to explore Fingal's Cave on the island of Staffa, a place I had been imagining since listening to a scratchy 78 of Mendelssohn's *Hebrides* overture on a wind-up gramophone while staying with my friend Brenda in Cornwall, circa 1945. Staffa did not disappoint. Fingal's Cave, a cathedral in stone, was profoundly impressive.

*　*　*

I still take refuge in work. Writing this book has been a blessing. Work for me is no longer the intense team effort it used to be. The Aldeburgh Festival engages me occasionally to introduce historical music films which have a Britten connection and I also enjoy organising occasional musical celebrations off my own bat. Thus in 2006 I planned a season of Mozart concerts and films for the 250th anniversary of his birth. My friend and Suffolk neighbour Christian Blackshaw featured in a cycle of Mozart's enchanting piano sonatas which I arranged at our much-loved Jubilee Hall. Christian's insight into Mozart is uncanny. And he played the sonatas on the Steinway of another great Mozartian, Benjamin Britten; the composer's piano was brought down from the Red House for the season. That was a real privilege. Nowadays, with every inch of Britten's home watched over with eagle eye by the conservation people, his Steinway is, I suspect, forbidden to travel. Five years later, for my eightieth birthday, I organised a Simply Schubert weekend. We started on Friday evening at the Jubilee Hall in Aldeburgh with a fun Schubertiade, for which I recruited all my local musical friends; we then moved to Snape where (as already mentioned) I conducted the Prometheus Orchestra in the 'Unfinished' Symphony; in the second half Edmond Fivet, our tireless music director, conducted the Aldeburgh Music Club Choir – I had been named its president a few months previously – in Schubert's E flat Mass. It's an honour to serve as president of this choir, which Britten and Pears established at their Crag Path home in 1952, with Pears as its first president, followed by Imogen Holst. For another Schubert event that weekend I brought down my beloved Schubert Ensemble of London – they had never before appeared at the festival – to play the B flat Trio and the Trout Quintet; for a master class that weekend the late Martin Lovett (father of Sonia Lovett, my vision-mixer, and the only survivor of the Amadeus Quartet) kindly coached some young cellists in Schubert's great C major Quintet. Two singer friends, Susanna Hurrell and Pippa Berry (Philippa Dames-Longworth), sang Schubert *Lieder*; I accompanied a gifted local violinist Jeanine Thorpe in one of the sonatinas I had been playing since my Long Dene days; and Christian Blackshaw played two heavenly late sonatas; it was the most agreeable of Schubert occasions.

Every winter since 2005 I have presented three or four illustrated conversations about opera and music in our state-of-the-art Aldeburgh Cinema under the title *Matinées Musicales* – a deferential nod to our local hero Mr Britten, who used that title for a dashing ballet suite of Rossini-based orchestral miniatures. For these matinées I dream up new ways of recycling my old television programmes, mostly using excerpts from what I laughingly call my personal archive – when we moved up from London I stored about a thousand VHS cassettes in our less than perfectly dry garage. The *Matinées*, which never run less than two hours, have proved to be an ego-massaging exercise. Coronavirus has forced the closure of so many cultural activities but the *Matinées* have had to stop for a different reason: my video cassette tapes are slowly crumbling into white dust. I have had the programmes I treasure the most converted into DVDs and hundreds more have been disposed of at the local dump, but for those that remain on the archive shelves it is a race not against time but against apathy. In the words of another Gershwin song: 'Who cares?' Well, I am doing my best and Aldeburgh is a wonderfully appreciative constituency.

After eighteen months of living in this little town my wife and I decided we liked the place enough to settle, so we bought the freehold of the house we were renting and used most of our much-diminished cash mountain to add on a large kitchen-cum-dining room facing west to catch the Suffolk sunsets. We employed a very sympathetic building contractor, Andy Kernahan, who designed the perfect space. The high ceiling he built for the kitchen helps to create a friendly acoustic for madrigals; a group of about sixteen of us used to assemble every month or so for an evening of singing, feasting and good company. Our garden has two lawns divided by a wall whose purpose we have never understood: the south-facing lawn is adequate for crude croquet matches and the larger one, facing west, had the proportions for riotous games of football and cricket. But that was some years ago, when waves of grandchildren were still growing up and coming to stay: these days the place is quieter. Being octogenarians, my wife and I should of course be downsizing. By the same token, pigs should fly …

I have had my share of health issues in the twenty-first century – replacement valve heart surgery, a new knee and so on – but I manage to stay mobile for most of the time, indeed with my travel-besotted daughter Helena I have made wish-list trips in my eighties to Venice, Machu Picchu, Iceland and the Taj Mahal. Nowadays Christina and I like to think of ourselves as operating on a sort of plateau, holding back to a minimum the pace of our inevitable decay: 'keep your fingers crossed', our German friends used to say, and this is our motto.

* * *

In December 2019 I was named a knight in the New Year Honours. The citation they sent me for my information said the award was for services to the media. I asked if that could be changed: it sounded as if I had invented a new form of email. 'What would you prefer?' asked the friendly mandarin. 'Well, what about "services to classical music"?' said I, lacking inspiration, and so it came to pass, with the addition of 'and the arts' as a sort of afterthought.

Thinking them over, before I close these pages, I wonder whether I may have failed – even when staking a claim to have been 'useful to the living', to echo a phrase of Benjamin Britten's. From a quick re-read the impression emerges – old codger that I am – that I believe things to have been better 'in my day'. Certainly they ain't what they used to be. But when one takes a step back to consider the place of classical music in today's tech-dominated world one has to take into account the fact that we have been through a revolution in how we listen to music. In the 1930s Constant Lambert referred in his scintillating book *Music Ho!* to the 'appalling popularity' of music – mostly heard then via radio and gramophone recordings. Today's digital world is much, much worse than Lambert's. What with Spotify and all the streaming services to be found online these days, we are not just swamped with music: nowadays we are seriously spoilt by choice, pampered, cast adrift on a sea of sound. Choice, choice, choice – there's far too much of it! There should be degree courses on how to exercise choice, and pamphlets on its deployment should be available from the Citizens Advice Bureau.

When one considers the position of classical music on today's television then I submit there is very little to be pleased with. One glimmer of hope: a new independent company is producing the BBC's televised Proms; one is especially grateful to the Corporation for that exuberant summer festival, if not always for the inconsequential way an individual concert is presented or for the jumpy style in which the music is sometimes presented on video. One is also grateful to the BBC for protecting its great symphony orchestras. Giving them a corporate existence and providing work for hundreds of classical musicians is a noble cause. On the medium of radio, the BBC's Radio 3 and the commercial station Classic FM are too often plagued by presenters desperate to share their feelings with us about what they have just heard. On balance I can't help feeling that music programmes on today's television are often less interesting than what was being produced in *Omnibus* and *Workshop* half a century ago. I will bite the bullet and complain that ambitious and expensive music documentaries such as *The Golden Ring* (which I made almost sixty years ago) are no longer being commissioned. Another disappointment is that very few creative communicators are being discovered to replace such eminent figures as Pierre Boulez and H.C. Robbins Landon. In the field of opera, Sir Tony Pappano is marvellously articulate about the art of singing in front of his great orchestra, but where is the spokesman for contemporary music to rival what Simon Rattle gave us on Channel 4 in that service's pioneering days under Jeremy Isaacs? Shouldn't Rattle and the LSO (national treasures) be in a regular TV slot? That would be more useful, dare it be said, than the building of a new and acoustically satisfying concert hall for central London or the construction of an even faster train service to Birmingham.

I can see now that I should count my lucky stars for having had the opportunity to work with Leonard Bernstein, fulfilling as it was to preserve for posterity his performance archive as an interpreter of Beethoven, Mahler, Stravinsky and Brahms. I took an easier path, accepting outside contracts to work on my performance films of such conducting luminaries as Solti and Karajan. And I probably should also have fought to keep an influential place in the BBC's management hierarchy so that what I think of as my type of programme, the tradition of revelatory programmes *about* music and musicians – the area I explored for a couple of decades at the end of the last century – could have gone on being developed (as they still are intermittently) by the next-generation directors such as John Bridcut, Dominic Best (Pappano's director) and Tony Palmer. What is missing now, in this time-consuming era of commissioning editors and independent production companies, is the team *ethos* which existed among directors and producers in Music and Arts back in the 1970s.

So yes, defiantly I must admit that behind this book is a defence of what I see – looking back in my eighties – as the Good Old Days of British television. The most encouraging thing about the *current* decade, the 2020s, is the strength of our musical institutions, by which I do not mean merely the music colleges, the BBC and our national symphony orchestras. I have described how my own membership of the National Youth Orchestra of Great Britain was a major source of inspiration when I first had the idea of the *BBC Young Musician of the Year* competition. I knew we had a colossal pool of performing talent and that it was not just a product of the public schools, with their admirable tradition of quality music-making. Today's NYO is a great source of inspiration both to the young public and to the players who participate. Sarah Alexander, their visionary chief executive, rightly insists on choosing conductors and concert programmes which will give the orchestra a sense of purpose in society, an intimation of the immortality that comes with making music together, particularly when inspired by great conductors. And of course I am proud of the Young Musician competition, which continues to discover players of terrific talent such as Nicola Benedetti and the cellist Sheku Kanneh-Mason.

Staring me in the face, however, is a vital consideration: the difference in mindset between today's 'controllers', the administrative planners in charge of television's channels, and my own mid-twentieth-century bosses, Wheldon, Peacock, Attenborough, Wenham and Co., men equipped with the vision and culture to 'inform, educate and entertain', as Lord Reith put it, to whom I hope I have paid adequate tribute in these pages. I am aware that all those inspirational colleagues were men. Women had a lesser role in broadcasting, it is true, but Grace Wyndham Goldie has an honoured place in my pantheon, along with the dedicated planner Joanna Spicer. By comparison, today's television bosses seem so anonymous: I don't even know their names.

* * *

Leonard Bernstein's first musical, *On the Town*, has a wistful number near the end entitled 'Some other time', lyrics by Comden and Green. 'Where did the time all go to?' ask the lovers poignantly as they bid each other goodbye at a deserted subway station. I suppose this book – *In My Own Time* – is my response to that eternal question.

ILLUSTRATIONS

Chapter 3. Boyhood Turns Sour

Chapter 4. National Service

Chapter 5. Cambridge

Chapter 6. L'Année Française

Part Two

Part Three

Chapter 13. LWT: Not Such a Brave New World

Chapter 14. The Age of Aquarius, 1970–1975

Chapter 15. 1970: Bernstein's Annus Mirabilis

Part Four

Chapter 16. In Make-Up or Munich

Chapter 17. Discovering My Métier

Chapter 18: Hooray for Hollywood

Chapter 19. On the Musical Merry-Go-Round

Chapter 20. Hitting My Stride

Chapter 21. Bernstein's Endgame, 1989–1990

Part Five

Part Six

Chapter 26. A Life on the Ocean Wave

The author would like to thank Andy Nicholson of Directors Cut Films Ltd for his assistance in preparing selected images for publication.

The author and publisher are grateful to all the institutions and individuals listed for permission to reproduce the materials in which they hold copyright. Every effort has been made to trace the copyright holders; apologies are offered for any omission, and the publisher will be pleased to add any necessary acknowledgement in subsequent editions.

INDEX

References to illustrations are indicated in *italics*.